ISRAEL IN
THE MIND OF
AMERICA

ISRAEL IN THE MIND OF AMERICA

PETER GROSE

ALFRED A. KNOPF

NEW YORK · 1983

Library of Congress Cataloging in Publication Data

Grose, Peter.
Israel in the mind of America.

Bibliography: p.
Includes index.
1. United States—Foreign relations—Palestine.
2. Palestine—Foreign relations—United States.
3. Zionism—United States. 4. Jews—United States—
Politics and government. 5. United States—Ethnic
relations. 6. Palestine—History—Partition, 1947.
I. Title.
E183.8.17G76 1983   327.7305694   83-47937
ISBN 0-394-51658-3

In memory

of my parents

CLYDE LECLARE GROSE

Professor of History

1889–1942

CAROLYN TROWBRIDGE GROSE

Student of History

1899–1981

CONTENTS

8 pages of photographs follow page 144

AUTHOR'S NOTE

THE UNITED STATES and Israel are locked in a strange and special relationship, operating through international politics and personal emotions, sometimes in harmony, sometimes not. Over the decades both sides have found solace and security in the other, even as they grew frustrated in their cross-purposes. Americans have derived inspiration from a national redemption—and despaired at the shortfall of the reality from what might have been. Be it strategic asset or strategic nuisance, Israel embodies an ideal deeply embedded in American thought from the earliest years of life in the New World. How this unique bond came about is the subject of this history.

The arguments for and against the Jewish state display a remarkable durability. Current disputes are not new; in large part, they re-create sentiments voiced with great conviction by previous American generations. The anti-Zionism of the State Department in the 1940s, the idealism of Brandeis and his American Jewish followers in the 1920s, the forebodings of American consuls in Jerusalem in the nineteenth century —such relics of past American experience have come to life again in the political climate of today.

Two circumstances at the turn of the 1980s established the need for this book: First, the political leadership that had dominated the Jewish national movement for three-and-a-half decades had fallen, replaced through democratic elections by a militant minority faction with a vision of Israel quite different from that to which Americans—Jews and Christians alike—had grown accustomed. Second, the seals were finally broken on three rich collections of archives, making available for the first time full official documentation of the drama of Israel's restoration. This detailed and authoritative historical evidence—American, British, and Israeli—is reflected in the pages that follow. Triangulation of the working documents of the climactic years has permitted a fresh examination of the numerous memoirs and unofficial archives on which previous histories of this period have been based.

I came to this research from the Policy Planning Staff of the State Department, so I was fully mindful of the protocols and limitations of official records. Bureaucrats learn quickly—and so, obviously, must historians—how to read formal memoranda, how to spot code phrases that convey unstated assumptions and, most of all, how to note what is *not* said, but could have been, at any particular juncture. The memories of key players in the drama also have their limitations, for it is a human trait to remember things just the way we want to remember them, in the light of everything that followed. Conversations with surviving participants were valuable on matters of color and atmosphere (these interviews are noted in the essay on sources), but when it came to assessing judgments and decisions made under the pressure of the times I relied more on what was actually said or done, as revealed in the records, than on what individuals remembered saying or doing.

When I started this research, I had no idea where it would lead me. What I found was that the news columns I had written as a reporter in the 1960s and '70s were incomplete without an understanding of the tensions and conflicts of the 1940s, and these in turn made little sense without knowledge of the way unstated assumptions were built into the attitudes of the participants. So even though this is the story of earlier times, it completes the news stories of today. Being history, furthermore, it can treat sensitive issues with more information and detachment than we can bring to current developments; the most sensitive of these problems will strike all-too-familiar chords with today's politicians and opinion-makers.

I claim no personal memories of the events of 1948; I was thirteen years old at the time, the nearsighted son of a midwestern Baptist family, and try as I may to conjure up some contemporary awareness of this drama which was to play such a role in my professional life, the effort is absolutely in vain. But from an earlier time, 1940 or so, two things a little boy sensed, and remembered, about his father are relevant: his love of history, and his anguish in his last years of life over terrible things happening to people called Jews, somewhere far away from our home in Evanston, Illinois. It took me many years, and many personal encounters, to understand these two memories.

The Middle East Institute at Columbia University provided me with a congenial home in which to pursue this study. But I owe a prior debt of gratitude to the publisher and responsible editors of *The New York Times,* under whose care I became absorbed in the realities of American foreign policy and Jewish statehood. I was managing *The Times'* Moscow bureau in June 1967 when they summoned me back for the next decade of immersion in the problems of the Middle East, as diplomatic and foreign correspondent and member of the editorial board. The Rockefeller Foundation later provided generous support for my research, and I look back with special appreciation to Mishkenot Sha'ananim for a home and welcome while I was examining the relevant records in Jerusalem.

A study as eclectic as this could not have developed without prodding and guidance from patient friends. I think with enduring gratitude of the intellectual support I received from Michael Janeway, who first stimulated me into action, and J. C. Hurewitz, who kept me moving along. My State Department colleagues Samuel Berger and Paul Kreisberg shared their judgments with me on both style and substance, and so, over more years and in more situations than either of us cares to remember, did Anthony Lake. Their loyalty conveys to me the true meaning of friendship. Aron Chilewich showed the kindness of his nature in more ways than I can describe. Lois Wallace and Charles Elliott came along with encouragement just when I most needed it, and provided continuing wise counsel. Working with the professionals at Alfred A. Knopf has been an author's dream.

One of the joys of writing history is encountering those who are ready to help. A good research librarian is a treasure to be sought and shared. Among all the libraries and collections I consulted, I am particularly grateful to a few individuals who showed extra patience in ferreting out responses to my arcane requirements: William R. Emerson, director of the Franklin Delano Roosevelt Library at Hyde Park; Malka Newman and Michael Avizohar at the Ben-Gurion Library and Archive in Sde Boker, Israel; John Taylor at the National Archives in Washington; and Sylvia Landress at the Zionist Archives and Library in New York. The staff at the Harry S. Truman Library in Independence, Missouri, and the Public Record Office in Kew Gardens, London, helped in the excitement of discovery. In the final stages, the research staff at the Council on Foreign Relations in New York offered constructive criticism and support.

A number of experts read all or parts of this manuscript and offered valuable suggestions. I quickly offer the assurance that no one is responsible for anything written here except the author himself. Besides those already mentioned, Moshe Arad, Jonathan Sarna, and Richard Bulliet all shared with me their perceptive insights. At several key points in my work, Arthur Hertzberg, Lincoln Bloomfield, and Howard Morley Sachar stimulated my thinking along productive lines. Others who provided specific guidance or information are noted in the essay on sources. To all of these, and dozens of others willing to humor my enthusiasm, I offer my thanks.

Throughout four years of a father's obsession, Carolyn B. Grose and

S. Kim Grose have been eager companions, ever providing the special insight of the teenager and the most serious quality of all, a sense of humor. I thank them for their fortitude and love. To Claudia I owe everything: as co-worker in research, she brought discipline and integrity, and then firm support month after month for my absorbing preoccupation. This shared endeavor has given us our happiest years, so far.

PETER GROSE

Vineyard Haven,
Massachusetts
June 1983

ISRAEL IN
THE MIND OF
AMERICA

PROLOGUE

A T FIRST, the more romantic European explorers guessed that the red-skinned hunters in the North American woods might be remnants of the Ten Lost Tribes of ancient Israel. This was a thrilling speculation; abandoned by history in 722 B.C., the Lost Tribes had been an obsession of medieval Christendom, and the faithful believed that with their rediscovery would come redemption for all mankind.

The theory failed to prove out. North America's actual encounter with Jews began the first week of September 1654, when twenty-three of them—four men, six women, and thirteen children—climbed from the hold of a creaky French vessel to join the little settlement of the New Netherlands on Manhattan Island. In sickness and squalor, they had barely weathered the stormy passage from Brazil.

In South America, European settlers had already won their first battles of colonial survival, and a life of culture and commerce seemed in the offing, not only for Christians but for Jews as well. But it was not to be. The Inquisition of the Church had crossed from Spain to the colonies and, facing intolerance in unyielding form, the Jewish traders decided to move on. The Dutch community on the North American coast offered higher promise—or so this little band of wandering Jews hoped.

They were quickly disillusioned; the civil liberties of the Dutch heritage, it seemed, were an unnecessary luxury in the New World. Some 750 Christians already settled in Manhattan greeted these first Jews with suspicion, hostility, and bigotry. Within a fortnight of their arrival the settlement's pastor articulated the general repugnance: "These people have no other God than the Mammon of unrighteousness, and no other aim than to get possession of Christian property, and to overcome all other merchants by drawing all trade toward themselves."

The autocratic governor, Peter Stuyvesant, a man not known for piety, felt free to denounce the intruding Jews as "hateful enemies and blasphemers of the name of Christ!" Their "customary usury," their

3

"deceitful trading with the Christians," rendered them unworthy to share in the blessings of the New World. On September 22, Stuyvesant addressed an official petition to his superiors at home, the Dutch West India Company of Amsterdam, demanding that Jews be barred from Manhattan forever.

For seven months the Amsterdam Chamber of the company considered the problem, receiving counter-petitions from Jewish merchants of Amsterdam who noted with pride that "many of the Jewish nation are principal shareholders in the Company." Stuyvesant, meanwhile, had turned his zeal against troublesome Lutherans and Quakers, but the reply from Amsterdam still rankled when it finally reached the New World.

No, said the company directors, exclusion of the Jews would be "unreasonable and unfair." Their role in support of the Dutch conquests in Brazil had to be taken into account, to say nothing of the large amount of capital which the Amsterdam Jews still provided to the company that kept Stuyvesant and his pioneers in business. Mindful of such considerations, the Amsterdam Chamber scolded its man on the spot: "You will now govern yourself accordingly." Stuyvesant's Manhattan and its surrounding boroughs would ultimately nurture the largest Jewish community of any city in the world.

The pattern was established in these earliest years—an uneasy sense of coexistence, mutual misperception and mistrust that would mar relations between Jews and Christian society in North America far into the future. Over the ages Christendom had regarded Jews as a separate and alien body in its midst. In enlightened western Europe, wealthy Jews had been accepted. Their support was welcomed; *in extremis,* even sought. Yet these "respectable" Jews perversely insisted on defending their less endowed relatives, the humble and coarse, the rag peddlers and grinds who offended the sensibilities of polite society.

To Jews solidarity was only natural, part of their age-old covenant. To Gentiles it smacked of conspiracy. Proper authorities like Stuyvesant, seeking to suppress the distasteful elements, found their efforts thwarted by seemingly nefarious powers, financial and even political, pulling strings across oceans and national borders. For three centuries to come, many American Gentiles would be troubled about this strange class of citizens.

THE PURITANS OF NEW ENGLAND found romance in linking Jewish and Anglo-Saxon destinies. They identified with the people of the Old Testament, casting their self-image in terms of the Book. Their new land they called Canaan. Their preachers, endlessly imaginative in their stark pulpits, compared the trials of the early settlers to the plagues of Moses' Egypt. A knowledge of Hebrew was a sign of erudition among the men who came over on the *Mayflower* and for generations thereafter. Not until 1787 were Harvard undergraduates excused from compulsory Hebrew study and permitted to substitute French in fulfilling their academic requirements. Ezra Stiles, president of Yale, was fluent enough to converse in Hebrew, and used it to deliver his commencement greetings. His personal letters were replete with mellow musings about the geography of faraway Jerusalem, of Hebron and other biblical sites in Judea and Samaria, as if he knew them firsthand. When the colonists rallied against the English, their enemies became in their eyes the Philistines; King George III was Rehoboam or Pharaoh. "We Americans are the peculiar, chosen people, the Israel of our time," wrote Herman Melville as he looked back upon the mind of early New England. "We bear the Ark of the liberties of the world." Henry Ward Beecher later noted that both Puritans and Jews "scarcely ever separated patriotism from religion."

The imagery of ancient Israel captivated the Continental Congress in 1776. Benjamin Franklin proposed a device for the Great Seal of the new confederation featuring a heroic Moses lifting his wand to divide the Red Sea while Pharaoh is overwhelmed in his chariot by the rushing waters. Thomas Jefferson preferred a less bellicose design, with the children of Israel struggling through the wilderness, led by a cloud and a pillar of fire.

George Washington recognized, as a matter of course, the civic identity of the scattered Jewish communities following the Revolution. At proud and cosmopolitan Newport, for instance, on August 17, 1790, he received the greetings of Moses Seixas, head of the Hebrew congregation and heir to one of the most illustrious Jewish names of New England. Taking his place among the councils of the town with the Christian clergy and the Society of Freemasons, Seixas greeted the new President in the name of "the children of the stock of Abraham." Washington replied in language of solemnity and simplicity remembered from the prophet Micah: "May the children of the stock of Abraham who dwell in this land continue to merit and enjoy the good will of the other inhabitants, while every one shall sit in safety under his own vine and fig tree and there shall be none to make him afraid."

Pressing the campaign to separate state and religion, Washington declared that "the United States is not a Christian nation, any more than it is a Jewish or Mohammedan nation." For the first decades, such soothing words gave the Jews of the New World nothing to fear and everything to anticipate. "I will insist that the Hebrews have done more to civilize man than any other nation," John Adams wrote Jefferson. To a Jewish petitioner, he expressed the wish that "your nation may be admitted to all the privileges of citizens in every country of the world. This country has done much. I wish it may do more, and annul every narrow idea in religion, government and commerce." Later, in his blind old age, Adams uttered a sentiment that became a signal: "For I really wish the Jews again in Judea an independent nation." (A century later, Jewish nationalists would stir their faithful by recalling this message from America's second President, discreetly omitting the remainder of it: "Once restored to an independent government and no longer persecuted they would soon wear away some of the asperities and peculiarities of their character, possibly in time become liberal Unitarian Christians.")

It was the idealized Jew of Scripture, rather than the contemporary reality, that inspired early America. Numbering no more than 1,500 out of a total population of nearly four million in the census of 1790, the first Jews of the United States were mostly merchants, brokers, and handicraftsmen of little or no distinction. Relatively few of the Americans who praised and claimed the Hebraic heritage actually knew any of these Jews personally. An early patriot, Thomas Kennedy of Maryland, could declare, even as he championed the civil rights of Jews as of all other citizens, "I don't have the slightest acquaintance with any Jew in the world."

The use of biblical imagery was in fact no more than rhetoric, employed to claim an identity for the early Americans as "the chosen people," to convey Puritanical scorn for Anglican and Roman Catholic worldliness in the European society left behind. Pride in the Hebrew language was an affirmation of cultural sophistication, not a statement of ideology; early Americans were no more enamored of the Jewish nation as such than a modern-day Latin teacher is a secret advocate of the restoration of Imperial Rome. Nor did an obsession with the Old Testament heritage reduce in the least the popular fear of an ineffable Jewish conspiracy at work to undermine Christian society.

Yale's President Stiles was fascinated to know the twenty Jewish families of eighteenth-century Newport, but he was also ready to believe idle talk from others about an "international Jewish intelligence system" controlled from a back street of London. Jefferson willingly conceded the Christian debt to the Jewish faith, but he sadly acknowledged in a letter to a Jewish acquaintance that "the prejudices still scowling on your section of our religion, altho' the elder one, cannot be unfelt by yourselves." In a less guarded moment, he lamented the Jewish condition: "among them ethics are so little understood."

For their part, the Jews of colonial America were far too busy making their own way in the fresh air of the New World to be overly concerned with prejudice and ignorance, particularly as the expression of such sentiments was so innocuous compared with the virulent strains that Jews had known for generations in Europe.

"We live here in the country of America, in New York and in the other places, in great security," wrote two Jewish community leaders to coreligionists abroad in 1795. "And Israelites together with Gentiles preside in court, both in civil and criminal cases." Personal acquaintance with Christian Americans broadened gradually; "indeed," wrote an 1812 chronicler, "the seats in a Jewish synagogue are often crowded with visitors of every denomination."

Nonetheless, between the early American Christian and the early American Jew there hung an awkward ambivalence. On the one hand, the Jew was a free man, entitled to all the rights of man on which the republic was built. John Wesley, founder of Methodism, maintained that some of the Jews he had encountered in his travels "seem nearer the mind that was in Christ than many of those who call him Lord." At the same time, the Jew was still marked by a strange and alien quality; somehow there was the assumption that he need not be treated in quite the same way as a Gentile. It was not only his deftness in commerce that had so troubled Stuyvesant and the magistrates of New Amsterdam. It was the deeply troublesome fact that the Jew had refused to accept the Lord Jesus. The early American was fixed in his belief that for that error the Jew had forfeited his full rights in Christian society.

This forfeit was a matter of the most intense and active concern to the early Christian settlers. In 1696, Cotton Mather confided to his diary his fervent prayer "for the conversion of the Jewish Nation, and for my own having the happiness, at some time or other, to baptize a Jew, that should by my ministry be brought home unto the Lord." Conversion of the Jews took on the force of a social crusade in the early years of the American republic. One of its champions was the frail Hannah Adams, a distant cousin of the Presidents, compelled by the poverty of her side of the family to seek an income from writing as a self-styled "compiler of historical information." Among her studies was a sympathetic history of the Jews; she could not understand why such a noble race should persist in rejecting the Messiah. After sending her manuscript off to the printer, she threw herself into a campaign to remedy this unholy situation, and in 1816 formed the Female Society of Boston and Vicinity for Promoting Christianity Among the Jews. The movement quickly spread among the intelligentsia of the young American republic—no fewer than twenty affiliated clubs were registered in New York alone—and John Quincy Adams and De Witt Clinton stood among its early backers.

From the longing to convert the Jews, and thus to complete the work of the Lord, came an enduring theme of American social history, concerning nothing less than the redemption of all mankind. One sign of the happy moment would be the rediscovery of the Lost Tribes; another sign would be the ingathering of the Jewish nation at Holy Jerusalem. Jews in exile had longed for this, of course, since the loss of their sovereignty and temple in A.D. 70. But the theme of the Jewish restoration had a place in Christian doctrine as well. It was a totally apolitical concept, remote in time and space, far simpler and far less troubling than the latter-day political movement known as Zionism. The "restoration of the Jews" was not a geopolitical goal, it was a symbol of grace.

Mundane political considerations were never totally absent from the crusade, nor was its impulse confined to the United States. Would restoration, for instance, require that the Jews regain national sovereignty in Palestine? And if so, which world power would sponsor their aspiration? Napoleon of France stood within twenty-five miles of Jerusalem in 1799 (his closest approach, as it turned out) and proclaimed: "Israelites arise! Now is the moment . . . to claim your political existence as a nation among nations!" It was not the last time a Christian leader would attempt to mobilize Jewish national sentiments in pursuit of his own political interests.

Some saw danger in the idea of Jewish restoration, in the Holy Land or anywhere else. An English parliamentarian warned in 1753 that "if the Jews should come to be possessed of a great share of the land of the kingdom, how are we sure that Christianity will continue to be the fashionable religion?" But in the intellectual and religious optimism of the young United States of America, such doubts faded before a vision of a special role for America in the Jewish destiny. It appeared with prophetic clarity in a modest pastor's study in Albany, New York, and spread across the Christian land to attain the exaltation of prophecy redeemed by the year of the Lord 1948.

PASTOR JOHN MCDONALD was perusing the Book of Isaiah in preparation for another of his popular morning lectures at Albany's Chapel Street Presbyterian Church. The American republic, a mere twenty-five years old, was torn once again by war with Britain. It was 1814, the new capital city of Washington was in flames under British occupation, and the young nation was struggling to find its own destiny free of entanglements in Old World power rivalries. Even in a quiet street of Albany, it was a time for thought about the Apocalypse.

The Presbyterians of Albany were an earnest congregation, managing in their zeal to attract more and more of the townspeople, even though in social standing they were far overshadowed by the Episcopalians a few blocks away. McDonald had been the first pastor of the church to be formally installed, back in 1785, and he gradually gathered around him a personal following that transcended denominational loyalties. Like the Puritans, the pastor and his flock were fascinated by Old Testament prophecies, particularly those of Isaiah which presaged the restoration of the Jews to their own land and the ensuing redemption of all mankind.

Yet for two years past, McDonald admitted in 1814, the true meaning of Isaiah's obscure Chapter 18 had eluded him. One of the shortest chapters of the Hebrew Scriptures, it amounted to barely 250 words. It had been composed more than two millennia before, at a time when ancient Israel had finally managed to come to terms with Egypt and was seeking an uneasy alliance against aggressive powers to the north. Suddenly, as McDonald pondered Isaiah's poetry once again, a remarkable new prophecy leaped from the allegorical language of old.

The first verse of Isaiah 18 evokes "the land shadowing with wings, which is beyond the rivers of Ethiopia," and there the pastor found his first clue. "Beyond Ethiopia" is clearly far, far away, perhaps even across a great ocean. Huddled under the shadow of wings? Where else but the land under the outstretched wings of the mighty eagle, the newly adopted sign of the United States of America!

From verse 2 the Albany congregation learned that this was a land "that sendeth ambassadors by the sea." Intoned the prophet: "Go, ye swift messengers, to a nation scattered . . . a nation meted out and trodden down, whose land the rivers have despoiled." For McDonald there was no turning back. The nation to be sought by the ambassadors from afar was obviously the Jewish nation, scattered and downtrodden.

"Jehovah . . . dispatched swift American messengers to the relief of his prodigal children," McDonald declared. "Rise, American ambassadors, and prepare to carry the tidings of joy and salvation to your Savior's kinsmen in disgrace!" The Jews, by the end of days, shall be returned to the land of Zion—and it shall fall to Christian America to lead the nations, to "send their sons and employ their substance in his heaven-planned expedition!"

There, in 1814, the American mission was clear. Someone had probably thought of this interpretation before, but it was new to the Presbyterians of Albany, and the published version of McDonald's sermon won a wide audience in the city and beyond. Isaiah's Chapter 18 became a call to faith and to action.

Two years before McDonald's death in 1821, the first of the American Protestant missionaries left for the Holy Land, then under the rule of the Ottoman Turks, to help prepare the way for the Lord's work. "There

exists in the breast of every Jew an unconquerable desire to inhabit the
land which was given to their Fathers," declared Levi Parsons on the eve
of his departure, "a desire which even conversion to Christianity does not
eradicate. Destroy, then, the Ottoman Empire, and nothing but a miracle
would prevent their immediate return from the four winds of heaven."

The theological symbol became a political plan, and as the decades
passed more and more of the faithful answered the call. Elder Orson
Hyde of the new Mormon sect reported in 1841 that "the idea of the Jews
being restored to Palestine is gaining ground. . . . The great wheel is
unquestionably in motion, and the word of the Almighty has declared
that it shall roll." Some, to be sure, dissented; William Miller, founder
of the Seventh-Day Adventists, declared that "the Jew has had his day."
But the mainstream of the movement known as fundamentalism maintained the vision and refined it. No longer was the Jews' restoration
necessarily contingent on conversion. Arno C. Gaebelein, a pioneering
fundamentalist leader who lived on well into the twentieth century, stated
that the Jews might even return to their land "in unbelief." Restoration
is a cause worthy unto itself, he said, and conversion can come later at
the hand of the Messiah.

Old Pastor McDonald of Albany had it a little wrong. When the
diplomats of the American nation assisted in the deliverance of the Jewish
people in Zion, they were not as fervent as the preacher had expected.
Yet the seed was sown, to flourish and multiply until the day of decision
134 years later.

BIBLICAL PROPHECY is not for everyone, and the America of Andrew
Jackson and the expanding frontier was rapidly turning secular in its
interests. The ideas and hopes of an obscure clergyman like John Mc-
Donald made little impact on the emerging political elite of the United
States. This critical audience soon heard of the cause of the Jewish restoration from another quarter, one that was to them far more persuasive
than biblical exegesis.

Through the first half of the nineteenth century, the most influential
organ of political information and opinion in the United States was the
newsmagazine *Niles' Weekly Register*. Required reading for Presidents,
legislators, and community leaders, this journal was authoritative and
comprehensive. Its Quaker editor, Hezekiah Niles, refused all advertising
or other blandishments from the mighty that might influence the independence of his judgments on the issues of the day. Among the topics
that most consistently fascinated Niles and his readers was the status of
the Jews.

A man of his times, Niles displayed the old ambivalence about the Jewish character. Stereotypes appeared throughout his columns. Jews "will not sit down and labor like other people," he wrote. "They create nothing and are mere consumers. They will not cultivate the earth, nor work at mechanical trades, preferring to live by their wit in dealing."

"But all this has nothing to do with their rights of men," he argued. This was Niles' real message. As early as 1816, he gave his influential Gentile readership a striking foretaste of what the movement called Zionism would stand for a full century later. Learning from European correspondents that Jews were considering emigrating to Palestine, Niles expressed astonishment that "this singular and interesting people, scattered all over the world and everywhere despised and maltreated, have continued as a separate race of men in all nations, having a home in none."

Why should they not have a national home, their own country? he asked.

> Many of them are possessed of princely talents and when to the force of their numbers and wealth should be added a portion of that religious zeal which caused their ancestors to perform such deeds of desperate courage, who shall calculate the effect? . . . The deserts of Palestine brought into cultivation by patient industry may again blossom as the rose, and Jerusalem, miserable as it is, speedily rival the cities of the world for beauty, splendour and wealth.

This was no allegory culled from the obscurities of Holy Writ. It was the nearest thing to hard-nosed political analysis the times could offer, and it came from the most authoritative public commentator of the land. The Gentile leadership of America was stirred, in the twenty-seventh year of the republic, to pay heed to the Jewish national dream, to make the desert bloom.

The Jews of early America noted all this Gentile fervor in their behalf with an interest best described as guarded. Within their own communities, to be sure, the age-old ideal of the return to Zion was kept alive. But it was not something to be discussed with strangers. The dream was recounted and embroidered from the pulpit. From time to time, living reminders would appear to lend it substance.

One by one these revered emissaries, known as *shadarim,* traveled from Zion to the New World to prick the consciences and (more to the point) to tap the resources of the young American Jewish communities. The ground was rich. For centuries Jews of the Diaspora had felt the obligation of *halukkah,* a regular contribution of funds for the support of the backward little Jewish community holding on in the Holy Land. *Halukkah* was not a burden; it was a deeply ingrained and joyful abstraction, like the idea of the restoration itself. Such abstractions brought comfort and a sense of identity to the Jews of early America; when flesh-and-blood realities intruded, America's Jews tended to become uneasy.

It was a strange and unappealing community which the *shadarim* asked the Jews of America to support with their charity. Close to 5,000 Jews clung to their Jerusalem hovels in the early decades of the nine-teenth century, surviving at the brink of extinction, pious old men and women whose only wish from life was to meet death in the city of David and Solomon. "There is no business to be done here," wrote a midcentury Jewish correspondent from Jerusalem. Most of the community was sick or blind; "one out of every three has diseased eyes . . . they have no hospital to go to, except the one belonging to the English missionaries, which to the pious Israelites is worse than death itself." No common language—literally—allied this ancient settlement with the dynamic Jews of early America; a prominent Jew of New Haven, Isaac Hart, had to ask the Reverend Stiles of Yale for help in translating the Hebrew script.

Some of the *shadarim* were truly impressive—for example, Rabbi Cohen from Hebron. When this learned personage appeared on the street outside New York's Elm Street Synagogue, turbaned and robed in the loose gown of the Orient, a Jew of the town asked his elders for enlighten-ment about "this noble Jew from some Eastern clime . . . this person finely proportioned . . . this patriarchal dignity."

More often, the Jews of early America saw the *shadarim* as money-grubbing scoundrels. Rabbi Isaacki from Tiberias arrived in 1825 and proceeded to raise the impressive sum of $179.75 from New York Jews. When he insisted that the money be handed to him personally, and not dispatched through a trusted London intermediary, the board of the congregation promptly sent the money to London anyway and paid Isaacki another $45 to get out of town. The contributions collected by Enoch Zundel of Jerusalem in 1832 were used up in defraying the emis-sary's expenses. Even when the *shadarim* were scrupulous in remitting to Palestine, it was understood that they could retain one-third of what they had collected as their personal commission. By midcentury the situ-ation had got so far out of hand that a powerful voice rose to call for an end to the abuse.

Scholar of the Scriptures, learned preacher, Rabbi Isaac Leeser of Philadelphia was also editor of the journal most read among Jews, the *Occident and Jewish Advocate*. "It is time that this constant soliciting for the Holy Land were put a stop to; it seems to be a quagmire into which the treasures of the world could be sunk without producing a visible effect," wrote Leeser. The rabbi-editor's concern was heartfelt, for beneath his business sense was a deep devotion to the cause of the restoration. Prim and sedate behind rimless glasses, he was pained to see the national destiny distorted by the grubbing of charlatans.

So far, however, the Jews' call to Zion was essentially a religious concept, just as McDonald's had been for the American Protestants. Before the striving Jewish community of the new United States could be convinced that a practical political program lay in the promise of Scripture, a new type of Jewish leader would have to emerge, a charismatic figure capable of stepping from the reverie of the synagogue into the marketplace of politics, from the pulpit to the broadsides. A scarcely credible personage named Mordecai Manuel Noah was such a man.

A FLAMBOYANT and freewheeling activist in American political life, Noah has been lost to the history books of his native land. But his memory lives on in the Jewish homeland that he envisaged. Some Israeli scholars conducted a poll in 1970 and discovered that nearly half of Israeli high school students questioned recognized his name. Yet when it was put to adults from the United States who had emigrated to Israel, and thus presumably had some interest in their American Jewish heritage, fully 80 percent said they had never heard of him.

Mordecai M. Noah was born in Philadelphia in 1785; he died in New York in 1851, and his funeral drew one of the largest crowds of mourners that the city had yet known. Successively, usually not successfully, he was a playwright, diplomat, politician, essayist and maverick social critic, editor, lobbyist, friend and adversary of governors and Presidents. "A great literary and political lion in the City of New York," wrote a chronicler of the day; everyone knew "that he told the best story, rounded the best sentence and wrote the best play of all his contemporaries; that he was the life and spirit of all circles; that his wit was everywhere repeated, and that, as an editor, critic and author, he was looked up to as an oracle."

An early factotum in the party apparatus of Tammany Hall, Noah became a disastrous sheriff of New York. In a fit of humane and civil-libertarian concern, he impulsively freed all the debtors in his prison, thus becoming personally responsible for their debts. His appointment had raised some eyebrows, for there were Gentiles who found it unseemly that a Jew should have authority to hang a Christian—to which Noah cheerfully retorted, "What kind of a good Christian would have to be hanged?"

One of his schemes for the well-being of his people was the abortive attempt to found a Jewish colony near Buffalo, New York, to serve as a way-station to the Holy Land. At its dedication ceremony, amid the bands, cannon salutes, parades of bemused citizenry, Noah stood resplendent in a black costume covered with judicial robes of crimson silk trimmed with ermine.

Many of his fellow Jews dismissed Noah as another in the long string of false Messiahs. His career, nevertheless, made him the clear prototype of the leading players in the forthcoming drama of the Jewish restoration. He anticipated Theodor Herzl, for instance, comrade in flamboyance, literary passion, and Jewish vision, who would succeed (where Noah failed) in framing the national dream to capture the world's imagination. In his political hustling, he anticipated Chaim Weizmann, the shrewd activist confronting skeptical Gentile authority, ever ready to evoke a shimmering humane vision, to lobby, agitate, cajole, or bombard with letters and petitions anyone who might help to promote the cause.

On April 17, 1818, Noah stepped to the pulpit of the New York synagogue Shearith Israel to deliver a statement far more practical than the congregation was used to hearing, or than Protestants had heard from the likes of Pastor McDonald. He made the first statement recorded in the United States of a political platform that would eventually become known the world over by the name of Zionism.

"I would ask you to accompany me to the early periods of the history of our nation," he began slowly. "Eighteen hundred years have passed without shedding a ray of happiness upon the Jews." He recalled the oppressions, the wanderings, the prejudices. Then he unveiled his revolutionary program: intensive Jewish education, especially in Hebrew, lest new generations succumb to Gentile society; return to the agricultural pursuits from which Jews had been so long barred; vocational training in skills other than "those crooked paths of traffic, miscalled commerce." He reached his peroration:

> There are upwards of seven millions of Jews known to be in existence throughout the world, a number greater than at any period of our history, and possessing more wealth, activity, influence and talents, than any body of people of their number on earth. . . . They will march in triumphant numbers, and possess themselves once more of Syria, and take their rank among the governments of the earth.

"This is not fancy," Noah assured his dubious congregation. Jews

> hold the purse strings, and can wield the sword; they can bring 100,000 men into the field. Let us then hope that the day is not far distant when, from the operation of liberal and enlightened

measures, we may look toward that country where our people have established a mild, just and honourable government, accredited by the world, and admired by all good men.

Why did a New York Jewish politician, on an April day of 1818, pick the figure of 100,000 Jews to march on Palestine? This is an inquiry for the numerologist mystics of the Jewish science of gematria, for it is the same figure that would resound through the diplomatic channels in the same month 128 years later, the number of potential Jewish refugees to emigrate to Palestine.

Noah the visionary left the pulpit and Noah the publicist sprang into action, spreading the text of his remarks far and wide, eliciting responses from, among others, John Adams. "If I were to let my imagination loose," wrote the retired second President of the United States, "I could find it in my heart to wish that you had been at the head of a hundred thousand Israelites"—that figure again—"and marching with them into Judea and making a conquest of that country and restoring your nation."

From where did this strange proto-Zionism come? Noah had suffered in a mysterious episode earlier in his career which led to his public repudiation by the Department of State—simply, it was said, because he was a Jew. There was an uproar of protest and an official cover-up; documents were destroyed or conveniently disappeared, President and Secretary of State hastened to concoct cover stories. More than 150 years passed before the answer was finally pieced together.

Before choosing politics as a career, Noah had managed through influential friends in the administration of James Madison to gain appointment in 1813 as United States consul to the Barbary States of North Africa. This was hardly the comfortable diplomatic post in Europe that he had been angling for, but it was not degrading, for it had just been vacated, under dubious circumstances, by one of the most socially prominent men of Washington, one Tobias Lear. To be Lear's successor in any post was acceptable. The Barbary pirates were a terrible nuisance to American foreign policy at the time, and Noah reasoned that his ambitions for high office might be well served by success in dealing with the menace. Stout, sandy-haired, sporting large red whiskers, the young aspirant set off for North Africa and spent the next two years wheeling and dealing through layers of obscure machinations and casual payments to diverse Arab and Berber potentates.

Then, without warning, a special envoy arrived from Washington bearing a sealed letter from James Monroe, Secretary of State. Excusing himself from the presence of the courier, Noah read:

At the time of your appointment as Consul at Tunis, it was not known that the religion which you profess would form any obstacle to the exercise of your Consular functions. Recent information, however, on which entire reliance may be placed, proves that it would produce a very unfavorable effect. In consequence of which, the President has deemed it necessary to revoke your commission. On the receipt of this letter, therefore, you will consider yourself no longer in the public service.

Both in what it said and in the way it said it, this letter to the Jew Mordecai Noah could hardly have been more insulting; it went squarely against everything then known about Noah's performance on post, against the civil-libertarian convictions of Jefferson and Madison, and against the spirit of freedom of conscience which so marked the young American republic.

A political storm erupted among the powerful Jewish leaders in Charleston, South Carolina, Noah's boyhood home, when the news became known. Madison had to dispatch a trusted army officer, a Jew, to pacify the community. Both Noah and the diplomatic establishment plunged into self-justification; the relevant documents were promptly destroyed (at least they have never been found in the official archives) and the insult which the United States government delivered upon an American Jew was lost in a morass of political charges and counter-charges.

Unraveling a cover-up in the administration of James Madison is not an easy task for investigators in the late twentieth century. Certain points are clear, nonetheless. In the first place, the fact that Noah was a Jew had never been concealed across official Washington, even before his appointment. Indeed, in angling for a diplomatic job, Noah had tried to turn his religion to advantage. "I wish to prove to foreign powers that our government is not regulated in the appointment of their officers by religious distinction," he had written the Secretary of State in 1811. "I know of no measure which can so promptly lead foreign members of the Hebrew nation to emigrate to this country with their capitals [sic] than to see one of their persuasion appointed to an honourable office attended with the confidence of the people."

Madison himself tried to soften the bluntness of his Secretary of State's letter of recall—though he had personally authorized it—when he wrote Noah after the furor that "it was certain that your religious profession was well known at the time you received your commission, and that in itself could not be a motive in your recall." (The antisemitism of the later American diplomatic corps was not an issue in the Washington of

Madison and Monroe. They appointed at least two other Jews to consular posts, including one who refused to transact business on his Saturday sabbath.)

Secondly, in attempting to justify Noah's recall, the government made reference to financial irregularities in his official ledgers. The accounts were indeed complex, since part of his mission involved secret ransom payments to the Barbary pirates. But after two years of audit and litigation the State Department granted Noah's claims, and even reimbursed him $5,216.57 for out-of-pocket expenditures. Neither peculation nor religion could have been the true grounds for Noah's recall.

What, then, was the "recent information . . . on which entire reliance may be placed" which moved Madison and Monroe to action? The story is a classic glimpse into the dark side of bureaucratic behavior, an operation of government that goes unnoticed by civics textbooks but which was destined to play a crucial role in the drama of Zionism, even as it did in the sacking of the American who first anticipated the Zionist program.

It is the simple and unquestioned reliance on information acquired through what bureaucrats call the "back channel"—gossip, innuendo, sometimes even factual information, which for one reason or another the purveyor prefers to keep out of official files. Though back-channel maneuvers seldom leave traces for historians, they can be decisive in creating the attitudes of officials, who then act upon what they have learned.

The nexus of the back channels in Noah's case was that mainstay of the early American establishment, Tobias Lear, the man who had preceded him as consul to the Barbary States. Lear was a social leader in Dolley Madison's Washington, longtime private secretary and confidant in his youth to George Washington himself. Two of Lear's three wives were nieces of Martha Washington and he shared in the first President's estate. To Dolley Madison's set, the last Mrs. Lear was Aunt Fanny; Lear himself always had the President's ear.

Diplomacy had been a new venture for Lear. His strategy for dealing with Arabs was to buy them off, to slip them ransoms and expect thereby to gain their loyalty. The strategy failed, and both in Washington and in Algiers, Lear fell under a cloud for the clumsiness of his representations. In 1811 the Dey of Algiers ordered him to leave. For all his social prominence, Lear's failure dogged him upon his return to the capital. He was not consulted on the selection of his successor, the Jew from Charleston, even though he still considered himself the government's ranking expert on Barbary affairs.

In 1814, just as Noah was getting started in North Africa, Lear received a personal letter from Algiers. (The "personal letter" between statesmen has always been a favorite back-channel technique.) His friendly correspondent was John Norderling, the veteran Swedish consul, who had represented the United States' interests in the interval between Lear's abrupt departure and Noah's appearance on the scene. Norderling disliked the newly arrived Jew, who had tactlessly not bothered to seek the guidance of those who had preceded him before assuming his duties, and he relished passing on to the congenial Lear all the gossip about the difficulties Noah was facing in his delicate dealings.

Conveyed in personal letters over distance, back-channel information may survive in family papers; in the form of salon talk and after-dinner chats, it seldom leaves definite traces. In the Washington circles frequented by the Lears, the Madisons, and the Monroes, the gossip stimulated by this letter, and Lear's undoubted embroideries upon it, could easily have been elevated to the status of "recent information . . . on which entire reliance may be placed." No one in that glittering social set would be inclined to speak on behalf of the young and pushy Jew who had taken Tobias Lear's job. Secretary Monroe tacitly acknowledged that the subject had been discussed when, some time later, on learning of anti-Jewish sentiments encountered by American emissaries on the Barbary coast, he wrote a memo to Madison saying that now "the reason for removing [Noah] is stronger."

Noah was sacked, in short, because of informal and perhaps maliciously distorted reports that reached Madison and Monroe from their social friends. Noah, they said, was bungling his delicate mission. Yet since this mission involved under-the-table payments which the United States government could not officially acknowledge anyway, Noah's behavior on the job could not be discussed publicly.

Strangely enough, one key presidential document did survive the subsequent sweep of the files, and it was the message that launched the whole cover-up. On April 24, 1815, on the basis of earlier conversations with his Secretary of State, Madison wrote: "Tunis will be vacated by the recall of the Jew. . . . In recalling Noah it may be well to rest the reason pretty much on the ascertained prejudices of the Turks against his religion, and it having become public that he was a Jew, a circumstance which it was understood at the time of his appointment might be awkward."

So, for all the early American devotion to freedom of conscience, religious profession was considered an acceptable pretext for action when other reasons could not be stated. Later generations of officials reversed the proprieties: they would seek out other pretexts for their decisions rather than admit to anti-Jewish prejudice.

Noah subsequently conceded that all had not gone well in his brief foray into diplomacy. "The real cause of disapprobation was probably a just one," he conceded privately in 1820; perhaps his ministrations to the Barbary pirates had been a little careless. But the circumstances of his recall, involving a blatant slur on his heritage, touched off in him nothing less than the ambition to lead a crusade. If being a Jew led to humiliation, then a Jew he would be—and he would fight back.

The rebuff led him to the pulpit of Shearith Israel, to an assertion of Jewish national destiny, and to a place in history far more interesting than anything he might have achieved on the Barbary coast. The final irony, considering the grief which Zionism would bring to the State Department a century or so later, is that it was the Department's own action which unwittingly provoked the first clear statement of Zionist aspirations in the United States.

Noah never found his way back into diplomacy. Instead he became a crusading newspaper editor, aspirant at Tammany Hall, activist over the range of civic good works, Jewish and Christian alike. He was one of the community luminaries approached for an initial subscription to found New York University in 1831; his work in Jewish philanthropic movements led to the establishment of Mount Sinai Hospital on upper Fifth Avenue.

Making enemies as heartily as friends, Noah was branded by *Niles' Weekly Register* as "a notorious shuffler . . . the most incompetent man that ever dabbled in party politics." In the feisty columns of his own newspaper, the *Evening Star,* he never let slurs on Jewry pass, whether they came from political allies like Daniel Webster or journalistic foes like James Gordon Bennett. To a critic maligning Jewish bankers, Noah remarked that quite a few "New Testament Jews" earned a good living in banking too. To a fellow editor who disparaged his religion, Noah recalled that the man's anti-Jewish sentiments had not prevented him from cheerfully accepting the $200 contribution which Noah himself had made to help start the rival newspaper.

The theme of the Jewish restoration was never absent for long from his writings, as he darted from one so-called practical scheme to another, impatient with those of his coreligionists whose interest in their national destiny seemed confined merely to talk. "The Jewish people must now do something for themselves," he thundered; "they must move onward to the accomplishment of that great event long foretold—long promised —long expected."

Noah's most famous, most measured statement of his proto-Zionist vision came at the height of his civic fame in 1844, just seven years before his death. New York's largest meeting hall, the Broadway Tabernacle, was not big enough to accommodate the crowds who flocked to hear him —Christian clergymen and civic leaders among them—and the well-

publicized "Discourse on the Restoration of the Jews" had to be repeated
for a second overflow audience. As in his earlier address, he developed
themes of Jewish sufferings over the ages, the hope for a return to agriculture and all the creative pursuits from which Jews had been so long
excluded. Now, he said, "the Jews are in a most favorable position to
repossess themselves of the promised land, and organize a free and liberal
government."

Then he added a new theme, an appeal to Christian America to join
in promoting the Jews' return to Palestine. He even seized upon Isaiah
18, though in terms less fanciful than those of Pastor McDonald:

> Christians can thus give impetus to this important movement; and
> emigration flowing in, and actively engaged in every laudable pur-
> suit, will soon become consolidated, and lay the foundation for
> the elements of government and the triumph of restoration. This,
> my friends, may be the glorious result of any liberal movement
> you may be disposed to make in promoting the final destiny of the
> chosen people.

Considering the state of geopolitical knowledge at the time, it is not
particularly surprising that Noah found no need to comment on the fate
of the Arab residents of Palestine once the Jews returned in force. Nor,
obviously, did he wish to say anything about the Christian interest in
converting the Jews—in any case, the conversion impulse had lost much
of its popular allure by the 1840s. But Noah did address head on a
question that would only grow in sensitivity as the campaign of Zionism
gained strength: Will the Jews of the world actually want to move to
Palestine?

It was—and would remain—a particularly awkward question for the
comfortable Jews of America, confident and buoyant in their expectations
of the good life in freedom and prosperity. Noah gave the soothing answer that would remain a firm tenet of American Zionist thought, as
opposed to the rival Zionist ideologies of Europe, for more than a century: Jews who seek freedom will go; all who are already free, such as
those of the United States, will have no need to migrate, but will feel
more secure and comfortable in their identity for knowing that the Jewish
homeland is there.

"Let the people go," Noah declared.

> Point out the path for them in safety, and they will go—not all,
> but sufficient to constitute the elements of a powerful government;
> and those who are happy here may cast their eyes towards the sun

as it rises, and know that it rises on a free and happy people beyond the mountains of Judea, and feel doubly happy in the conviction that God has redeemed all his promises to Jacob. . . .

Noah savored the adulation that came to him in the last years of his life. "Our friend Noah . . . seems mellowing into a type of the patriarchs of old," wrote a columnist in 1850. Holding court in his New York town house at Broadway and Franklin Street, across from the residence of William Waldorf Astor, Noah was seen "flushed and puffing like another Falstaff." When he set out for a stroll, cane in hand, "everybody observed him, and it seemed as if every third or fourth man we met gave him a respectful salute." Crowds many persons deep lined Broadway between Houston and Bleecker streets on March 24, 1851, to observe the passage of his funeral cortege.

Mordecai Noah spoke for the Jews to the Gentiles. Among his own people, he was not quite respectable, a little too flamboyant and provocative. His more scholarly contemporary, Rabbi Leeser, represented an opposite pole in the definition of the Jewish identity. They shared, ultimately, a conviction about the destiny of their people, but they spoke to and from different worlds. Noah was secular and mundane, Leeser was exclusive and religious. As Noah tried to blend the followers of his faith into the mainstream of Christian America, Leeser insisted on the maintenance of Jewish group identity, calling constantly for vigilance against the dangers of assimilation.

Leeser's journal gave respectful attention to the declarations of his senior journalistic colleague, but his commentaries were guarded. He had none of Noah's confidence that the nations of the world would permit Jewish nationhood in Palestine; he argued that the Jews themselves, moreover, were too disunited to attempt their restoration. Leeser worried more than Noah about the oft-expressed Christian interest in conversion.

The revolutions of 1848 in Europe softened Leeser's political skepticism and gradually his editorials in the *Occident and Jewish Advocate* came to look more favorably on a prospect that he had earlier thought possible only through divine intervention. "Is it then so unlikely," he asked in 1864, "that an effort will be made to place in Palestine and the countries immediately north and south and east of it an enterprising race, which shall keep it as a highway to all nations?"

Leeser never used the phrase "Jewish state," though he anticipated a day when Jews would again have a "commonwealth of our own." But, like Noah, he was ever sensitive to the rising fear of divided loyalties among his Jewish readers. "Do not misunderstand me as saying that you should not regard the country in which you live as your own," he wrote as early as 1831. The love for Palestine in no way implied "diminished love for our present abode." Like Noah before him and generations of American Jews after, Leeser conceived of an enlarged Jewish settlement in Palestine as a solution for the oppressed Jews of Europe, not the comfortable and secure Jews of the New World.

Noah, Leeser, and the early American restorationists failed to ignite the populace. To the Jews of the young United States, Palestine and that still-promised land remained, at best, irrelevant. The calls to Zion marked the end of an era, not the beginning—the end of early American faith and confidence. For the next century, Jewish and Christian Americans would find themselves divided in their visions of the destiny of Israel.

1

THE OFFICIAL DISPATCH to the Secretary of State seemed a bit perfervid for a normal consular communication. "I have the honor to relate briefly for Your Honor's consideration some details of a most barbarous secret, for a long time suspected in the Jewish nation, which at last came to light in the city of Damascus. . . ."

The year was 1840, and with news of this "most barbarous secret" the government of the growing United States was confronted with an Old World controversy about the standing of Jewry in Christian society. It was not an issue that had loomed large in the experience of President Martin Van Buren or his Secretary of State, John Forsyth. They seldom had occasion to think much about Jews—until this strange dispatch appeared.

In breathless prose the American consul in Beirut relayed a lurid tale of massacre, the butchery of Jewish men, women, and children. The cause of the outrage, he explained, was the "secret" he was in a position to reveal: Jews, it seemed, routinely engaged in ritual murder to obtain Christian blood for use in their Passover worship. Thus reappeared the old "blood libel" that had been thrown against the Jews all through the Middle Ages.

To Forsyth and Van Buren, the Damascus reports amounted to precisely the kind of bigotry and superstition that the New World sought to escape. Moreover, behind it all was a tangled web of imperial rivalries through which the great powers of Europe were maneuvering for influence in the shambles of the declining Turkish empire. French agents on the spot, it emerged upon investigation, were responsible for the Damascus blood libel; it was they who had incited the Muslim residents to make the charge of ritual murder against the city's Jews, thus enhancing France's status as protector of the Christian population.

As far as proud citizens of the United States were concerned, this was a clear affront to the rights of free men, Jews included. Between the conflicting ambitions of great powers and the human rights of persecuted peoples the world over, the choice for American diplomats in 1840 was far clearer than it would be a century or so later. They sided unequivocally with the victimized Jews.

The anti-Jewish indignation of the gullible consular officer (a locally appointed Macedonian, not an American citizen) was turned off with a routine acknowledgment from Washington. When news of the Damascus persecutions reached London, the American minister there did not even wait for instructions before expressing his deep concern over "the cruelties practised towards the Jews in the East." And within a week of hearing how seriously the British were taking the incident, Forsyth ordered the American consuls in Alexandria and Constantinople to "interpose [their] good offices in behalf of the oppressed and persecuted race of the Jews."

All this took place before Noah or any of the other American Jewish leaders of the day had begun to speak out. When American Jewish congregations, encouraged by their brethren in the European capitals, finally managed to express their indignation, the State Department was able to inform them that official protests had already been lodged.

This was probably the last occasion on which the Department of State intervened on a major issue of Jewish concern on its own, without prodding from the Jewish communities of the nation. A century later, when America's Jews hesitated to raise their voices about persecutions of their brethren overseas, officers of the State Department were relieved at not being called upon to take action.

THE OLD AMBIVALENCE toward Jews in the United States grew more pronounced by the middle of the nineteenth century. Civil rights, even of Jews, was still a cause which Americans were prepared to support; if the offending parties were foreigners, and Old World imperialists at that, then indignation came easily and at low cost. But all the romantic talk of redeeming a special destiny for the Jews had long since faded before the practical challenges of building a new nation on an uncharted continent.

If, in the early decades of the republic, most Americans never had occasion to know a Jew, this was not true for the second American generation. In the 1830s and 1840s a great influx of Jewish immigrants arrived from Central Europe. By the tens of thousands they poured into New York, Baltimore, and Philadelphia. In just one year, 1847, no less than 50,000 Jews left the German states to settle in the new land of freedom and plenty.

"In a few months you will be here yourself," wrote a buoyant young immigrant to his fiancée back home. "To your own surprise you will see how your hatred of your fellow man, all your disgust at civilization, all your revulsion from the intellectual life, will drop away from you at once." The young lady arrived, they were married, and soon a son was born to them. Over his long lifetime as an American, and an American Jew, Louis Dembitz Brandeis would become a most satisfactory embodiment of his father's confidence.

But at the start, most of these German-Jewish immigrants seemed confused, dirt-poor, and appalled by the size and complexity of America. To the Christian society they entered, Jews now appeared in an altogether new light; instead of a romantic abstraction they were a reality—more often than not, a distasteful reality. Many of the new immigrants occupied themselves in squalid secondhand shops in the cities. Across the countryside they appeared as itinerant peddlers, shifty and rootless, plying the backwoods footpaths with cumbersome backpacks stuffed with the goods needed for daily life on the frontier. "Eleven times out of ten, the peddler is a Jew," quipped a midcentury European visitor; the stereotype of the "Jew peddler" took hold in the American mind.

Like Stuyvesant in New Amsterdam, civil and military authorities grew uneasy with this new class of citizens. During the Civil War a field commander telegraphed the capture of "150 rebels, 90 mules, 60 contrabands and 4 Jews." General Ulysses S. Grant (once a storekeeper himself) perceived a serious military threat in the frenetic commercial activity of the "Jew peddlers" during the Civil War. To this harried field commander, the Israelites were "an intolerable nuisance," engaging often in illicit commerce even across the lines of battle. In 1862 Grant took the impulsive step of expelling all Jews from his midwestern military region. This indiscriminate prohibition met the same fate as Stuyvesant's two centuries before; wealthy Jews supporting the Union war effort protested, and President Lincoln countermanded his general's order. "The President has no objection to your expelling traitors and Jew peddlers," Grant was informed, but as his order "proscribed an entire religious class, some of whom are fighting in our ranks, the President deemed it necessary to revoke it."

The idea of Jewish cunning flourishing amid the sacrifices of war was not confined to the military. The President could not come out and say so, but the romance of the Jewish destiny no longer found a sympathetic response in the Gentile mind.

Lincoln was personally confronted with the notion of restoring the Jews to Palestine during a brief encounter in March 1863. A wide-eyed mystic named Henry Wentworth Monk was lingering near the back of the throng crowding the President's office during one of the public audiences which Lincoln held three times a week even at the height of the war. When the presidential eyes happened to fall on him, Monk stepped forward to introduce himself as a visitor from Canada. Preliminaries accomplished, he launched into his appeal.

"Why not follow the emancipation of the Negro by a still more urgent step, the emancipation of the Jew?" Monk began.

"The Jew—why the Jew?" Lincoln replied. "Are they not free already?"

"Certainly, Mr. President, the American Jew is free, and so is the English Jew, but not the European. In America we live so far off that we are blind to what goes on in Russia and Prussia and Turkey," Monk said. "There can be no permanent peace in the world until the civilized nations . . . atone for what they have done to the Jews—for their two thousand years of persecution—by restoring them to their national home in Palestine."

This was not the kind of comment Lincoln was accustomed to hearing in his wartime audiences, and he turned it off in genial noncommitment. "That is a noble dream, Mr. Monk," he replied, "and one shared by many Americans. I myself have a high regard for the Jews. . . . But the United States is, alas, at this moment a house divided against itself. We must first bring this dreadful war to a victorious conclusion . . . and then, Mr. Monk, we may begin again to see visions and dream dreams. Then you will see what leadership America will show to the world!"

As THE JEWISH condition became more widely known among mid-century Americans, so did the Holy Land of Palestine. It was the era of travel literature, and the tales told by intrepid voyagers to the East gave a vivid sense of sacred sites known before only through the obscurities of ancient Scripture. Travel books about the Holy Land came out in England at the rate of several dozen a year, and many of them found their way onto the transatlantic packet boats.

America produced its own chronicler in John Lloyd Stephens, who thrilled his readers with an awed account of standing where Jesus once stood. Lieutenant William F. Lynch, U.S. Navy, captured the public imagination in 1847 with an official expedition to navigate the Jordan River and the Dead Sea. "The final dismemberment of the Ottoman Empire [would] ensure the restoration of the Jews to Palestine," Lynch reported. A few years before, Dr. Edward Robinson had started a systematic study of the archaeology of the biblical lands, and mingled with his scholarly descriptions of holy sites were pungent personal impressions. He was disgusted at the "eagerness of Jericho ladies for intercourse with visitors; the sins of Sodom and Gomorrah still flourish upon the same accursed soil." But from the travel literature Americans learned that the Holy Land was not totally barren—there were actually people still living there, and very few of them were the Jews of Scripture. Mark Twain reported this "discovery" with particular gusto. Imbued from boyhood with romantic fantasies of the roaming Arab of the desert, Twain found the reality shattering: sore-eyed children, filth, squalor. "Arab men are often fine looking, Arab women are not," he wrote. "From Abraham's time till now, Palestine has been peopled only with ignorant, degraded, lazy, unwashed loafers and savages"—a bit strong, perhaps; that passage from his original articles was deleted from the collection *Innocents Abroad,* published afterward.

Twain noted talk "of the long prophesied assembling of the Jews in Palestine from the four quarters of the world, and the restoration of their ancient power and grandeur." But he warned that poetry and tradition were doing a disservice to anyone who actually thought of settling there. "Palestine is desolate and unlovely. . . . Palestine is no more of this work-aday world," he concluded. "It is a hopeless, dreary, heart-broken land."

Other literary notables—Herman Melville, William Cullen Bryant, Lew Wallace—were less caustic in their accounts of travels through Palestine, but no less moved by the contrast between the inspiration they sought and the reality they found. In Melville's allegorical poem "Clarel," the Holy Land discovered by a young American theology student lies in wilderness and darkness, the degradation of mankind. Only at one site was there light: the little town of Bethlehem.

THE JEWS of mid-nineteenth-century America numbered about 150,000 in a total white population (as it was then counted) of 27 million. Many of them, risen from their humble beginnings, were firmly embarked on an upward course, fanning out from the crowded ports of entry to the American interior. Cincinnati, Louisville, St. Louis, and Milwaukee soon became centers of small but growing Jewish communities. From peddlers, the immigrants achieved the status of tradesmen, eventually "store princes." The new American society gave them unaccustomed freedom to live where they wanted, to dress the way they wished, even to employ non-Jews if they had the means to pay them. The occasional visitations of the *shadarim* from Zion were little more than emotional and financial nuisances. This was the setting that greeted, in 1846, a twenty-seven-year-old German-trained rabbi from Bohemia who would emerge as the most magnetic, and most enigmatic, Jew of America's late nineteenth century.

Isaac Mayer Wise poses a problem to sympathetic observers of American Jewry a hundred years later. He was as impressive a Jew as America has produced. He epitomized self-confidence in the Jewish community. He spoke out, he talked back, he founded the institutions by which a people survived. But, in retrospect, he was wrong as often as he was right.

Wise was bitterly hostile to Abraham Lincoln. In electing this man President, "the people of the United States just committed one of the gravest blunders a nation can co.nmit," Wise declared. Throughout the Civil War he lambasted "Abe Lincoln and his thousand-and-one demonstrations of imbecility." He was horrified at the destruction of national unity, for in his view unity of the Republic was a goal superior to any other cause, even including the abolition of slavery. He condemned abolitionists—"Protestant priests," he called them—who would rather "see this country crushed and crippled than discard their fanaticism or give up their political influence."

Wise justified slavery in this way: "Either one must believe the Negro was created to be a beast of burden to others, or you must say he is just as good as you are." It is not "absolutely unjust to purchase savages, or rather their labor, place them under the protection of law, and secure them the benefit of civilized society and their sustenance for their labor." Petulant and snobbish, he saw virtue in what slavery was doing for the Negro: the race "might reap the benefit of its enslaved members if the latter, or best instructed among them, were sent back to the interior of Africa."

That was one side of I. M. Wise. Another was his lifelong and—given the times and traditions—courageous efforts to enhance the status of women in Judaism. He led the battle for ordination of women as rabbis, for female suffrage, and never in performing the marriage ceremony would he order the bride to "obey" her husband. In these and other liturgical innovations, Wise's Reform movement brought down the wrath of traditional congregations, involving him in turmoil, lawsuits, and even physical violence from the faithful. Wise never avoided a fight, and rare was the issue on which he would not cheerfully proffer an opinion that was bound to upset convention and tradition.

So it was with Palestine and the idea of restoring the Jews to their biblical glory and nationhood. With venom and irony, Wise attacked Noah and Leeser and their yearnings for the ancient homeland. He "praised" a proposal to build a railroad from the Mediterranean coast to the Palestinian interior: "this improvement does away with the ass for the coming Messiah—he can ride in a railroad car clear into the city of Jerusalem." His sarcasm fell upon receptive ears. While centuries of persecution had strengthened the mystical bond of the Jewish Diaspora to their Holy Land, the opportunities offered by nineteenth-century America broke it.

Wise and his followers had no real objection to Jewish settlement in Palestine—for those who had nowhere better to go. They disdained the movement for its impracticality and were bored by all the talk, by the *shadarim* and their unending demands for diversion of precious resources. But the hackles rose when the early Palestine settlers tried to claim that their cause was universal in Jewry, that all Jews should uproot themselves and move to the Holy Land if they were to remain good Jews. For Wise and his flock this was too much.

"The idea of the Jews returning to Palestine is no part of our creed," he declared. "The land of our fathers of two thousand years ago appears to us no better than that of our own and of our children. The political restoration of Israel cannot be accomplished in Palestine." For nineteenth-century Reform Judaism, "Palestine" was a concept, not a location. "This country is our Palestine, this city our Jerusalem, this house of God our Temple," Wise declared with finality. "American and European Jews would not immigrate to Palestine, not even if the Messiah himself, riding upon that identical ass upon which Abraham and Moses rode, would come to invite them."

Central to Wise's conviction was the assumption of Christian goodwill, particularly that of the new American society where Jews could at last live both as freemen and as Jews, without apology or conflict. This confidence often clouded his vision. "The present antisemitic craze will be overcome, which will take but a few years," he wrote in 1894. "It is all a momentary furore." Wise and the Reform leadership were convinced that the political movement of Zionism was itself playing into the hands of the antisemites, posing the ever awkward question of where the Jews' national loyalties would come to rest. Only when Jews proved their loyalty to their present homelands, the Reform leaders argued, would antisemitism abate.

To be a Jew, in Wise's view, meant to practice a religion, like a Catholic or a Methodist. There was no such thing as a Jewish nationality. "Outside the synagogue we are citizens of the lands of our nativity or adoption, and do not differ from our fellow men," he said. "In religion alone are we Jews, in all other respects we are American citizens."

Wise's proclamations poured forth from his home base of Cincinnati from 1854 until his death in 1900. With his muttonchop whiskers and bandy-legged gait, he was a distinctive presence in the booming Jewish communities of the American heartland. Like Noah and Leeser before him, he used the press to propagate his views. His newspaper, the *American Israelite,* had a sprightly tone; it built up a following that left Leeser's staid *Occident* far behind. But Wise was too gregarious and energetic to be content with the printed word; between editorial deadlines he was constantly traveling, appearing as a guest speaker, as a prize attraction for the dedication of new synagogues. He loved an audience, and he never was without one. I. M. Wise, it was said, had more personal contact with more Jews in America than any other man of his time.

A curious inversion of historical memory over a hundred years marks the relative standing of Noah, Leeser, and I. M. Wise, the three most prominent Jews of America's nineteenth century. Wise became a period piece. Yet the great institutions of Reform Judaism which he founded, including Hebrew Union College, keep his memory alive even as his anti-Zionist ideology lingers on as an embarrassment. Leeser's more sober approach to Judaism and the world led to the founding of the Jewish Conservative movement and the assertion of Jewry as a compatible—but separate—segment of the American dream.

It was Noah's proto-Zionist vision that became the dominant credo of American Jewry in the century after his time, yet the visionary himself disappeared from sight. Mordecai Noah planted his feet firmly in midair; he left no thriving institutions, no body of eloquent writings to sustain the memory of his name.

IN 1881 BEGAN one of the great migrations of modern times. From that year to 1920, more than three million Jews left their Eastern European homes to seek safer lives in America. The German-bred Jewish community of the United States found itself submerged by a twelvefold increase in Jewish numbers, just as it was beginning to feel secure in social status. In a single generation, the composition and outlook of American Jewry were transformed. The base was laid for an outpouring of intellectual energy that would alter the course of American culture in the twentieth century; so also was created the social and economic distress that would divide American Jewry into bitter, warring camps.

Tsar Alexander II of Russia was assassinated in 1881, and the ensuing tumult unleashed a flood of antisemitism and pogroms (the word comes from the Russian verb *pogromit'*, "to destroy"). A few intellectuals among the Jews of the Russian Pale pointed to the Holy Land as the source of a new life, but the mass of the *shtetl* peasantry was guided by a practical common sense hardened through generations of daily life struggle. To them, the dynamism of America offered a better prospect for survival than the deserts of Palestine. In the first two decades, to 1900, half-a-million Jews landed on America's shores. The tidal wave came in the next fourteen years, up until the outbreak of world war. In that period, one and a quarter million Jews poured past the immigration counters.

It was the era of the Golden Door, the chaotic scenes at Ellis Island, the sudden creation of a vast and teeming new Jewish community on the Lower East Side of New York City. "There she lies, the Great Melting Pot," wrote the playwright Israel Zangwill. "Listen! Can't you hear the roaring and the bubbling? There gapes her mouth—the harbor where a thousand mammoth feeders come from the ends of the world to pour in their human freight."

Romantics like Zangwill celebrated the human experience. Emma Lazarus, bookish poetic daughter of an old and secure American Jewish family, adopted the faith and legacy of the newcomers as her own. Who dared to call the Eastern European Jews "tribal"? she asked. "Our national defect is that we are not 'tribal' enough; we have not sufficient solidarity to perceive that when the life and property of a Jew in the uttermost provinces of the Caucasus are attacked, the dignity of a Jew in free America is humiliated."

Others, less secure than Miss Lazarus, were not so sure. These newcomers were Jews quite different from the Western Europeans who had been coming to America ever since Stuyvesant's day. Particularly—and painfully—they were different from the emancipated immigrants of a generation before, whose first lowly ventures into commerce had grown into prosperous family enterprises.

The newly arriving Jews came from an alien, closed society. In eighteenth- and nineteenth-century Europe, from the German states westward, Jews had been permitted to blend into the prevailing culture. But the Jewish concentrations in Russia and Eastern Europe were required to maintain their separate, isolated, and, inevitably, primitive existences. These were the people now arriving in America. They were bearded, unwashed, strangely clothed; they jabbered away in a loud and harsh dialect. To polite Americans, cultured Jews as well as Gentiles, they were unpleasant. They were observed "obstructing the walks and sitting on chairs"—of all the nerve—in Battery Park, complained the New York *Tribune* in 1882. "Their filthy condition has caused many of the people who are accustomed to go to the park to seek a little recreation and fresh air to give up this practice."

It was I. M. Wise, typically, who broke the silence of the established Jews as they saw what was happening to the good name of their faith. From the fresh air of Cincinnati, Wise observed the noisy, smelly scenes in the eastern seaports and was revolted. "It is next to an impossibility to associate or identify ourselves with that half-civilized orthodoxy which constitutes the bulk of the [Jewish] population in those cities," he stormed. "We are Americans and they are not. We are Israelites of the nineteenth century and a free country, and they gnaw the dead bones of past centuries." Wise was never a man to mince words. "The good reputation of Judaism must naturally suffer materially, which must without fail lower our social status." The prosperous "Uptown" Jew of New York found identification with the unsavory "Downtown" Jew dangerous in the extreme. It was in the Uptown salons of the German-Jewish aristocracy that the word "kike" first appeared, to deride the uncultured and unclean immigrants. Yet the emotional dilemma was acute, for the Uptown Jew was not without a sense of obligation and guilt.

"On the one hand, here are his true relatives who are dear to him and whom he wants to help; on the other hand, what a blemish!" Thus did one Jewish periodical describe the mood of 1893. "All his aristocratic neighbors, and he, himself, will again become aware of his descent, of his past and his poverty. . . . Our friend spends a great deal of money and tries to rehabilitate his relatives. But, after this first party of relatives, there arrives a second, third and fourth and there seems to be no end to the influx."

The American Jewish community of 1881 had been called "perhaps the happiest community in the long history of the Dispersion." The change was abrupt and devastating, and resented. Three Uptown luminaries, Jacob Schiff, Oscar Straus, and Jesse Seligman, paid a formal call on President Benjamin Harrison in 1891 to urge a government protest to Russia for forcing "groups of its people to seek refuge in another country." Even Miss Lazarus weakened. "For the mass of semi-Orientals, Kabbalists and Hassidim who constitute the vast majority of east European Israelites," she wrote, "some more practical measure of reforms must be devised than their transportation to a state of society [the United States] utterly at variance with their time-honored customs and most sacred beliefs." She came up with an idea: "They must establish an independent nationality."

So it was that previously aloof American Jews began to discover the desirability of settling Jews in Palestine—not themselves, of course, but the "other" Jews. I. M. Wise did not shrink from uttering aloud thoughts that were in the minds of many in the German-Jewish establishment. He urged readers of the *American Israelite* in 1887 to support a charity created to send Rumanian Jews to Palestine, "to protect us here against an immigration too large and too expensive for the common good." In case anyone still missed the point, he spelled it out: "We think it is the best and the cheapest thing we can do: . . . it liberates the oppressed

. . . it carries European civilization into Asia; it protects us here against a class of immigrants we do not want."

So spoke the acknowledged dean of American Jewry during the German ascendancy. But the voice of this happiest of Jewish communities was being drowned out by the cruel realities of social and generational change. On Wise's death in 1900, leadership of America's Jews passed from his Cincinnati base back to the East Coast cities; here the American-born sons of the German immigrants were taking a far more sympathetic view of the Jewish newcomers—the sons, after all, had been born into the security and comfort which their fathers had had to achieve for themselves.

As issues of civil rights and foreign wars would provoke social responsibility in later Jewish generations, the care and upbringing of the Russian immigrants became the cause of Uptown Jewish youth. In the soup kitchens and noisy social centers of the Lower East Side, the future leaders of American Jewry got their first taste of a wider world. One of the well-heeled students who rode the bus Downtown for social work was a Columbia University undergraduate named Joseph Proskauer. There he met a brilliant young immigrant, Abba Hillel Silver. For all their shared experiences on the Lower East Side, Proskauer and Silver would become arch-foes in maturity, representing opposite poles in the campaign for a Jewish state. Another of this new generation, a glamorous young rabbi with impeccable Uptown credentials named Judah L. Magnes, shocked many of his family friends by throwing himself into self-help organizations among the Russian immigrants. But then Magnes would spend his whole life doing the unpopular thing.

On the teeming Lower East Side, the Uptown Jews absorbed the contagious enthusiasm of their Downtown relatives. They promoted the urban night schools from which grew an intellectual dynamism, an energy and creativity which gave the literary and performing arts of twentieth-century America men like Irving Berlin, the Marx brothers, George S. Kaufman, S. N. Behrman, and George Gershwin. And the Uptown crowd began to learn more than I. M. Wise had ever told them about the new European political movement called Zionism, officially founded in 1896 by the assimilated Austrian-Jewish journalist Theodor Herzl.

The Russian immigrants were not all Zionists—they had, after all, just rejected the option of migrating to Palestine. The Socialist Labor movement, the Bund, had been formed in Poland the same year as Herzl's Zionism, and the Bundists had as little sympathy for Jewish Orthodoxy or bourgeois nationalism as did the Reform Judaism of I. M. Wise. Yet the organizational zeal of the Zionists, the clubrooms and endless political discussion groups, provided a comfortable social setting for people otherwise adrift in noisy and perplexing America. The young social activists from Uptown found that talk of Zionism gave them more access to the new Eastern European community than any of the other causes of the day.

The death of Herzl in 1904 brought general mourning to the Jewish neighborhoods of the Lower East Side. "I was amazed at the almost unanimous display of sentiment, and enquired of the man I was visiting whether all these people belonged to the Zionist movement," remarked a Jewish visitor from Uptown. "He replied that few, if any, would so much as buy a *shekel* . . . let alone join a Zionist society; nevertheless the news . . . had touched at the hearts of Zionist and non-Zionist alike."

From the puzzling human experience came a change in intellectual direction. The Russian immigration jolted America's Jews out of preoccupation with their New Palestine, stimulating renewal of interest in the old-fashioned visions of Noah and Leeser and the Jewish restoration. To some, the newfound interest grew from desperation to settle these primitive and alien Eastern Europeans somewhere—anywhere, almost—other than here. But more and more comfortable young American Jews found themselves caught up in the revolutionary cause they discovered in the Lower East Side Zionist clubs.

Gentile society of the day could hardly summon up the same fervor toward a return to Zion, but intellectual curiosity had already been provoked by numerous reports from Europe. In October 1870, readers of *The Atlantic Monthly* learned that "benevolent and public-spirited Jews" of Europe were launching schemes for the return of their people to agriculture. "The scene of the first experiment is Palestine itself," wrote the influential journal. "The disuse of eighteen centuries cannot be overcome in a year or two, but there is reason to believe that the people who once made their land a proverb for its abundant harvests are about to recover their skill in the cultivation of the soil."

The first eighteen pages of *The Atlantic* that October were devoted to an article called "Our Israelitish Brethren," by a popular writer of the day, James Parton. Jewish history shows "how uniformly they rise and expand and ennoble when the stigma is removed and the repressive laws are abolished," Parton explained. "America can boast no better citizens, nor more refined circles, than the good Jewish families of New York, Cincinnati, St. Louis, Philadelphia."

If a tone of protesting too much seeped through these remarks, it was for good reason. America after the Civil War saw the rise of intense status consciousness among immigrant groups jockeying for position within the Anglo-Saxon preserves. Of all the ethnic parvenus, the Jews, that strange race apart, posed the readiest target for social discrimination. In 1877 one of the nation's most prominent bankers, Joseph Seligman, a Jew, was turned away from the Grand Union Hotel in Saratoga, New York. Resort advertisements announced "Jews not admitted"; the shakier the social standing of the establishment, the more scrupulous were their proprietors in preserving the genteel and Gentile composition of their clientele. The *Saturday Evening Gazette* of Boston examined the city's Jewish citizenry in 1879 and concluded, "It is strange that a nation that boasts so many good traits should be so obnoxious." Then came the tidal wave of immigrants from Eastern Europe, and many American Christians displayed the same revulsion as Uptown Jewry, without the guilt feelings. There was even a new ideology afoot—a German publicist named Wilhelm Marr had just coined its title: "antisemitism."

The notion of implanting the Jewish nation in Palestine had appealed to early American Protestants on religious grounds; in this latter day no such delicacy was required. Striving Gentile Americans looked at the eastern immigrants and said, "Better Palestine than here."

As Pastor McDonald opened America's nineteenth century with a vision, another churchman came forward at the century's end with a plan for action. The word "Zionism" had yet to gain currency among the social and political elite of the nation, and America's Jews were not about to stir up any trouble over it. But the message came through from a spellbinding Protestant evangelist who captured the attention of the leaders of the land.

BORN A METHODIST in upstate New York in 1841, William Eugene Blackstone became an avid student of the Bible in boyhood. After the Civil War he followed the path of fortune to the West and established himself in Oak Park, Illinois, with a construction and investment company. Self-earned wealth gave him the space and security to pursue a sense of mission that reached far beyond the confines of a balance sheet. He threw himself into his lifelong avocation, the preparation for the Second Coming of Christ.

In 1878 Blackstone published his major work, *Jesus Is Coming,* and quickly assumed the stature of prophetic hero along the national circuit of revival meetings. The evangelical communities called him Reverend, though he never attended a theological seminary. His book sold over a million copies and was translated into forty-eight languages, including, eventually, Hebrew.

Blackstone's literal interpretations of Scripture may have offended mainstream American Protestantism, which had long since adopted a more flexible theology. But with his friends Dwight L. Moody and Cyrus I. Scofield, Blackstone clung to the Holy Text word for word, holding that the Jewish people remained to become once more God's elect, the chosen people. The evangelist took his daughter on a grand tour of Palestine in 1888, and with one eye on the inspiration of the Holy Land and the other on the social pressures of restive Russian Jewry crowding into the United States, this born-again businessman devised his plan.

Eventually, no less than 413 prominent Americans joined in his appeal, among them John D. Rockefeller, Cyrus McCormick, J. Pierpont Morgan, the Chief Justice of the Supreme Court, the Speaker of the House of Representatives, senators, clergymen, newspaper editors. It was a formidable listing of the American elite. Absent from their text were the inspirational, doctrinal arguments which generated such excitement on the revival circuit. The petition which Blackstone handed to President Benjamin Harrison on March 5, 1891, appealed to humanitarianism and, though hardly stated explicitly, the need to do something lest teeming crowds of immigrants would make life too uncomfortable for American society, socially endangered Jews as well as Gentiles.

"What shall be done for the Russian Jews?" Blackstone began, going straight to the point. "Why not give Palestine back to them again?" Under Jewish cultivation that land had once been remarkably fruitful, he argued. It had been a nation of commercial importance, the center of culture and religion.

If they could have autonomy in government, the Jews of the world would rally to transport and establish their suffering brethren in their time-honored habitation. For over seventeen centuries they have patiently waited for such a privileged opportunity. . . . Let us now restore to them the land of which they were so cruelly despoiled by our Roman ancestors.

Part promoter, part visionary, Blackstone anticipated objections to his plan—and dismissed them. The alternative of inviting persecuted Jews to America, for instance? "This will be a tremendous expense, and require years," he argued—the Palestine solution would seem not to be so burdened with practical difficulties. Is Palestine "ours" to give? Well, the Treaty of Berlin in 1878 "gave" the Turkish provinces of Bulgaria to the Bulgarians and Serbia to the Serbians—"does not Palestine as rightfully belong to the Jews?"

Blackstone knew, to be sure, that there were already other, non-Jewish, inhabitants of Palestine. "No expulsion of the present inhabitants of the land was contemplated," he explained. The new Jewish state would be founded only on public lands ceded by the Turkish state, just as

Bulgaria and Serbia had been. Blackstone was sure that the European powers sympathized with the Jewish restoration, for they had no wish to see Jews "crowded into their own countries." Nor could anyone charge that the United States, by taking the lead, was seeking imperial aggrandizement. "Her efforts for Israel would be recognized as entirely unselfish and purely philanthropic," Blackstone declared.

The Blackstone Memorial, as it was called, is a remarkable document: in its timing, 1891, half a decade before European Jewry heard the call of political Zionism; in its source, a fundamentalist Christian from the American heartland; and in the grandiose sweep of its naïve vision. It was a Christian document; prominent Jews whom Blackstone approached refused to sign, fearful of the trouble it might cause. In public discussion and editorial comment it generated more ferment in turn-of-the-century America than any other program dealing with the Jews and their fate, more even than a book published five years later called *Der Judenstaat* by Theodor Herzl, a mere café-hopping journalist in Paris and Vienna at the time Blackstone was holding forth.

Blackstone, in fact, was annoyed with Herzl's Zionism, for it found no sign of God's purpose in the call for a Jewish state. Indeed, as far as Herzl was concerned, it did not seem to matter where the state would be established—Palestine or Argentina or wherever. The Illinois churchman sent the founder of political Zionism a copy of the Old Testament, carefully marking those passages in which the prophets designate Palestine as the chosen land for the chosen people.

Modern Israelis hold convocations from time to time to commemorate Blackstone. The marked Bible is on display at Herzl's tomb in Jerusalem; a forest in Israel is dedicated to Blackstone's memory. Like Mordecai Noah, Blackstone is one of those bit players in the American epic whose memory is all but lost in his native land, while it is revered in the Jewish state that later came to be.

The Blackstone experience contained one lesson that would be learned and relearned over the coming half-century of Zionist agitation: the futility of grand public statements unaccompanied by pointed and discreet political pressures. For the fact is, nothing ever came of the Blackstone Memorial. Acknowledging its receipt, President Harrison promised "to give it careful consideration," but there is not the slightest evidence that he ever did so.

Blackstone himself continued preaching his message, undeterred by the lack of official response. Like the fundamentalist faithful who hearkened to his words, he used the growth of Zionism, the ingathering of the Jews, as evidence for his belief that the Second Coming was at hand. As time passed, many Christian enthusiasts grew annoyed at Zionists who insisted upon putting their secular political interests ahead of their God-given mission. Blackstone complained in his later writings that the Jewish national movement had fallen into the unworthy hands of atheists who ignored or even scorned the deep religious significance of their return to Zion.

Some fundamentalists succumbed to the mood of antisemitism which took hold in America in the 1920s and 1930s, but Blackstone himself held the line until his death in 1935. In the last two years of his life he wrote to his old Chicago mission urging them on toward the political solution he had first espoused decades before and, indeed, toward the religious mission assigned to America by the Puritans and old Pastor McDonald in the distant past. "I am more than ever interested in Israel's awakening," he wrote, "with prayers that many may come to know their true Messiah through your work."

Blackstone had tried to persuade the President of the United States by recalling the Persian monarch Cyrus, who permitted the Jewish nation to return from Babylon and build their Second Commonwealth in Jerusalem. "Not for 24 centuries," Blackstone told Benjamin Harrison, "has there been offered to any mortal such a privileged opportunity to further the purposes of God concerning His ancient people." Harrison himself was unmoved, but no one could then know the impact which the Bible story of Cyrus and the restoration of the Jews would have upon a later holder of presidential office, then a seven-year-old farm boy in Missouri.

SUCCESSIVE PRESIDENTS' professions of respect for the Jewish citizens of America could be dismissed as one of the mandatory hypocrisies of politics; though small relative to the whole electorate, the Jewish population was concentrated in large eastern cities where the popular vote was a critical electoral factor. It was a population, moreover, burdened with generations of insults and disrespect—recognition and kind words from Gentiles were eagerly sought and treasured when they came.

Yet among more sophisticated Jews there was a problem. In the egalitarian and idealistic society of America, the assumption was that a person of merit should rise on the strength of his own virtues, whatever his background or family position. To be singled out for recognition just for being a Jew, therefore, was not necessarily desirable. President Theodore Roosevelt once blundered in this regard. Shortly after he had named Oscar Straus, a Jew, to his Cabinet, a testimonial dinner was given in Washington under the sponsorship of the dean of Uptown Jewry, Jacob Schiff. All was mellow and patriotic, and Roosevelt seemed to hit just the right note in his speech when he praised Straus's ability and "devotion to high ideals." "I did not name him because he was a Jew," Roosevelt declared. "I would despise myself if I considered the race or the religion of a man named for high political office. . . . Merit and merit alone dictated his appointment." The dinner crowd applauded in appreciation of this testimonial to Straus and to America.

Then Schiff stood up to make the host's concluding remarks. Though he was practiced in looking alert and applauding at the right time, the venerable Jewish financier was in fact stone-deaf; he had been sitting on the dais without hearing a single word Roosevelt had said. Thus he knew no reason to skip over the following passage in his prepared statement: "Before making up his Cabinet, President Roosevelt sent for me and informed me that he wished to appoint a Jew as a member of his Cabinet, and asked me to recommend the ablest Jew who would be most acceptable to my race. I recommended Oscar Straus. He was appointed, and he has more than justified the recommendation." The crowd applauded nervously, Theodore Roosevelt stared into space.

PRESIDENTS AND POLITICIANS responded to one set of sensitivities. A quite different outlook moved the professional foreign policy experts.

Secretary of State James G. Blaine must have regretted all the bother he injected into the placid diplomatic preserve by taking "the Reverend" Blackstone to see President Harrison that March day of 1891. Concern for persecuted Jews was a constant element in the American diplomatic program, ever since the Damascus affair of 1840, but the newly emerging elite corps of diplomats could summon up little enthusiasm for the simplistic notions of an evangelist from Chicago.

State Department expertise on the remote Turkish province of Palestine had been slow in developing, though America had maintained nominal official representation in Jerusalem since 1832. At first the consular office was an honorary post bestowed casually on someone belonging to the expatriate community in the Ottoman lands. Even by the mid-nineteenth century, when Washington got around to dispatching American citizens to outposts in the Turkish empire, the type of person interested in serving in as backward a post as Jerusalem tended to be odd indeed.

The first full-time American consul in Jerusalem was Warder Cresson, eccentric son of a respected Quaker family of Philadelphia, friend and admirer of both Mordecai Noah and Isaac Leeser. Smitten by the missionary impulse in 1844, he used family influence to get an official appointment and set off for the Holy Land with his favorite dove, leaving wife and eight children behind. When alarming reports of his freewheeling representations to the local pashas reached Washington, the State Department canceled his commission. But Cresson stayed on, converted to Judaism—not the direction of conversion envisaged by the missionaries—and fought off his shocked family's attempts to have him declared legally insane. Noah fired off a deposition to the court in his friend's defense; "That a Christian court would decide that adopting Judaism as a religion would be a proof of insanity," Noah declared, "we can never believe."

A decade after Cresson the Department appointed a more conventional consul, a Boston physician named John Warren Gorham, who was so overcome by the disease and squalor of the Holy City, as well as the petty intrigues of the local religious communities, that he promptly succumbed to drink.

By the 1860s, a more serious breed of American representatives in Palestine began sending back discouraging dispatches about the movements afoot in Europe to resettle Jews in Palestine. "It will be impossible to bring Jews of different nationalities together and make them live in harmony," said an 1867 consular report. "It will require a greater miracle to bring all the Jews together than was required for their dispersion, and a greater miracle still, each day, to prevent their eager departure to the countries of their birth."

Not all the early diplomats were so sour on the matter. Lew Wallace, a Civil War general who won popular acclaim with his novel *Ben Hur,* served as American minister in Constantinople from 1881 to 1885 and was impressed by the efforts of the new Jewish settlers in Palestine; on his return home he championed the cause of large-scale Jewish colonization. Another consul in Jerusalem, Edwin S. Wallace (no relation), won a wide readership in turn-of-the-century America for his diplomatic memoir, *Jerusalem the Holy.* He argued that "the subject of Israel's restoration . . . is not a popular one now, but the unpopular of today is the universally accepted of tomorrow."

But for all their diplomatic titles, these were amateurs speaking. The United States diplomatic service was striving for professionalism, and enthusiasm did not seem professional. When the Blackstone Memorial reached the State Department, the man to whom the policymakers turned for advice on what to do about it was the most serious and influential of the nineteenth-century Jerusalem consuls, a former army chaplain named Selah Merrill.

Merrill first arrived in Jerusalem in 1882; with occasional breaks, he served as consul there for much of the next three decades. He wrote his share of the day's popular travel and antiquarian literature about the Holy Land, but his influence in Washington rested upon his extensive reportage of the growing Jewish settlements in Turkish Palestine. His reports were detailed and vivid; they were also highly prejudiced.

"Palestine is not ready for the Jews," Merrill concluded, and "the Jews are not ready for Palestine." As a race they are incapable of living on the land, he declared; they want only the life of the cities, "where they can live on the fortunes or the misfortunes of other people." The vision of the Blackstone Memorial filled him with disgust. "To pour into this impoverished country tens of thousands of Jews would be an unspeakable calamity both for the country and for the Jews themselves," he informed the Department of State in October 1891. "When and where have they learned the art of self-government? The quickest way to annihilate them would be to place them in Palestine with no restrictions or influences from any civilized government, and allow them to govern themselves; they would very soon destroy each other."

Given this perspective, the first considered assessment of the Jewish restoration in the State Department files, it is hardly surprising that Merrill would give his superiors in the diplomatic establishment no reason to take the Blackstone petition seriously. "Turkey was not in the habit of giving away whole provinces for the asking," he noted wryly. It was one thing to raise a general protest against distant persecutions; it was quite another to engage the honor of the United States in the practical plight of "degraded and undesirable persons" (in the words of Secretary of State Walter Quintin Gresham in 1893), unholy persons from Tsarist Russia who were at that time flooding through Ellis Island, "unfitted in many important respects for absorption into our body politic."

The death knell to the Blackstone campaign came in a penciled notation from Alvey A. Adee, head of the professional diplomatic service: "For thirty years and I know not how much longer, Turkey has writhed under the dread of a restoration of the Judean monarchy. Every few months we are asked to negotiate for the cession of Palestine to the Jewish 'nation.' The whole project is chimerical."

Adee was a professional's professional. Over an unprecedented thirty-eight consecutive years as Assistant Secretary of State, from 1886 to 1924, he dominated the conduct of American foreign affairs. His protégés were placed throughout the diplomatic service; his influence was discreet but far-reaching, and his curt dismissal of the Jewish national movement would echo through the official dispatches for years to come.

Taken as a class, the generation of American diplomats aspiring to high professional standing in the early twentieth century could scarcely have been less fitted to answer the questions about world Jewry that would press upon them and their successors. Clubby, a self-chosen elite, moving with hauteur through closed circles of the like-minded, these diplomats came almost without exception from a patrician society which had no taste for the immigrants descending upon America's shores, no taste for the Irish or the Poles, above all none for the Jews.

Blackstone and his lower- and middle-class Christian fundamentalists could still summon up visions of grandeur in the Jewish destiny. But such notions lacked the sophistication necessary to stir interest in the eastern boarding schools and colleges from which came the first leaders of America's diplomatic profession. (Adee, just to prove the rule, was educated at home by private tutors; his only college degree, from Yale, was an honorary M.A.)

More to their liking were the sentiments of, say, James Russell Lowell, who at first shared the atavistic Hebraic interests of his New England ancestors, but matured into a monomaniacal antisemite. "He detected a Jew in every hiding place and under every disguise," wrote a contemporary acquaintance. Asked at a dinner party what would happen when his hated Jews got control of all the world's affairs, Lowell replied in a melodramatic whisper, "That is the question which will eventually drive me mad." Nothing was at risk in discussing Jews in the Brahmin salons, for, contrary to the case with other immigrant groups like the Irish, there was little likelihood that anyone around the table had ever actually met one. Patrician antisemitism ranged from Lowell's obsessive concern with illusory Jewish power to the sheer snobbery of a Henry James: "There is no swarming like that of Israel, when once Israel had got a start."

This attitude reached its nadir in the nastiness of Henry Adams, a self-professed anachronism through most of his adult life. Adams had hoped to make his mark in the diplomatic service, but for all his illustrious family connections his career went nowhere. He took out all his bitterness on the parvenus whom he saw supplanting his own class in setting the tone of the nation. "In a society of Jews and brokers, I have no place," he mourned. "We are in the hands of the Jews. They can do what they please with our values. One does not want it any more."

Adams was an irascible fanatic, and recognized as such; among the critics of fashionable antisemitism were public figures of equally patrician cast, men like John Hay or William James or William Dean Howells. But they spoke in a rarefied world of intellect; the popular literature of the day, and most particularly the children's literature, was permeated with antisemitic stereotypes. Jews were routinely ridiculous figures, either old and shabby or ludicrously ostentatious. "Poor Auntie used to say nobody could ever get justice from a Jew dealer," said a character in a popular children's novel. Or, as argued by Annie F. Johnston, with her wide following among turn-of-the-century youth: "People who have been living in a ghetto for a couple of centuries are not able to step outside merely because the gates are thrown down."

This was the sort of literary diet available to an adolescent Wallace Murray (b. 1887) or Breckinridge Long (b. 1881) or Loy Henderson (b. 1892), future diplomats whose decisions would play such a large part in the Jewish fate in the twentieth century. Nothing they, or others like them, would learn or hear in their maturity could wholly erase its effects.

BETWEEN 1903 AND 1906, the press reported no less than 300 pogroms in Eastern Europe. All hopes of stemming the tide of immigration to the United States had disappeared, and the German-Jewish establishment began to face squarely the need to organize itself to represent Jewish interests and to integrate the newcomers into American life at the least possible social cost. The reluctance to assert themselves as Jews, a reluctance which had inhibited even Mordecai Noah as he made his way upwards in Gentile society, fell away.

By 1906, some of New York's most prominent Jewish leaders were ready to take a public position; they formed the blue-ribbon American Jewish Committee. Self-appointed, unabashedly elitist, they were on guard from the start against any suggestion of democratic procedure that might allow the growing Eastern European majority to take control. "Is it necessary that this Committee represent the riff-raff and everybody?" stormed Adolf Kraus, president of the Jewish fraternal order B'nai B'rith. "If the Committee represents the representative and high class Jews of America, that is enough." His colleagues agreed that unless the group "be composed of the most conservative men, the standing of the Jews in the American nation will be seriously affected for the worse."

Holding itself aloof from the mass of American Jewry, the American Jewish Committee nevertheless became an influential and articulate defender of Jewish interests through the first half of the twentieth century. With a patrician sense of noblesse oblige, the luminaries of the AJC espoused the cause of the Russian immigrants; "they became their spokesmen, they defended their politics for them, they looked after their physical and intellectual needs, they 'Americanized' them—and they despised them cordially," wrote one Jewish commentator.

The preferred technique of the AJC was always quiet diplomacy, the sophisticated use of personal contacts, the same method of "back channel" access that Jews had seen used against them in the past. This was the age-old Jewish tradition of the *shtadlan,* the smooth and well-placed petitioner who could move through Gentile society more comfortably than could the Jewish masses whose interests he professed to represent.

The excitable and impatient Russian Jews came to regard the gentility of the American Jewish Committee as inexplicable, if not downright cowardly. For decades past, humble voices had been raised against the seeming "sycophancy" of approaches to Gentile society. Now, from the Lower East Side, came articulate and vocal Jewish intellectuals who demanded aggressive assertion of Jewish interests—not just Zionism, but defense against antisemitism and equality of respect for differing faiths in public life. The strains between the two camps, the advocates of quiet *shtadlan* diplomacy and the champions of Jewish self-assertion, would provoke dissension and bitterness within the American Jewish leadership for many decades to come.

But there were other sources of conflict that cut far deeper: American Jewry found itself hopelessly divided over the fundamental concept of the Jewish identity: Does being a Jew mean membership in an exclusive race of mankind, or the profession of a particular faith? Does "Jewish" define a nationality, or a religious denomination? Even to pose the question brought discomfort, for it signaled the clash of two great Jewish traditions, the assimilationist yearnings of the emancipated and the minority nationalism of those left behind in Eastern Europe. The question of identity threatened the process of Americanization through which all the nineteenth-century immigrant groups sought to pass; it was brought to a head by the troublesome issue of Zionism.

Touring in Europe, Jacob Schiff met with Herzl; that pillar of the American Jewish establishment came home and dismissed the whole cause of political Zionism as a "sentimental theory," having no future whatever. Others were not so sure, and in the parlors of the respectable Uptown Jews, Zionism loomed as an irritant, "a disturber of their peace of mind . . . an offense to their Americanism . . . an obstacle to Jewish adjustment in a democratic environment; it revived memories they wished to forget." I. M. Wise fired his parting blast two years before his death, in the name of the socially respectable Reform movement: "We are unalterably opposed to political Zionism. . . . Zion was a precious possession of the past . . . but it is not our hope of the future. America is our Zion." At the other extreme, the religious Orthodox synagogues also condemned Zionism as a secular "Torah-less" movement, in which man presumed to do the work of God. And among the zealous Eastern European immigrants the strong Marxist contingent regarded the Zionists as nationalist reactionaries; come the world revolution, there would be no place for narrow bourgeois nationalism.

But Herzl had lit a spark which would not die out, and ironically it was the younger generation of I. M. Wise's own Reform movement that produced the American leaders of the Jewish national cause. From the

Lower East Side clubhouses the word began to spread. "When you see a Jew who is not a Zionist, hand him a Zionist pamphlet," advised the Zionist newspaper *The Maccabaean;* "if you haven't one with you, hand him an argument." Editorials in the journal endlessly attacked the prevailing conceptions of the Jewish establishment: "The Jewish nation cannot . . . be maintained in the religious form. It must re-establish itself on its own territory, re-assume its normal national life, before it can be freed from the delusions of compromise, 'catholic Judaism,' and the like."

The *shtadlanūt* of the American Jewish Committee came in for special scorn from the Zionists, even when it sought government action against European antisemitism. Quiet Jewish diplomacy to influence one government to influence another was futile, *The Maccabaean* argued. "The Jewish people must emancipate themselves; they must do their own philanthropy; they must solve their own problems."

By the outbreak of World War I, American Jewry was "split into two warring camps," Joseph Proskauer recalled. For all the heat and noise of the Zionists, they counted for little in the American Jewish community. No more than 20,000 of America's 2.5 million Jews belonged to any Zionist organization. The movement could claim a certain enthusiasm among the faithful, but it languished in administrative shambles, lacking managerial talent, a clear sense of direction, a dynamic leadership that could capture the imagination of the masses, both Jewish and Gentile.

Into this unpromising situation stepped the son of that mid-nineteenth-century immigrant couple from Bohemia.

2

AN ENDURING MYSTERY in the story of America and the Holy Land is why Louis Dembitz Brandeis suddenly became a Zionist. It was a strangely impulsive step for him, well into middle age, on the eve of World War I. Given the times and his reputation, Zionism was not the sort of cause that would come naturally to him. Doubts about his motives were raised from the start and have lingered on, half a century after his death. But whatever his motivation, Brandeis' act was to transform the Jewish national cause in the American mind.

Brandeis was born in Louisville, Kentucky, in 1856. Both mother and father, natives of Prague, came from dignified and emancipated families; they transplanted the cultivated air of their upbringing, and their new home in America remained a place where learning was respected. As a teen-ager, Brandeis went to Europe for two years of rigorous study at Dresden's Annen Realschule, then made his way at the age of eighteen to Harvard Law School without even earning an undergraduate degree.

The intellectual intensity of Cambridge was captivating. Instead of returning to Kentucky, Brandeis founded a Boston law firm with a classmate of the most proper New England lineage. This was in 1879. Their practice flourished. By the age of thirty-four Brandeis had achieved financial independence and was free to devote the bulk of his energies to causes that genuinely stirred his interest.

Brandeis was the prototype of the public interest lawyer, known in his day as the "people's advocate," champion of the minimum wage and the rights of the workingman against the giant combines of capital and industry. In his private life he was the typical assimilated Jew, totally unlettered in the Talmud or any formal religious instruction. He never attended synagogue; his relatives had married Gentiles without inhibition. As he later told British Foreign Secretary Lord Balfour during one of their long and mellow conversations, his entire life "had been free from Jewish contacts or traditions." Brandeis' speeches were full of literary allusions, but they rarely came from the Bible and those that did were as likely to be from the New Testament as from the Old. His brother-in-law was Felix Adler, founder of the Society for Ethical Culture, but even that offshoot of emancipated Judaism held no interest for him.

It is in the influence of another relative that the first clue to Brandeis' belated interest in the Jewish destiny may be found. His maternal uncle Lewis Dembitz, an eminent legal scholar and an abolitionist in the Kentucky borderland, conveyed the sense of the world to his nephew. The young Brandeis called him "a living university"; he took up the legal profession under his uncle's influence and formally changed his middle name from David to Dembitz. That this awesome uncle happened to be a devout Jewish nationalist, long before the cause had gained any prominence, could hardly have been overlooked.

Whatever talk may have passed between mentor and protégé on the prospect of the Jewish restoration, the subject never affected Brandeis' early career. As late as 1905, he was a prophet of the melting-pot vision for America, dismissing any role for the "hyphenated American"—the Protestant-American, the Catholic-American, the Jewish-American. Then, in 1907, Dembitz died. Within three years, still feeling his loss, Brandeis found himself enmeshed in the affairs of a type of Jew quite new to him, the working-class immigrants from Eastern Europe, so different in so many ways from the upper-class German-Jewish society of Boston and Uptown New York. A garment workers' strike in 1910 brought Brandeis to New York as arbitrator. The experience seems to have had a profound effect. "I am inclined to think there is more to hope for in the Russian Jews than from the Bavarian and other Germans," he wrote his father.

Brandeis' task was to mediate between nouveau riche garment manufacturers, who were Jewish, and their workers, also Jewish. "What struck me most was that each side had a great capacity for placing themselves in the other fellow's shoes," he recalled long afterward. "Each side was willing to admit the reality of the other fellow's predicament." It occurred to Brandeis that in the Jewish character might lie some special genius for democratic self-government.

In December 1910, Brandeis was interviewed by a Jewish newspaper editor named Jacob De Haas. A decade before, De Haas had been a close aide of Herzl, and the founder of political Zionism had sent him to America to mobilize the Jews to the cause. De Haas made little headway at first and drifted into pursuits more lucrative than grass-roots political action, but he never overlooked an opportunity to carry out Herzl's mission.

As Brandeis recited his melting-pot philosophy, De Haas asked about

Zionism. "I have a great deal of sympathy for the movement and am deeply interested in the outcome," Brandeis replied casually. "These so-called dreamers are entitled to the respect and appreciation of the entire Jewish people." De Haas grabbed at his chance and put the headline in the Boston *Jewish Advocate:* "Brandeis Sympathizes with Zionism." Brandeis' remarks reflected his warm feelings toward the cause of his late uncle and his own attitudes toward the Eastern European Jewish communities where Zionism was making such headway. But what he actually said in that interview hardly justifies the headline's definitive tone. For months to come, Brandeis had little contact with Zionism.

Early in 1912, he found himself in a casual dinner-table conversation about an agricultural experiment station in Palestine. "The talk was the most thrillingly interesting I have ever heard," Brandeis wrote to his brother, "showing the possibilities of scientific agriculture and utilization of arid or supposedly exhausted land." Here, for the first time, was a sign of the enthusiasm that could lead a man into a cause; significantly, it was not a point of ideology or traditional European Zionist principle that caught his interest, but a practical, pragmatic project already underway. Ever the foe of "bigness" in social and economic affairs, touched already by a belief in the Jewish capacity for self-government, Brandeis was drawn by the prospect of a small, dynamic, progressive Jewish community in the land of Palestine.

The sequence of what happened next is important for an understanding of the controversy that later developed over Brandeis' "conversion." A foray into national politics reached a dead end in the spring of 1912 when Brandeis' favorite, the Progressive Robert La Follette, failed in his drive for the Republican presidential nomination. During the summer Brandeis met the Democratic candidate, Woodrow Wilson, and decided to throw himself into Wilson's campaign instead.

On Cape Cod, where Brandeis spent almost every August of his adult life, who should arrive to talk about Democratic Party fund-raising but the eager journalist De Haas. Their ostensible business completed, Brandeis was driving his visitor to the train station when De Haas casually referred to the late Lewis Dembitz. "He was a noble Jew," De Haas remembers saying, and the remark caught Brandeis up short—what did he mean by that? And what was the man Herzl like, whom De Haas had served in his younger days? Brandeis turned the car around, urged De Haas back home for lunch and more talk. From this conversation, August 13, 1912, is traditionally dated Brandeis' "conversion" to Zionism.

Nothing could be done immediately in the heat of a presidential campaign. Brandeis figured high on the list of potential Cabinet members after Wilson's election, first for the post of Attorney General, then Secretary of Commerce; Wilson was eager to have this brilliant mind at his side. But he took the political precaution of sounding out the Jewish community, as he knew it, for their reaction to the possible appointment. From Jacob Schiff and the magnates of the American Jewish Committee came back the word that Brandeis, whatever else he might be in American life, was not a "representative Jew." This was a code phrase. A "representative Jew" would bring with him significant Jewish community support; no such support could be anticipated from appointment of a Jew who was not "representative." On March 4, 1913, the Wilson Cabinet was announced, and Brandeis was not a member.

Sixteen days later Brandeis agreed to introduce a visiting European Zionist at a public meeting at Boston's Faneuil Hall; it was his first appearance at a Zionist function. Declining an invitation to speak himself, Brandeis nevertheless listened carefully to the Zionist orator and impulsively went forward to shake his hand. "Thank you," the people on the platform heard him say, "you have brought me back to my people." On April 17, 1913, he formally joined the Zionist Association of Boston. For the next two and a half years, Louis D. Brandeis lectured all across the country, lending his prestige and zeal to the hitherto obscure European ideology of Jewish nationalism. In January 1916, when Wilson named him Associate Justice of the Supreme Court, the Jewish community leaders gave him their unqualified support. What had changed their minds?

The cynical implication in this sequence of events is that Brandeis used the cause of Zionism for his own political advancement; checked in his political ambitions by his lack of a personal base in the Jewish community, he set about (within sixteen days!) to build that base and become a prominent "representative Jew."

William Howard Taft, former President of the United States, was an early purveyor of this charge of political opportunism. Taft was just the kind of political enemy that Brandeis enjoyed collecting. Champion of the conservative monied interests, head of a Republican administration blemished by financial intrigues which Brandeis had helped expose, Taft had wanted for himself the seat on the Supreme Court. When it went instead to his radical Jewish adversary, Taft wrote a long letter giving the story as he had heard it from one of his sympathetic contacts in the American Jewish Committee.

Brandeis, Taft declared,

was no Jew until he was rejected by Wilson as Attorney General, because the leading Jews of the country told Wilson that Brandeis was not a representative Jew. Since that time, Brandeis has

adopted Zionism, favors the New Jerusalem, and has metaphori-
cally been recircumcised. He has gone all over the country making
speeches, arousing the Jewish spirit, even wearing a hat in the
Synagogue while making a speech in order to attract those bearded
Rabbis. . . . If it were necessary, I am sure he would have grown
a beard to convince them that he was a Jew of Jews. All this has
made it politically difficult for not only the Jews but for anybody
looking for office where there are Jews in the constituency, to
hesitate about opposing Brandeis. The humor of the situation I
cannot, even in the sorrow of the appointment, escape.

Brandeis' long and distinguished career in the Supreme Court was
not troubled by the charge of political opportunism, but long after his
death historians began reviving the innuendoes, particularly historians in
the state of Israel. American defenders of his memory rushed to his
defense, and the controversy among scholars has simmered ever since.

The most telling point in Brandeis' defense involves the contradictions that existed within the Jewish community's higher reaches. Notable
among notables of the Uptown Jews, Jacob Schiff would obviously not
consider Brandeis a "representative Jew"; Schiff considered himself the
"representative Jew." In their social and economic outlook, Schiff and
the patricians of the American Jewish Committee were much closer to
the moneyed anti-Brandeis interests than they were to the common folk
whom Brandeis championed. For all his admitted lack of Jewish associations, Brandeis' philosophy drew him far closer to the Russian-Jewish
immigrants than to the likes of Schiff.

Next, if Brandeis had consciously set out to obtain proper Jewish
credentials after his rejection for the Wilson Cabinet, he would hardly
have espoused a cause which had virtually no standing, was even considered repugnant, among the influential Jews of the country. Being a
Zionist in 1913 was no positive recommendation among men of influence.
And even when the popular mood had changed by 1916, largely because
of Brandeis' own efforts, conservatives at the AJC held to their cynical
anti-Brandeis opinions.

From his position of Olympian gentility, Taft can perhaps be forgiven
for failing to grasp these internal Jewish concerns. But modern Israeli
scholars understand full well the family quarrels that cluttered the path
to the Jewish state. There must be some other reason why an analysis
that diminishes the stature of Brandeis, even in small measure, finds a
sympathetic response.

Perhaps it is this: Brandeis was a stranger to the European Zionist
mainstream, the doctrinal tradition that culminated in the establishment

of Israel. He was a brusque and authoritarian newcomer with ideas of his own. When, belatedly, he embraced Zionism, he redefined it to his own liking. Instead of accepting the style and outlook of the Russian Pale, the root source of Zionist strength, he attempted to impose the values of American progressives. The grafting did not take, and today, looking back, Israelis view Brandeis' Americanized Zionism with bemusement; his short-lived movement is regarded as an unsympathetic and alien dead end, and his place in the Zionist pantheon is, at best, a modest one.

SEVEN YEARS PASSED before the confrontation between American and European Zionism broke into the open, years of world war and upheaval. For all the latter-day arguments about whether Brandeis used Zionism to serve his own interests, no one disputes that Brandeis served Zionism's interests at the moment when it most needed help. In prosperous neutral America, he brought visibility, respectability, and, above all, organizational zeal to a near-moribund cause. Zionist membership in America grew from 20,000 to nearly 200,000 during World War I; even Jacob Schiff found himself willing, by 1918, to raise money for the Jewish colonies in Palestine.

To the typical established American Jew beyond the Lower East Side, Zionism was vaguely unsavory; it seemed another of those airy *fin-de-siècle* political movements from a contentious Europe, ill defined and quixotic, played out in endless debates, coffeehouse intrigues, obscure manipulations in a dozen chancelleries. With its Central Office in Berlin, there was even confusion about which side Zionism would take as the empires of Europe slipped toward war.

August 1914 found Brandeis at his South Yarmouth resort home— the assassination of an Austrian archduke a month or so before could hardly upset the vacation habits of a lifetime. Though officially a member of the American Zionist Federation, Brandeis rejected repeated urgings that he assume a post of national leadership, much to the despair of De Haas and his colleagues. But in his vacation reading that month was a hastily assembled brief on the "Jewish problem," and by the end of August, events had converged upon him in unexpected fashion.

In the last days before the outbreak of war, Herzl's successors in England and France had managed to remove the Zionist Central Office from Berlin, and De Haas secured its transfer to neutral America. That determined newspaperman even had a thought about who the new provisional leader of the movement might be. "The welfare of seven-tenths of the Jewish race" is at issue, he pleaded, knowing how Brandeis liked precision of number; toward other possible claimants to emergency wartime leadership, De Haas was disdainful. "We already know what we can expect of the men of the Schiff type." Brandeis cut his vacation two days short and set out by overnight boat for Manhattan. On August 30, 1914, at New York's Hotel Marseilles, an extraordinary conference of 150 American Zionist delegates established the Provisional Executive for General Zionist Affairs to assume the functions of the abandoned Berlin office. The meeting pledged to raise $200,000 for an emergency fund, and it formally elected Brandeis chairman. Scarcely a year after joining its Boston branch, Brandeis found himself chief executive officer of an international political movement.

His acceptance speech at the Hotel Marseilles made plain the pragmatic, non-doctrinaire approach that would be his from this point onwards. "Throughout long years which represent my own life, I have been to a great extent separated from Jews," he admitted.

> I am very ignorant of things Jewish. But recent experiences, public and professional, have taught me this: I find Jews possessed of those very qualities which we of the twentieth century seek to develop in our struggle for justice and democracy; a deep moral feeling which makes them capable of noble acts; a deep sense of the brotherhood of man; and a high intelligence, the fruit of three thousand years of civilization. These experiences have made me feel that the Jewish people have something which should be saved for the world; that the Jewish people should be preserved; and that it is our duty to pursue that method of saving which most promises success.

This was a far different tone from the overblown rhetoric and folk mysticism that the Zionist faithful were used to hearing. Instead of the usual belabored abstractions, Brandeis proposed leading Zionism toward the outcome "which most promises success." The Brandeis revolution had begun.

In the disarray of war, the European Zionist leaders were in no position to challenge America's provisional leadership. Indeed, many cabled their satisfaction in this distinguished new convert to their cause. No longer did Brandeis plead the pressure of other work; "Zionist affairs are really the important things in life now," he wrote his brother.

Even before letting the delegates disperse he called for reports on the membership of their diverse organizations, their budgets, the activities they were prepared to undertake. For two more days he sat in his room at the Hotel Marseilles, interrogating the faithful, briefing himself on the administrative shambles which he had suddenly agreed to direct.

Drawing on all the professional, social, and political connections at his disposal, Brandeis overturned the habits of a generation. He closed down the ramshackle old Zionist offices on lower Second Avenue and brought the headquarters into the mainstream, to Fifth Avenue and Eighteenth Street. "He would come to the Zionist offices in New York early in the morning and remain for hours, receiving visitors, questioning them, and assigning tasks," recalls a co-worker. "He would take his coat off, loosen his tie, ruffle his hair, use his hands actively and twist his body in the chair as he carried on a hearty discussion with infinite patience."

Unabashedly the intellectual snob, Brandeis pursued the "college men," preferably those from Harvard Law, hoping to bring quality and political drive to the cause—and offering them the chance to further their own careers in the process. "A summons to meet . . . Brandeis was like nothing else," recalled one young recruit; "to me it was like being invited to meet a Moses, a Jefferson, a Lincoln." Headed by one so close to the Wilson administration, the reinvigorated Zionist movement offered young lawyers promising ground for pursuing their professional and political ambitions. Felix Frankfurter, Benjamin V. Cohen, Julian Mack—these were just a few of the young aspirants who followed Brandeis as a Pied Piper to prominence.

Brandeis devised an exclusive channel for exercising his magnetic leadership, parallel to the official network of Zionist organizations across the country. This was an elitist secret society called the Parushim, the Hebrew word for "Pharisees" and "separate," which grew out of Harvard's Menorah Society. As the Harvard men spread out across the land in their professional pursuits, their interests in Zionism were kept alive by secretive exchanges and the trappings of a fraternal order. Each invited initiate underwent a solemn ceremony, swearing the oath "to guard and to obey and to keep secret the laws and the labor of the fellowship, its existence and its aims."

Brandeis himself eventually tired of the sophomoric trappings of ritual and oaths, but he used the Parushim as a private intellectual cadre, a pool of manpower for various assignments that might have been smothered by the rhetoric and debate of the public Zionist clubs. "An organization which has the aims which we have must be anonymous," explained an early recruiter, "must work silently, and through education and infection rather than through force and noise, and can gain results only insofar as its standards are made to live in the lives of the people to whom they are brought. But nothing could be more suicidal than the announcement of such an object, so that the secrecy is inevitable."

Stripped of the ritual and regalia, the Parushim were a sort of precursor of the informal Zionist discussion groups that coalesced in official Washington during the 1940s. The members set about meeting people of influence here and there, casually, on a friendly basis. They planted suggestions for action to further the Zionist cause long before official government planners had come up with anything. For example, as early as November 1915, a leader of the Parushim went around suggesting that the British might gain some benefit from a formal declaration in support of a Jewish national homeland in Palestine. It seemed an unlikely idea at the time.

The leader and guiding spirit of the Parushim, and one of the most important formative influences on American Zionism, was a social philosopher named Horace Kallen. Modest and self-effacing—a rarity among Zionist leaders—Kallen has never received the credit due him for the phenomenal upsurge of Zionist activity in the Brandeis years. Son of an Orthodox rabbi, he attended Harvard, turned secular in his interests, and while still an undergraduate in 1903 met Brandeis. Though the student and the eminent lawyer had many long and mellow talks together about the nature of man, justice, and society, Kallen never revealed at that time that he had secretly taken up the cause championed by Herzl in Europe.

Kallen left the intellectual comfort of Cambridge for a junior faculty post at Princeton; his appointment there was not renewed after it became known that he was a Jew. He settled as instructor of philosophy and psychology at the University of Wisconsin, but there he grew lonely for old friends, and found in the idea of a secret order the chance to maintain Harvard associations and assert at the same time his own modern Jewish identity.

In 1913, hearing of Brandeis' emerging interest in Zionism, Kallen wrote to his old mentor about his own philosophy: "In Palestine we aim at a new state and a happier social order." No giant corporations would control society, there would be no class struggles or predatory wealth. "There are . . . in Jewish Palestine . . . exploiting and exploited classes," Kallen said. "None of these is necessary; all are avoidable by right beginnings."

This was just the kind of progressive idealism that Brandeis liked. Embarked on his own search for the "right beginnings," he invited his old student friend to South Yarmouth in August 1914. Kallen accompanied Brandeis on the overnight boat to New York on the eve of the Zionist conference that elected him to the chairmanship of the movement. In their long conversations emerged the philosophical underpinnings for Brandeisian Zionism.

First, Brandeis had to modify his old faith in the melting-pot vision for America, his scorn of "hyphenated Americans." Kallen pressed upon him another vision, the then novel idea of "cultural pluralism," arguing that America promised opportunity for growth not only for individuals

but for ethnic groups as well. Brandeis did not resist for long, for exposure to the community of Russian immigrants had shaken his earlier
beliefs. On July 4, 1915, he declared his new conviction, his leap from
the melting pot to the salad bowl as the vessel for the American dream:

> America . . . has always declared herself for equality of nationali-
> ties as well as for equality of individuals. America has believed
> that each race had something of peculiar value which it can con-
> tribute. . . . America has always believed that in differentiation,
> not in uniformity, lies the path of progress.

Now the way lay open for Brandeis to link Jewish group identity,
through Zionism, with the American dream. Assimilation to the majority
culture, he argued, would be national suicide. With a stroke of rhetoric
he cut through the dilemma of dual loyalties. "Let no American imagine
that Zionism is inconsistent with Patriotism," he declared. "Multiple
loyalties are objectionable only if they are inconsistent. . . . A man is a
better citizen of the United States for being also a loyal citizen of his
state, and of his city. . . . There is no inconsistency between loyalty to
America and loyalty to Jewry. The Jewish spirit . . . is essentially modern and essentially American."

Brandeis delighted in the links of early America with the values of the
Old Testament. The nouveau Brahmin of Boston invoked the Puritans,
their struggles against nature and mankind to build their ethical society;
"Zionism is the Pilgrim inspiration and impulse over again," he declared.
"The descendants of the Pilgrim fathers should not find it hard to understand and sympathize with it." Repeatedly, as he crossed the country,
Brandeis merged the American and Jewish heritages. "Only through the
ennobling effect of [Zionist] strivings can we develop the best that is in
us, and give to this country the full benefit of our great inheritance," he
concluded. "To be good Americans, we must be better Jews, and to be
better Jews, we must become Zionists."

The more alert in Brandeis' audiences might have noticed the little
trick in his eloquence, his almost interchangeable use of the terms "Jewish" and "Zionist" in invoking ancient values and future destiny. This
"carelessness"—which it certainly was not—conveniently disregarded
the struggle going on within Jewry, the uphill battle which the Zionist
minority was fighting to identify their cause with their whole people. His
eloquence had a devastating effect on the Jews in his hearing who had
not believed that Zionism was what Judaism had to offer the modern
world.

By rooting his conception of Zionism so firmly in Americanism, Brandeis set himself apart from the ideology of the European Zionist move-

ment. Herzl's Zionism had grown out of a heritage of antisemitism, which European Jewry regarded as universal in Christian society. From the security of the *Goldene Medine,* Brandeis rejected that belief. Though he had himself experienced genteel forms of antisemitic prejudice in his Boston law practice and from his Christian neighbors in the fashionable suburb of Dedham, he did not let his emotions carry him into a sweeping judgment on the Jewish fate in Christendom. Like I. M. Wise, Brandeis always assumed the goodwill of the Christian majority. America may not have become the new Palestine—Brandeis stopped short of Wise on that score—but it still offered a welcome and an opportunity for Jewish survival at least as promising as that of the ancient homeland.

In short, Brandeisian Zionism stood for the enrichment of Jewish life in America as well as in Palestine. Like American Jews from Mordecai Noah onward, Brandeis never believed that a Jew would have to move to Palestine in order to remain a Jew. His Zionism "was almost entirely philanthropic in nature," wrote a Jewish leader long after the Brandeisian revolution had died out. "It was no more than a desire to 'help others.' They did not feel that they needed Zionism for themselves in any way." I am my brother's keeper, said the Brandeisian, but I am not my brother.

Zionism was a great social experiment, representing "in Jewish life what Progressivism does in general American life," said Brandeis. It sought to create a model new society in a small and sacred land, where exciting new forms of democratic social institutions could flourish on the soil of the ancient heritage, offering equal justice, self-government, and economic opportunity for the common man in the land of his fathers. And it could provide refuge for the Jews of Europe who were not welcome in the United States.

Brandeis, the controversial "people's advocate," put Zionism on the agenda of public debate in America, but his identification with the Jewish cause also stirred criticism from all the forces that had long regarded him as a radical enemy of American capitalism. "Brandeis, the Boston butterin, is a high-grade opportunist," commented the *Los Angeles Times,* adding its hope that Brandeis would "open real estate offices in Jerusalem and thrive there—and stay there, above all, stay there."

Zionists "believe that the Russian Jews should be experimented upon," commented I. M. Wise's heirs on the *American Israelite.* "If Mr. Brandeis and one hundred prominent Jews go to Palestine and live, then will their example cause thousands of others to follow suit; will the Zionists accept this challenge?" The *Israelite,* for one, did not miss the trick in Brandeis' rhetoric: "Mr. Brandeis is entitled to his opinion that Zionism is the panacea for all Israel's ills. But when he says that all those who do not agree with him 'are against their own people,' he is guilty of uttering that which is not true and of being grossly impertinent at the same time. Who is Mr. Brandeis to judge his brethren?"

Brandeis tried to stay aloof from the organizational rivalries that had so immobilized the Zionist movement in the prewar decade, the clash of the Uptown *Yehudim* and the Downtown *Yidden.* Coming from neither society, he nevertheless could not long conceal his contempt for the monied magnates of Uptown. He decided to lend his support to the drive for a democratic body, the American Jewish Congress, to supplant the American Jewish Committee (the similarity in names was not accidental) in speaking for American Jewry. The Congress was just what the Committee notables had feared; "the riff-raff and everybody" were presuming to usurp leadership. The American Jewish Congress signaled the revolt of Downtown; its success caught the attention of political analysts in Washington and abroad who were in the habit of looking Uptown for "representative Jews." A new group seemed to have taken charge of the Jewish vote, if there were such a thing, and with Brandeis at its head it seemed firmly committed to the cause of Zionism.

Brandeis said his appointment to the Supreme Court proved that "in the opinion of the President there is no conflict between Zionism and loyalty to America." This may have impressed those who were still troubled about dual loyalties, but it did not impress the immigrants down on the Lower East Side. They muttered about a Brandeis betrayal—that, given the chance, he turned his back on his people and accepted a position in the Gentile power structure. But Brandeis had no intention of turning his back; he fully intended to remain at the helm of the Zionist organization. The fact that he saw no conflict of interest confirmed that his concept of Zionism was philanthropic at heart. It apparently did not occur to him that the global political movement of which he was provisional head could one day—in fact, soon—clash with the government of the United States.

Brandeis' many enemies among both Jews and Gentiles came forth during his confirmation hearings. A rival Zionist leader, Judah Magnes, attacked him angrily for his political maneuverings on the issue of summoning the democratic American Jewish Congress. The Ochs and Sulzberger families' *New York Times* echoed the Uptown establishment in urging him, as a sitting Justice of the Supreme Court, to withdraw from "activities of a political or social nature." Hurt by the criticism, Brandeis resigned on July 21, 1916, from all his posts of authority in Zionism. It was just short of two years since he had assumed active leadership.

But he remained the power behind the scenes of American Zionism. Daily reports from the New York headquarters, including financial statements, went to his Supreme Court chambers in Washington. For his associates and successors, he was still "the chief." And within a year of his arrival in the nation's capital he would be called upon for another act of service to Zionism.

WASHINGTON, the capital of the American republic, was a placid community in those years before the Great War. Motorcars were rarities, long avenues of trees brought beauty and shade to leisurely strollers along wide promenades. The business of government was civilized and not really time-consuming, at least compared with what it would later be; particularly was this so in the realm of foreign affairs. As the Old World empires slipped into their war, the little club of professional diplomats was well ensconced in its own sheltered preserve.

During working hours, gentlemanly short, the diplomats inhabited the grandiose granite block next to the White House, four stories of columns, porticos, and mansard roofs evoking the grandeur of Second Empire France. Silent functionaries in cutaway coats strode up and down the wide, semicircular stairways with the huge bronze balusters, intent upon obscure missions of presumed import.

Away from the demands of office, the most elite of the elite, men like the young William Phillips, Joseph Grew, and Hugh Gibson, would gather at the genteel rooming house at 1718 H Street, in northwest Washington, where the bachelors among them maintained a pied-à-terre. They called themselves "the Family"; these civilized young men formed the nucleus of what would become the Foreign Service of the United States. It was a life of comfort and composure.

Occasionally, moments of tension intruded. When Britain and France found themselves at war in 1914 with the Ottoman Turkish Empire, lackluster ally to Germany, neutral America was asked to represent their interests in the obscure Turkish province of Palestine. Routine operations were hampered by a Turkish ban on international communications in an "enemy" language, including English. The American ambassador's complaints elicited a decree from Constantinople authorizing use of "the American language," and a missionary publication heralded the triumph: "Great is diplomacy!"

The Christian missionaries were one of three groups in American society that paid attention to developments in the Ottoman lands; the other two were oil men and Jews.

From its modest beginnings as a romantic crusade, the American missionary community had grown into a formidable educational force in the Middle East. Robert College in Constantinople, founded in 1863, and the Syrian Protestant College, founded in 1866, later named the American University of Beirut, were emerging centers of national awakening among the diverse minorities under Ottoman rule. The missionaries had shed their simplistic fundamentalism and become an establishment of well-endowed educators. With contacts at all levels of Ottoman society, they could rightly claim an expertise in the affairs of the region that eluded the representatives of government and commerce.

One of the minority groups of the Turkish empire, the Jews of Palestine, had lost their appeal to the Christian missions. They were so few in number—at the most 80,000 before World War I, compared with the millions of surrounding Arabs. More to the point, these Jews were absolutely intransigent about clinging to their group identity; even the secular pioneering immigrants from Europe showed no interest in a modern Christian education.

The oil and commercial entrepreneurs were equally frustrated in their attempts to exploit the anarchy of the Ottoman Empire. Bribes and ministrations to the court of the Sultan by American venture capitalists were abruptly undermined by the Young Turk coup d'état of 1908, and for all their continuing effort American commercial interests found themselves regularly outmaneuvered by the wily cartels of Europe.

But among the diplomatic professionals in Washington, the Christian missionaries and the venture capitalists were respectability itself compared with that third group of concerned Americans. The Zionists made a certain amount of noise, particularly after Brandeis took over the movement, but their interest was too parochial to be taken seriously by the makers of foreign policy. As far as the Turkish province of Palestine was concerned, for all except those who thrived on romantic travel literature about the Holy Land, it was only a nuisance.

The life of the American consul in Jerusalem had become tedious, consumed in petty disputes among rival commercial and religious groups of Jews claiming the protection of the American flag. Under the Ottoman system of "capitulations," foreign consuls were permitted to dispense extraterritorial justice among their own nationals. Whichever rival faction the hapless consul might choose, partisans of the losers in the United States would bombard the State Department with complaints.

The Department of State had created a Near East Division in 1909, parallel to the more established divisions for the Far East and Western Europe. The sense of politics and geography in those days was such that the new division's purview spanned the empires of Russia, Germany, Austria-Hungary, and the Ottomans, plus Italy, Greece, the Balkans, Abyssinia, Persia, Egypt, and the French and British colonies in the Mediterranean. In this galaxy, concerns of Palestine did not loom large. Secretary of State William Jennings Bryan's ideas for the Holy Land began and ended with his suggestion that an American group of investors should obtain an option to buy the Galilean hillside from which Jesus delivered his Sermon on the Mount. Revolutions and coups d'état in the Balkans and the Near East counted for little, in the diplomats' view; the map of the Near East on the Secretary of State's office wall was fully fifty years out of date.

As long as the various Zionist representations to the Department dealt with humanitarian relief matters, as they generally did under Brandeis' leadership, the diplomats responded sympathetically. The State Department protested Turkish attempts to expel Jewish settlers as potential enemy aliens; it urged similar measures of protection for the Armenian and other minorities. In rare recognition of domestic political interests, the Department obliged President Wilson in his 1916 reelection campaign by producing a public memorandum of all the international representations made in defense of Jewish civil rights the world over. The statement had a certain effect in metropolitan areas where the Jewish vote could well be important to the President.

But the Department cast a wary eye upon any approach from the Zionists that implied political engagement. The Near East Division dismissed one Zionist proposal in 1913, noting that it "would involve American political activity in the Ottoman Empire." Even a letter from Brandeis conveying the Zionist political program in May 1917 seems to have been ignored by the State Department officers responsible for the area.

To preside over this unruffled foreign policy establishment came an unruffled Secretary of State. Reserved, proper, and conservative, Robert Lansing may once have had President Wilson's confidence, but their relationship failed to survive the rigors of high office. Neither intellectually nor temperamentally could Lansing compete for influence with the shrewd and manipulative Edward M. House, the reserve colonel from Texas who, without title or staff, superseded the State Department in charting the foreign policy of the Wilson era. It was through Colonel House, and not Secretary Lansing, that Britain and the Zionists worked on the first great diplomatic act of the Jewish national cause.

It would become known as the Balfour Declaration. But as it was taking shape, the Department of State was off on another tangent, a venture that left scarcely a trace in diplomatic history and served only to renew that old suspicion of international Zionism as a nefarious conspiracy.

The episode began casually enough. One day in May 1917, in his second-floor office overlooking the White House gardens, Secretary Lansing placed a telephone call, then dictated a letter (he could never be sure that Wilson would return his calls). "My dear Mr. President: I had yesterday two conversations in relation to Turkey which are worthy of consideration . . ."

The first was with the private secretary of the United States ambassador, just returned from Constantinople—Lansing did not note the gentleman's name. Turkey had broken relations with the United States the month before, but the two countries were not formally at war. The secretary's information was that the weary Turks might be induced to break with Germany and reach a separate peace. Could the United States mediate in this delicate undertaking?

Lansing had been impressed and, by chance, he received a second report later the same day, this time from a man whose name he knew well: Henry J. Morgenthau, former American ambassador to the Ottoman Empire. Morgenthau, then sixty-one, was one of those nineteenth-century German-Jewish immigrants who had thrived in the New World; his fortune was secured when he managed to buy up promising plots of land at the future stops of the advancing New York City subway system. His appointment to Constantinople came in recognition of his financial help to Wilson in the presidential campaign. Though retired from diplomacy by 1917, Morgenthau remained eager to be of service, and he succeeded in persuading Lansing that, with his many old contacts, he was the man to sound out the Turks about peace.

As it happened, Wilson did return the Secretary of State's call, three days later, and the two reached rather absentminded agreement that Morgenthau should be sent off to see what he could do. What seemed like a harmless idea quickly turned awkward as it became apparent what it meant to the forces more directly concerned. Britain was about to launch an invasion of Turkish Palestine, and separate peace moves could be inconvenient for her imperial designs upon the Ottoman territories. Even more alarmed were the diverse nationality groups agitating for postwar liberation from the Turkish yoke—Armenians, Arabs, and Jews— all of whom saw a separate peace as a threat to their aspirations.

Morgenthau had no sympathy for Zionism, but he agreed to accept as traveling companion a protégé of Brandeis', a thirty-five-year-old Harvard law professor named Felix Frankfurter, whose presence ensured that the Zionists were kept fully informed about the envoy's actions. Britain moved discreetly to scotch the American initiative by dispatching an immigrant chemist from Russia named Chaim Weizmann, who was gaining influence in the Zionist movement, to intercept the Morgenthau party at Gibraltar. There he and Frankfurter succeeded in talking the would-be peacemaker out of proceeding any further.

The whole affair fizzled out, leaving the American diplomatic establishment convinced that the failure was the direct result of a Zionist conspiracy in the imperial chancellories of Europe. Never mind that Morgenthau himself was an avowed anti-Zionist; never mind that the Zionists' opposition succeeded only because Britain had arranged Weizmann's scuttling errand; never mind that Lansing and his advisers had regarded the mission as a long shot anyway. To the diplomats at State, the episode rankled. To them, as to Stuyvesant centuries before, it seemed one more ominous proof of that strange power which international Jewry could call upon to thwart national governments and achieve its own ends. The instincts of antisemitism lurking among the class of diplomats received a new note of encouragement—and just at the moment when international Zionism was poised for a genuine diplomatic triumph.

Of that greater drama, going on parallel to Lansing's modest efforts, the American Secretary of State knew absolutely nothing.

EARLY IN MAY 1917, the same month that Lansing began thinking about sending Morgenthau to Turkey, two distinguished gentlemen lingered over breakfast at a Washington hotel. They had met a few days before at a formal White House luncheon, and each had his own professional reasons for wanting to pursue a relationship. One man at the breakfast table was Brandeis; the other was His Britannic Majesty's Secretary of State for Foreign Affairs, Arthur James Balfour. Sitting as always in aristocratic languor, legs stretched straight out in front, Balfour could not conceal his curiosity about the brilliant, controversial Jew across the table. "You are one of the Americans I had wanted to meet," he said.

Balfour had been well schooled in Jewish history and civilization; to him the destruction of ancient Judea by the legions of Rome stood as "one of the great wrongs" of history. As early as 1906, Balfour had struggled with the political dilemma of the Jews. "My anxiety is simply to find some means by which the present dreadful state of so large a proportion of the Jewish race . . . may be brought to an end," he told a meeting of English voters. (Balfour was fighting for reelection, and an opponent in a nearby constituency, Winston Churchill, was making a big play for the large Jewish vote.)

Not that Balfour himself had personal acquaintance with the Jewish people—a companion recalls him watching motley crowds of London Jews flocking toward a Zionist meeting at the Albert Hall, then turning in vague wonderment to ask, "But who *are* all these people?" Through his studies of history and politics, Balfour, like Blackstone, understood better even than Herzl the symbolic aspirations of Zionism. "If a home was to be found for the Jewish people, . . . it was in vain to seek it anywhere but in Palestine," he said.

By the spring of 1917, British diplomacy had more than philosophical reasons for learning about Zionism. The European allies were closing in to deliver the *coup de grace* to the collapsing Ottoman regime; the disposition of the Turkish lands, including Palestine, weighed heavily in the calculations of empire. At the same time, American support for British war efforts was a top priority in Whitehall, which is why Balfour had rushed over for talks with President Wilson immediately upon America's declaration of war.

From what London had learned about American political life, the Jews seemed to offer a promising means of promoting pro-British sentiment. "They are far better organized than the Irish and far more formidable," cabled the British Embassy in Washington. "We should be in a position to get into their good graces." At the head of organized Jewry appeared to be this newcomer Brandeis, an intimate of the President, popular enough with the Jewish masses to make his movement a threat to the supremacy of the old-line American Jewish Committee. The British Foreign Secretary had ample reason to be curious.

Balfour and Brandeis started their breakfast with generalities. The American jurist stressed the ethical purposes and practical aspirations of Zionism, and the power of the dream of a Jewish homeland. He had said it many times before. Then, as Balfour gingerly turned the conversation toward political considerations, Brandeis grew uncomfortable. For the fact is that, as late as April 1917, Brandeis had given no thought whatever to the international political consequences of a Jewish state. Such issues were superfluous to his concept of Zionism.

To be sure, he had contemplated approaches to the Turkish government about securing leases and concessions for Jewish settlement, and he had pressed Wilson as early as 1914 for sympathetic consideration of these efforts. But he spoke only in terms of relief for refugees, of capital investment and progressive social change among the struggling little Jewish communities of Palestine. For the rest, the political future of the Arabs and the Jews in the Ottoman province—that was a matter on which he had yet to focus. The Zionists of Europe, the leaders of Russian Jewry and others who had gravitated to wartime London, were far ahead of him.

On April 25, 1917, just a few days before he met Balfour, a cable arrived from James de Rothschild, one of the leaders of English Zionism, suggesting a postwar political goal: a Jewish Palestine under a British protectorate. Did Brandeis and his American colleagues agree, and could they secure President Wilson's endorsement? Brandeis was uneasy about launching into this uncharted political territory, and a quick check with the Zionist Provisional Executive in New York revealed that they too had given no thought to postwar political planning.

Thus, in his first meeting with Balfour, Brandeis felt at a certain disadvantage. Early in May the Provisional Executive hastily discussed how Brandeis should reply to Rothschild, and Brandeis himself went over to the White House after lunch on May 4 for a forty-five-minute talk with Wilson. It was their first substantive conversation about the politics of Jewish national aspirations. When Brandeis met Balfour a second time, on May 10, he felt more comfortable about dealing with specifics.

Balfour had been hesitant to suggest a British protectorate to his American contacts, fully mindful of the fears in Wilson's Washington of getting sucked into the imperial rivalries of the European belligerents. Moreover, the idea that the Foreign Office had been turning over for a year past was that the United States might itself be induced to assume a protectorate over the Holy Land. This would keep out the French and any other colonial rival, and Whitehall had every reason to be comfortable with a benign American presence in the neighborhood of the Suez Canal.

Fresh from his meeting with Wilson, Brandeis knew just what to say about the idea of an American protectorate. The President and everyone else he knew in official Washington were flatly opposed to any United States responsibility for Palestine or Armenia or any of the other Turkish territories. Responsibility of empire, under whatever legal guise, was not the vision of Woodrow Wilson's America. As for a British protectorate, the scheme on which the European Zionists were working, Brandeis was able to promise Wilson's wholehearted support, including his readiness to speak out in public at the appropriate time.

Balfour left Washington deeply satisfied with his mission. Brandeis, he confided to an associate, "was probably the most remarkable man" he had met on his visit to the United States, not only for political prowess but for "high moral tone" on the subject of Palestine. To Brandeis directly, at the end of their Washington meetings, Balfour said bluntly, "I am a Zionist."

As an illustration of back-channel diplomacy at its most effective, the Balfour-Brandeis encounter was exceptional. A Foreign Minister seeking understanding on a delicate political issue turned not to his official opposite number, the Secretary of State, or even to the other foreign policy advisers known to be close to the President. He sought out instead a member of the judiciary having neither official nor unofficial standing in the matter, but a deep personal interest—and the sympathetic ear of the President. Brandeis, for his part, saw no impropriety in discussing a humane, philanthropic issue.

Assured of American sympathy, British policymakers turned to the next step in their strategy, a public declaration of support for the establishment of the Jewish national home in Palestine. The idea had come to them from an unlikely source. In November 1915, long before the United States was involved in the war, the fertile brain of Horace Kallen out in Madison, Wisconsin, had come up with the idea of an Allied statement supporting, in whatever veiled way was deemed necessary, Jewish national rights in Palestine. Such a statement, he argued to a British friend (who he knew would pass the idea along), "would give a natural outlet for the spontaneous pro-English, French, and Italian sympathies of the Jewish masses." It would help break down America's neutrality, Kallen argued, knowing full well that this was precisely the aim of British diplomacy. Kallen's idea lit a spark of interest in Whitehall.

As charters for a modern nation-state go, the sixty-seven words of the Balfour Declaration of November 1917 are surely among the most modest and unassuming. Conveyed in the form of a personal letter from the British Foreign Secretary to a prominent British Jew, Lord Rothschild, it said:

> His Majesty's Government view with favor the establishment in Palestine of a national home for the Jewish people, and will use their best endeavours to facilitate the achievement of this object, it being clearly understood that nothing shall be done which may prejudice the civil and religious rights of existing non-Jewish communities in Palestine, or the rights and political status enjoyed by Jews in any other country.

Perhaps no other paragraph of the twentieth century has been so exhaustively analyzed and parsed to its subtlest nuance, of which there are obviously many. One early draft spoke of the "Jewish race," but Zionist lobbyists persuaded the Foreign Office draftsmen to substitute "Jewish people" and thus bypass a controversy between race and religion. The Zionists would have liked Balfour to advocate the "re-establishment" of the Jewish national home, adding the legitimacy of ages past to the modern campaign.

Most significant was the phrase "in Palestine." An earlier draft was more forthright, calling for the "reconstitution of Palestine as a Jewish State." Acting on a hunch more than any deep reasoning, Lord Milner, an influential member of the War Cabinet, whittled this unambiguous formulation down to the final form, "in Palestine," which shaped the diplomatic and political struggle for decades to follow. The promise of a Jewish national home "in Palestine" opened the way for the partition of Palestine into separate Jewish and Arab states.

. . .

IN WOODROW WILSON'S second term, the American presidency lost its innocence on the matter of the Jewish destiny. The Balfour Declaration elevated the cause of Zionism from a romantic vision to a political campaign, and the leader of the United States could no longer take refuge in vague pleasantries designed to assuage the feelings of the Jewish constituents. As of November 1917 church and state were both engaged in the restoration of the Jews to the Holy Land, and the President had to take a stand. Given his background, Wilson could have gone either way.

The son of a clergyman, imbued with a deep Christian commitment, Wilson displayed a messianic streak from the start of his public career. "He believes that God sent him here to do something and God knows what. . . . I am sorry I cannot penetrate the mystery," wrote Britain's ambassador at the start of Wilson's presidency. Wilson's friend, financial mentor, and spiritual colleague was Cleveland H. Dodge, pillar of the Protestant missionary community, devoted to the emotional and educational interests of Arab nationalism.

The upper-class Christian milieu of Princeton, where Wilson and Dodge had been classmates, was thoroughly antisemitic. To the old ideological themes of the Wandering Jew and the Ever-alien Jew, these well-brought-up young men added a new concern with the Ubiquitous Jew— the specter of numbers far larger than the reality. As late as 1918, Wilson operated under this influence; an entry in the personal diary of Colonel House relates an after-dinner conversation at the White House. They were discussing "how ubiquitous Jews were"; House remarked that it was particularly surprising since there were so few Jews in the world. How many were there? House guessed 15 million, Mrs. Wilson suggested 50 million, and the President said the correct figure must be 100 million. Even House's estimate was high; the world Jewish population in the early decades of this century was slightly over 11 million.

But this was dinner-table talk. When Zionism first came to Wilson's serious attention, in 1916, Dodge and the missionary community had not fully perceived the threat of the Jewish national movement. It was the plight of the starving Armenians, their massacres by the Turks, that was uppermost in the conversations of Wilson and Dodge at their mellow weekends together at Dodge's estate in Riverdale on the Hudson.

The first serious talk Wilson heard of the Jewish homeland in Palestine came from pro-Zionist friends. One, Norman Hapgood, editor of *Harper's Weekly,* became "converted" to Zionism—he was not Jewish— in 1914, arguing that the movement had, at the least, "forced nations of the world either to welcome Jews or to take the risk of losing such energetic citizens." Simon Wolf, a *shtadlan* of Washington who had made it his business to be on friendly terms with every President from Lincoln onwards, sent Wilson a little essay about Mordecai Noah in 1916, with the recommendation that he give sympathetic consideration to the Zionist position. Most influential, however, was the voice and intellect of Brandeis, who, though not a member of the Wilson Cabinet, had free entree to the White House. When Brandeis spoke, Wilson listened.

"It has been said of the President," wrote a British diplomat, "that when he takes up a new subject, the first thing he does is to make up his mind." As early as March 1916 Brandeis felt confident enough of Wilson's position to be able to assure a colleague that the President "would support Zionist aspirations seriously and actively."

There were good political reasons for doing so. The American Federation of Labor, under Samuel Gompers, was endorsing the principle of a Jewish homeland, as Jewish immigrants threatened to glut the American labor market. Theodore Roosevelt and his Republicans were leaning toward the Jewish national cause, and no Democrat would willingly abandon the potential Jewish support in the big eastern cities to the opposition. Zionist leaders were members of Wilson's political family— Brandeis, his protégé Frankfurter, the crusading New York rabbi Stephen Wise (unrelated, in family or ideology, to the late I. M. Wise); to wish to satisfy their Zionist interests was only normal for a political leader, especially in the absence, before 1917, of arguments to the contrary.

Zionism also fit into Wilson's global scheme for self-determination of the world's peoples, at least at first glance. Indeed, in the nervous months before America's entry into the war, when Wilson was being drawn toward alliance with Britain, support for the Jewish national cause came a little easier than support for the self-determination of, say, the Irish or the Hindus. Those peoples were struggling against Britain, while the Jewish cause—so Brandeis and Balfour assured him—was Britain's own interest.

Finally, the prophetic stream of Christian thought had its effect on Wilson, with his daily Bible readings, his romantic visions of the people of the Book. The evangelist Blackstone, undeterred by the lack of interest of previous Presidents, persisted in his campaigns for the Jewish state; in 1916 he persuaded the Presbyterian General Assembly, governing body of Wilson's own church, to endorse the Zionist goal. "To think that I, the son of the manse, should be able to help restore the Holy Land to its people," Wilson once remarked.

Under this barrage of influences, and with only the tiresome Lansing and his diplomats to argue the opposition, Wilson took his natural first step: he made up his mind. "Whenever the time comes," he told Rabbi Wise in June 1917, "and you and Justice Brandeis feel that the time is ripe for me to speak and act, I shall be ready."

The time was so soon in coming that Wilson was not, in fact, quite ready. On September 3, 1917, the British government inquired as to how he would react to their plan to issue a statement supporting Zionist aspirations to the Holy Land. Aware of the delicacy of the query and the fact that there was a war on, Whitehall made use of a back channel— Colonel House, as close to the President as any man. House, as usual suspicious of the imperial power game, told Wilson that he regarded it as an attempt to lure the United States into British colonial designs upon the disintegrating Turkish empire. Wilson decided to temporize.

For the next six weeks, House repeatedly fed Wilson's suspicions, urging against any partition of Turkey among the belligerents and mincing no words at the annoyance he felt about Zionist pressures. "The Jews from every tribe have descended in force," he advised his chief, "and they seemed determined to break in with a jimmy if they are not let in."

But in time Wilson was given a second chance to look at the British proposal. Aware of the American President's suspicions, Foreign Office promoters of the Zionist connection sought a way to resurrect their initiative by placing it in a more acceptable context. Perfect for the purpose were some vague but convenient intelligence reports from inside Germany.

In their efforts to woo the international Zionist movement, the British had long been mindful of that faction of Zionism which still looked to Berlin, rather than London, as its natural mentor. By October came reports that the German government might itself be contemplating a declaration in support of Jewish settlement in postwar Palestine. These hints were all that was needed. On October 6 a second inquiry went off to Wilson, through House, in the private code reserved for the most sensitive communications. The Germans "are making great efforts to capture the Zionist movement," Balfour advised the President, stretching vague hints into a grand design. Would he now consider the time ripe for a declaration, to pre-empt the enemy?

This intelligence made the plan far more appealing, as the British knew it would. Wilson promptly forgot his, and House's, fears of a colonial ploy and saw instead a timely British move to secure the loyalty of influential Jews for the Allies. Harassed and preoccupied with other matters, he concurred in the British initiative.

Woodrow Wilson's prior support for the Balfour Declaration was a significant milestone in the long struggle of Zionism. It actually happened in a casual way. "I find in my pocket the memorandum you gave me about the Zionist movement," the Chief Executive wrote House on October 13. "I am afraid I did not say to you that I concurred in the formula suggested from the other side. I do, and would be obliged if you would let them know." House knew his place, overcame his scruples, and did as he was told.

Twenty days later, the British War Cabinet gave final approval to the Balfour Declaration. Nineteen years after Herzl first raised the banner, Zionism received the official endorsement of a major power. Without bothering to clear it with anyone, the President of the United States joined in a foreign policy initiative that would shape the course of world affairs for the rest of the century. And his Secretary of State knew nothing about it.

ON DECEMBER 15, 1917, more than a month after the Balfour Declaration was issued, Lansing sent instructions to Ambassador Walter Hines Page in London: "Investigate discreetly and report fully and promptly to Department reasons for Balfour's recent statement relative Jewish state in Palestine."*

Page knew where power lay in Washington, and did not take the Secretary's request very seriously. Nor did he choose to reveal that he had in fact been relaying secret diplomatic exchanges directly to House and the President. He sent Lansing a perfunctory reply. Later the London embassy asked for a report on the American Jewish reaction to the Balfour initiative; Lansing felt so ill equipped to respond that he asked the President what he should say. The White House sent the Secretary of State a page torn from a periodical containing various published comments, pro and con.

For all his lack of involvement in the Balfour Declaration, Secretary Lansing wished to leave Wilson in no doubt of the State Department's opposition. Having no idea that the President had already concurred in the British move nearly two months before, Lansing dashed off a formal letter in December citing three reasons for withholding American endorsement: First, as it was not formally at war with Turkey, the United States should avoid the appearance of carving up the Ottoman territories. Second, the Jews themselves were not of one mind in support of Zionist aspirations and nothing would be gained by siding with one faction over

* The wording of this laconic cable is of considerable interest in light of the subsequent decades of dispute over the precise intent of the Balfour Declaration. Whatever the British government actually meant, whatever the various Zionist and Arab factions would later argue, there was no doubt in the minds of the American diplomats on the sidelines that what was envisaged was nothing less than a full-fledged Jewish state.

another. Finally, reaching his most sensitive point, the Secretary of State argued that "many Christian sects and individuals would undoubtedly resent turning the Holy Land over to the absolute control of the race credited with the death of Christ."

Lansing was warned as soon as he sent the letter off that it was not the sort of thing to be left behind for historians to find in the State Department archives. When news of it leaked out some three years later, after Lansing's downfall, a Department spokesman announced that a search of the official files had revealed no such document. In retirement, Lansing himself denounced the leak as a "flagrant fraud." Yet the letter was there, in the former Secretary's personal files. Wilson, somewhat embarrassed by it, had returned the original to its author when they met at a Cabinet meeting the next day. As he filed the letter away, Lansing had attached a note stating that Wilson had "very unwillingly" agreed with the views expressed, but had added his "impression that we had assented to the British declaration." Thus the President informed his Secretary of State that the United States had concurred in making the political platform of Zionism the official policy of a world power.

There is no indication that Wilson ever felt regret over his casual decision. On the contrary, four months later he specifically reaffirmed a pro-Zionist position over the objections of the State Department. Lansing took every opportunity to resist Zionist requests. In February 1918 he advised Wilson against permitting a Zionist medical unit to visit Palestine, noting that it might have political motives. Wilson went ahead and authorized the medical mission.

Wilson's dedication to Zionism does not withstand close examination. He seems to have given it little thought. Friends and political supporters, distinguished gentlemen whose opinions he respected, put their pro-Zionist arguments to him cogently and sensitively. There were good political reasons for going along; a gesture to the Jews made him feel good in his daily Bible meditations. In the early period when he was making his mind up on the matter, no one was on hand to warn of the problems that Zionist aspirations could create.

Later, at Versailles, with the opponents of Zionism deployed in force on all sides, Wilson had moved on to far bigger things. He took no interest in the detailed negotiations for the settlement of the former Turkish territories, and was oblivious of the efforts of his own experts to chip away at Zionist advances. "I never dreamed that it was necessary to give you any renewed assurance of my adhesion to the Balfour Declaration," Wilson wrote a frantic Felix Frankfurter, "and so far I have found no one who is seriously opposing the purpose which it embodies."

The President was clearly out of touch, and with his physical collapse

in September 1919, he could no longer arbitrate for the Jewish homeland
—or any other aspect of his idealized world vision. One last time, in
February 1920, he ordered Lansing to defend a pro-Zionist position at
the peace table. Thereafter, plagued with breakdown in mind and body,
Wilson grew testy with seemingly endless Zionist importunings. With
feeble, shaking fingers, the President penciled his refusal in May 1920 to
send yet another message affirming his support of the Balfour principles.
In the drama of the Jewish restoration, Woodrow Wilson's role was at an
end.

3

AMERICANS TOOK no great note of the Balfour Declaration. The United States was already firmly committed to the Allied cause, and the subject of the Jewish restoration was relatively unimportant in the mood of November 1917. Within a week came the Bolshevik Revolution in Russia, ten days that shook the world. Zionism and Bolshevism became linked in the public mind, partly through the coincidence of timing, with results that would be costly to Jewish nationalism.

The prospect of a Jewish national home was not welcomed in every part of American Jewry. The Jewish Socialists of the Downtown sweat-shops persisted in their disdain for bourgeois nationalism. The ultra-Orthodox Agudath Israel movement warned its faithful that Zionism "is the most formidable enemy that has ever arisen among the Jewish people." From Uptown, the wealthy and assimilated Henry Morgenthau called Zionism "wrong in principle and impossible of realization . . . an Eastern European proposal . . . which, if it were to succeed, would cost the Jews of America most that they had gained of liberty, equality and fraternity."

Brandeis, the most prominent American Jew, stayed in the background. His own role in the Balfour Declaration was not widely known and was marginal anyway; he recognized that the real credit should go to the persistent Russian-born chemist Chaim Weizmann, who somehow had gained the confidence of the British War Cabinet. Zionism benefited from its well-placed zealots.

Once the Balfour episode was over, Brandeis' attention returned to defining the shape and structure of the visionary community that would emerge in Palestine. His working day at the Supreme Court was spent on measures of social reform; when he got home to his little study, the size of a large coat closet, he was consumed by Zionism. As always, he turned for intellectual stimulation to Horace Kallen, and as always, Kallen was at work anticipating events and trying to control them.

By early 1918 a document emerged from their discussions, written by Kallen and reworked by Brandeis, called "Constitutional Foundations of the New Zion." After being presented to the national Zionist convention in Pittsburgh, in June 1918, it became the Pittsburgh Platform, the codification of Brandeisian Zionism at the apogee of its triumph. In six succinct sections, it described a progressive Jewish homeland in Palestine: political and civil equality of all inhabitants, irrespective of race, sex, or faith; public ownership of land, natural resources, and utilities; land-leasing policies to promote efficient economic development; cooperative management of agriculture, industry, and finance; free public instruction at all grade levels; Hebrew, the Jewish national language, to be the medium of public instruction.

This posed problems—for it was an American, not a Jewish, manifesto. Where was the faith, the religious and mystical unity of the Jewish people, the centuries of struggle, the creative spirit of the folk? The Hebrew language was assigned a prosaic functional place in Brandeis' New Zion, with none of the shimmering affirmations of culture that inspired generations of Jewish nationalists. Where was the space for political factions, for the countless hard-fought ideological diversities that so consumed the energies of the European Zionists? Where were the business opportunities for the middle-class Jewish entrepreneurs who might want to invest in Palestine? Brandeis even seemed to be offering political and civil equality to residents of Palestine who were not Jewish! There was always something " 'far-off' in the American way of looking at things," wrote a European Zionist intellectual. "Whatever ideas our lawgivers and prophets had, they were not twentieth-century American democrats." Brandeisian Zionism met the needs of Harvard intellectuals, inheritors of the progressive traditions of turn-of-the-century America. It was an anodyne construction, rooted firmly in minds of logic and erudition but not at all in the deep human experience of a people.

On the Lower East Side, the Brandeisian vision fell flat. The Yiddish press virtually ignored the Pittsburgh Platform, with which so few of its readers could identify. And the Zionists of Europe, longing for redemption from centuries of despised exile, found the American program for mere social progress to be bloodless and vapid.

Within three years this vision came under frontal attack from the one personage in the world movement who might claim to match Brandeis in stature. On April 2, 1921, Chaim Weizmann arrived in the United States.

THE S.S. ROTTERDAM was more than four hours late in tying up at the Holland-America Line's Hoboken pier, but the welcoming throngs of

Downtown Jewry made no move to disperse. On board the liner, as their Zionist organizers had been telling them for days past, was a delegation from the World Zionist Organization, the new postwar high command of the international movement for a Jewish state, headed by Weizmann himself.

Weizmann wanted his arrival noticed by more than merely the Jews of New York. With his well-developed instinct for catching the public eye, he saw to it that the possessor of a far bigger name than his was at his side when he first set foot in the United States.

Weizmann and Albert Einstein had not met before they boarded the *Rotterdam* together in England, but the excitable scientist had happily accepted the Zionist leader's written invitation to join the delegation for the purpose of promoting the founding of a Hebrew University in Jerusalem. That was half of Weizmann's purpose on his journey; the other half was nothing less than to break the Brandeisian leadership of American Zionism.

It was midday Saturday, and the Jewish party chose to remain on board until the ending of the Sabbath at sundown. The pilot boat had intercepted the *Rotterdam* down-harbor carrying official reception committees and hordes of newsmen attracted by the glamor of the scientist whose theory of relativity was revolutionizing man's concept of time and space. "Prof. Einstein Here; Explains Relativity," exclaimed *The New York Times* in a deceptively definitive headline on Page One. Weizmann recalled that "the whole of that afternoon we were subjected to an endless series of grueling if well-meant interviews."

Then a police boat carried the Zionist delegation across to Manhattan and the welcoming throngs. Deeply packed against the Battery wall, they waved little Jewish flags of white with two blue bars, "cheering themselves hoarse," wrote *The Times*. All the way up Second Avenue, the police escorts and motorcade attracted the waves and shouts of crowds lining the sidewalks. Even as he acknowledged the well-orchestrated cheers, Weizmann's thoughts were elsewhere. "I knew that this magnificent popular reception was only one part of the story," he wrote in his memoirs. On the boat deck of the *Rotterdam,* as the newsmen and dignitaries were swirling around the shabbily dressed little physicist, another delegation of American Jews had quietly handed Weizmann a memorandum, a statement of the terms on which Brandeis would receive him.

The clash between the onetime colleagues in Zionism was now open and acrimonious, for each of the two visionaries approached the matter of the Jewish destiny from the perspective of his own background, the one from Boston and the power centers of Washington, the other from the timeless depths of the Russian Pale. "I do not agree with the philosophy of your Zionism," Weizmann told the Americans. "We are different, absolutely different. There is no bridge between Washington and Pinsk."

Actually, Weizmann was overstating his origins a bit. Pinsk was a mighty metropolis, quite unreachable from the *shtetl* village of Motol where the future President of Israel was born in 1874. No railway, no paved road, passed within twenty miles of Motol's two hundred Jewish families, only a little river cutting through the great Pripet marshland of Byelorussia. Here in the Pale of Settlement the Jews lived as they had for generations past, in poverty and fear of all but each other, estranged from the world around them.

It was an astonishing departure from tradition when eleven-year-old Chaim, third of fifteen children of the village timber trader, moved twenty-five miles away to attend a Russian school in Pinsk. Equally startling was his impulsive decision, at the age of eighteen, to investigate the world outside Russia. Signing on as a member of a raft crew floating downriver to Danzig, Weizmann picked up his bundle and jumped ship the moment they tied up at the first stop outside the Tsar's domain. It was 1892. For the next decade, he roamed Germany, Switzerland, and the Russian western provinces, working for cash and studying for ever higher degrees in exciting new fields of chemistry. He demonstrated early an exceptional brilliance, selling his first dye patent to I. G. Farbenindustrie, later the industrial force of the German war machine. By 1905, when he finally settled down as an industrial chemist in Manchester, England, the son of Motol enjoyed a modest financial independence.

His research carried him into the process of fermentation with starches and bacteria, and he evolved an efficient method of mass-producing acetone, necessary to the manufacture of smokeless gunpowder in World War I, and the butyl alcohol that would make possible synthetic rubber in World War II. For these scientific contributions, Weizmann secured a place in history. But it was the feverish activity in which he reveled at night after leaving his laboratory that made a still more lasting mark on the course of the twentieth century.

Weizmann had been captivated by the cause of Zionism during his schoolboy days in Pinsk. It became an obsession with him in turn-of-the-century Berlin and, over endless student lunches of beer and sausages (on credit) at the Hotel Zentrum on the Alexanderplatz, he led a group of young radicals who challenged the great Herzl for failing to move decisively toward the Jewish state. "Herzl's pursuit of great men, of princes and rulers, who were to 'give' us Palestine, was the pursuit of a mirage," Weizmann charged, an anticipation of precisely the complaint that a later generation of Zionists would level against Weizmann himself.

Leaving Berlin for Manchester, he became a lonely figure on the fringe of organized Zionism. Weizmann grew convinced that the Jewish national interest was firmly linked to the Allied cause against Imperial Germany. He was summoned to London as a scientist by a desperate Ministry of Munitions in 1915, and began the double existence that he would maintain for the rest of his life. From his little flat at 3 Justice Walk, Chelsea, he pursued his sensitive and confidential scientific career by day, a sensitive and discreet diplomatic campaign by night.*

As a minor provincial functionary, Weizmann could only applaud from afar the assumption of wartime Zionist leadership by a personage as distinguished as Brandeis. But soon his own access to the corridors of power in Whitehall, as a scientist, coupled with an innate ability to persuade, made him a match for Brandeis in the transatlantic maneuvering leading up to the Balfour Declaration.

Weizmann was never a spellbinding public speaker; he never fully lost the manner of the shiftless refugee, even as he successfully courted the statesmen—and their ladies—of the highest international society. But his was the genius of making the most implausible proposition seem straightforward and sensible. He claimed to have conducted more than 2,000 interviews leading up to the Balfour Declaration.

Each of his arguments for the Jewish state would be delivered in just the tone that he knew would appeal to his interlocutor of the moment. With Balfour he dwelt on the philosophical background of Zionism, with the Welsh-born Prime Minister Lloyd George he compared the land of Palestine to the small mountainous land of Wales. To the British diplomats interested in empire he spoke of the extension of British power; to others, intrigued by the Wilsonian vision, he placed Zionist aspirations in the glowing context of world order. Nor did he ignore the junior officials on the staffs of the mighty; as one of them, who would later become a distinguished diplomatic historian, recalled, Weizmann "always indicated by a hundred shades and inflexions of voice that he believed that I could appreciate better than my superiors other, more subtle and recondite arguments."

Weizmann and Brandeis established a working relationship during the autumn of 1917 at long distance; when they finally met, in London during the summer of 1919, first impressions were good. Weizmann found "something Messianic" in Brandeis' face. Brandeis found Weiz-

---

* Among his sometime Chelsea roommates, hanging around for endless post-midnight disputations, was a fellow Zionist activist named Vladimir Jabotinsky, who later broke with Weizmann to found the militant Revisionist movement, the inspiration for the anti-British underground of the 1940s and the Israeli government of Menachem Begin in the 1970s. Weizmann wrote of Jabotinsky: "He lacked realism. . . . He was immensely optimistic, seeing too much, and expecting too much."

mann "neither as great, nor as objectionable, as he was painted. . . . He is very much of a man and much bigger than most of his fellows." Then both discovered that things would not always go well between them. As he came to know his European colleagues in Zionism, Brandeis found that they were objectionable after all. Their personal styles were repugnant. When Brandeis pressed for action, the Europeans insisted that before action must come analysis.

Presiding over the first postwar congress of world Zionism in London in July 1920, Brandeis grew disgusted. The speeches were long, windy, and, worst of all, imprecise. There was no formal agenda; delegates arrived late and wandered out early. To the Europeans this was the norm, the way all the Zionist congresses had been since Herzl's day. Brandeis knew nothing of Herzl's day, and to him the whole affair lacked proper parliamentary decorum.

At one moment of enthusiasm Weizmann impulsively grasped Brandeis' hand, bent down and kissed it—not a usual gesture in the Boston society to which Brandeis had accustomed himself. And when Brandeis spoke, as he often had at home, of the parallel between the Jewish settlers in Palestine and the early Puritans of New England, Weizmann and the other Russian Zionists wondered where this strange "Anglo-Saxon Jew" could possibly be coming from.

The differences that flared into the open between Brandeis and Weizmann, between Washington and Pinsk, ran the gamut of the personal, philosophical, and organizational. To Weizmann, the political intrigue, the maneuvers through a dozen chancellories, was Zionism and life itself; to Brandeis, the international politics leading to the Jewish state was a secondary concern. Their priorities diverged sharply in the aftermath of the Balfour Declaration and the assignment of the Palestine mandate to Britain in 1920. At that point, Brandeis said, politics became the responsibility of the settlers on the spot in Palestine, not the Diaspora Zionist groups which had carried the cause thus far. "Politics as such may now be banished," Brandeis said.

His language seemed almost a deliberate slur upon the talents of Weizmann. "There is nothing that can be accomplished from this time on by ingenious political action, however great our diplomats and however wise the individual may be in manipulating this portion of the population or that, or this official or that." For the Diaspora Jews choosing to remain in their own countries, the task was merely practical and supportive, a matter of the efficient construction of the model Jewish community in Palestine and its social and economic expansion. This view, of course, undercut the entire position of Weizmann and the European Zionist leaders who argued—correctly, as it turned out—that a great political effort among the governments of the world was still necessary to realize the promise of Balfour.

Brandeis steadily resisted Weizmann's attempts to enhance the role of the World Zionist Organization, to convert it from the union of philanthropic societies that the Americans envisaged into something like a government-in-exile. To Americans such plans smacked of the old European "Diaspora nationalism," the theory that Jews of the world should be organized into a coherent political entity.

A second basic difference between the philosophies of Washington and Pinsk related to operating style. Brandeis and the Americans spoke of practical industrial and commercial development, of anti-malaria projects and forestation; the Europeans inevitably chose to conduct theoretical reviews of policy in rigorous academic formulations. Demonstrated loyalty to Zionism counted for much more in choosing leaders than professional competence. Brandeis was horrified to learn that an obscure doctor had been recommended for an important hospital post in Palestine because he had given good speeches on Zionism. For their part, the Europeans were dismayed at American presumption in complaining about such technicalities as faulty budgeting, a lack of strict financial accounting, or the casual mixture of donation and investment funds, when it was the Jewish destiny at stake!

With his single-minded emphasis on discipline, professional competence, and efficiency, Brandeis seemed to Weizmann to be stripping Zionism of all its potential for a spiritual and cultural renaissance of traditional Jewish values. In this, unknowingly, Brandeis was clearly closer to Herzl than the post-Herzl European Zionists; it was, in fact, one of the issues on which the youthful Weizmann had challenged the founder of the movement. Herzl, like Brandeis after him, sought first and foremost to develop the land of Palestine. Weizmann and his colleagues pursued a far more sweeping vision, an almost mystical destiny with the Zionist movement as its driving force.

Brandeis and Weizmann held to different levels of personal commitment. In the milieu from which Weizmann came, every Zionist intended sooner or later to take up residence in the Jewish state. Brandeis argued that Zionism was "not a movement to remove all the Jews of the world . . . to Palestine." Instead, it was to give Jews the same rights as other free men, "to live at their option either in the land of their fathers or in some other country." Weizmann settled his mother in Palestine in 1920 and prepared a home there for himself soon afterward. Brandeis seems never to have given thought to settling in Palestine himself.

In sum: for Weizmann, Zionism was central to his own life; for Brandeis, it was important to Jewish life. The distinction endures between Israelis and American Jews of the 1980s. Israel is important to the lives of American Jews; Jewish statehood is the central preoccupation of existence for the citizens of Israel.

All these differences lurked beneath the surface of transatlantic Zionist discussions during 1919 and 1920. Brandeis was infuriated at reports sent back by one of his young Harvard protégés, Benjamin V. Cohen, of petty incompetence among the Palestinian Jewish leaders. Inefficiency, factional power plays, local hierarchies, and personal prerogatives were already entrenched; the concept of a politically neutral civil service was unknown among the Zionist settlers, even under the British Mandate. For a time it even looked as though the Zionists were jockeying for power in commercial rivalry—European and American investors were each seeking to claim the best business opportunities in the emerging Jewish homeland. It was not what Kallen considered the "right beginning."

The final break between Washington and Pinsk came on the issue of money. The Americans came to believe that all the European and Palestinian Jews wanted from them was their dollars, given freely and without strings. Whenever Brandeis and his associates pressed for greater control over the disbursal of funds, they were confronted with a solid wall of resistance. Weizmann later tried to paint the issue solely in terms of Brandeis' fund-raising goals, which he considered too modest. "If this was all he could find in America," Weizmann recalled telling Brandeis to his face, "I should have to come over and try for myself."

As their dispute festered through the closing months of 1920, the American Zionists kept advising Weizmann that the timing for his visit was inopportune. In April 1921 Weizmann took matters into his own hands. With his newsworthy scientific colleague in tow, the chemist from Pinsk confronted the Americans on their home ground. He rejected the initial terms laid down for a meeting with Brandeis, and the shrewdly engineered hero's welcome accorded him by the Jews of the Lower East Side only strengthened his hand. Emissaries of the two rivals passed back and forth, trying to arrange some sort of reconciliation, even if only for the sake of appearances.

The scraping of Einstein's violin filtered through the Hotel Commodore's walls as the arguments raged. "We have been asked to meet Dr. Weizmann . . . on the bridge, but he and his colleagues have already made sure that if we accept the offer, we shall be walking the plank," one of Brandeis' men reported. Slyly, the Brandeis group managed to lure the politically naïve Einstein over to their side against his traveling companion. On May 19 Weizmann met with Brandeis' representatives for a last attempt at compromise; Weizmann acted in an "extremely impatient and intolerant" manner, Cohen told his chief, but Frankfurter had not helped matters by accusing Weizmann to his face of behaving like a dictator.

The schism was complete. Weizmann went public—convinced, as he later wrote, "that the great masses of American Zionists resented the attitudes of their leaders." The man from Pinsk did indeed have a better sense of the mood of Downtown Jewry, which now dominated the American Jewish scene, than did Brandeis and his Harvard intellectuals. In June 1921 Weizmann made a dramatic appearance at the 24th Convention of the Zionist Organization of America in Cleveland. "Thirsting for his words," as one delegate described the scene, "were the relatives of the Jews of Vilna, of Warsaw, of Bucharest, of Krakow and of Vienna." These were Zionists who were newcomers to the American experience; they knew little and cared less about the Puritans, or Kallen's "cultural pluralism." The concerns of Brandeis were not their concerns. "They were not aware of any double loyalties. They had become Zionists through the passion of their leaders in Russia, in Poland, and in Rumania. They had not been separated from other Jews by time and distance. They were not the Lost Tribes of Israel. They were kinsmen who had wandered from home and who had found freedom in a new land, but they remembered their origins."

By a vote of 153 to 71, American Zionism formally repudiated Brandeis' leadership. The prophet who had fought for democracy against the oligarchs of Uptown Jewry was defeated by the democracy, "the riff-raff and everybody," whom he had himself championed. More than forty members of the American Zionist administration, the "college men" who had been managing the movement in the name of their behind-the-scenes chief, walked out of the Zionist movement. Pinsk had won.

The progressive impulse of an American generation, the social idealism and yearnings for new forms of political and economic relations, were thus repudiated by traditional Zionism in 1921. They would find their eventual release instead in domestic American politics, in the liberal movement of the New Deal, with Felix Frankfurter, Benjamin V. Cohen, and a dozen other Brandeis protégés among its intellectual driving forces. As Jews, they never turned their backs on the Jewish national movement —indeed, two decades later many of them would play critical roles in the final act of state-building. But it would be as private Americans that they acted, no longer as officers of Zionism.

BRANDEIS HIMSELF visited Palestine just once, in 1919. "The problems and the difficulties are serious and numerous," he wrote home, "even more so than I had anticipated."

One of those problems he gravely misjudged. "So far as the Arabs in Palestine are concerned, they do not present a serious obstacle. The conditions under which immigration must proceed are such that the Arab question, if properly handled by us, will in my opinion settle itself," he wrote. Brandeis seemed to regard the Arab community as a future partner and resource; he used to speak of Palestine as a bridge between the values of East and West, an associate recalled, "where Western science and technology would cross-fertilize Eastern mysticism and religion, . . . a country where Jew and Arab would live peaceably side by side as they developed a common culture drawn from the distinctive heritage of each."

In another of his long conversations with Balfour, on his way back from Palestine, Brandeis urged that Arab nationalists be told directly that they could not expect sympathy if they directed their efforts against the Jewish settlers. The Foreign Secretary ordered the British military commander in Jerusalem to discourage all displays of Arab opposition to the development of the Jewish national home, a basic point of British policy. Only later would Whitehall start expressing its doubts on that score.

Brandeis played no further role in Zionist politics. But he remained active in the social and economic construction that he so favored for Palestine. He headed a private Palestine Development Council, which sponsored an association of Jewish savings banks; one of their early clients for a home-building loan was a young labor leader named David Ben-Gurion. A group of American immigrants founded a kibbutz between the Jezreel and Sharon valleys in 1937, naming it Ein Hashofet, "The Judge's Brook," in Brandeis' honor.

Alert and erect well into his eighties, his eyes as wide and piercing as ever, Brandeis would hold court in his Washington apartment, serving weak tea and watercress sandwiches to the energetic intellectuals of the New Deal. The old regulars would be there—Ben Cohen, Horace Kallen, and Felix Frankfurter; the wealthy jurist paid Frankfurter a regular retainer to continue the pro bono legal work that Brandeis had to abandon when he joined the Supreme Court. New protégés entered the scene— Henry Morgenthau, Jr., who became much more interested in the subject of Zionism than his father had been; a rising lawyer in the Washington establishment named Dean Acheson, who respectfully asked to differ with Brandeis on the subject of Jewish nationalism when he was named to high office in the State Department. An occasional visitor was the junior senator from Missouri, Harry S. Truman, who concurred in the elder statesman's support for the little man against the monopoly power of big capital. Even a mellowed Chaim Weizmann paid a call of reconciliation on his adversary. "What a perfect setup for the antisemites," quipped Frankfurter to break the ice. "No doubt the 'Elders of Zion' were hatching a conspiracy."

Brandeis died on October 5, 1941, just a month short of his eighty-fifth birthday. "Brandeis was the first Jew to be great both as an American, quite apart from what he did for the Jews," said Ben-Gurion, "and great as a Jew, quite apart from what he did for America."

The boldness of the Brandeis vision has been somewhat diminished in retrospect. He was, after all, repudiated by the movement that he had adopted as his own. Beyond that, however, so much that was bold in the vision has become commonplace for later generations; it is hard to recapture the daring novelty of a Jewish state as Brandeis advocated it. The mood of the times in which he spoke was deeply suspicious.

If Uptown Jews found Zionism offensive and "un-American," their Gentile neighbors were downright shocked at the anti-capitalism explicit in Bolshevism and implicit in the ideology of Brandeis. Zionism and Bolshevism were indeed revolutionary movements, and both emerged from the collapse of the European order that had kept the peace, more or less, for a century. They both seemed to threaten the comfortable old polity of Christian statecraft. For decades to come, the onrush of Zionism and of Communism would become a dual specter haunting the minds of the American diplomatic corps.

As WORLD WAR I drew to a close, the State Department possessed a unique source of intelligence about the emerging Zionist movement. Established in Geneva in 1917, the source was named the "Near Eastern Intelligence Unit." It consisted of one man. Samuel Edelman was thirty-one years old, a vice-consul, busy rising in the diplomatic service. A Jew, he had served in the Jerusalem consulate before the war, and he was trying to build for himself a reputation for expertise on Jewish nationalism. Of all the diplomatic dispatches to the State Department that sounded the alarums against Zionism, there were none more hostile and vitriolic than Edelman's.

"It is true that here and there a successful orange orchard or vineyard has flourished," he informed Washington in November 1917, "but if the books were balanced, it would be found to have returned little or no interest on the money invested." The leaders of Zionism were men "with narrow ideas and high personal ambitions," he said, who had collected vast sums of money "excessively out of proportion" to the real needs of their cause. "A Jewish state should not be tolerated," Edelman warned, for above all there was the "sacredness of the Christian memorials in

Palestine," and a Jewish predominance in that land would be "polluting and intolerable."

This was the sort of argument that he hoped would appeal to his superiors in Washington. Two Jews who had served the government in senior positions—Henry Morgenthau, Sr., ambassador to Constantinople, and his successor, Abram I. Elkus—had tended to ignore the Jewish minority within the Ottoman lands, for fear of exhibiting bias. Edelman chose the opposite tack.

Senior diplomats of the Wilson era, of course, did not need Edelman's unsympathetic assessments to know where they stood on Zionism. Walter Hines Page, ambassador to Britain, was intimately involved in secret official correspondence about the Jews and the Balfour Declaration. But even as he dutifully performed his official mission, he wrote personal letters home to his son. "I have never been able to consider the Zionist movement seriously," he wrote. "The whole thing is a sentimental, religious, more or less unnatural and fantastic idea, and I don't think will ever trouble so practical a people as we and our Jews are. . . . I don't think anybody in the United States need be the least concerned about the Zionist movement."

Apart from the pastiche of newspaper clips, personal memories, and prejudiced analyses that flowed in from Edelman during 1917 and 1918, there were experts just outside the diplomatic service in a position to make their views known. Beginning in the autumn of 1917, Wilson had started a brain trust under the direction of Colonel House to help him make the world safe for democracy. Called "the Inquiry," this group of scholars and specialists composed some ten lengthy studies of the Palestine problem before Wilson departed for the peace conference of Paris at the end of 1918.

In one study, a professor of Old Testament exegesis began with the Paleolithic period in the land of Canaan; other papers surveyed the geography, history, ethnology, religions, economics, domestic life, and government of Palestine. Some of the commentary was rapturously pro-Zionist. "Among the surprises of the war there is perhaps none more striking than the emergence of Zionism, the Jewish national movement, from comparative obscurity into the sunshine of popular acclamation and international sanction. . . . The demand of the Zionists for a British or American protectorate would meet with a welcome from all classes, and it is the only obvious solution." Others, however, found Zionist aspirations neither obvious nor welcome. The Protestant missionary leader Dr. James Barton fell into the latter group. Instead of a Jewish state, he proposed a vast autonomous Arab federation across the Near East, under the international protection of the United States.

The usual reception granted to academic analyses inside government is a polite nod of interest, followed by oblivion; the fate of much of the Inquiry's paperwork was no exception. But one collection of memoranda submitted between November 1917 and June 1918 acquired particular influence over the peacemaker's plans for the Middle East. It also made a reputation for its author, a prewar oil explorer and resident agent for Standard Oil of New York named William Yale.

Realizing that the output of Edelman in Geneva left something to be desired, the State Department dispatched Yale to Cairo as an American diplomatic agent, to report on political trends of the region. Yale's energy, range of contacts, and hardheaded perspicacity turned out to be impressive. Over the months he confirmed the pattern of great-power rivalry affecting the entire Middle East, a pattern that cut through all the romanticism and sentiment. "In plain English," Yale wrote on the eve of the peace conference, "in spite of a widespread camouflage propaganda in regard to the liberation of oppressed races and the rights of small nations, the British and French are thinking and working only for their own interests in the Near East."

AND SO THE STATESMEN of the world converged upon the palace of Louis XIV, prepared to build a new order of peace upon the ashes of the Great War. There were David Lloyd George of Britain and Georges Clemenceau of France, each hoping to enhance his own nineteenth-century colonial order, and there was Woodrow Wilson, radiating the moral authority of an America long passive on the international scene but now possessed of a vision of leadership.

The functionaries swung into action. Wilson had decided within days of the November armistice that he would attend the peace conference in person; typically, he never thought to discuss this decision with Secretary Lansing or even to inform him of his plan. The first word the State Department got was a message from the White House asking that appropriate stationery be printed for the President's use in Paris. The Assistant Secretary of the Navy quickly refitted a transport ship for the President's party, ordering a replica of George Washington's desk at Mount Vernon to be placed in Wilson's study on board. (When all the peacemaking was over, Assistant Secretary Franklin D. Roosevelt bid $100 for the desk and chair, and sent them to his home at Hyde Park, New York, intending to use them himself one day.)

To the statesmen in Paris, the fate of Palestine was no more than a minor sideshow. Wilson sympathized with Zionism sentimentally and politically; Lansing and the other diplomats saw a British imperial ploy hiding behind the rhetoric of Jewish nationalism. It was difficult to focus on Palestine when their minds were on the structure of the whole world.

But among the Americans at the peace conference were two groups who cared, and cared deeply, about the ultimate disposition of the Holy Land. One group, naturally enough, was the Zionists, speaking the message of the Balfour Declaration. Inspired to optimism by the prestigious leadership of a Supreme Court Justice and presidential intimate, the Zionists' delegation to the peace conference was also richly endowed with talent: Brandeis' "college men," Frankfurter, Cohen, and Rabbi Stephen Wise, men who knew how to maneuver through the thickets of politics and among the competing claims of zealots.

In corridor conversations and countless social encounters that constituted the working life of the peace conference, they maneuvered and pressed. Their strategy was to ally themselves with the various European nationality groups; if the rights of other small nations were recognized, the interests of the Jewish nation would benefit too. They could not look for help to the government of the United States; State Department officers and Colonel House's consultants firmly opposed any further steps along the lines of the Balfour initiative.

A second group of articulate Americans in Paris was just as well placed as the Zionists to get the ear of President Wilson, and also a far more sympathetic hearing from the diplomatic professionals. These were the Protestant missionaries. They had been slow to grasp the devastating impact that Zionism would have upon the national ambitions of "their" Arabs. Back in 1905 a professor at the Syrian Protestant College had preached a message of welcome to Jews returning to their ancient land. On their side, the early American Zionists had no grudge against the Protestant missionaries, once their old purpose of converting Jews had been abandoned.

By the time the statesmen gathered in Paris, however, the lines were clearly drawn. Within months of the Balfour Declaration, Christian and Muslim Arabs of Syria made common cause against the new threat of Zionism. With alumni of its great educational institutions scattered in key positions throughout the Middle East, the missionary community was solidly committed to Arab nationalism. Zionism seemed to post competitive claims in the postwar settlement, so the missionaries turned against the Zionists.

The most respected and influential American in the Middle East at the end of the war was Howard Bliss, president of the Syrian Protestant College, son of its founder. Two families, the Blisses and the Dodges, shared the leadership of the missionary community; in the World War I period, Howard Bliss worked in the field and his old family friend, Cleveland Dodge, managed the American end of the missionary operations—attracting, not incidentally, the sympathetic attentions of his old classmate, Woodrow Wilson.

In January 1919, with Wilson already in Paris, Dodge cabled Bliss urging him to proceed to the French capital, to assist and organize the disparate Arab nationalists gathered there to pick up the pieces of the Turkish empire. Most important of all, he was to prevent Palestine from being bestowed upon the Jews for lack of any concerted counterclaims.

For the anti-Zionist alliance, the missionary move came just in time. January 1919 marked the high-water mark of Zionist influence over the statesmen in Paris, with one draft recommendation circulating among the American delegation proposing something close to the most optimistic Zionist program:

- establishment of a separate and independent Palestine, under British mandate from the League of Nations;

- recommendation "that the Jews be invited to return to Palestine and settle there . . . being assured that it will be the policy of the League of Nations to recognize Palestine as a Jewish state as soon as it is a Jewish state in fact."

At least some of the American experts had apparently been persuaded to encourage unrestricted Jewish immigration and carry the spirit of the Balfour Declaration to the logical—but not inevitable—outcome of full Jewish sovereignty. Even Edelman had overcome his earlier hostility and began assuming in his continuing "intelligence" papers that the eventual creation of a Jewish state had become official American government policy.

Then Bliss arrived on the scene. From the moment he reached Paris late in January, the missionary college president cut a formidable figure. He quickly made cordial contact with the academic experts attached to the American delegation, with the British champion of Arab nationalism, T. E. Lawrence, and with diplomats who had long relied on the missionaries as their best advisers on the inscrutabilities of Levantine politics.

Immediately these diverse forces began countering the Zionist advances. The United States was not in a good position to take an active role in the Middle East settlement in the first place, since it had never declared war on Turkey. Now the American analysts became ever more convinced that Balfour was merely attempting to utilize American influence as a counterweight to French claims upon Ottoman territories. The alternative solution proposed by the missionary community was to maintain the Turkish province of Syria intact, including Palestine, and to recognize it as an independent Arab state under United States—not British or French—protection. This was simply a non-starter in Wilson's scheme of things.

By this time the problems of managing the world had finally led to a complete break between Lansing and Wilson. Scarcely on speaking terms, Secretary of State and President passed one ten-day period in Paris together without exchanging a single word. Whatever the President may have said or done, the diplomats were fond of stating, "the United States [i.e., the Department of State] had never accepted or approved" the Balfour Declaration. For years to come, they would take comfort in reiterating this assertion.

Lansing allowed himself to become almost mawkish in his partisanship, as he listened to the rival testimonies of Zionists and Arab nationalists. He sat through Weizmann's presentation to the statesmen in Paris on February 27, 1919, with almost no comment. Then came the Emir Faisal, soon to become King of Iraq, a "noble Arab" who stirred the emotions of the dry and legalistic Secretary of State as few other men ever would. Faisal's "voice seemed to breathe the perfume of frankincense," Lansing mused, "and to suggest the presence of richly colored divans, green turbans and the glitter of gold and jewels." The Zionists were colorless pedants by comparison, and their case was not helped by the testimony of other Jewish spokesmen, assimilationists and Orthodox religious figures, who flatly rejected the idea of an independent Jewish state in Palestine.

Bliss and the other missionary strategists, however, understood that evoking pro-Arab sympathies from Lansing and his diplomatic analysts would do little good in the long run. Wilson was the man to reach, and soon after his arrival on the scene Bliss hit upon a tactic: establish a commission of inquiry to poll the residents of the Holy Land and learn how they wished to be governed after the peace settlement. Central to the President's vision, Bliss noted, was the principle of self-determination; if carried out in Europe, why not in Syria and its southern province of Palestine?

Thus from the American missionary community came the impetus for what would eventually represent the Arab nationalists' answer to the Balfour Declaration. The commission named after lengthy negotiations in the councils of Paris was headed by the president of Oberlin College, Henry C. King, and a wealthy industrialist and financial backer of President Wilson named Charles Crane. The King-Crane Commission set off in May 1919; in sixty days these hardy fact-finders visited forty towns in Palestine and Syria, meeting the notables, receiving the petitions, testing the grass-roots sentiments. Their conclusion was just what Bliss knew it would be. The Arab majority in the region was unalterably opposed to Zionist designs upon their lands.

The fallacy in the commission's approach was obvious: Turkey had long been restricting Jewish immigration into Palestine; the Jews were a minority only because their potential growth had been stifled. Would it not be fair to poll the Jewish people the world over, rather than simplistically heeding the views of a majority on the spot that retained its majority position only through artificial restrictions? When an academic member of the commission staff tried to point this out, he was ignored. Crane later declared his pro-Arab sentiments in terms that no one could miss: the Arabs had come to trust America through the work of the missionary institutions, and America owed them something in return, he argued. Those Arabs who had emigrated to the United States, furthermore, were good and loyal citizens; "they did not try to run our politics or anything else," unlike certain other immigrants.

The final report of the King-Crane Commission rallied an entire generation of anti-Zionist forces. Balfour's promise of a Jewish national home "is not equivalent to making Palestine into a Jewish state," the commissioners argued, nor could such a state come into being "without the gravest trespass upon the civil and religious rights" of the Arabs. "The fact came out repeatedly in the Commission's conference with Jewish representatives that the Zionists looked forward to a practically complete dispossession of the present non-Jewish inhabitants of Palestine, by various forms of purchase." The report dismissed Zionist claims to the land, "based on an occupation of two thousand years ago." Armed force would be required to make these claims stick.

Then King and Crane reached their telling, climactic point:

> There is a further consideration that cannot justly be ignored. Millions of Christians and Moslems all over the world are quite as much concerned as the Jews with conditions in Palestine. . . . It may be doubted whether the Jews could possibly seem to either Christians or Moslems proper guardians of the holy places, or custodians of the Holy Land as a whole. The reason is this: the places which are most sacred to Christians—those having to do with Jesus—and which are also sacred to Moslems, are not only not sacred to Jews, but abhorrent to them. It is simply impossible, under these circumstances, for Moslems and Christians to feel satisfied to have these places in Jewish hands.

Professing, in conclusion, "a deep sense of sympathy for the Jewish cause," the King-Crane Commission urged the Paris peace conference to dismiss Zionist claims. "Jewish immigration should be definitely limited and . . . the prospect for making Palestine distinctly a Jewish common-wealth should be given up."

FULLY TWENTY-FOUR YEARS LATER—in 1943—as the Near East Division of the State Department briefed senior officers on the question of Palestine, large sections of the King-Crane report were cited verbatim; "every word is as valid today as when written," the diplomatic specialists argued. The report "was and remains a notable document."

In terms of its contemporary purpose, however, the King-Crane report failed utterly. Wilson had already sailed for home when the commissioners returned to the peace conference, and no one else in Paris had the slightest interest in hearing what they had to say. British and French colonial designs upon the Ottoman territories had prevailed while King and Crane were away, and Wilson, ailing and discouraged, had lost all interest in the Turkish settlement by the time the report arrived at the White House. He suffered a physical collapse the very next day, and apparently never saw the commission's work.

Recognizing an idea whose time had come and gone, the State Department suppressed the King-Crane report for nearly three years, until it was leaked to the press in 1922. In its effort to quash the international movement of Zionism, the American missionary community had overplayed its hand.

PARIS IN 1919 was a hotbed of ideas—competing, converging, tangential, farfetched, profound, empty, visionary. All were expressed in the lofty tones, the passionate eloquence, of zealots. Realpolitik, of course, rather than ideals dictated the Middle East settlement. Yet in the dossiers studied over the peace tables, the intellectual justification for Zionism was not totally blanked out by Howard Bliss's onslaught. Indeed, the most persuasive argument against the King-Crane position, perhaps the most eloquent defense of Zionism ever to reach the Department of State, came in July 1919 from the prolific William Yale.

Attached to the King-Crane Commission as an expert consultant, Yale remained outspoken and iconoclastic. As Lansing was being swept off his feet by the Emir Faisal's claims of 100,000 Arabs under arms, Yale coolly reckoned the size of the Arab army at a mere 2,000. Not that he was in any way partisan toward the Zionist settlers—"young, hot-headed Jews," he called them, "overbearing and arrogant in their treatment of the felaheen."

His initial skepticism about Zionism faded as he toured the area and absorbed the grand politics of the issue. Submitting a carefully reasoned dissent from the King-Crane recommendations, Yale conceded that the majority of residents in Palestine and Greater Syria were indeed opposed to the establishment of the Jewish national home. But Syria was not a nation with a strong national history, he argued, and due consideration should be given to "the wishes and desires of 14,000,000 Jews who have a national history, national traditions, and a strong national feeling." The United States and the Allied governments had made formal promises to the Jewish people, Yale contended, and "to retract such promises would be unjust and unwise. . . . The promises must be fulfilled and the Jews must be given their chance to found in Palestine a Jewish Commonwealth."

Yale gave the makers of American foreign policy a shrewdly nuanced assessment of Jewish nationalism. If the movement remained in the hands of "that disagreeable arrogant type of their race," bitter conflict would be inevitable. "On the contrary, if the Zionists' leaders be that broad-minded, liberal high-type Jew which western Europe and America have developed, the feeling in Palestine might be ameliorated and the bitterness toned down." Yale, the Gentile diplomat, had no reason to be reticent about distinctions of class and style within Jewry; for Brandeis and other "high-type" Jews, such candor would have seemed churlish.

Yale well knew that he was swimming against a strong tide of anti-Zionist sentiment among his professional diplomatic colleagues, if not their political masters. He sketched a glowing vision of what he thought might be accomplished:

> Jewish energy, Jewish genius, and Jewish finance will bring many advantages to Palestine. . . . An Eastern race well versed in Western culture and profoundly in sympathy with Western ideals will be established in the Orient. Furthermore a Jewish state will inevitably fall under the control of American Jews who will work out, along Jewish lines, American ideals and American civilization.

Yale and Brandeis came from different worlds, but they shared the idealistic aspirations of the times. Both minimized the threats of Arab resistance to the Jewish settlers; Yale argued that much scare talk emanates from antisemitic and anti-Zionist quarters. His conclusion was prophetic: "The Arabs may never become reconciled to Jewish immigration, but they will become reconciled to the fact that they must accept it as inevitable."

Not for another three decades would a dispatch to the Department of State make such a sympathetic case for the establishment of the Jewish state. Even as Yale submitted his report, the dossiers were filling with contrary arguments reiterating the traditional fears. The consul in Jerusalem in 1919, seventy-four-year-old Otis A. Glazebrook, was a worthy successor to old Selah Merrill; he informed the Department that the Jews were boasting in the cafés of Jerusalem that when their time came they would destroy the Holy Sepulcher, for "commemorating events in the life of an illegitimate person." Through the 1920s, the Jerusalem consulate's reports would dwell on Jewish threats to Christian shrines, and at the same time the "Communistic tendencies" of the Zionist pioneers. As the American diplomats on the spot saw it, Palestine was the convergence of the double specter unleashed upon the God-fearing world in that epic month of November 1917.

THE PEACE SETTLEMENT of World War I marked the turning point, the transformation of Zionism from a vague and parochial longing to an international political cause, controversial and chilling to many in Christendom but blessed, apparently, by the leaders of the new world order. In April 1920 the statesmen in Paris awarded a mandate over Palestine to Britain, and the terms of Balfour's 67-word letter to Lord Rothschild were formally enshrined in international law.

Balfour himself had departed the scene. For all the complex and devious motives that had led Britain into sponsorship of the Jewish national cause, the aristocratic diplomat himself expressed guarded satisfaction over developments since his first meetings with Brandeis. On the eve of his retirement in August 1919, he wrote a long and pensive memorandum. "The four Great Powers are committed to Zionism," he said, "and Zionism, be it right or wrong, good or bad, is rooted in age-long traditions, in present needs, in future hopes of far profounder import than the desires and prejudices of the 700,000 Arabs who now inhabit that ancient land. In my opinion, that is right." Balfour was willing to rise above the principle of self-determination. "I do not think that Zionism will hurt the Arabs, but they will never say they want it," he wrote. And he added a strong recommendation to his successors: "If Zionism is to influence the Jewish problem throughout the world, Palestine must be made available for the largest possible number of Jewish immigrants."

That was the Balfour vision. Into the language of statecraft were translated the dreams of Pastor McDonald and William E. Blackstone, more mundane and tentative, of course, but the beginning of the long-prophesied Jewish restoration.

But Balfour was retired, Wilson sick and disheartened; the missionaries and diplomats whose campaign against Zionism had faltered at Versailles found new hope. Balfour's successors in London rejected his advice. "The Balfour Declaration appears to be rendered less and less objectionable each time some principle of it is enunciated," cabled an exultant American consul from Jerusalem in 1923. And when Brandeis and Weizmann had their public falling out, it seemed that even the Zionists were growing fragmented in their dedication to the cause that had been so simple to state, so complicated to realize.

4

Hugh Gibson, United States minister to Warsaw, as urbane and promising a young diplomat as the professional service could offer, had two reasons for rushing to ·Paris in June 1919. There were the last refinements of language on the Polish peace treaty to be signed at Versailles. And there was a more personal matter which threatened to become very serious indeed: Gibson was finding himself under attack from leading American Jews, on charges of antisemitism. Such personal attacks were a new experience for a young gentleman diplomat. A brief and stormy confrontation in Paris that June set the stage for a hostility and distrust between diplomats and Jews that would continue through America's interwar decades.

Warsaw, capital of the new Polish republic, was a training ground for diplomatic expertise. As an up-and-coming member of "the Family" on Washington's H Street, the bachelor pied-à-terre where the young diplomats nursed their ambitions, Gibson was the professionals' choice for the challenge of Warsaw. It was all exhilarating and exhausting—the near-anarchy of postwar Poland, the sputtering war with the new Soviet Union. Much of what he saw was disquieting. After his first excursion into the countryside along the Vistula, he wrote home to his mother of his first encounters with an exotic and alien populace: "There were nothing but Jews to be seen in their black caps, their long coats and long red or black beards." How totally different they were, he added, from "the Jewish friends we have at home."

In Poland was gathered one of the largest—and least assimilated—Jewish communities in the world. The plight of this unkempt minority became Gibson's first big problem, and he found the interruptions to orderly diplomatic life most upsetting. "I am blessed if I think it is worth the time as our Jewish friends come dashing in and tell us every time they hear of anybody who made a face at a Jew," he complained. Antisemitic incidents were frequent after the 1918 armistice, and telegrams of protest

came pouring in from American Jewish groups. They were surely embroidered in the telling, but the reality of Polish antipathy toward the
Jewish minority had deep historical roots—and was most inconvenient
for diplomats who looked upon the reconstituted Polish state as a test of
democracy. "It is ridiculous as we are told about every incident where
the Jew gets the worst of it and a great many incidents that never happen
at all," Gibson wrote home. "These yarns are exclusively of foreign manufacture for anti-Polish purposes."

Gibson arrived in Paris on June 24, 1919. He reported in at Colonel
House's hotel suite—not Secretary of State Lansing's, of course—and
found two gentlemen already there: Felix Frankfurter of the Zionist
delegation to the peace conference, and Louis D. Brandeis, Associate
Justice of the Supreme Court, passing through Paris on his way to Palestine. The atmosphere was heavy, Gibson noted, and "the Colonel nim-
bly slipped out of the room and left me to defend myself."

Brandeis and Frankfurter "opened the prosecution by saying that I
had done more mischief to the Jewish race than anyone who had lived in
the last century," Gibson related. "They said . . . that my reports on the
Jewish question had gone round the world and had undone their work"
to alert the public to rampant antisemitism. "They finally said that I had
stated that the stories of excesses against the Jews were exaggerated, to
which I replied that they certainly were and I should think any Jew would
be glad to know it."

The interview was not off to a good start. "Felix Frankfurter insisted
over and over that I 'had no right' to make reports to the Department in
regard to Jewish matters and should have 'refused' on the ground that I
could not possibly learn enough about them to make even general observations." The Jewish spokesmen "seemed to be interested in the agitation
for its own sake rather than in learning of the situation," Gibson complained. "Their efforts were concentrated on an attempt to bully me into
accepting the mixture of information and misinformation which they
have adopted as the basis of their propaganda."

Gibson felt his dignity under attack, and he said as much to one of
his patrons in Washington. "Felix handed me a scarcely veiled threat that
the Jews would try to prevent my confirmation by the Senate [then still
pending]—I didn't consider it worthwhile to take notice of this," he
noted. "I am still a good deal in the dark as to what this important group
of American Jews wants. . . . They made it clear to me that they do not
care to have any diagnosis made that is not based entirely on Jewish
statements as to conditions and events and does not accept them at face
value. If they are not ready to go into the question honestly I don't see
how they can hope to accomplish anything for the good of their people."

Word passed speedily through the professional service that one of their number, a rising favorite, had suffered browbeating and humiliation from influential Jews. The old fears of that murky conspiracy rose to the surface. Gibson wrote out his suspicions—over twenty-one pages—to his friends in the State Department. By whipping up emotions between Jews and Poles, he said, American Jews were embarked on "a conscienceless and cold-blooded plan to make the condition of the Jews in Poland so bad that they must turn to Zionism for relief."

Eventually an independent committee was set up to propose relief measures for Polish Jewry and prepare a controlled emigration to the West. But on Gibson's legation staff, the cynicism only increased. "I have been having a delightful time holding the hands (figuratively, of course) of our numerous Hebraic friends who are in trouble," wrote the third secretary, Jay Pierrepont Moffat. "Jewish movement to America presents a serious menace to our civilization," wrote Major T. W. Hollyday, a U.S. Army observer in Poland. Many of the prospective immigrants are "radical agitators or Bolshevik agents," he reported. They are "filthy from a sanitary viewpoint"; they are "international in their tendencies and do not strengthen, but rather weaken, our national spirit." They will only settle in cities, in "filthy Jewish quarters," instead of helping to cultivate the land. Major Hollyday much preferred "the great Nordic race which founded and built up our civilization."

By 1923 the Warsaw legation's distaste for its Jewish petitioners had become a well-rehearsed litany. "It is common knowledge that this race of people [Jews] are continually and constantly spreading propaganda, through their agencies over the entire world, of political and religious persecution," commented Vice-Consul Monroe H. Kline. "It is true that the Pole hates the Jew. . . . The Jew in business oppresses the Pole to a far greater extent than does the Pole oppress the Jew in a political way."

American diplomats and public officials thus fueled—they certainly did not create—the mood of racism, isolationism, and simpleminded populism that infected the public mind for the next two decades. Anti-semitism arose in America in many forms, some crude and blatant, some more genteel and intellectual but just as pernicious.

The most notorious vendor of simplistic prejudice in middle America was Henry Ford, the automobile entrepreneur, embodiment of the capitalist dream, for whom stereotypes became an obsession. In 1919 Ford bought a weekly newspaper, the Dearborn *Independent,* to serve as a sounding board for his diverse and generally half-baked ideas on public issues.

Jewish "subversion" of Christian society was one of Ford's favorite themes, along with the "lasciviousness" of Hollywood, the destruction of

family, church, and school at the hands of freethinking radicals, and the
"endless stream" of immigrants who were polluting American society.
For all these varied vices gripping society, Ford's journal laid the blame
on "the International Jew." Week after week for nearly two years, starting
in 1920, the Dearborn *Independent* poured out lurid theories of the
conspiracy by which international Jewry was gaining control over public
life.

Ford's basic text was the mysterious tract called *The Protocols of the
Elders of Zion,* supposedly the transcript of secret meetings at which
leading Jews of many lands planned a drive for world domination. The
document emerged from Russia in several versions after the Bolshevik
Revolution. In one, the alleged meetings occurred during Herzl's First
Zionist Congress in 1897—Zionism was, it said, the cover name for the
conspiracy. Other versions left the time and place of the meetings more
obscure. Though some commentators were willing to take the tract seriously, a little analysis showed up so many contradictions, anachronisms,
and downright silly errors that it was soon dismissed as a crude forgery.
But not by Henry Ford; to him the *Protocols* were just the "evidence" he
needed. With his subsidy, the Dearborn *Independent* reached a regular
circulation of 700,000, and a series, *The International Jew,* was separately reprinted in various editions of several hundred thousand each.

American intellectual leaders awakened belatedly to the malevolent
allure of this crude slander. Norman Hapgood, influential editor of *Harper's,* lambasted Ford for setting loose "a malicious force that added fury
to similar forces already in existence." Over one hundred prominent
Christians, ranging from former President Taft to William Cardinal
O'Connell, signed a statement calling on Gentiles to halt "vicious propaganda" against Jews.

Yet the church leadership itself was not free from anti-Jewish sentiment, rising first out of the old grounds of Christian doctrine and reinforced through the 1920s and 1930s by reaction to the political assertions
of Zionism. The *Christian Century,* a leading journal of American Protestantism, was particularly nervous about encouraging "aggressive Jews
to claim the country [of Palestine] as a 'homeland' for their people."
Nationalism among the Jews was an ominous trend, the *Christian Century* commented, for "it was nationalism that crucified Jesus." The journal explained its stand in a frank admission: "The Christian mind has
never allowed itself to feel the same human concern for Jewish sufferings
that it has felt for the cruelties visited upon Armenians, the Boers, the
people of India, American slaves or the Congo blacks. . . . Christian
indifference to Jewish sufferings has for centuries been rationalized by

the tenable belief that such sufferings were the judgment of God upon the Jewish people for their rejection of Jesus."

The liberal American intelligentsia rejected both Ford's bigotry and the doctrinal explanations of the conservative churchmen, but its journals also raised questions about the standing of Jews in American society. "There is really a Jewish problem," noted *The Atlantic Monthly*. "The feeling against the poor [Jews] is an outgrowth of the fear of Bolshevism, while the feeling against the rich ones is a part of the general post-war clamor against profiteers—the feeling in both cases being greatly intensified by the popular nationalistic suspicion that the Jews are willfully resisting assimilation."

Here was yet another form of anti-Jewish pressure. Were Jews in fact resisting assimilation? Or was Christian America refusing to assimilate them? In the late nineteenth century America's social leaders had criticized the Jews for trying to break in; a generation later they criticized them for holding aloof. It seemed almost as if the desired solution to the "Jewish problem" was simply for Jews to stop being Jewish. To call this widespread attitude "antisemitic" weakens the force of the word as applied to the outright genocide that subsequently occurred in Nazi Germany. But the calls for assimilation amounted to a form of intellectual genocide. As the liberal Christian theologian Reinhold Niebuhr argued, "The majority group expects to devour the minority group by way of assimilation. This is a painless death, but it is death nevertheless."

American society was proud of its pluralism, but tolerance seemed to stop short of Jews. Quotas against Jewish students were discussed noisily, and implemented quietly, at Ivy League universities in the 1920s. The president of Harvard, A. Lawrence Lowell, committed the indiscretion of advocating such quotas in public, and he was met with a storm of criticism. But nothing could stop the private slurs. A distinguished judge recalled hearing that 50 percent of the thefts reported at Harvard's Widener Library were committed by Jews. Upon investigation, he discovered the accuracy of the report: precisely two thefts had been reported, one by a person with a Jewish-sounding name.

Industrialist Charles Crane, smarting over the eclipse of his anti-Zionist recommendations to Wilson, promoted "a sort of pact with the Islam world [*sic*] whereby the followers of Mohammed may be protected against the Jews who are taking Palestine." After discussing the Jewish threat with no less an authority than Adolf Hitler, in 1933, Crane urged American officials to "let Hitler have his way." The retired Colonel House was more circumspect as he advised a new ambassador to Berlin: "You should try to ameliorate Jewish sufferings. They are clearly wrong and even terrible; but the Jews should not be allowed to dominate economic or intellectual life in Berlin as they have done for a long time."

Inside the corps of professional diplomats, patrician antisemitism became steadily less genteel. Hugh Gibson stepped carefully after his traumatic encounter with Brandeis and Frankfurter in Paris, but the friends who corresponded with him had no such scruples. "They are, all of them, Democrats and Republicans and Socialists alike, truckling to the Jews," a gushing lady friend wrote Gibson in 1936. "The Republican National Convention was opened by the prayer of Rabbi Snigglefritz of the Congregation of Some-Kind-of-a-Torah. . . . the Jew is 6% of the population, and he is 60% of the present administration and I should say he is 96% of Communism. . . . No one knows better than you!" Franklin DuBois, chief of the State Department's visa office, capped his complaints about the new Soviet trade office, Amtorg, by noting that they had retained "low class Jew lawyers to represent them."

Aspiring young diplomats in Foreign Service training were lectured repeatedly about the dangers which immigrants, and most notably Jews, posed to American society. "The unassimilability of these classes . . . is a fact too often proved in the past to bear any argument," the head of the Consular Service, Wilbur J. Carr, told a congressional committee. As late as 1938 the head of the Georgetown Foreign Service School, Father Edmund A. Walsh, argued that "the Jew was not the cause of the Russian Revolution, but the entrepreneur, who recognized his main chance and seized it shrewdly and successfully."

Graduates of this training became the all-powerful consuls and visa officers of the late 1930s who passed judgment on the applications for American entry permits filed by the refugees from Nazism.

AFTER THE BRIEF FLURRY of Wilsonian internationalism, Washington settled back into the leisurely comfort of a southern town. The diplomats on State Department duty returned to their clubby and contented ways; they routinely left their offices at four-thirty, like all other government workers. "They know the 'ropes,' they know one another, and they know all sorts of little tricks to protect one another and to cover up deficiencies," wrote Washington observers. "They stuck to precedent, clung to routine, passed the buck, wrote the weasel-worded cable, and took another glass of sherry." As late as 1929, the State Department's entire professional staff could be assembled on the back steps for a group photograph after lunch. They chafed at the lack of public recognition for their professional skills. Hugh Gibson used to argue that diplomats were far more than "cookie-pushers," coining an image that would cling to the diplomatic profession like a crumb of buttered tea cake on starched linen.

United States interests in Palestine were not momentous for these diplomatic professionals. The politics of the Holy Land could be left to Britain, which had assumed a League of Nations mandate over the former Turkish province. As for economic interests, it was the same three groups of Americans who cared—missionaries, oil men, and Jews. Among the three, the lowest of the State Department's priorities was not in doubt.

The most influential specialist on Middle Eastern affairs in the post-Versailles years was Allen W. Dulles, nephew of former Secretary Lansing. Dulles fumed at the Zionists, just as his uncle had, and he refused to grant that the late President Wilson had ever given any shred of support to the Balfour promise. Dulles and his division fought tenaciously to keep any reference to the Balfour Declaration or the phrase "Jewish national home" out of the legal record.

Indeed, from 1917 all the way to 1948, United States policy toward Palestine was hung up on a contradiction. One set of statements would be forthcoming from Presidents and congressmen, "for public consumption," supportive of Zionism. Then another set of "official" policy statements would come from the State Department, presenting more guarded attitudes toward Jewish aspirations. Which statements represented the policy of the United States government? That is what no one could know with certainty. Friends and foes of Zionism could seize upon whatever signals of American policy would best serve their interests, but never with any sense of confidence. After Congress passed a strong pro-Zionist resolution in 1922, putting at least the legislative branch on record in support of the Balfour Declaration, a European diplomat inquired of the State Department whether the resolution was an expression of United States government policy. The American diplomat only smiled and uttered no reply.

At the start of the British Mandate in the early 1920s, the State Department had obtained assurances that American economic interests would be appropriately safeguarded. Zionists assumed that these guarantees would apply to Jews as much as to oil men. In those years, American Jews were still inclined to trust the good intentions of Gentile government. If United States citizens residing in Palestine had economic interests, surely they were entitled to the protection of the flag, the Zionists reasoned, whether they were oil entrepreneurs or idealistic Jews.

This is not the way the State Department saw it. The Jewish contributions to the building of Palestine were private and politically inspired, in the view of the diplomats, "artificial and chimerical," scarcely solid economic investments like oil concessions. "It requires little discussion," said the State Department lawyers, to establish that the proper function of government does not include "encouraging its nationals to deplete the national wealth by contribution of funds or investment of funds in foreign countries."

The State Department made only perfunctory attempts to learn the scope and nature of Jewish investment in Palestine, and not until 1939 did the consulate in Jerusalem report that of all the American citizens in the Middle East, fully 78 percent were in Palestine—9,100 United States citizens, 84 percent of them Jewish settlers. Dollar investment in Palestine amounted to $49 million, $41 million of it from American Jews. Palestine was far and away the largest American interest in the entire Middle East during the interwar decades. In fact, from the 1920s to the outbreak of World War II, more American private capital and more American citizens were concentrated in Palestine than in all the other countries of the Arab Middle East combined (excepting only, at the end of the period, Saudi Arabia). Yet it was artificial and discountable in the State Department's eyes, because it came from Jews who were only promoting their own narrow and parochial nationalistic aspirations.

BUREAUCRACY GRINDS along at its own pace, toward the goals it perceives in its own interests, distracted as little as possible by outside influences that might prove inconvenient. Civil servants always have to contend with elected officials, the political leadership charged with making policy, but as a practical matter such leadership can be exercised over only a few issues at any one time. Whenever the White House or the top political echelons of the Department of State chose to intervene, the bureaucrats would generally fall in line. But unless such a show of interest was forthcoming, the closed circle of specialists tended to go its own way.

Thus it was that a small, unremarkable group of professional diplomats managed to formulate American policies toward Palestine in the 1930s, in the absence of interest or concern from the politicians. Even American Jews caused the experts little real bother, once the flash of Brandeisian glory had sputtered away.

American Zionism between the wars was a mediocre endeavor. Chaim Weizmann may have accurately sensed the objection of American Jewry to the elitist leadership of Brandeis, but he totally misjudged the mood of the immigrant sons and daughters in their encounter with American life, with the lures of assimilation mitigating the various forms of antisemitic pressure. Jewish separateness, the aspiration to distinct nationhood, ran counter to the mood of the 1920s in the United States. The typical Jew of the first native-born generation preferred to join the work- and fun-loving majority and let others worry about the survival of their heritage. Those few who were truly committed acted on their convictions and emigrated—a young Milwaukee schoolteacher named Goldie Meyerson, for example. Discounting the pessimism of her plodding husband, a free-lance sign painter who argued that Jewish nationalism was a hopeless dream, she took off for Palestine in 1921 and eventually adopted the Hebrew name of Golda Meir.

Inflation in Europe, then global depression, brought a halt to large-scale transfer of capital to Palestine in support of the pioneering settlers, and it looked to many as though Zionism had failed, just a few years after Balfour. In August 1929, the anger of the Palestinian Arabs broke into the open under the inflammatory leadership of the Mufti of Jerusalem, and a wave of terror attacks against the Jewish settlements raised serious doubts about the viability of the Zionist effort. Two months later came the crash of Wall Street, the collapse of a decade of self-satisfied buoy-ancy, and American Jews began wondering where they could safely turn. Arab unrest or no, more than 3,000 of them emigrated to Palestine in the years 1933–35, driven by the hope of building better lives than depressed America could offer.

It was unemployment and sheer economic distress that provoked them to action, not any inspirational stirrings from the leaders of orga-nized Zionism. For with the loss of Brandeis, his "college men," and the dedicated young idealists of the immigrant families, the Jewish national movement lost its most dynamic executive talent. Contrary to Weiz-mann's expectations, American Zionism became a do-good society of halfhearted merchants and executives, no longer men of charisma, of conviction and rhetoric that could move the masses.

Jews of the interwar years drew a sharp distinction between the tedi-ous political crusade of Zionism and the exciting practical enterprise of Jewish settlement in Palestine. The slogan of all but the most doctrinaire Jewish press became "Scrap Zionism and Build Palestine." There was no contradiction in this stance, for it had never been established with finality that the Jewish restoration required the creation of a sovereign Jewish state—only a benevolent political regime that would receive and encour-age Jewish social and intellectual development. The task that captured the imagination of American Jews was the building of the land—in ab-sentia, of course—the design and support of the educational and public health systems, the housing and employment of the new immigrants. This was the pragmatism of Brandeis, and the impulse survived him. When it came to the politics of it, the grubby partisan maneuvering among the Jewish factions and the British mandatory administration, the eyes of busy Americans glazed over.

American philanthropy and technical advice fell heavily on the settlers in Palestine. Frankfurter pursued the campaigns of Brandeis for efficient practical projects, and was criticized for "meddling" ("He gives orders like an omnipotent Sultan," complained one Palestinian Jew). In their private correspondence, the Zionist pioneers poured their sarcasm upon "the mentality of the stay-at-home American Zionist who sends his alien experts to ennoble Palestine." There is none more self-righteous than the American fighting for "100% efficiency," complained a Jerusalem intellectual. "Americans are supposed to be missionaries adapting Palestine to America, especially if they are good hospital experts, or good 'case workers' in the American social workers' jargon." Pinsk and Washington were fighting it out again, and sometimes it became ugly. "If you take away the money of a Russian Jew, there is a Jew left," quipped an Eastern European ideologist. "If you take away the money of an American Jew, there is nothing left." The bitterness of the Zionist pioneer obsessed with a mystical folk mission knew no bounds against the practical man of affairs interested only in getting the job done with no nonsense.

The fallow years of American Zionism after Balfour and Brandeis nevertheless scored two strategic conversions to the cause.

In September 1925, Abraham Cahan paid a visit to Palestine. Cahan was called the "Socialist Pope" of the Lower East Side. Founding editor of the Yiddish newspaper the *Jewish Daily Forward,* he was the latest in the line of Jewish publicists in the tradition of Noah, Leeser, and I. M. Wise, whose newspaper columns brought intellectual solidarity to vast numbers of otherwise voiceless Jews. The *Forward* was the favored journal for immigrant comrades of the Bund, the General Jewish Workers' Organization of Russia and Poland. Founded in 1897, the same year as the Zionist organization, this Marxist movement established a firm foothold among Polish Jewry. Bundists scorned Zionists as capitalist exploiters, reactionary nationalists in the dawning era of Socialist internationalism. In New York, the *Forward* mocked the bureaucratic politics of Zionism, covering its contentious meetings with the flippancy of the gossip columnists rather than the self-conscious intensity of the ideologues. "How many years must we bore Eretz Israel into the hearts of the Jewish masses in order to be recognized up there?" wearily asked a *Forward* reporter.

Recognizing a legitimate news story in the experiences of Polish Jews as they sought a better life in Palestine, Cahan set off for a firsthand look. He was welcomed by David Ben-Gurion, leader of the branch of the Jewish labor movement that espoused Zionism instead of, like the Bund, opposing it. Amid the round of official receptions and meetings befitting a comrade of such immense influence over American Jewry, Cahan found himself deeply impressed with the facts of everyday life among the Jewish settlers. "Everything smacked of beginning," he wrote home in his dispatches, of newness and hope. "Tel Aviv is already a Jewish home in the fullest sense of the word." Even the ultra-Orthodox Hassidic Jewish settlers came in for praise from Cahan.

These dispatches brought intense displeasure to Cahan's Bundist colleagues in New York. In their view of the world, nothing could be more reactionary than the exploitation and commercialism of Tel Aviv—unless it was the primitive superstitions of the religious Hassidim. Cahan, it seemed, had been taken in by both. On his return, he stood firm. "I am not a Zionist in the accepted term, but I sympathize with them," he declared. "I will do all in my power to help Palestine Labor to lighten its burden. They hunger too much and work too hard and have too little sunshine in their lives, except for the spiritual sunshine."

Among Downtown Jewry, Cahan's "conversion" gave an unexpected respectability to Zionism. Then, with the Depression, lingering skepticism among Jewish-American labor leaders gave way before sheer economic distress: if workers could be siphoned off to settle in Palestine, that would mean less competition for scarce jobs here at home.

The second quiet "convert" to Zionism in the 1920s held a position as influential as Cahan's—but at the other end of the social scale. If Cahan was the Socialist Pope, his opposite number was the capitalist pontiff, Felix M. Warburg.

Warburg acceded to the leadership of the Uptown Jewish community in 1920 upon the death of his father-in-law, Jacob Schiff. From his office high in the financial partnership of Kuhn, Loeb & Co., Warburg continued the philanthropic tradition. He helped found and served as longtime chairman of the Joint Distribution Committee, that formidable international machine for giving succor to homeless Jews in Poland and the world over. As a Jew, Warburg was interested in Palestine; as a secure American, his interest had its limits. The ancient homeland was merely one of the several possible places for settlement of Jewish refugees, along with the Soviet Crimea, Latin America, and various other alternatives put forward during the troubled 1920s. Among the Uptown notables, of course, Zionism continued to have a motley, lower-class image. But the impetus to build Palestine, to help needy Jews from oppressed Europe with investment and enterprise in a new land of settlement, was appealing.

The "government" of Palestinian Jews under the British Mandate was the quasi-official Jewish Agency. At the start Weizmann and the Zionists considered this institution to be their own. As the 1920s roared on, Weizmann realized that his victory over Brandeis and the Harvard intellectuals had cut the movement off from the influence and wealth of American Jewry. In 1923 he returned to the United States, making a special point of meeting the non-Zionist Warburg. Six years of sensitive negotiations ensued before the wary Uptown crowd were persuaded that they could affiliate with the Jewish Agency for economic development without becoming embroiled in Zionist politics. By 1929, businessmen and ideologues were ready to work together—for Palestine.

Warburg held no brief for a sovereign Jewish state. He described the political objectives of Zionism as "impractical and foolhardy"; a Jewish state, he joked, would have to appoint an ambassador to Kuhn, Loeb & Company just to negotiate its annual budget. He wanted the Jewish Agency to abandon Zionist political goals so that the Arab community of Palestine could be engaged in joint endeavors. Economic development, he said, should be the "hand-to-hand work of the whole population of that little country."

Doctrinaire Zionists in Palestine and Europe recognized that they needed the financial clout of Warburg, even as they harbored the same doubts about him that they had about Brandeis: Palestine was important to Warburg; it was not the central obsession of his life. "It was only one among the fifty-seven varieties of Warburg's philanthropic endeavors," said one. But, reluctantly, they admitted that they were glad to have him taking part in the management of the Jewish Agency.

The "conversions" of Cahan and Warburg allowed Zionism to survive the traumas of the 1920s—but at a cost. The messianic political mission found itself so watered down that Socialist workers and capitalist bankers alike could participate—and there was even the naïve wish to draw in the Arabs of Palestine as well! Both Cahan and Warburg were ready to bring their resources to the aid of the Jewish restoration, but they were not the sort to champion the cause. With Brandeis gone, American Zionism needed a leader, someone capable of stirring both Gentile and Jewish society with epic passion. That man finally emerged, an "exile" who had followed the Brandeisians out of the Zionist movement but could never manage to stay aloof for long.

THE ZIONIST CAREER of Stephen Samuel Wise stretched from the pioneering days of Herzl through the exhilaration of Brandeis, the despair of the Holocaust, to the establishment of the state of Israel. As Brandeis had made Zionism respectable to American Jewry, so Wise projected the Jewish destiny into the mainstream of Christian American political thought.

Stephen Wise was born in Budapest in 1874; his paternal grandfather had been Chief Rabbi of Hungary, his mother's father founder of the Hungarian porcelain industry, a man named Baron of the Empire by the Hapsburg Emperor Franz Josef. Brought to America at the age of sixteen months, the distinguished old family name of Weisz properly Anglicized, the high-strung and bookish boy passed his youth amid the gaslights and horse-drawn wagons of New York's dusty streets. Wise spoke English, German, and Hebrew interchangeably; he went through public schools and graduated from Columbia University at the age of eighteen. In postgraduate study at Vienna and Oxford he added Arabic, Syriac, and Sanskrit to his repertoire.

Ordained a rabbi in his early twenties, he assumed the pulpit of the fashionable Madison Avenue Synagogue, New York's second oldest, but in 1899 decided that he was not yet ready to settle down into the comfortable life of a New York spiritual and social leader. He accepted a more adventurous pulpit in Portland, Oregon, and threw himself into the campaigns of the American Far West against gambling, prostitution, and exploitation of cheap labor. Along with his pastoral duties, he became Oregon's unpaid State Commissioner of Child Labor.

New York did not forget this promising young man, and in 1905 he was offered the lucrative and prestigious spiritual leadership of Temple Emanu-El, citadel of the Uptown Jewish aristocracy. A fierce struggle ensued between Wise, who demanded complete freedom to pursue his various causes from the Emanu-El pulpit, and the domineering trustees Louis Marshall and Jacob Schiff, who insisted that all sermons be cleared by the board before delivery. "It is the Rockefeller-Morgan method of buying up everything in sight, including men's scruples," Wise complained to his young wife. He turned the offer down, and proceeded to found his own "Free Synagogue" across Central Park. Ensuring that the fracas at Emanu-El received wide publicity (to his advantage), Wise soon became a respected and revered public figure.

Early every morning he strode resolutely through Central Park to his Free Synagogue office on West Sixty-eighth Street, topped by a large black felt hat, enveloped in the long, heavy folds of a Prince Albert coat. Encountering children of his congregation on their way to school, he would sweep the hat from his head and accomplish an exaggerated low bow, to the nervous titters of the awed youngsters. The doors of his office would be open for the first forty-five minutes of each working day, as he opened his mail. Students would flock to the large, shadowed room, putting their special concerns to the rabbi as he sat in a large circle of light shining upon his corner desk.

Then he stepped out in public, and every villain that crossed his path felt the brunt of his rhetoric, the full leonine roar of his voice. His long arms spread wide, his huge frame rocked back and forth on his heels with the power of his eloquence. He walked the picket lines in support of labor. He thundered from the Free Synagogue pulpit against the corruptions of Tammany Hall. With Margaret Sanger he championed the daring cause of birth control. He was one of the founders of the National Association for the Advancement of Colored People. In the midst of the tense steel strike of 1919, Wise denounced the president of United States Steel as the "most prolific breeder of Bolshevism" in the land, so shocking the wealthier members of his synagogue that many of them resigned forthwith.

Wise was a journalist's dream, always ready with a quick opinion and a colorful quote on any issue of public concern. With his views cited in the press alongside those of established Protestant and Catholic churchmen of distinction, Stephen Wise was the first rabbi that most twentieth-century Christian Americans ever heard of in public life. He stood as a symbol of the confident and effective Jew who could move with the Christian mighty without hesitation or apology. When an unknown Jewish refugee in the turmoil of Hitlerite Europe addressed a plea simply to "Rabbi, United States of America," the postal service promptly delivered the letter to Stephen Wise's New York home. In the decades when the mass of American Jewry sought to disappear inside the melting pot, the prominence of this eloquent Jew enhanced the image of an entire people.

Yet Wise had his detractors. Eclectic and outspoken, he was branded "phony" and "demagogue" by rivals for public adulation, including fellow clerics—Jewish and Christian alike—whose quotes for publication were never quite as succinct or catchy. He was particularly suspect in the narrow Jewish community Downtown. It was not only that he flouted religious law in his Free Synagogue, holding Sabbath services on Sunday instead of Saturday. The more telling fault in traditional eyes was that Wise was too comfortable in Gentile society. Campaigning for the League of Nations, he showed no discomfort in touring the nation in company with President Lowell of Harvard, the man who had just attempted—in public—to limit the number of Jews to be admitted to his university. He backed Al Smith in his campaign for the presidency, a Jewish rabbi endorsing a Roman Catholic!

Too radical for Uptown Jewry, Wise failed to understand that Downtown Jews still viewed Christian society as the perpetrator of pogroms. He had little patience with the religious Orthodox, no more than he had with the materialism by which many insecure Jews sought social standing among the Gentiles. "How money vulgarizes!" he wrote his wife after a visit to Miami Beach. "Thank God the Jews are in a small minority." Wise saw nothing wrong with paying a visit to the Bavarian village of Oberammergau, the setting for the centuries-old and—until recently— strongly antisemitic Passion Play. He wrote home in a lighthearted vein of his delight at being allowed to try on some of the traditional costumes. "I wore both the crown of the High Priest (and suitably enough that was too small) but the crown of thorns was too large." These, of course, were private remarks. But in 1925 he delivered a sympathetic public sermon about Jesus, just a few days before Christmas, and the wrath of the Orthodox descended upon him. They branded him "a grave menace to Judaism," and he was forced to resign, for a brief time, as head of a fund-raising campaign for Palestine.

Among Wise's countless crusades, beginning in his teen-age years at turn-of-the-century Columbia, had been the daring cause of Zionism, then just attracting attention. Wise became an official American delegate to the Second Zionist Congress in 1898, serving alongside Jacob De Haas in the secretariat. There he met the great Herzl, who assured the young American that the Jewish state would come in his lifetime.*

Wise's interest in Zionism paled alongside his other causes in the empty decade after Herzl's death and before the emergence of Brandeis. Once the movement again caught fire, he plunged into the Brandeis whirlwind and worked his way, in the company of the Supreme Court Justice, into the inner councils of the Wilson administration. Ever trusting in the goodwill of his Gentile friends, Wise was blind to the anti-Zionist leanings of Wilson's foreign policy advisers, Colonel House and Secretary of State Lansing, going so far as to call Lansing a "tested friend of the Zionist cause"—oblivious to Lansing's real views.

When Brandeis walked out, so did Wise. But he never could drop any cause for long, and soon he was back in the leadership of the Zionist organization trying to play the role of peacemaker among the feuding factions. He was, after all, the American Jew most recognized and admired in Gentile society—and the time was rapidly approaching when Jewry needed help more than it had ever anticipated.

"EVEN IF THE HITLERITES should get into power," Warburg wrote a friend in 1932, "the moment responsibilities rest on their shoulders and they are in the government, they will sober down, just as much as the

* By a matter of months, it did.

Communists have in Russia and the Laborites have in England." So spoke the optimistic voice of German Jewry, in the United States and in Germany. Stephen Wise only reinforced his standing as a radical when he condemned this complacency as "just incredible . . . a policy of silence and cowardice." Yet even Wise could not grasp the real magnitude of the threat. In 1933 Justice Brandeis said flatly, "The Jews must leave Germany." Wise, as he wrote a friend a few months later, "could hardly believe my ears. . . . I could hardly believe that he was sane. A people to migrate!"

Migration was a troublesome matter on many scores. America of the 1930s was in the grip of isolationism and economic distress. The Immigration Act of 1924 had imposed a rigid quota system that discriminated against Jews of Eastern Europe. American Jewish leaders had opposed the 1924 legislation, but they subsequently acquiesced, mindful that a renewed flow of immigration would only repeat the social agonies their fathers had known and intensify the crippling unemployment. Native-born Jews were already finding it hard to get jobs, and the word spread that Jewish employees were being fired when non-Jews became available.

Jews who could afford it fulfilled their communal responsibilities, not by pressing for freer immigration to America, but by donating to refugee organizations that would help foreign Jews in need, as long as they stayed where they were or went somewhere other than the United States. Zionism suddenly became attractive once again, for Jewish settlement in Palestine was an obvious and pleasing alternative to a new migration to the *Goldene Medine*. As late as 1943, when the right of immigration to Palestine had become a rallying cry of a nearly united American Jewry, proposals for the right of immigration to the United States were roundly shouted down.

Official Zionism began to emerge from the post-Brandeis doldrums with Stephen Wise's assumption of leadership in 1935. The growing menace of Nazi Germany stirred new concerns for Jewish survival; Zionism, offering one possible answer, increased in membership and energy. Yet the focus of Zionist attentions remained diffuse. Zionists were anti-Nazi, of course, but they were also hostile to Britain, where the cause of Arab nationalism was gaining supporters and inhibiting the growth and development of the Jewish community in the Palestine mandate. Zionists did their best to raise money, but in the 1930s this was not an easy task. Moreover, many American Jews continued to be troubled by the manners of those unkempt Jews in Palestine, by the high-handed attitudes of Ben-Gurion's labor movement, and the Zionists' call for a sovereign state. With all the great powers maneuvering and Arab factions increasingly restive, Palestine simply did not seem to be a good bet for ensuring Jewish survival.

One Jewish community, that of San Francisco, held back donations, for fear that "all the sums raised will be spent on Palestinian politics." A $5,000 check to a relief organization from Spokane, Washington, came with the restriction that it not be used "in whole or in part for Zionistic or Palestinian purposes." Warburg's Joint Distribution Committee complained about Zionist attempts to politicize its work. "The principle that our help should follow the refugees wherever they may be brought, is being twisted to mean that the only help and the only solution lies in Palestine," wrote one officer of the Committee. Warburg himself complained in 1936 that the Zionists were interested in relief work only if "done through its political organization in Palestine. That group goes so far that, if very important work is done in the economic field, along non-political lines, they love to minimize it and, in fact, interfere with it."

When interest in Jewish resettlement was finally aroused, moreover, it concerned resettlement primarily for German Jews, with whom the American establishment felt some cultural affinity, and most certainly not the more primitive, alien Jews of Poland and Eastern Europe. "Our program in Eastern Europe [is] primarily devoted to economic reconstruction and relief and support of necessary institutions and organizations in those countries," reported the Joint Distribution Committee in 1937. "It does not cover emigration." Americans committed to this philanthropic endeavor felt little sympathy with the shadowy activities of that Zionist intelligence network known as *Aliyah Beth,* at work from 1939 onwards trying to organize illegal immigration from Eastern Europe to Palestine.

What, then, to do about the Nazi threat to Jewry, as it gradually became more than a pre-election tactic? Some American Jewish leaders proposed an economic boycott of all German trade, "the pinch in the pocket-book region," as Warburg called it. Yet the Jewish establishment opposed such a "provocation," warning that success would only confirm the antisemitic charges of an international Jewish conspiracy. Even militant Zionists were inhibited by their knowledge that the Jews in Palestine were themselves actively trading with the Nazis. Blocked funds of recent emigrants from Germany were quietly being transferred, to become a crucial economic buttress in the development of the Palestine community.

Stephen Wise was at the height of his influence in the late 1930s as the fate of European Jewry under Nazi rule became of acute concern to Americans, Christians as well as Jews. Calling for a mass migration of historic proportions, the liberal Gentile writer Dorothy Thompson warned in 1938 that "millions of Jews are in danger of becoming pariahs." More than any of his colleagues, Wise was troubled by the dilemma that Nazi antisemitism posed for Americans, and particularly for Zionists. One of the most painful memories burdening the conscience of American Jewry is the resettlement drama of 1938–42.

Zionist doctrine had long required unremitting pressure for Jewish settlement in Palestine—and only Palestine. Proposals over the years for Jewish resettlement elsewhere were regarded as diversions, detracting from the campaign for a national homeland. As the Nazi menace became ever clearer, however, bleak questions arose. Were doctrinaire Zionists still right to insist on their political goals? Or did the imminence of danger to European Jewry justify any rescue and resettlement plans, even at the cost of deferring the campaign for the building of Palestine?

Wise, for one, was ready to moderate doctrine. In 1937, he wrote a friend that "Being a Semite I would be willing to do a little bargaining with Britain if we get two things," meaning the British colonies of Uganda and Kenya for unrestricted Jewish settlement. If Arab pressures were making the growth of Jewish Palestine impossible, Wise said the next year, then the Jews should be given "some great additional English colony." These ideas were heresy, of course, recalling the "territorial" crisis of early Zionism, when Herzl himself had been willing to settle for a Jewish homeland somewhere other than Palestine.

In 1938 was formed the International Colonization Society, to provide endangered Jews of Europe with new homes wherever they could be found. Wise was an early supporter. Something of the same outrage greeted this philanthropic effort as had struck Herzl back in 1902. Abba Hillel Silver of Cleveland, a rabbi of whom Zionism would soon be hearing much, expressed a typical reaction: he wrote Wise in a fury, refusing to pledge a single dollar for resettlement, lest Palestine get the "short end of the bargain." Weizmann in London fired off warnings to American friends. "Visions of settlements in South America will be conjured up; it will all prove a disappointment . . . but the Assimilationists will catch on to it." And so they did. Bernard Baruch, perhaps the most prominent of the assimilated American Jews, drew up a detailed plan to resettle European Jews in British Africa or Portuguese Angola—prompting the aged Brandeis to remark to President Roosevelt that "Baruch would be more likely to consider colonization of Jews on some undiscovered planet than Palestine."

Britain and the Arabs were adamant against opening Palestine to refugees from Hitler, and journalist Dorothy Thompson sadly concluded that "all hopes of anything like Jewish mass migration to Palestine have to be buried." She proposed alternative resettlement in Canada and Brazil; hers was a lonely voice in calling even for increased Jewish immigration to the United States. Wise proposed the development of a Jewish colony in the Dominican Republic, and five hundred families were actually settled there. As late as November 1941, Under Secretary of State Sumner Welles addressed a Jewish audience at length about the Dominican project, making no more than a single reference to Palestine. Zionists in the hall were disappointed and angry.

The strangest of the resettlement proposals came from the military government of Emperor Hirohito's Japan. From early 1939, Japanese diplomats had been intrigued with the possibility of building sympathetic ties to the American Jewish community. What better bait than an offer to resettle European Jews in the Japanese-controlled territories of Manchukuo or China? And whom better to approach with this offer than the revered Stephen Wise, a humanitarian known for his influence and access in high places? "He goes anywhere the President goes as the shadow follows the form," wrote one Japanese diplomat to his superiors. Wise received an unofficial envoy in his office early in 1940 and listened politely; but to him Japan was "as truly Fascist a nation as Germany or Italy," and as he showed his visitor out the door, he exploded to an assistant, "I have no time for this nonsense!"

The fact remained that even if the ultimate need of world Jewry was a homeland of their own, the immediate need of the Jews of Europe was survival—and Wise was not the only Zionist who recognized it. A splinter group of Jews, loosely allied with a Palestinian underground army, the Irgun Zvai Leumi, dropped the political goal from the program it argued before the American public. Injecting the idea of Palestine into the discussion would only harm the refugees, argued one of the Irgun group's well-placed friends, Congressman Will Rogers, Jr.

American Jews, even devoted Zionists, were deeply divided between political and human values. Campaigning singlemindedly for the Jewish homeland in Palestine, Rabbi Silver and his dedicated partisans minimized the "immediate problem" of saving Jewish lives. For centuries, Jews had ignored the underlying causes of their distress to concern themselves only with "immediate problems," argued one of his associates in 1943. Had there been a Jewish state, "either a Hitler would not have arisen in our time or, if one had, we might have had a country under Jewish control in which the Jews of Germany and other lands could have been received—and received in large numbers. It has been our misfortune throughout our history that we have not been able to look ahead, to plan ahead, and to provide this radical solution."

The conflict devastated the sensibilities of a generation which had worked hard and grown comfortable in American society. American Jews were "showing signs of cracking up," wrote *The Jewish Spectator* in May 1941, "under the mental and physical strain of 'news from Europe.' " A non-Zionist of the Joint Distribution Committee looked back in bitter rebuke: "If the Zionists had helped in leadership, perhaps tens of thousands could have been saved." Wise himself confessed, long after it was all over, to "a harrowing sense of guilt"—that if perhaps the Zionist movement had been more willing to compromise long-term goals for immediate needs, many of Hitler's victims might have survived. Other Zionists argue to this day, as they did at the time, that none of the alternative resettlement sites stood a chance of success anyway. The sense of guilt lingering among American Jews is not that they failed to rescue their besieged brethren in Europe, for that was clearly beyond their abilities. It is rather that too many were unready or unwilling even to take the risk of trying.

By 1942, the basic human issue had become moot. For millions of Europe's Jews there was no longer any need for rescue and resettlement —in Palestine or anywhere else.

5

STEPHEN WISE and his colleagues in the leadership of the Zionist Organization of America were elated as they emerged from the White House one day early in 1939. They had discovered that Franklin D. Roosevelt had started taking an interest in the political destiny of the Jews. Justice Brandeis had called on him twice recently to focus his attentions; Zionist aspirations had come up in conversation with two of his New Deal loyalists, Felix Frankfurter and Benjamin V. Cohen. "We have every reason to believe that the President has the finest understanding of, and the deepest sympathy with, our movement," wrote one of Wise's colleagues to his worried associates in Europe.

For years to come, American Zionists would eagerly accept all reassurances of Roosevelt's fidelity. As late as 1944, a powerful White House functionary named David Niles told Zionist petitioners that Roosevelt was "completely with you." Palestine's future would be settled in a "highly satisfactory" way, the sympathetic Niles told his visitors.

Yet not five years later, the same David Niles confessed to "serious doubts in my mind that Israel would have come into being if Roosevelt had lived." Bernard Baruch, no Zionist but concerned with the Jewish destiny nonetheless, surveyed the choice in 1944 between Roosevelt and his Republican presidential challenger, Thomas E. Dewey, and said bluntly, "I would rather trust my American Jewishness in Mr. Dewey's hands than in Mr. Roosevelt's." Secretary of State Cordell Hull wrote that Roosevelt "at times talked both ways to Zionists and Arabs, besieged as he was by each camp."

Something odd happened between the living Roosevelt, trusted and revered by America's Jews, and the portrait of political hypocrisy that came out after his death. What is the fair judgment to be made about Roosevelt and the Jews? The role of the thirty-second President of the United States in the long drama of the Jewish restoration poses a challenge to the historian. The reality is stranger and more complex than either critics or defenders suppose.

FRANKLIN DELANO ROOSEVELT was a product of patrician America. "Every one of my ancestors on both sides," he joyfully informed the Daughters of the American Revolution, an audience who would appreciate the point, "every single one of them, without exception, was in this land before 1776. And there was only one Tory among them!" The Daughters cheered. Roosevelt money was old money, about as old a family fortune as any in the Republic. It grew from real estate speculation on Manhattan Island early in the eighteenth century, and was multiplied by entrepreneurship in the sugar trade—and the sugar trade, in those days, meant slavery. As their wealth mellowed, and sons came to feel a touch of guilt in remembering the deeds of fathers, the family evolved a tradition of public responsibility. In a sophomore essay at Harvard, the future President noted that Roosevelts "never felt that because they were born in a good position they could put their hands in their pockets and succeed. They have felt, rather, that being born in a good position, there was no excuse for them if they did not do their duty by the community."

Franklin was brought up by governesses and tutors at Hyde Park, on the banks of the Hudson in Dutchess County. At fourteen, he was allowed to leave the family estate to attend Groton, the highly principled Massachusetts boarding school headed by the Reverend Endicott Peabody. There all but a token few were from Social Register families. Worship of God and Christian virtue was uncritical and wholehearted. "I studied Sacred Studies for six years at Groton," recalled one of Franklin's schoolmates. "I was never told that the Old and the New Testaments are full of the most potent contradictions."

At Groton, and later at Harvard, Franklin held back, socially aloof. Entering school two years later than his classmates, "he felt left out," recalled his fifth cousin and future wife, Eleanor. "It gave him sympathy for people who are left out." He was turned down by Porcellian, the most aristocratic of the Harvard clubs. He discovered that cheerful banter was often a useful technique for concealing shyness; he never for the rest of his life lost the almost obsessive craving to be liked by the people around him, and he sought reassurance a dozen times a day of just how much he was liked. By 1930 he had joined no less than forty-seven different clubs, associations, and societies.

The patrician antisemitism of his circle was not Roosevelt's style—looking down on people was not a way to make them like you. His future wife did not have the same inhibitions. "I am anxious to hear about the first day," she wrote her cousin as he started work at Columbia Law School, "and whether you found any old acquaintances or had only Jew Gentlemen to work with." Through her correspondence was sprinkled the gossip of a well-bred young lady in society—the party for Bernard Baruch that she had to attend, "which I'd rather be hung than seen at. . . . the Jew party was appalling—I never wish to hear money, jewels and sables mentioned again." Among Roosevelt's early and longtime intimates were Henry Morgenthau, Jr., and Felix Frankfurter, whom Eleanor described on first meeting as "an interesting little man but very Jew." (Eleanor Roosevelt thus unwittingly put her finger on the lifelong complexes of the short and wiry jurist: "There were matters one never talked about but always thought about," Frankfurter once remarked, "one was your height, another was your Jewishness.")

A rising political figure in World War I Washington, Roosevelt was happy to accept membership in the Metropolitan and Chevy Chase clubs. They excluded Jews from membership, along with Negroes and businessmen, but Roosevelt always sought friends outside the snobbish club crowd. Long afterward, as President, he would chide the professional diplomats for confining their social contacts to the club establishment. Ambassadors ought to come home from time to time and be sent to Tennessee for a year, he said, just to find out how Americans really lived.

Religious upbringing played a powerful role in shaping the attitudes of American Presidents toward the destiny of the Jews; this was as true of Roosevelt as of the more openly devout Woodrow Wilson and Harry S Truman. Roosevelt's religion, like his political and social thought, was eclectic. "He had little, if any, intellectual or theological understanding," wrote Frances Perkins, his Secretary of Labor, who may have understood Roosevelt's mind as intimately as any other associate. "His sense of religion was so complete that he was able to associate himself without any conflict with all expressions of religious worship. Catholic, Protestant and Jew alike were comprehensible to him, and their religious aspirations seemed natural and much the same as his own."

In Roosevelt, love of geography merged with old New England's fascination with the lands of the Bible. On his way to meet Prime Minister Churchill and Marshal Stalin in Tehran in 1943, the President ordered his pilot to fly low over Palestine; in mounting excitement he proceeded to pick out sites known from Scripture. "We've seen it all from Beersheba to Dan," he exclaimed. "You know this country as though you were raised here," said a bemused aide, and Roosevelt proudly replied, "So I do!"

Roosevelt was no intellectual, but he did not waver in respect for intellectual ability, and he grew testy with attempts to inject irrelevant factors into personnel decisions. When a delegation of influential Jews urged him not to name Frankfurter to the Supreme Court, for fear of provoking antisemitism, Roosevelt angrily rejected their appeal. The New Deal drew in so many Jewish intellectuals that his reactionary critics called it the "Jew Deal," a slur that annoyed the President almost as much as the substantive criticism of his policies. American democracy, he said in his second inaugural address, will never "hold any faithful and law-abiding group within its borders to be superfluous." The phrase had been suggested by Stephen Wise, and Roosevelt used it verbatim.

The President would delight Jewish intimates by teasing them in a manner that no one suspected of antisemitism could carry off. His friend "Stevey" Wise, for one, floated through the corridors of the White House like an overawed courtier, not minding in the least Roosevelt's imitations of his hortatory pomposities. Nahum Goldmann, a diplomat of the Jewish Agency, told of a wartime weekend when he and Wise were summoned to Hyde Park by Roosevelt's aide Samuel R. Rosenman, who stayed in a cottage near the President's main house. "It was a sweltering day, and we were all in our shirtsleeves on the verandah when we heard the blare of a car horn and Roosevelt's car drew up in front of us," Goldmann recalled. "When he saw us together the President said, 'Oh, oh! Rosenman, Stephen Wise and Nahum Goldmann conferring together. Carry on, boys. Sam will tell me what I'm supposed to do on Monday.' The car was drawing away when Roosevelt stopped it and called out: 'Imagine what Goebbels would pay for a photo of this scene —the President of the United States taking his instructions from the three Elders of Zion!' "

The record of Roosevelt and the Jews must obviously be reckoned on more substantial evidence than memories of personal charm. During his presidency, the Jewish people suffered the Holocaust and glimpsed national redemption. Retrospect tends to blur this double drama of the 1940s into a single epic. But to people living through it, Jews and Gentiles alike, the two facets of the Jewish destiny seemed separate and distinct. The fate of European Jewry in the face of Nazi genocide was one issue; the political future of Palestine was a different matter. In common with most of his countrymen, Roosevelt saw the two issues from quite different perspectives.

ROOSEVELT AND HITLER came into office the same year. The new American President named an idealistic historian from Chicago, William E. Dodd, as his ambassador to Nazi Germany. Dodd went fully prepared to understand and work with the puzzling new German leadership, though his predecessor had taken the initiative of warning the Nazi leaders that, of all their revolutionary programs, mistreatment of Jews would have a "disastrous effect in America and in molding world public opinion." It took the scholarly new ambassador less than a year in Berlin to recognize that he was dealing with ruthless men.

The career diplomats on his staff and back in Washington were not impressed, for they matched Dodd's contempt for the Nazis with their own contempt for a rank amateur treading upon their professional turf. The ambassador's performance, noted embassy counselor John C. White, was pleasing only to the American press and to the Jews. Not that the embassy staff was blind to Nazi intentions. "It is definitely the aim of the [Nazi] government . . . to eliminate the Jews from German life," wrote one political officer. By 1937 the dispatches from Berlin were conveying clear warnings that Hitler's persecutions of the Jews were not casual or incidental.

Until then, Nazi antisemitism had aimed at expelling Jews from Germany; some 120,000 had been uprooted, a third of them reaching Palestine. A young career diplomat in the embassy, Jacob D. Beam, described a new trend in German policy that year which only hinted at the eventual reality: "The Nazis' unstated but ultimate purpose, failing the possibility . . . of getting rid of the Jews by mass emigration, is that life in Germany should be made so uncomfortable, if not impossible, for them that they shall be discouraged from reproducing their kind and shall hence die out in the course of one or two generations." One of Beam's embassy colleagues, Second Secretary George Kennan, advised against any American protests over this policy, saying it would be an ineffective interference in another country's internal affairs. Beam concurred, reporting to Washington that "the day would seem to be past, if indeed it ever existed, when disapproval from abroad could moderate the fixed and ruthless lines of Nazi domestic policy."

An obvious alternative presented itself to American policymakers, if they were really concerned about the plight of European Jewry. Indications were clear that millions of Jews were in danger of their lives, their community in danger of extinction, under Nazi rule. At the same time, a political movement existed, one with an illustrious heritage, that sought to resettle Jews in a homeland of their own. In retrospect, the question asks itself: Why were problem and solution not brought together? Why did policymakers express no serious interest in resettling the threatened Jews of Europe in the land of their forebears, where a community of their faith and nation was eager to receive them? As Blackstone had asked half a century before, why not give Palestine back to them again?

Neither then nor now is there an easy answer, and even to pose the question triggers complex political, emotional, and psychological responses.

On the most practical level lies the argument that settlement in Palestine would not really have "solved" the problems of European Jewry, given its inhospitable geography and the hostility of the surrounding Arab population. Arab goodwill was important to British and American policymakers—more important, perhaps (though one could not comfortably say it aloud), than the fate of those alien Jews who fell under Hitler's power. In and out of government there were those who were still fearful that Eastern European Jewry represented a Communistic, revolutionary cancer that would distress and disrupt any land they inhabited. Charles Crane was not the only prominent American who wondered if Hitler might not have some grounds for his paranoia.

Even Jews harbored strong doubts about whether the Zionist vision was in fact realistic or desirable. If Jews themselves could not clearly analyze the situation, the Gentiles in Washington had little interest in stirring up emotions.

In terms of foreign policy, it was not only emotions that would be aroused by an official call for Jewish rescue and resettlement in Palestine; there would be inconvenient and downright dangerous stirrings of anti-British sentiments, already at large among American isolationists. A massive Jewish resettlement program in Palestine would fly straight in the face of British policy. How could Washington policymakers defy Britain on that score, yet at the same time summon up the emotional support that Britain needed in its struggle against the Nazi enemy? Privy to the political sensitivities of the Roosevelt White House, Under Secretary of State Welles argued in 1941 that "for reasons of policy as well as for reasons of expediency, I consider it in the highest degree important that everything be done by this government to prevent Jewish groups within the United States from opposing the British war effort."

America's unwillingness to consider the Palestine alternative for European Jewry was, for the record, brought about by reluctance to put pressure on the British ally as she stood squarely in the front line of Western democracy against the totalitarian threat. But under the surface remained that nagging feeling, already noted openly by the *Christian Century,* that somehow the sufferings of Jews need not be taken quite as seriously by Christendom as the plight of other, less tainted, peoples.

Practitioners of public policy, pressed into countless minute decisions daily, do not often reflect on the real meaning of their acts. To the diplomats of the late 1930s and early 1940s, mundane bureaucratic considerations determined that the two issues of rescuing Jews from Europe and resettling Jews in Palestine had to be regarded separately in isolation.

Direct-line responsibility fell to two different bureaus of the State Department, each headed by a domineering and adept administrator endlessly jealous of any intrusions upon his domain. To bring them together, someone at a higher political level would have had to push, at great cost in time, energy, and perseverance. A harassed Chief Executive would sooner arrange for Arabs and Jews of Palestine to sit down and reason together than pound together the heads of the State Department's Near Eastern and European divisions.

Whatever the policy in Palestine, decisions about rescuing Jews and other refugees from Europe fell into the sprawling bureaucratic empire of a frustrated politician named Breckinridge Long, who watched over the problems of the Old World and decided what was best for America.

He hailed proudly from the Breckinridges of Kentucky and the Longs of North Carolina. His diplomatic career began in 1917 with a minor post awarded for a major contribution to Wilson's campaign. Though he rose to greater eminence in World War II, after uneventful forays into politics, it was the Washington of the earlier day that he found more to his liking. "Washington then was gay and confident. Now it is sober," he confided to his diary in 1942. "Then it had many aspects of social as well as intellectual leadership. Now it is intellectual without the social setting." Long's social credentials were impeccable; his intellectual distinction less so. Among his undergraduate papers at Princeton was an impassioned argument entitled "The Impossibility of India's Revolt from England." Later, when assuming control of a new section in the State Department, he noted with a disarming frankness, "I am surprised how much can be done without any knowledge of it on my part."

Long was antisemitic, but this misses the point a little. He was also anti-Catholic, anti-liberal, anti-Communist, anti-Nazi, anti-New York, anti-voter, anti-everybody, in fact, whose background differed from the gentility of his own. Hitler and Mussolini were "obdurate, ruthless and vicious" men, Long believed, but they were efficient and should be appeased. It was "Breck" Long in 1933 who raved to Roosevelt that Mussolini deserved recognition for making Italy's trains run on time. After the fall of Paris in 1940 he warned that "if we are not careful we are going to find ourselves champions of a defeated cause. . . . We may have a war thrust upon us if we antagonize the military machine which is about to assume control of the whole continent of Europe."

Not everything about the ruthless Nazis was bad, in Long's book; with Hitler he shared an almost hysterical anxiety about Communists and Jews. *Mein Kampf* he found to be "eloquent in opposition to Jewry and to Jews as exponents of Communism and chaos." Through the extraordinary personal diaries which he kept daily run strings of extravagant epithets to describe his many opponents in the Washington power games, disgusting people like "communists, extreme radicals, Jewish professional agitators, refugee enthusiasts." In a 1942 tirade he wrote: "Each of these men hates me. I am to them the embodiment of a nemesis. They each and all believe every person, everywhere, has a RIGHT to come to the United States. I believe NOBODY anywhere has a RIGHT to enter the United States unless the United States desires."

This was the man named by Roosevelt to head the State Department's visa section, with its consular officers empowered to decide which among the refugees from Hitler should be granted American entry permits. In December 1939, when he was appointed, he enjoyed powerful political backing, including that of Joseph P. Kennedy, ambassador in London, and could claim old friendship with the President. He needed a job, and refugee policy was not a matter that yet commanded much interest in the Roosevelt administration.

Long came to call himself, accurately, the "policymaking officer and the executive agent of the government" for decisions about the fate of refugees. His philosophy was simple: keep them out—they are all troublemakers. Yet, as he moved to halt the desperate human flow, it cannot be said that he faced much opposition from other Foreign Service professionals down the line. A prominent journalist was approached by a secretary in one of the American embassies in Europe with the admonition "I hope you're not helping Jews get into the United States." Another American diplomat was asked what he thought should be done with Jews fleeing from Hitler; he replied only with his hands, simulating the sweep of a machine gun across the room.

Nor were Long's attitudes totally out of step with the times. A *Fortune* survey concluded that 83 percent of Americans opposed any increase in United States immigration quotas; even Jewish leaders concurred in restrictive measures. For all the British restrictions on immigration to Palestine, more were settled there than were granted entry to the United States; some 258,000 Jews entered Palestine between 1931 and 1942, compared with only 169,000 arriving in the United States. For the decade after Hitler came to power, State Department obstructionism ensured that the quotas for immigrants from Germany and Austria were never more than half filled.

Long was proud of his record, and he tolerated neither criticism nor interference. Shortly after taking office, he explained what he proposed to do: "We can delay and effectively stop for a temporary period of indefinite length the number of immigrants into the United States. We could do this by simply advising our consuls to put every obstacle in the way and to require additional evidence and to resort to various administrative devices which would postpone and postpone and postpone the granting of the visas." Long instructed his consular officers, "in the interest of public safety," to deny visas to any "alien who has close relatives or who is acquainted with other persons" residing under Nazi control. Thus the gates were slammed shut, for the applicant who could deny relatives or acquaintances in occupied Europe was rare indeed. A few striking individuals in the consular corps, notably in Marseilles and Casablanca, bent Long's regulations as far as they dared to rescue intellectuals in flight, but the larger consulates in Vienna, Berlin, Rotterdam, Zurich, and Lisbon enforced the restrictions with impressive zeal.

When Stephen Wise and a delegation of Christian liberals tried in September 1941 to alert Roosevelt to what was happening, the President merely referred the matter back to his friend "Breck" Long, whose diary reveals what he thought of the complaint: "I got a little mad and I fear I betrayed it. . . . The exclusion of any person is objectionable to those eminent gentlemen. . . . They would throw me to the wolves in their eagerness to destroy me—and will try in the future as they have in the past to ruin my political status."

Long was convinced that the pool of refugees contained dangerous fifth columnists and Gestapo agents, a notion eagerly encouraged by the British to justify their restrictive immigration policy. Unbeknownst to American diplomats, however, the British Foreign Office well knew the spurious nature of their arguments. "I cannot help feeling that we have been sailing a little close to the wind in several telegrams we have sent to the United States," noted one British diplomat involved in the confidential internal traffic. "Neither the authorities in Palestine nor here know definitely that a single enemy agent has arrived in this way." Another British diplomat sized up the mentality of Long and those around him:

> The argument about enemy agents has such a fatal attraction— like the candle-flame for the moth—though they get burnt every time they come near it. If one has a personal conviction that the Jews are our enemies just as the Germans are, but in a more insidious way, it becomes essential to find reasons for believing that our two sets of enemies are linked together by secret and evil bonds, and it becomes our duty to say that they are so linked, irrespective of the evidence we can produce.

Under the determined indoctrination of Breckinridge Long, reinforced by the prejudices of the age, officers of the United States government were not receptive or sympathetic when ominous reports started filtering out of Nazi-occupied Europe, something about a "final solution" to the Jewish problem.

.   .   .

ONE DAY EARLY in January 1942, the nerve ends of the nation still
numbed by the surprise Japanese attack on Pearl Harbor a few weeks
before, a world-famous German writer sat down at a recording machine
in his new exile home in California. It was his monthly contribution to
the war effort, an anti-Nazi propaganda broadcast to be beamed by the
British Broadcasting Corporation to the German population at war. A
modest effort, but it "does the heart good," he told a friend.

Microphone live, shellac transcription disk turning, he began:

> The news sounds incredible, but my source is good. Four
> hundred young Dutch Jews have been brought to Germany to
> serve as objects for experimentation with poison gas. . . . They
> are dead; they have died for the New Order and the martial ingen-
> iousness of the master race. Just for that they were, at best, good
> enough. After all, they were Jews.

The sarcasm in the voice of Thomas Mann was a message in itself.
Mann was an eloquent symbol of pre-Nazi Germany. In his younger days
conservative and antisemitic ("That's the way it was in Germany," ex-
plained his wife, herself Jewish), he had joined that distinguished band
of exiles from Hitler, Gentiles and Jews alike, who became in midcentury
America a fount of artistic and intellectual creativity. There was Einstein,
settled at Princeton; Mann's fellow novelist Erich Maria Remarque; Max
Reinhardt, the theatrical producer; the brilliant symphonic conductor
Bruno Walter; and many more. To the ordinary Germans left behind,
Mann was in a class by himself—and here he was relaying one of the first
authentic reports to leak out of the Nazi councils of a holocaust against
the Jews.

"I said the story sounds incredible, and everywhere in the world many
will refuse to believe it," Mann went on. Of atrocity stories there had
been many, scattered through the public press. News of pogroms was
nothing new to readers of the Jewish press and, if the victims were really
numerous, they might even rate a few lines in the Gentile press as well.
"There is little doubt," the American Jewish Committee concluded early
in 1940, "that the ultimate aim of the Nazi government is to eliminate the
Jews as quickly as possible in any way short of direct mass execution."
By October 1941 the United States government had heard enough about
Nazi atrocities on the Eastern Front to raise the matter timorously with
the Vatican. The Holy See replied that it was unable to provide any
further information or suggest a useful response.

But the report that came to Mann seemed different; it did not actually report "direct mass execution," but suggested that something calculated and systematic was going on, directed against a civilian population away from the field of battle. As Mann's broadcast went out, the *Jewish Chronicle* of London named Mauthausen as the concentration camp where the gas experiments were being conducted. The British consul general in Bern picked up his version of the same reports in February. *The New York Times* of March 1, 1942, printed the testimony of a distinguished Polish banker and writer, Henry Shoskes, under the headline "Extinction Feared by Jews in Poland." Shoskes told *The Times* of reports smuggled out of the country that "about 3,000,000 Polish Jews are doomed to annihilation"; the article appeared on page 28. In May a radio signal was received in London from the Bund, the Marxist Polish underground, stating flatly that "from the day the Russo-German war broke out, the Germans embarked on the physical extermination of the Jewish population."

In fact, it was in March 1941 that Hitler's top secret decision had been reached for the ultimate disposition of the Jews within his extended grasp. In July, Nazi security forces were ordered to "take all preparatory measures" to effect the "final solution" of the Jewish problem. The following January, the month of Mann's broadcast, a conference of fifteen top Gestapo and SS officers convened at the Wannsee police headquarters in Berlin to review plans for "liquidation." During the winter of 1941–42 an estimated 90 percent of the Jews in Nazi-occupied Soviet cities were killed; major deportations from Holland and occupied France began in July 1942, and in August the industrial park at Auschwitz was designated the central extermination camp for the western Jews who remained.

Bits and pieces of this news gradually leaked out of the Nazi sphere of control, through underground radio broadcasts, coded personal messages, and the firsthand testimony of German businessmen, commercial travelers, and roving functionaries who had little concept of the whole story but had overheard or picked up enough hints of it to be concerned. Some reached Mann, probably from other exiles who paid him courtesy visits. Government services everywhere listened for new pieces to fit into the pattern.

A key crossroads of intelligence was the Swiss banking center of Zurich, and there in July 1942 one Benjamin Sagalowitz received a disturbing visit from an old friend, a Swiss businessman who had just heard something important from a visiting German business contact, an industrialist—he mentioned the name quickly—who seemed to know what he was talking about.

"Benno" Sagalowitz was a man of many parts. Called a free-lance journalist, he was a sometime press agent for the various Jewish organizations in neutral Switzerland; he also wrote articles for world press organs that could not afford to station a full-time correspondent at the listening posts. He was, in addition, a tipster to official agencies of several governments who wanted someone reliable to relay gossip and facts, and who understood how to distinguish between the two. In short, Sagalowitz knew his way around.

The name mentioned to Sagalowitz rang a bell; it was a man he had known vaguely in the past, a man who had provided timely and accurate intelligence about the German attack on Russia in June 1941, and later about some important personnel changes in the Nazi high command. The man's latest information was even more striking; planning was underway in the Führer's headquarters, he reported, to arrange that "all Jews in countries occupied or controlled by Germany, numbering 3.5 to 4 million, should after deportation and concentration in the East be exterminated at one blow, to resolve once and for all the Jewish question in Europe." The extermination was to be accomplished in the coming autumn, through the use of lethal prussic acid. The German informant was so convinced of the accuracy of his information that he passed the word to his Swiss business contacts with the request that it be conveyed urgently to Roosevelt and Churchill.

For Benno Sagalowitz, this was a heavy load. Substance aside, his normal reporting channels did not include access to Roosevelt and Churchill. But he immediately thought of one friend who might provide that access: Gerhard Riegner in Geneva, a scholarly thirty-year-old bachelor, Swiss representative of the World Jewish Congress. Riegner reported directly to the head of the Jewish Congress in the United States, Stephen Wise, and in Switzerland they knew as well as in Japan that access to Wise meant access to Roosevelt.

Cool-headed and professional, Riegner sought corroboration. No, the German industrialist would not meet Riegner directly, but he did agree to meet Sagalowitz briefly to convey the same intelligence passed earlier through the Swiss intermediary. For a week, Riegner probed sources in the little community of professional Nazi-watchers in Geneva, among them Professor Paul Guggenheim of the Institut des Hautes Etudes, who also served as legal adviser to the World Jewish Congress. Guggenheim's further inquiries elicited parallel information from such well-placed authorities as Carl Burckhardt, distinguished Swiss historian and official of the International Red Cross.

Riegner had previously obtained contingency permission to send sensitive messages to Wise through the American consulate. Unfortunately, his contact at the consulate was on vacation, so on August 8 Riegner walked into the office of Vice-Consul Howard Elting, Jr., whom he had not met before. Riegner "was in great agitation," Elting reported, and when the diplomat pressed for details to assure himself that the alarming information was worth passing on, Riegner was convincing. "My personal opinion is that Riegner is a serious and balanced individual," Elting informed the Department of State, "and that he would never have come to the consulate with the above report if he had not had confidence in his informant's reliability and if he did not seriously consider that the report might well contain an element of truth." Elting urged that the Department relay the message to Wise.

The State Department had a long tradition of skepticism about reports of Jewish persecutions, ever since Hugh Gibson's days in Poland. Elbridge Durbrow of the Division of European Affairs saw the Riegner message and advised that it not be passed on to Wise, "in view of the fantastic nature of the allegations and the impossibility of our being of any assistance if such action were taken." The assistant division chief, Paul Culbertson, was also nervous and wrote: "I don't like the idea of sending this on to Wise but if the Rabbi hears later that we had the message and didn't let him in on it he might put up a kick." After discussion, the State Department decided that that was a risk they could take, and the Riegner message was locked away without a word to Wise.

Riegner, no innocent in the matter of dealing with the State Department, had taken a precaution. He was also authorized to report to the British branch of the World Jewish Congress, and the same day he sent the message to Wise he dropped a copy through British diplomatic channels to Sydney Silverman, a member of Parliament, chairman of the Congress's British section. As an afterthought, Riegner added a line to Silverman's message: "Inform and consult New York," just in case Wise never heard from the State Department. The Foreign Office was as troubled by the report as the State Department, but after hesitating a week or so, Whitehall chose to pass the telegram on as instructed.

Rabbi Irving Miller was alone in the New York office of the World Jewish Congress on the Friday afternoon before Labor Day of 1942 when the telegram arrived from Silverman in London. He immediately called Wise at home and read the message over the telephone. After a brief discussion, Wise called Washington and set up an urgent appointment with Under Secretary of State Welles for the following week. Wise and his Zionist colleagues had long considered Welles to be about the only sympathetic contact they had in the State Department. When they met, however, Welles pleaded with Wise to keep silent about the alarming report until the Department could obtain further confirmation. Reluctantly, harboring his own doubts about "fantastic allegations" and fearful of stirring up antisemitic resentments over unverified rumors, Wise agreed to join the State Department in suppressing the report of the plan "to resolve once and for all the Jewish question in Europe."

By August 1942, when Riegner sent off his message, an estimated 1,500,000 of Europe's Jews were already dead. In the three months that followed, as Wise and the State Department maintained silence, another million died.

How could the report be verified? Wise contacted an acquaintance on the World Council of Churches who would be traveling to Geneva in a few days and, swearing him to secrecy, asked him to pose a one-sentence query to Professor Guggenheim, a man Wise knew more intimately than he did Riegner and whose word he would consider authoritative. Wise and the American Jews had heard about the Nazi policy of "deportations," which alarmed them quite enough. Now, Wise wanted to know from Guggenheim: "Are you absolutely satisfied that 'deportation' means 'extermination'?" Guggenheim gave the visiting churchman a one-word reply to carry back to Wise: "Yes." Riegner, meanwhile, collected affidavits and assembled a brief of evidence that he, with his legal training, knew would convince the sternest of judges. This he submitted to Leland Harrison, the American minister in Bern, and handed over to him also, in a sealed envelope, the name of his original German informant. Harrison, who well understood the reception that would be forthcoming from the Division of European Affairs, conveyed his reports in personal letters directly to Welles.

Late in November the Under Secretary summoned Wise back to the State Department and grimly passed over the thick dossier that, he said, would "confirm and justify your deepest fears." He released Wise from the pledge of secrecy, and the weary rabbi went out to announce to the American press the confirmed report of Holocaust.

Years later, an American journalist recalled that day:

> There were many things happening in Washington and many things happening in the world. We were fighting in Europe. We were fighting in Asia. There were gasoline shortages. There were all kinds of home-front economic problems. There were people dying and living. I went to a press conference with Stephen Wise and he talked about mass murder of Jews in Europe. And he had what he said was evidence of that. There were perhaps five or six other reporters at the place. There were many other events happening at the time. Did I write a story about it? Yes. Did it make one of the wires? Yes. Did papers pick it up? Yes. Did anybody believe it? I doubt it. Did I believe it? Yes, perhaps halfway I

believed it. I believed a little bit of it. I didn't believe all of it. It was beyond the comprehension of everybody in this country.

Wise's announcement made page 10 of *The New York Times.* A few days later, the rabbi wrote directly to Roosevelt—it was fully four months since the lone German informant had asked that his news be conveyed to the highest leaders of Britain and the United States. Even with this ghastly message Wise could not suppress the sycophancy with which he invariably approached the President. "Dear Boss," he began. "I do not wish to add an atom to the awful burden which you are bearing with magic and, as I believe, heaven-inspired strength at this time . . ." Then he told of the slaughter of two million Jews. He called it "the most overwhelming disaster of Jewish history."

Wise and his Zionist colleagues probably did all within their capacity to alert an apathetic and suspicious public over the following months. Weizmann was called in to address a mass rally at Madison Square Garden on March 1, 1943, and he concluded solemnly, "When the historian of the future assembles the black record of our days, he will find two things unbelievable: first, the crime itself; second, the reaction of the world to that crime."

Wise was personally chastised by the Jewish establishment, the American Jewish Committee, and the editors of *The New York Times* for giving such credence to wartime atrocity stories. As late as December 1944, a Roper poll indicated that the majority of Americans still did not believe reports of a mass murder of European Jewry.

BRECKINRIDGE LONG was furious to find himself bypassed. Soon after Welles had given Wise confirmation of the Riegner report late in 1942, a remarkable telegram went from the State Department to Minister Harrison in Bern: "In the future we would suggest that you do not accept reports submitted to you to be transmitted to private persons in the United States unless such action is advisable because of extraordinary circumstances." But while Long may not have considered the systematic slaughter of Jews an "extraordinary circumstance," others in the Department were more attuned to changing political realities. A year later, when Treasury Secretary Henry Morgenthau, Jr., finally started investigating the State Department's role in the fate of European Jewry, he was denied access to this telegram on grounds that it did not relate to Treasury business.

The persuasive, documented verdict on the State Department response to Nazi antisemitism was finally put before Roosevelt in January

1944. The investigators were two Gentile officials of the Treasury Department, Randolph E. Paul and John Pehle, financial experts who normally would have had no involvement in refugee matters, but Morgenthau suspected something was amiss and had given them a mandate to look into the situation. Entitled "Report to the Secretary on the Acquiescence of This Government in the Murder of the Jews," Paul and Pehle's conclusions were chilling:

> Certain State Department officials are guilty of the following:
> 1) They have not only failed to use the governmental machinery at their disposal to rescue Jews from Hitler, but they have even gone so far as to use this governmental machinery to prevent the rescue of these Jews.
> 2) They have not only failed to cooperate with private organizations in the efforts of these organizations to work out individual programs of their own, but have taken steps designed to prevent these programs from being put into effect.
> 3) They have not only failed to facilitate the obtaining of information concerning Hitler's plans to exterminate the Jews of Europe, but in their official capacity have gone so far as to surreptitiously attempt to stop the obtaining of information concerning the murder of the Jewish population of Europe.
> 4) They have tried to cover up their guilt by:
>   a) concealment and misrepresentation;
>   b) the giving of false and misleading explanations for their failures to act and their attempts to prevent action; and
>   c) the issuance of false and misleading statements concerning the "action" which they have taken to date.

With a little editing to tone down the most lurid passages, Secretary Morgenthau sent the Paul-Pehle report to President Roosevelt. Six days later, on January 22, 1944, Roosevelt created the War Refugee Board, with John Pehle as executive director, to take all rescue and resettlement efforts out of State Department hands.

Of course, by that time, the problems had diminished in Europe; there were about four million fewer Jews left to be rescued.

THE ACTIONS AND THE INACTIONS of Roosevelt's administration as it witnessed disaster befalling the Jews cannot be justified by document or memory. Ignorance, apathy—even prejudice—are unconvincing as excuses. A fair understanding of Roosevelt's sorry record in the Holocaust comes only through consideration of his particular style of leadership, a style not entirely in keeping with the qualities that have been assigned to him. Heroic visionaries are supposed to press ever forward toward their clearly perceived goals, surmounting all opposition set up by man and circumstance, ignoring resistance from the small and petty-minded. Roosevelt was not like that. The visions were there, in his head, but not very well organized, not thought out, rarely articulated in more than a random and haphazard fashion.

Roosevelt functioned as overseer of competing forces, the orchestrator of countless strains of social and political thought. He was not the conscious initiator of a particular ideology, unless it were the simple idealism of his family, the tradition of leaving the community in better shape than before. He was often naïve and ignorant before being briefed on a particular matter, recalled his Brains Truster Rexford G. Tugwell, but he would then quickly assimilate new information, particularly the details that he found useful to his purpose of the moment. Unless a certain course of action was such as to be directly indicated for any good Christian gentleman, Roosevelt would temporize or experiment, throw out an idea tentatively, then watch to see how the forces and intellects around him would respond.

Frances Perkins wrote that Roosevelt loved to use his imagination, "and yet he wanted to be sure that he checked himself, or that somebody else checked him against undue enthusiasm." Sincerity was hard to find in Roosevelt. "He would have flashes of almost clairvoyant knowledge and understanding," Perkins wrote. "He couldn't always hold that or verbalize on it. . . . It would stay only a minute or two; sometimes long enough to solve the problem, sometimes only enough to give him a hunch. Sometimes it would disappear."

Roosevelt's initial instincts on the plight of European Jewry were bold enough to be shocking. During the later 1930s, he repeatedly bucked the nativist tide of American society by stressing the benefits which immigrants had always brought to the United States. He stunned the Daughters of the American Revolution, having first established his genealogical credentials, by exhorting them to "remember always that all of us, and you and I especially, are descended from immigrants and revolutionists."

"Population never made a country unprosperous," he told Perkins at one point, "not so long as our farmers can grow enough for that population—we may have to think of our immigration policy in those terms some day." Some day—the Roosevelt style of tentative suggestion; he withdrew this time as his political advisers warned him that he would win no friends or voters by calling for freer immigration. But he came back to it. To his Cabinet in 1938, when the Nazis had just marched into Vienna, he said, "America was a place of refuge for so many fine Germans in the period of 1848—why couldn't we offer them again a place of refuge at this time?" Once more the provocative idea thrown out to test the waters; none of the officials around him—except Perkins—saw fit to pick it up, so Roosevelt shrugged his massive shoulders and moved on to other things. Maybe it was only a hunch.

This competitive interplay of fragmented forces, rather than any grand historical vision, guided Roosevelt's leadership. And if any one viewpoint, any one of the possible options for action, was insufficiently argued and pressed in competition with the vying alternatives, then it simply fell off the President's agenda by default, forgotten until his manipulative instinct led him to raise it again.

In the late 1930s and the early 1940s, Roosevelt spent hundreds of hours absorbed in the possibilities for resettling Jews and other refugees from Nazism. His wife, Eleanor, regularly petitioned the President and every other official with relief requests for individuals of whom she had heard heartrending stories. Quite apart from the attractive human potential of the European intelligentsia, the idea of resettlement appealed to his love of geography. "The possible field of new settlements covers millions of square miles situated in comparatively young republics and in colonial possessions," he told an Intergovernmental Committee on Refugees in 1939.

With his geographers he would pore over world maps and bellow into the telephone as he came upon an exciting new locale. (Roosevelt was one of those who never seemed to grasp that telephonic communication involved a degree of electronic amplification—he would shout into the mouthpiece as if only his lung power would carry the message onward, and the person at the other end would have to hold the receiver far from the ear.) A Jewish community in the Cameroons appealed to him; "some very wonderful high land, tableland, wonderful grass . . . and all of that country has been explored and it's ready." Another plan submitted was too paltry; "it does not stimulate my imagination—somebody has to breathe heart and ideals on a large scale into this whole project." But no one did. He had the President-elect of Paraguay on the telephone at one point and in great excitement called in Morgenthau to try getting "two or three people together . . . to work out a plan." He would have it called the Roosevelt Plan, if that would help, and if Morgenthau would only give him a list of the thousand richest Jews in the United States, he personally would tell each one how much to contribute. Morgenthau did not pursue that particular notion.

In time, Roosevelt's geographical task forces had come up with no less than 666 possible sites around the globe for resettlement of the Jews of Europe. They included Northern Rhodesia, Tanganyika, Nyasaland,

Angola, Kenya, Cuba, Ethiopia, Cyrenaica, northwestern Brazil, Santo Domingo, Bolivia, Mexico, and British Guiana. Formal international conferences were held to ponder the possibilities; attending one with the title "Jewish observer from Palestine" was a young American emigrant who became known as Golda Meir. "Sitting there in that magnificent hall, listening to the delegates of 32 countries rise, each in turn, to explain how much they would have liked to take in substantial numbers of refugees and how unfortunate it was that they were not able to do so, was a terrible experience," she recalled.

Roosevelt set up a President's Advisory Committee on Refugees, but whenever operational decisions had to be made he would maintain that Breckinridge Long at the State Department had the whole matter under control. On several occasions he assured Breck Long that he shared the State Department's concern over politically unreliable refugees.

Roosevelt preferred to think of the "refugee problem," not the "Jewish problem." It was, he found, politically expedient to keep the issue generalized instead of dwelling on the needs of one particular and problematic group. For all his personal disdain for bigotry, Roosevelt believed that Jews in the mass might well stir up socio-political difficulties. He was impressed when his favorite geographer, Isaiah Bowman, president of Johns Hopkins University, proposed that European Jews should be resettled sparsely in scattered places around the world rather than in one large concentration, so as to minimize the antagonism of Gentiles.

In one of his rare discussions of Jews specifically, at the Casablanca Conference in January 1943, Roosevelt proposed that North African resettlement projects restrict the number of Jews allowed to practice such professions as law and medicine to a quota based on Jewish representation in the whole population. Such a limitation, Roosevelt said, would "permit the Jews to engage in the professions, and at the same time would not permit them to overcrowd the professions, and would present an unanswerable argument that they were being given their full rights."

The blind faith of Wise and Roosevelt's other Jewish intimates would have been sorely tried had they been privy to the secret deliberations at Casablanca. "The President," noted the official transcript, "stated that his plan would further eliminate the specific and understandable complaints which the Germans bore towards the Jews in Germany, namely that while they represented a small part of the population, over 50% of the lawyers, doctors, schoolteachers, college professors, etc., in Germany were Jews."

In confronting the crisis of European Jewry, Roosevelt's humanitarian instincts failed him. Intrigued with individual cases and obsessed above all with his sophisticated world maps, he could never bring himself to face the real problem. On July 28, 1943, he received an unusual visitor, a young agent of the Polish underground named Lieutenant Jan Karski, recently escaped from occupied Poland. Karski, a Gentile, had personally visited the concentration camp of Belsen and could also give authentic firsthand testimony about Auschwitz, Dachau, and Treblinka. "I am convinced, Mr. President, that there is no exaggeration in the accounts of the plight of the Jews," Karski reported. "Our underground authorities are absolutely sure that the Germans are out to exterminate the entire Jewish population of Europe. Reliable reports from our own informers give the figure of 1.8 million Jews already murdered in Poland up to the day when I left the country."

Karski remembered Roosevelt's exact words in response, even thirty-seven years later. "You tell your leaders in Poland they have a friend in the White House. We shall win the war. The guilty will be punished." Then he turned to another topic and the discussion ended. "If something was unpleasant and he didn't want to know about it, he just ignored it," said Eleanor Roosevelt of her husband. "I think he always thought that if you ignored a thing long enough, it would settle itself."

Roosevelt allowed the fate of Europe's six million Jews to "settle itself." To be fair, his critics have the obligation to note that the President was not alone. Roosevelt was not the only person, for instance, to whom Karski gave his report.

During his Washington visit, the young agent was presented by the Free Polish ambassador to Supreme Court Justice Felix Frankfurter. The jurist bore down upon his youthful visitor like a schoolmaster confronting an errant sixth-former. "Do you know who I am?" "Yes, sir, my ambassador told me," Karski replied. A short silence. "Do you know that I am a Jew?" "Yes, sir, my ambassador told me." "So, my man, tell me. What happens to the Jews in your country? I am interested to hear."

Karski spoke for fifteen minutes, his eyes closed or staring up at the ceiling. Not once did Frankfurter interrupt him. "He sat quietly," Karski recalled. "Then he got up. He started to walk in front of me and Ambassador Ciechanowski on my left. Then he stood in front of me and said: 'A man like me talking to a man like you must be totally honest. So I am. So I say, I do not believe you.' The ambassador broke in, 'Felix' (they were good friends), 'Felix, how can you say such a thing? You know he is saying the truth, he was checked and rechecked in London and here. Felix, what are you saying?'

"Frankfurter answered, 'Mr. Ambassador, I did not say that he is lying. I said that I don't believe him. There is a difference. My mind, my heart, they are made in such a way that I cannot conceive it.' And he outstretched his arms. 'No, no, no, I do not have the strength to believe it.' "

Information is not knowledge. Roosevelt failed to act on the information available to him; so did many others, Jews and Gentiles alike, who might have been able to goad the President into action had they tried. The options for action open to the United States government were pitifully few. But even the possibilities scarcely came up for discussion. There was none of the competitive give-and-take, none of the brainstorming, through which Roosevelt exercised his leadership. Roosevelt's guilt, the guilt of American Jewish leadership and of the dozens and hundreds of others in positions of responsibility, was that most of the time they failed to try.

6

THE ROOSEVELT RECORD on the Jews does not end with his neglect of the Holocaust. For the thirty-second President of the American republic had special thoughts about Palestine, for a Jewish restoration more ambitious than even his Zionist contemporaries dared to advocate. He never seems to have connected this vision with the reality that the Jews of Europe were enduring. But in the midst of contrary circumstance and apathy, disillusioned repeatedly by the skepticism of others, he kept returning to it, and it stayed with him to his death.

The roots of his vision reached back to the simple Christianity of his boyhood. Groton's Endicott Peabody was no fundamentalist, to be sure, but the schoolmaster was enough of a spiritual descendant of the Puritans to be full of the idealism of prophecy, and he passed on this faith to his charges. From his first years in the presidency, Roosevelt expressed secular interest in the ingathering of the Jews. In 1936 he urged British Prime Minister Chamberlain not to cut back on Jewish immigration to Palestine. Again, in 1938, under prodding from Stephen Wise, Felix Frankfurter, and Benjamin V. Cohen, Roosevelt sent a signal to London insisting on adherence to the Balfour Declaration. "I was at Versailles," he reminded Secretary of State Cordell Hull, "and I know that the British made no secret of the fact they promised Palestine to the Jews. Why are they now reneging on their promise?"

This was the first basic theme in Roosevelt's thinking on the Middle East: Britain, and by extension the world, had promised Palestine to the Jews.

The President's interest in Palestine was sporadic and superficial in the early New Deal years, as with other foreign policy issues. The Middle East was one of those subjects on which he had not yet found it necessary to be briefed. In 1939 Roosevelt took the kind of little step that signals a major turning point in the thinking of a busy executive: he instructed his secretary to open a file entitled "Palestine." It was to be for his own personal use, he told Grace Tully, and would be only temporary. As it turned out, over the next five years the "Palestine" folder fattened into boxes and dossiers scattered through all three of the archive collections in the White House offices.

OVER AT THE Department of State, Palestine was not uppermost. The Near East Division was "not often marked with excitement," commented *Harper's Magazine* in 1937; "our relations with these peoples are not important." Outsiders to diplomacy were content to leave this backwater in the care of a domineering personage named Wallace Murray, who headed the division without interruption from 1929 until 1945. With his clipped British accent and an explosive temper, Murray ran a bureaucratic fiefdom embracing the entire Arab world, Turkey, Iran, and Afghanistan. Like Breckinridge Long down the black-and-white marble corridor—a world apart, for all the physical proximity—Murray controlled each detail of his division with his own firm hand. He permitted no interference from below and accepted it only disdainfully from above.

The fate of world Jewry was of no particular interest to Murray; indeed, younger associates conceded, he shared fully in the antisemitic attitudes of his class and times. The officers of the Near East Division were veterans of service in Beirut, Damascus, and Aleppo; they spoke Arabic (knowledge of Hebrew or Yiddish had no place on an aspiring diplomat's résumé) and enjoyed comfortable friendships among the missionary officials who were so knowledgeable about the lands of the East. To these Arabists, the European Jews were most unwelcome intruders into Palestine, bent only on overturning a placid and traditional way of life. Moreover, as Murray blandly remarked at the end of one long conversation with Weizmann, "a Jewish state would necessarily have distinct Bolshevik tendencies." Murray encouraged the Department's well-established animus against the Balfour Declaration; he concurred in the convenient view that Palestine was solely a British responsibility and need not concern busy American diplomats, whatever hypocrisies persons involved in politics found necessary for their own electoral purposes.

Roosevelt was not alone in letting Murray and his handpicked team cope with the obscurities of Middle Eastern affairs during the late 1930s. To Secretary of State Cordell Hull, Palestine was a parochial matter; given its political sensitivity—plus the fact that Hull's wife was Jewish— the Secretary saw wisdom and discretion in busying himself with other matters. Thus, whenever a Palestine matter came up for a policy decision, it would fall to Under Secretary Sumner Welles.

Like Roosevelt, Welles was a patrician, a product of Groton and

Harvard. He was a close personal friend of the President (Hull was not) and possessed a fine political sense. American Zionists looked to him for sympathy, and he, almost alone in the Department, was cordial and careful to keep American Zionist leaders informed about matters of concern to them. He listened to their entreaties; on at least four occasions he blocked Murray's anti-Zionist policy recommendations from reaching Roosevelt. Yet Welles never advocated Zionist positions while in office, as he did later in retirement. He was less critical of Britain's pro-Arab policies in Palestine than Roosevelt, and he was as slow as anyone else to grasp the grim meaning of the Nazi threat to European Jewry.

Welles, Murray, and their staffs of experts were the President's natural sources of information to fill his Palestine file, along with tidbits from political friends like Wise, Cohen, and Frankfurter. But the State Department did not press the Middle East upon the President's attention. His energies were consumed in other matters. New oil concessions in Saudi Arabia in 1939 and 1940 stirred wider interest in Murray's backwater duchy, and during World War II American oil, trade, and airline interests became potentially competitive with those of Britain in the Middle East. But these did not require presidential attention. Whenever representations came to the Department from oil companies or other economic interests, off went a flurry of diplomatic notes asserting the rights of American nationals and reiterating the Open Door trading policy. When American Zionists raised a protest over British restrictions on the Jewish community of Palestine, the State Department would do nothing, on grounds of not wishing to complicate the problems of a wartime ally.

For one brief moment in 1942, as part of a long-range planning exercise, the State Department considered the theoretical possibility of encouraging Jewish settlement, "so as to make Palestine an unquestioned sphere of Jewish influence by reason of the numbers of Jews who will be settled there." The author of this unorthodox proposal—he called it a "radical solution"—was none other than Ben Cohen. To his four-page memo were promptly affixed two pages of objections by Murray, including a veiled warning which was to become an obsession in official Washington—that United States military forces might be required to set up and maintain a Jewish state in Palestine. Cohen's speculations about a Jewish state fit into a context in which Maronite, Kurdish, and Assyrian states were also considered. The planners finally concluded that such "Balkanization" would not serve United States interests, and that was the end of it.

From the earliest period of active American involvement in Middle Eastern politics, the experts of the State Department saw United States interests tied to the cause of Arab nationalism. So fundamental was this tenet that the Department's experts saw no reason to consider the possibility that Arab nationalists might be willing to pay a price for American support. When a few public figures suggested that a quid pro quo might be Arab acquiescence in Jewish national rights in Palestine, State Department planners did not regard the idea as worthy of consideration.

Starting in 1941, in fact, a move got underway in the Department to issue a new declaration, a sort of "reverse Balfour," to signal Arab nationalists that the flirtation with "ill-considered Zionist aspirations" no longer represented American policy. It was Alexander C. Kirk, minister in Cairo, who raised the idea. Arriving in the Middle East after serving as chargé d'affaires in Berlin, Kirk worried about Nazi inroads among anti-British Arabs. The situation, as Kirk saw it, was the reverse of 1917: then, a pro-Zionist declaration had seemed helpful to the war effort; in 1941, Kirk argued, disavowal of Zionism would aid the Allies in the Middle East. "Despite the noble sentiments which may have characterized the idea of the Jewish national home at its inception," he wrote, "the project in its present form has not only failed in the past but is incapable of realization in the future unless imposed by force on an unwilling native population." Two months later, Kirk proposed steps "to bring Zionist leaders in the United States to revise their views on the Palestine problem in the light of the demonstrated impracticability of the present policy." Murray considered Kirk's proposal to be "very important."

This was one of the recommendations that Welles refused to forward to the White House. American Zionists do not see the Jewish settlement in Palestine as a failure, he sternly informed Kirk, nor do they see their movement as a handicap to the British war effort. The United States "can hardly be expected to adopt an attitude or policy which is more pro-Arab than the British." Thus political leadership made bureaucracy stop in its tracks, or at least stall in seeming compliance. Good bureaucrats know that high-level interest soon fades and the momentum of their expertise can once again resume its desired course. In the annual pro forma statement on the anniversary of the Balfour Declaration in 1942, the Department managed somehow to omit any reference to Palestine.

PRESIDENT ROOSEVELT, meanwhile, was filling his Palestine file. A tip reached his desk in the spring of 1939—not, it need hardly be said, from the State Department—about an impending British parliamentary study, a so-called White Paper, calling for a drastic reduction in Jewish immigration to Palestine as a sop to the Arab majority. His information came through a back channel: Justice Brandeis, who had heard it from Weiz-

mann in London. The two old Zionist adversaries had resumed the correspondence they had started in 1916. At that time, their purpose had
been to nudge President Wilson into sympathy for a British initiative that
became the Balfour Declaration; in 1939 they were hoping to prod President Roosevelt into blocking an anti-Zionist initiative.

Roosevelt reminded Whitehall in April that he was concerned about
the matter of Jewish immigration to Palestine, but the Foreign Office was
too far along in its own planning to let such a low-key approach deter
them. In May, Weizmann and Brandeis came in with harder information,
and Roosevelt wrote Secretary Hull that "I still believe that any announcement about Palestine at this time by the British government is a
mistake, and I think we should tell them that."

As always, Hull deferred to Murray in such matters, and the head of
the Near East Division was far more sympathetic to the British position
than to that of his own President. Instead of acting on Roosevelt's instruction, Murray let his officers be fully briefed by the British on their
new policy, and raised no objection to its intent of cutting back on Jewish
immigration. "It is our opinion," Murray informed Hull, "that the final
British decisions represent perhaps as reasonable a compromise between
Jewish and Arab aspirations as it is practicable to attempt to effect at this
time."

Roosevelt was incensed when he read the British White Paper. "In a
good deal of dismay," he wrote Hull that this "is something that we
cannot give approval to by the United States." Lest Murray once again
cheat on his instructions, the President put Hull on notice: "Before we
do anything formal about this please talk with me." Ambassador Joseph
Kennedy in London was instructed to convey United States displeasure
to the Foreign Office, but before doing so Kennedy gave private assurances that the American protest would not be pressed, despite the Zionists' public outcry. For all his dismay, Roosevelt's hands were tied. He
wanted to avoid any action that would weaken Britain's strategic position
in the Arab world on the eve of war. And at home he was anxious to
avoid fueling the anti-British sentiment among American isolationists.

But the Roosevelt imagination was quietly at work. An ambitious plan
was taking shape in his mind, a plan calling for the transfer of the entire
Arab population of Palestine to a nearby Arab land. He outlined his idea
to Brandeis in one of their talks. Iraq could be an appropriate new home
for the Arabs of Palestine, in Roosevelt's view. Two to three hundred
thousand of them should be resettled, at a cost of some $300 million.
Britain and France should together put up one-third of that, the United
States another third, and wealthy Jews of the Western democracies the
rest. Twice he raised this notion with British representatives, only to be

firmly told that no amount of financial inducement would move the Palestinian Arabs. Roosevelt was unconvinced, and told Zionist friends early in 1939, as they reported, that "as soon as he was somewhat relieved from the pressure of other affairs, he might try to tackle the job." Thus emerged a second theme in Roosevelt's Palestine vision—that once the pressures of war were lifted from his shoulders, he would solve the problem by his own personal statesmanship.

In February 1940 Roosevelt met Weizmann for the first time. In their half-hour talk the Zionist visitor pleaded for Jewish resettlement in Palestine, and Palestine alone. The President questioned him about the economic absorptive capacity of the land, and then tried out his idea about moving the Arabs out. "What about the Arabs?" Roosevelt asked breezily. "Can't that be settled with a little baksheesh?" Weizmann patiently explained to the President that uprooting the entire Arab population would not be quite as simple as that, but neither man completely dropped the idea that some kind of money settlement might be possible.

In December 1941, Japan attacked Pearl Harbor. The President's political and personal energies were at once fully engaged. What with mobilizing war production and manpower, sorting out all the Lend-Lease disputes with the Allies, and contending with Japan's military advances in the Pacific, the fate of the Jewish homeland fell to low priority. Frankfurter and Wise kept trying to turn the President's attention to Jewish issues, but so diffidently that it was easy for Roosevelt to avoid them.

Because Churchill asked him to, Roosevelt agreed to meet again with Weizmann in July 1942. Using a traditional technique for avoiding difficult discussions, Roosevelt preempted the conversation with a barrage of questions about another topic that he knew would command his chemist visitor's attention—synthetic rubber. Weizmann was stymied in trying to steer the conversation onto the subject of Palestine and that lingering possibility of financial inducements to Arab resettlement. Some days later, the President flatly refused to meet Ben-Gurion, explaining to Frankfurter that "the less said by everybody of all creeds, the better." To Hull he was more specific: "The more I think of it, the more I feel that we should say nothing about the Near East or Palestine or the Arabs at this time. . . . If we pat either group on the back, we automatically stir up trouble." Responding to the endless streams of requests for pro forma presidential greetings to Jewish testimonial meetings, the State Department worked up a routine draft and informed the President, "If anything at all is to be sent this is about as colorless as can be devised." Roosevelt put up no argument.

Yet the old dream was not entirely forgotten. Talking during the Christmas season of 1942 to his Hyde Park friend and neighbor Treasury

Secretary Morgenthau, the President mused again about what he wanted to do someday when the war was won. Morgenthau remembered Roosevelt's rambling words vividly:

> What I think I will do is this. First, I would call Palestine a religious country. Then I would leave Jerusalem the way it is and have it run by the Orthodox Greek Catholic Church, the Protestants, and the Jews—have a joint committee run it. . . . I actually would put a barbed wire around Palestine, and I would begin to move the Arabs out. . . . I would provide land for the Arabs in some other part of the Middle East. . . . Each time we move out an Arab we would bring in another Jewish family. . . . But I don't want to bring in more than they can economically support. . . . It would be an independent nation just like any other nation. . . . Naturally, if there are 90% Jews, the Jews would dominate the government. . . . There are lots of places to which you could move the Arabs. All you have to do is drill a well, because there is this large underground water supply, and we can move the Arabs to places where they can really live. . . .

Whether or not the amateur geographer really knew what he was talking about, one thing is clear: Roosevelt continued to think of Palestine as a strictly Jewish land, in which no Arabs (or very few of them) would remain as permanent residents.

The winter of 1942–43 brought the first strains of what would become known after Roosevelt's time as the Cold War, touched off by Stalin's suspicions about the Western Allies' tardiness in opening a second front. Roosevelt was a firm believer in the capacity of powerful nations, acting in concert, to "police the world." The United States would be responsible for the Western Hemisphere, he once told his aide William Hassett. Britain and Russia together would keep Europe under control, the United States and China would take care of Asia, and Africa would be the responsibility of Britain and, strangely, Brazil. So far as Palestine and the Arab Middle East was concerned, Roosevelt concluded that "Churchill and I [are] the only ones who could get together and settle things." This was in fact Roosevelt's conviction about how the Palestine issue would be resolved after the war. In one of his jaunty letters to the British Prime Minister later in 1943, Roosevelt looked forward to the day when "you and I are strong enough to carry Ibn Saud to Jerusalem and Dr. Weizmann to Mecca."

Churchill never made any secret of his support for Zionism during this period, contrary to the declared policy of his own government. "There is simply no arguing with him on this subject," said one exasperated British colleague. He felt free, moreover, to invoke Roosevelt's backing as well. "I am committed to the establishment of a Jewish state in Palestine," Churchill said during a visit to Cairo early in 1943, "and the President will accept nothing less." The remark quickly made the rounds of the diplomatic gossip mills, getting back to a horrified State Department in Washington. Roosevelt made no effort to refute Churchill's interpretation of his position, and left no doubt that he intended to stake out an advanced position for the United States in the postwar Middle East. "We can help those countries in the days to come," he wrote his old Groton headmaster, Endicott Peabody, "and with the proper management, get our money back."

State Department officials regularly tried to discourage the President from making pro-Zionist statements in public, little knowing how much more extravagant he was about a Jewish Palestine in his private musings. But except for Welles, his longtime protégé and friend, Roosevelt had little time for the professional diplomats, assuring Jewish visitors that he regularly discounted all their negative views. At Welles' suggestion he set about developing his own unofficial source of ideas to fill his Palestine file, a singular personage named Colonel Harold B. Hoskins.

During the years of World War II, Hoskins performed the kind of freewheeling diplomatic work that William Yale had done during World War I. Along with his British Arabist counterparts, T. E. Lawrence and H. St. John Philby (with whom he engaged in the sort of fierce professional feud that only like-minded scholars can sustain), Hoskins exerted back-channel influence on both British and American governments during the decade leading up to the climactic events of 1948.

Hoskins was a product of the missionary community, born in Beirut in 1895 and reaching the United States only as a teen-ager. He received a proper boarding school education, followed by Princeton. His subsequent career covered many fronts. A New York textile executive by profession, he served as trustee and later chairman of the board of the American University of Beirut. He was available for occasional diplomatic chores, became an officer in the Army, and, inevitably, an undercover American intelligence operative. He seemed a perfect choice as a presidential agent.

Hoskins' first mission for Roosevelt, in October 1942, was to build up "friendly contacts" (euphemism for an intelligence network) in the Arab world. He threw himself into the various anti-Zionist campaigns of the State Department; the Near East Division had initially been skeptical of this unorthodox, independent agent, but quickly recognized a kindred spirit who could be very useful indeed. While Murray and even Welles sent their arguments to Roosevelt in written memos, Hoskins would drop in at the White House for personal chats or occasional lunches with the President and Mrs. Roosevelt. The President was much taken with the man's panache and expertise, and sent Hoskins off again in July 1943 for the purpose of sizing up the strange but apparently powerful Arabian king, Ibn Saud.

Hoskins had never been at a loss in dealing with Arabs, but he was totally unprepared for his discoveries in Ibn Saud's desert court. Three years before, he learned, his old rival St. John Philby had launched an intrigue which could get Roosevelt into real trouble—for the President was at the center of the scheme, and knew nothing about it.

It seems that, late in 1939, Philby had approached Weizmann in London. For all his anti-Zionist leanings, the British scholar was seeking the basis for a deal that would serve Jewish and Arab interests alike. In great secrecy, Philby unveiled his plan to Weizmann: the Arabs would relinquish all of Palestine west of the Jordan River in return for complete independence from colonial rule in all other parts of the Arab Middle East. A large-scale transfer of Arab population out of Palestine was central to the plan, and to accomplish the resettlement, the sum of 20 million pounds sterling was to be put at the disposal of Ibn Saud, as executor of the transfer. Neither Philby nor Weizmann could have known how closely this idea paralleled Roosevelt's own thinking.

Weizmann was taken with the idea, and his general interest became more specific when Roosevelt subsequently spoke to him about using "a little baksheesh" to clear the ground for Jewish settlement. But Weizmann was hesitant to broach the vague plan of a British scholar to the President of the United States, and when he tried to talk about it at their next meeting in July 1942, all Roosevelt wanted to discuss was synthetic rubber!

Philby, for his part, took Weizmann's expression of general interest as a green light to test the other side; he approached Ibn Saud. The route of this back channel is long since buried in the sands of the Arabian Desert, but the King of Saudi Arabia apparently did not reject the idea out of hand. "On the contrary," Philby recalled afterward, "he told me . . . that some such arrangements might be possible in appropriate future circumstances." Meanwhile Philby was under royal injunction not to mention a word of the scheme to anyone else, "least of all to any Arab."

On further reflection over the ensuing months, the King suggested that if the British and American governments were as interested in the plan as Philby said they were, it should be presented in a more official form, and by someone other than a private, albeit respected, scholar. This presented a problem, for at the time Philby was talking with the

King, neither the American nor the British government had considered the Philby plan seriously, or for that matter knew much of anything about it.

Three years passed. Ibn Saud became skeptical about dealing with Zionists, and Arab independence came to seem a likely prospect even without the quid pro quo—or so he inferred from listening to anti-Zionist British and American diplomats. Furthermore, the exact purpose of the 20 million pounds became a little blurred; as time went on, it looked less and less like a fund to support resettlement of Palestinian Arabs and more like an outright bribe to the House of Saud.

In 1943, Ibn Saud was informed that President Roosevelt was sending a trusted personal envoy, Colonel Hoskins, to see him. Perhaps, at last, this was the official approach that he had invited. The problem was that Hoskins, when he arrived at the royal court, knew absolutely nothing about the Philby conversations. Waiting for a message that was not forthcoming, Ibn Saud erupted in fury. He told Hoskins his version of the story, as he had grown to understand it during his years of brooding— that Weizmann had attempted to bribe him, that Roosevelt himself had been invoked as guarantor of the whole plan.

Hoskins rushed back to the White House to report. His feelings were mixed; he was horrified by the high-level misunderstanding, but at the same time he relished the sinister light it cast on his old rival in Arabism. Any move of St. John Philby's would get no sympathy from Hoskins, and the presidential agent made his scorn clear in his conversation with Roosevelt. The President "expressed understanding of the King's refusal to see Dr. Weizmann in view of the attempted bribe," Hoskins reported to the State Department after he emerged from the White House. "The President also expressed surprise and irritation that his own name as guarantor of payment had been in any way brought into this matter since there was of course no basis in fact for doing so." The only remotely related point that Roosevelt said he could remember was a conversation with Stephen Wise some years before in which he had suggested that "if the Jews wished to get more land in Palestine they might well think of buying arable land outside of Palestine and assisting Arabs financially to move from Palestine to such areas," Hoskins reported.

Such are the dangers of building concrete plans on the talk of the back channel. Roosevelt had conveniently forgotten his notion of solving the Arab problem with "a little baksheesh," and his scheme to get $300 million from outsiders to resettle Palestinian Arabs in Iraq. The idea had apparently flashed through his mind and then disappeared without a trace, in just the manner Frances Perkins had described. Roosevelt angrily told his Cabinet of Hoskins' findings in the desert court. When an astonished Morgenthau asked if anybody had attempted to get Weizmann's side of the story, Roosevelt admitted that he thought not.

From frail little threads is woven the whole cloth. Ibn Saud's fury, which Hoskins surely did nothing to assuage, stopped the Philby plan dead in its tracks, along with the parallel notion which Roosevelt had conceived years before. But now, his imagination stimulated, the President wasted no time in coming up with a new idea. This one, Hoskins reported to the State Department, involved a new kind of trusteeship,

> making Palestine a real Holy Land for all three religions, with a Jew, a Christian and a Moslem as the three responsible trustees. . . . It might be difficult to get the agreement of the Jews to such a plan, but if Moslems and Christians of the world agreed [Roosevelt] hoped the Jews could also be persuaded. This concept to be successful would, he realized, have to be presented as a solution larger and more inclusive than the establishment of an Arab state or of a Jewish state. He realized that this idea, of course, required further thought and needed to be worked out in greater detail, but at least that was the line along which his mind was running.

Thanks to Hoskins, Murray and his experts in the State Department had finally acquired a direct glimpse into the President's thinking on Palestine; he was weighing the notion of an international trusteeship! As good bureaucrats, they promptly launched a two-week study to present their own ideas in a guise that would appear to be responsive to high-level interest. "The President's present suggestion of a solution of the Palestine problem is particularly timely," wrote Murray, as he proceeded to spell out the program for a trusteeship in which the three religious interests—Christian, Muslim, and Jewish—would be represented. Forgotten, of course, would be the old chimera of Jewish statehood with which the Balfour Declaration had saddled the British Mandate. But— following Roosevelt's lead—the Department experts said that Zionist objections need not be taken too seriously. "As the Zionists wish for political reasons to place as many Jews in Palestine as possible, it will be necessary to see to it that European Jews are not dragooned into emigrating to Palestine in excess of the emigration that is absolutely required by their situation." The study was produced in October 1943, when reports of Hitler's "final solution" were common knowledge.

Roosevelt never saw it. Murray's memo was stalled in the upper reaches of the Department—"It is pretty serious," noted one politically sensitive official—and Edward R. Stettinius, Under Secretary of State after Welles' retirement, prudently decided to probe the President's

MORDECAI MANUEL NOAH,
America's first "Zionist," a breezy,
aspiring young diplomat who was
fired by the State Department in
1815 on the grounds of his being
Jewish. The full story of the affair,
and its subsequent cover-up, was not
unraveled for a century and a half.
American Jewish Archives.

LOUIS DEMBITZ BRANDEIS, at about
the time he "converted" to Zionism in
1912. His vision of Jewish nationalism
was American-tinged, and while it
appealed to American Zionists it was
bitterly opposed by the Zionists of
Europe. *Zionist Archives and Library.*

ARTHUR JAMES BALFOUR, British Foreign Secretary—author of the famous Balfour Declaration of November 1917 calling for the "establishment in Palestine of a national home for the Jewish people"—visiting a Jewish settlement in Palestine after his retirement in 1919. "I do not think that Zionism will hurt the Arabs," he wrote, "but they will never say they want it." Balfour is the tall man in center. *National Archives.*

WOODROW WILSON, leading the United States delegation to the Peace Conference of Paris, 1919. The President (right) was scarcely on speaking terms with his anti-Zionist Secretary of State, Robert Lansing (center), and found the manipulative and malleable Colonel Edward M. House (left) to be more sympathetic. *National Archives.*

FRANKLIN D. ROOSEVELT and BERNARD BARUCH. A non-Zionist Jew and financier, Baruch (according to Brandeis) "would be more likely to consider colonization of Jews on some undiscovered planet than Palestine." By 1944, with news of the Holocaust received but not yet fully comprehended, Democrat Baruch was siding with Republican Thomas E. Dewey: "I would rather trust my American Jewishness in Mr. Dewey's hands than in Mr. Roosevelt's." *National Archives.*

ROOSEVELT and IBN SAUD, aboard the cruiser *Quincy,* February 1945. Roosevelt was determined to persuade the ruler of Saudi Arabia that the Arabs could yield a small part of Palestine without losing their national honor. He failed. *UPI.*

Three prophets of Zionism: STEPHEN WISE, whose oratory brought Jewish nationalism into the mainstream of American life; ABBA HILLEL SILVER, the militant from Cleveland who pushed Wise aside to found the American Jewish Lobby; DAVID BEN-GURION, leader of the settlers in Palestine who decided—no matter what the diplomats said—to declare the Jewish state in May 1948. *Zionist Archives and Library.*

STEPHEN WISE

ABBA HILLEL SILVER

DAVID BEN-GURION

EARL HARRISON, telling an Anglo-American Committee of
Inquiry about his experiences among the survivors of the Holocaust after World War II. This expert on refugee problems was
the first to argue on an independent basis that the way to do
justice to the memory of European Jewry was to establish a Jewish homeland in Palestine—advice not appreciated by either the
British Foreign Office or the U.S. State Department. *UPI*.

CHAIM WEIZMANN and ALBERT
EINSTEIN, before disembarking
in New York in 1921. Wanting
to catch the attention of more
than the Jewish community,
Weizmann saw to it that the
possessor of a far bigger name
than his was at his side when he
first arrived in the United
States. *Zionist Archives and
Library*.

DAVID K. NILES, whom a colleague described as "a most secretive individual," receiving an award from PRESIDENT TRUMAN for a lifetime of service to the Presidency. A White House administrative assistant, Niles was devoted for personal reasons to Stephen Wise and to the cause of Jewish nationalism, and played an important role in convincing the President to give it his support. *UPI*.

BRECKINRIDGE LONG, American diplomat who urged Roosevelt to appease the Fascists; the man responsible for the observation that at least Mussolini had made the trains run on time. As head of the State Department's powerful Visa Section, he did much to prevent the immigration of groups he considered undesirable, above all Jews. *UPI*.

Before the Cold War: The Soviet Union and the United States in harmony during United Nations debates on Palestine—Soviet delegate SEMEN K. TSARAPKIN and American JOHN H. HILLDRING. Hilldring was Niles' hand-picked choice to represent —discreetly—Zionist interests against the hostility of the State Department. *Zionist Archives and Library.*

LOY W. HENDERSON, ranking State Department expert on the Middle East after World War II. Determined in his opposition to Zionism, convinced that Jewish nationalism was inimical to American interests, Henderson opposed Truman's policies to the end. *UPI.*

CHAIM WEIZMANN, ailing and nearly blind, testifying before the United Nations in 1947 about his lifelong commitment to the establishment of a Jewish state. The Jewish settlers in Palestine had by that time grown suspicious of Weizmann's diplomatic approach, but he remained a formidable force in international affairs. *Zionist Archives and Library.*

EDDIE JACOBSON, Truman's longtime friend and former business partner, on vacation with his wife, BLUMA, from the haberdashery shop in Kansas City. They were elegantly received in Israel by the new country's first president, CHAIM WEIZMANN, whom Jacobson had once invoked as his "lifetime hero" in a successful attempt to influence Truman. *Zionist Archives and Library.*

thinking more fully before he would convey the views of the Near East Division.

STEPHEN WISE and the other American Zionists were not, of course, privy to internal State Department memoranda or the President's chats with Hoskins. Yet by October 1943 their sensitive antennae picked up clues that something was turning sour in the White House; it was proving difficult "to obtain a real understanding of what was in the President's mind," remarked one of their political strategists (a complaint not unique to the Zionists).

Seeking to open a new channel to Roosevelt, the Zionist leadership approached Eugene Meyer, publisher of the Washington *Post,* a friend of the President, a Jew but not a Zionist. Meyer agreed to make a sounding, but arranged for a mutual friend, a non-Jew, to go in first ("Two goyim could discuss things more freely," they agreed, "the President would let his hair down") and see to it that Roosevelt asked to see Meyer, rather than vice versa. All went according to plan, and on October 28, Meyer was invited to the White House. In a cordial forty-five-minute chat, the President corrected details of Meyer's plea for increased immigration to Palestine, thus impressing his visitor with his grasp of the subject, and begged Meyer "to tell the Jewish leaders to continue to put their faith in him, as he and Mr. Churchill between them would see them through." Roosevelt made no commitments. But the Zionists, seeing no alternative, went on trusting him—as he knew they would.

IN MARCH 1944—a presidential election year—the President invited faithful old Stephen Wise to the White House and, for good measure, asked that he bring along his new colleague in the Zionist leadership, Rabbi Abba Hillel Silver. Roosevelt knew that Wise and Silver had become bitter rivals, and he fully shared the senior rabbi's contempt for the militant upstart. But politics is politics, and two rabbis on the White House steps would look better than one.

The President avoided any promises about the political future of Palestine, but he authorized a comment about the British White Paper policy of restricting Jewish immigration, which had upset him from the start. Wreathed in smiles, the two rabbis emerged from the White House and read the authorized statement: "The American government has never given its approval to the White Paper of 1939. . . . When future decisions are reached, full justice will be done to those who seek a Jewish national home." The words had been as carefully crafted as a treaty of state. American Zionists roared approval at a testimonial dinner the same night, without pausing to question the ambiguity of the statement.

Predictably, however, within the week came urgent queries from American ambassadors in the Middle East and their Arab contacts: had the President actually said what the rabbis said he said? On Roosevelt's instructions, Secretary Hull sent out an unabashed reply. "While freely admitting that the Wise-Silver statement had been authorized," Hull explained, "the President pointed out that the statement mentioned only a Jewish National Home, not a Jewish Commonwealth, and added that although the United States had never approved of the White Paper, it had never disapproved of it either."

To the Jews, Roosevelt's assurances had been made in public; to the Arabs, in private. An election campaign was going on. In October, Wise submitted a draft for a pre-election statement by the President; Roosevelt actually strengthened the rabbi's language and sent it off to Senator Robert F. Wagner of New York to read at a meeting of the Zionist Organization of America. Again, the crowd cheered, and in November, some 92 percent of America's Jews voted for Franklin D. Roosevelt for a fourth term as President of the United States.

It is clear today, looking through the record, that no outsider—neither Jew nor Arab, neither diplomatic experts nor ordinary Americans—knew what Roosevelt was really thinking about Palestine toward the end of his life. Even as he was glad-handing Rabbis Wise and Silver in March 1944, he worried whether he could in conscience apply pressure on beleaguered Britain for the admission of more Jews to Palestine, should they miraculously be rescued from Nazi Europe. He confided to Morgenthau his concern about Arab hostility. To another confidant, Morris Ernst, he acknowledged the awkwardness of asking the Arabs to accept Jewish immigrants when the United States was showing its reluctance to do the same. And he also worried about the capacity of Palestine to support the immigrants; flying over the Holy Land, he had been struck by how rocky and barren it appeared, except for the narrow coastal strip. Would it really be productive enough to accommodate the millions of Jews that the Zionists sought to gather in? His son James expressed the same doubts after a brief visit to Palestine on an army inspection tour.

Judge Sam Rosenman, Roosevelt's longtime speechwriter and counselor, confided to a Zionist friend that the President was "beginning to think of [Palestine] as a nuisance." Rosenman had long been one of his favorites when it came to discussing Jewish subjects. Assimilated and secure, he was no Zionist, but he was ready to speak on behalf of Jewish interests. He reflected the cautious attitudes of the non-Zionist American Jewish Committee, and he harbored no illusions about the difficulty of transplanting European Jews into the desert. Once when Roosevelt threw out an old idea of his about erecting a barbed-wire fence around Palestine, Rosenman quipped that the fence would be as useful to keep the Jews in as to keep the Arabs out. But such banter dated from an earlier day; as Roosevelt's life energies were draining away, Rosenman remarked that "it is becoming difficult . . . , even for me, to talk to him," about Palestine.

Yet it was now, with the election over and won, that Roosevelt made some of his most extravagant remarks about Palestine and Zionism. They came during a relaxed private conversation with a newcomer to his official circle, Under Secretary of State Edward Stettinius. The President found it easier to talk with this genial steel executive than with the dour and dull Cordell Hull, who anyway was ailing and about to retire after nearly twelve years in office. Roosevelt said flatly that "Palestine should be for the Jews and no Arabs should be in it," Stettinius noted in his diary. "He has definite ideas on the subject. . . . It should be exclusive Jewish territory." This was not propaganda for public consumption, nor could it be construed as an attempt to charm a partisan. Roosevelt had been guilty of such things in the past, but this was a businesslike conversation between the President and his designated new Secretary of State. Stettinius carried no particular brief for Zionism though, like Welles, he did not share the prevailing anti-Zionism of the diplomatic establishment. The President, under these circumstances, had no need to dissemble or disguise his true sentiments—and these, as relayed by Stettinius, envisaged a Jewish Palestine in the original meaning of the Balfour Declaration.

Among many Zionists at the time, it had become prudent to speak of coexistence with the Arab population of Palestine under a Jewish government; some Zionists even spoke of the possibility of a binational state in which Arabs and Jews would share political power. Roosevelt would have none of it. In his vision, the Arabs must be moved out of Palestine, whether they liked it or not; whether by means of "baksheesh" or resettlement fund, a political deal with Arab nationalism or a barbed-wire fence, Palestine "should be exclusive Jewish territory."

But in these last months of his life Roosevelt understood the difficulties of realizing his vision. He wrote a private letter to Senator Wagner—with the election passed, so was the time for public letters. "There are about half a million Jews there [in Palestine]," he wrote. "Perhaps another million want to go. They are of all shades—good, bad and indifferent. On the other side of the picture there are approximately seventy million Mohammedans who want to cut their throats the day they land. The one thing I want to avoid is a massacre or a situation which cannot be resolved by talking things over." He even began to think of someone who might go out and mediate between Arabs and Jews, a retired President, perhaps, and his politically active wife, both experienced in "talking things over" among diverse political interests. That, however, was a bit premature at this point.

Stettinius kept Roosevelt's extravagant musings to himself and, hoping to capitalize on the easier post-election mood, the Near East Division tried to raise the Palestine issue on their own terms. Murray sent Stettinius another of his long memos, proposing yet another procedure by which Jewish "pressure groups" could be silenced and the entire problem solved. Stettinius carried the memo to the White House on December 23, in case the President was in a mood to talk again, but Roosevelt preempted the conversation by remarking that Palestine was an issue that he hoped he "would not have to get into again for some time." Stettinius left Murray's memo untouched in his briefcase.

The Christmas season was a time when Roosevelt could not avoid thought of the Holy Land. In his holiday reading was a long analysis of Soviet attitudes toward Palestine, Zionism, and the Arab world, prepared by a diplomat of undoubted political acumen, the ambassador in Moscow, W. Averell Harriman. As Harriman analyzed it, the Kremlin was ready to seize upon Arab resentment at the apparent Zionist sympathies of American politicians to increase Soviet influence in the region. Then Roosevelt received a personal letter from the director of American economic operations in the Middle East, James M. Landis, arguing "that the economic absorptive capacity of Palestine has been grossly exaggerated." Fear was widespread across the Arab world, he reported, that the Jews would inevitably seek to expand beyond the borders of Palestine, in search of ever more and better land.

Roosevelt brought up both these fears in a fifteen-minute meeting with Wise on January 22, 1945. The ailing rabbi, no longer as quick in conversation as in years past, replied to "the Boss" in writing two days later. First of all, Wise said, only about a million Jews would seek resettlement in Palestine in the near future, a number well within the absorptive capacity of the land. Moreover, with a Jordan Valley Authority patterned after the Tennessee Valley Authority (an idea that he knew appealed to Roosevelt), Palestine had enormous economic potential. Jews would not attempt to expand into nearby Arab countries, he assured the President; on the contrary, Jews in surrounding lands would probably emigrate to Palestine. Finally, as to Soviet designs, Wise reported a remark reliably attributed to Stalin: Moscow would raise no objections to a Jewish state, provided the United States and Britain could agree.

Whom was the President to believe? The arguments of Wise and the Zionists on the one hand, and those of the diplomats on the other, were so clearly colored by their special viewpoints that any hope of a disinterested judgment seemed futile. In his frustration, Roosevelt chose to try the technique that had carried him through prickly political disputes all his life—direct personal persuasion. "The President feels confident . . . he will be able to iron out the whole Arab-Jewish issue on the ground where he can have a talk," Stettinius noted in his diary. To Congressman Emanuel Celler, Roosevelt said, "Give me a chance to talk with Churchill and Stalin."

A summit meeting of the wartime Big Three was in preparation for early 1945—might it be symbolically useful to hold it in Jerusalem? Roosevelt asked. Harriman reported that Stalin would not leave Soviet territory, so the gathering took place in the Crimean resort of Yalta.

The three leaders had the entire postwar settlement to discuss, the fate of all Europe and a wider world beyond. When it came to the side issue of Palestine, Roosevelt concluded that it was not the leaders of Russia and Britain who really counted. Over that holiday season of 1944, the last Christmas of his life, the President made a secret decision to try working his personal charm in the heart of the Arabian Desert. Telling only a select few trusted aides around him, and ignoring the advice of men of long experience, Roosevelt decided to try settling the whole problem of Palestine in a face-to-face meeting with Abdul Aziz Ibn Saud.

KING OF SAUDI ARABIA since 1932, the same year that Roosevelt was elected President, Ibn Saud was a charismatic tribal leader. To him clung the romance of the Bedouin desert, the fierce and chivalrous warrior, shrewd, manipulative, personal lord of sand and oil. Churchill, pursuing his imperial interests, aspired to anoint him "boss of bosses" over Islam. Surely this was a man with whom Roosevelt could do business.

The President's strategy was to go back to the old bargain that he and St. John Philby had separately conceived, before it got corrupted with the silly talk of bribery: Palestine for the Jews, independence and economic development for the Arabs. On January 2, 1945, Roosevelt confided his plan to Stettinius. "The President said he desired to take with him a map showing the Near Eastern area as a whole and the relationship of Palestine to the area," Stettinius noted. On that basis, he intended "to point out to Ibn Saud what an infinitesimal part of the whole area was occupied by Palestine and that he could not see why a portion of Palestine could not be given to the Jews without harming in any way the interests of the Arabs." Roosevelt emphasized the need to guarantee "that the Jews would not move into adjacent parts of the Near East from Palestine."

Roosevelt knew that Weizmann and the Zionists understood economic and political trade-offs. Without having any notion of how closely they had approached the President's thinking, the American Zionist leadership submitted a memorandum even as Roosevelt took off for Yalta, noting "scope for Arab development and civilizing endeavor for a century to come. But assistance to this end must be predicated on the establishment of a firmly rooted Jewish nation in Palestine." Thoughts of "a little baksheesh" lingered in the President's mind. "President Roosevelt said to some of us privately he could do anything that needed to be done with Ibn Saud with a few million dollars," recalled his aide David Niles a year or so later. But, of course, there was to be no talk of bribery.

The King of the Desert and the leader of the Western Alliance had conducted a personal, if somewhat stilted, correspondence since 1943. They had never met, of course; Ibn Saud had never in his life left his peninsula. In May 1943, even before sending Hoskins on his exploratory mission, Roosevelt had written the pledge that became the orthodoxy of American policy for years to come: "I assure Your Majesty that it is the view of the Government of the United States that no decision altering the basic situation of Palestine should be reached without full consultation with both Arabs and Jews." The Arabian King always responded to Roosevelt in terms of respect and friendship, even as he dismissed suggestions that the Jews could have a homeland on Arab soil. In 1944, learning that Roosevelt was a philatelist, Ibn Saud sent him a packet of his kingdom's stamps. Roosevelt turned his thank-you note to political use: geography was as interesting to him as stamps. "I feel sure that the Kingdom of Saudi Arabia has a great future before it if more agricultural land can be provided through irrigation and through the growing of trees to hold the soil and increase the water supply." The President sought to prepare the ground in more ways than one.

Experts attempted to temper his enthusiasm. "You must be warned," wrote economist Landis in January 1945, "Ibn Saud both personally and as a political matter feels very intensely about [Palestine]." Suggestions of compromise were regularly rejected. Only recently, Landis went on, "he threatened in the presence of one of my people to see to the execution of any Jew that might seek to enter his dominion."

Undeterred, Roosevelt set off early in February for Yalta, with nothing said about the other meeting he planned afterward. In a day of preliminary talks with Churchill at Malta, before the two confronted Stalin, he casually brought up his hopes for an Arab-Jewish settlement. Even then he kept secret his plan to meet Ibn Saud. "Churchill was better informed on this complex controversy than the President," noted a Roosevelt aide, "and was somewhat doubtful that the Roosevelt goal could be achieved." Perhaps, but for Roosevelt it was too late to turn back.

Neither Western leader wished to engage Stalin in formal discussion of Palestine, given all the other issues to be thrashed out. But at dinner on the last night at Yalta, Roosevelt asked Stalin directly if he favored Zionism. Stalin "answered warily; yes, in principle, but he recognized the difficulty of solving the Jewish problem," according to the American interpreter, Charles E. Bohlen. Then, roguishly anticipating Churchill's annoyance at being caught unawares—and worse, in the presence of Stalin—Roosevelt casually announced that he was stopping on his way home the next day for a meeting with the King of Saudi Arabia. Churchill clamped down hard on his cigar; it was not the first time that Roosevelt had put on a little show designed to reassure Stalin that the two Western leaders were not ganging up on him. Stalin was amused at Churchill's discomfiture, just as Roosevelt intended, and asked what the King might get out of it. "The President replied with a smile that there was only one concession that he thought he might offer," Bohlen noted, "and that was to give Ibn Saud the six million Jews in the United States." Even bad jokes fell flat with Stalin. "The solution to the Jewish problem was difficult," he replied, according to Bohlen. "He called the Jews 'middlemen, profiteers and parasites.' "

IN SAUDI ARABIA, mysterious preparations had been underway for a royal journey. Considerations of both wartime security and intertribal politics required that the impending meeting between Ibn Saud and Roosevelt be kept totally secret. The site was to be the Great Bitter Lake, midway through the Suez Canal. An American destroyer, the *Murphy,* would bring the King and his retinue from Jidda; they would rendezvous with Roosevelt aboard the cruiser *Quincy.*

The commodore of the *Murphy* had an order to limit the royal party to four notables and eight servants and bodyguards, as futile an order as any in the annals of the United States Navy. When the King was ready to embark, he absolutely required an entourage of forty-eight, including chamberlain, majordomo, physicians, court astrologer, and personal coffee servers. This exceeded by thirty-two the authorized accommodations of the vessel, but the royal party, from the King on down, would not hear of leaving anyone behind. Once on board, the entire party shunned the staterooms, choosing to be sheltered by a tent of naval canvas set up on the deck, which was swathed in rich oriental rugs.

The real crisis arose in the last hours before embarkation, when a launch pulled alongside the *Murphy* laden with a hundred of the best and fattest sheep of the kingdom. Ibn Saud's concept of hospitality demanded that he supply the food for the entire journey, not only for his own party but for the *Murphy*'s American seamen as well. The American commodore delicately explained that he had ample food stocks already on board; the King brushed aside this irrelevancy and insisted that his American "guests" must eat from his table, from the produce of his domain. The impasse was complete. Finally, the American minister to Saudi Arabia explained that it was contrary to all the regulations of the United States Navy for the ship's crew to eat anything other than the rations provided for them. Reluctantly, the King deferred to the inscrutable practices of this foreign power. The commodore did, however, with dirty looks at the mediating American diplomat, allow seven of the sheep to be brought onto his ship for the royal party's own use. As needed, they were periodically slaughtered and roasted on the fantail.

The royal journey lasted two nights and one day. At 1000 hours on the morning of February 14, the *Murphy* hove to alongside the *Quincy,* where President Roosevelt waited on deck, in a wheelchair, enveloped in his customary cape despite the hot sun of the desert. The gargantuan monarch of Arabia made his way with difficulty across the narrow gangplank linking the two vessels. The two talked amiably and aimlessly for an hour and a half, each sizing up the other in his own way, then were summoned below for lunch. Official panic erupted when Roosevelt's elevator stopped midway between decks—and stayed there. It was one of the more joyful moments in naval history when mechanics and officers discovered that there had been no malfunction—the President had himself pressed the red emergency button, and was sitting alone in quiet contentment for just long enough to smoke two cigarettes. The use of tobacco in the presence of the King would have been a serious affront.

After lunch came business. "I had an exceedingly pleasant meeting with Ibn Saud," the President later remarked, "and we agreed about everything until I mentioned Palestine. That was the end of the pleasant conversation." Neither side found it prudent to recall the earlier contacts with Philby and Hoskins, but as Roosevelt tentatively launched into his scheme for a Jewish Palestine coupled with vast development programs for the Arab world, the King interrupted. "The Arabs and the Jews could never cooperate, neither in Palestine, nor in any other country," he declared. After a few minutes, Roosevelt made another try; the King declared with finality "that the Arabs would choose to die rather than yield their lands to the Jews." This was not the kind of conversation that the President had had in mind.

Roosevelt switched tacks and began to speak of "his great interest in farming, stating that he himself was a farmer," according to the official transcript. He spoke of water resources, of planting trees and developing water power and irrigation. "Stating that he liked Arabs, he reminded His Majesty that to increase land under cultivation would decrease the desert and provide living for a larger population of Arabs." This was a blunder. "Decreasing the desert" was no virtue in the eyes of Ibn Saud. "We are desert dwellers," said the King, "my people do not like trees." He could not, Ibn Saud said, "engage with any enthusiasm in the development of . . . agriculture and public works if this prosperity would be inherited by the Jews."

What was the point now in bringing out the map? Against the laconic intransigence of the King of the Desert, all of Roosevelt's aspirations were slipping through his fingers. The experts were right after all. Seeking to salvage what he could from the ill-fated encounter, the President reiterated his pledge to decide nothing about the fate of Palestine without full consultations with Arabs as well as Jews. Then, off the cuff, came a further comment which the King took to be a formal commitment: Roosevelt "wished to assure His Majesty that he would do nothing to assist the Jews against the Arabs and would make no move hostile to the Arab people." Soothing words, capable of varying interpretations, but to Ibn Saud they were enough to justify the whole adventure beyond his frontiers.

At 1530 hours the captain of the *Quincy* interrupted to say that the President's ship now had to depart for Port Said. Out of the question, said the King; frustrated in his proffered hospitality before, he insisted that the rules of his kingdom positively required that his honored guest, the President, visit his quarters on the *Murphy* and take a meal with him. Then Ibn Saud gazed at the gangplank that he had himself negotiated only with difficulty, and looked back at Roosevelt's wheelchair. "Will you at least drink a cup of Arabian coffee?" he asked. Before any reply was possible, two of the resplendent royal coffee servers elbowed their way past seamen, guards, and officers to pour out a symbolic bond between Arabia and the United States.

OF ALL the high-level meetings Franklin D. Roosevelt attended in his life, it was this one that gave him the least satisfaction. He admitted as much to Bernard Baruch. "I am sure the President did not realize what kind of man he was going to be entertaining," remarked Harry Hopkins. He was "greatly shocked" at the King's resistance to all the persuasive techniques that had served Roosevelt so well in the past. Ibn Saud clearly showed him that "the Arabs meant business," Hopkins said.

Reviewing the results of the meeting on board the *Quincy,* Roosevelt let Stettinius see his despair, concluding that "he must have a conference with Congressional leaders and re-examine our entire policy in Palestine." Stettinius noted in his diary that Roosevelt "was now convinced that if nature took its course there would be bloodshed between the Arabs and Jews. Some formula, not yet discovered, would have to prevent this warfare." The sixty-three-year-old President was failing in health, and many around him began to wonder if he would live long enough to discover what that new formula might be. The day after seeing Ibn Saud, Roosevelt met Churchill for what turned out to be the last time. Churchill had changed his own plans after Yalta and flown down to Alexandria to learn about the Bitter Lake conference. "The President seemed placid and frail," Churchill recalled. "I felt that he had a slender contact with life."

Back home on March 1, the weary President apologized to the Congress for remaining seated as he addressed a joint session; it was difficult, he said, to stand with "ten pounds of steel on the bottom of my legs." He reported on the momentous decisions reached with Churchill and Stalin and told of his meeting with Ibn Saud. Expanding on his prepared text, Roosevelt ad-libbed a sentence that sent shivers through the American Jewish community and puzzled even his own advisers. "On the problem of Arabia," he said, "I learned more about that whole problem, the Moslem problem, the Jewish problem, by talking with Ibn Saud for five minutes than I could have learned in the exchange of two or three dozen letters." It was a ridiculous remark, huffed Judge Rosenman; it must have just "popped into his head, for I never heard him say anything like that on the way home." Hopkins insisted that "the only thing he learned, which all people well acquainted with the Palestine cause knew, is that the Arabs don't want any more Jews in Palestine." Until he heard it himself, apparently, Roosevelt could not bring himself to believe it.

From the Arab world came triumphant versions of what had happened on the Great Bitter Lake. "President Roosevelt put his hand in the hand of King Ibn Saud," declared the Secretary-General of the newly formed Arab League, "and promised him that he would not support the Jews in Palestine."

Roosevelt had but one more month of life. Hoping to quiet the uproar from his unfortunate ad-lib, he summoned Wise for a comforting talk, a vivid account of his trials with the Arab King: "There was nothing I could do with him. We talked for three hours and I argued with the old fellow up hill and down dale, but he stuck to his guns. He said he could see the flood engulfing his lands, Jews pouring in from Eastern Europe and from America, from the Riviera and from California, and he could not bear the thought. He was an old man and he had swollen ankles and he wanted to live out his life in peace without leaving a memory of himself as a traitor to the Arab cause."

Roosevelt authorized Wise to go out and reassure the Zionists. A couple of days later he called in one of his anti-Zionist Jewish friends, Judge Joseph Proskauer of the American Jewish Committee, and asked his help in calming fears and lowering hopes for the early realization of a Jewish state. "He was now frightened," Proskauer recalled, believing that "either a war or a pogrom would ensue." Jewish statehood was absolutely out of the question under present circumstances, Roosevelt told Proskauer. But what about all your public statements? Proskauer asked. "Joe, you know I go out on a limb for my friends and I have done so here," Roosevelt replied. "You must help."

On March 3, Roosevelt had one last luncheon with Colonel Hoskins. It took place in the family dining room at the White House; Mrs. Roosevelt and their daughter, Anna Boettiger, joined them at the table. They reviewed the latest discussions with Churchill—"as strongly pro-Zionist as ever," Roosevelt said—and Ibn Saud, who "objected strongly" to every plan for resettling the surviving Jews of Europe in Arab lands. Mrs. Roosevelt intervened to remark that the Zionists had done "wonderful work" in parts of Palestine, but the President cut her off. Hoskins expressed his long-held fear that a "Zionist state would be installed and maintained only by force," and Roosevelt said he fully agreed. Mrs. Roosevelt said that she thought the Zionists were "much stronger, and were perhaps willing to risk a fight with the Arabs." "Mr. Roosevelt agreed that this was a possibility," Hoskins reported, "but reminded her that there were 15 or 20 million Arabs in and around Palestine and that, in the long run, he thought these numbers would win out."

Neither demography nor failing health could still the Roosevelt imagination, the capacity for those rapid flashes of intuition that carried him along in his vision of Palestine. To several visitors in these last days, the President threw out hints of the "new formula" taking shape in his mind. Postwar responsibility for Palestine might be beyond his and Churchill's power after all. Instead, perhaps the new United Nations Organization would create the Jewish state and underwrite its survival with an international police force. Clearly normal diplomatic procedures of sovereign states would not suffice. Palestine could become the first test of the community of nations; Roosevelt approved Zionist participation in the conference at San Francisco opening on April 25 to organize the United Nations.

"While there was a momentary sense of failure," Wise said after Roosevelt's death, "at the same time he said he had already planned for another and, as he believed, a more effective method of approach to the problem, the solution of which was bound to be the establishment of a free and democratic Jewish Commonwealth in Palestine."

And once again he spoke of his hopes of playing a direct role in the Middle East, after the presidency, after the war. "I think Eleanor and I will go to the Near East and see if we can manage to put over an operation like the Tennessee Valley system that will really make something of that country," he told Frances Perkins. "I would love to do it. . . . I don't know any people who need someone to help them more than the people in the Near East."

At the end of March, Roosevelt went to Warm Springs, Georgia, to rest. With him went the papers of state, encompassing the affairs of the world. To Stalin he wrote, "I feel sure that when our armies make contact in Germany and join in a fully coordinated offensive, the Nazi armies will disintegrate." Over the complimentary close "Your good friend," he signed a letter to Ibn Saud reiterating former assurances. On April 12 a new batch of draft letters arrived for his signature. There were messages to other Arab leaders similar to what had already been said to Ibn Saud. Reading over one of the drafts late that morning, Roosevelt looked up cheerfully and said, "A typical State Department letter—it says nothing at all." Three hours later, he was dead.

FRANKLIN D. ROOSEVELT's record on the destiny of the Jews is complex, marked with the imprint of his generation and of generations before. Yet, for all the inconsistencies, it reveals a single pattern, a pattern shaped by a personal vision that never matured but kept developing.

He had no particular interest in the romance of Jewish restoration. For that matter, the master of Hyde Park had no particular interest in Jews as such. The humanitarian instincts for which he is revered failed him in the case of the Jews of Europe. But like Presidents from John Adams onward, Roosevelt let the fate of the Holy Land occupy a place in his thinking far out of all proportion to its geographical significance or its objective relation to United States national interests. David Niles's doubts are not stilled. If Roosevelt had lived a few more years, would the state of Israel ever have come into being?

The consistent strain in his thought was that Palestine should be the homeland of the Jews—eventually, if not immediately upon their rescue from the clutches of the Nazis. Time and again, his instincts led him to consider ways to move the Palestinian Arabs off the land, to make way for the Jews wishing to return to their rightful home. Roosevelt believed that the Jews had an unchallengeable "right" to Palestine. In this belief the President was often more outspoken than many Zionists who seemed perfectly willing to embrace a significant Arab minority in their Jewish state. Roosevelt saw the Palestine of the future as Jewish. "No Arabs should be in it. . . . It should be exclusive Jewish territory." For three or four decades hence, not even Zionists would assert such a claim in a loud voice. This personal conviction was inconsistent with the declared policy of the United States government, at least as enunciated by the State Department over the decades. From this inconsistency, and the ambiguities of policy that arose from it, stemmed the unrealistic expectations—of all sides—in the disputes to come.

Roosevelt underestimated the intensity of Arab resistance to a Jewish Palestine. He was not alone. Even after learning the worst from Ibn Saud, he conceded only that the Jewish restoration would take longer than he had anticipated. He told Stephen Wise in their last meeting that the Arabs would ultimately have to be overruled. But Roosevelt said many things to many people, different things to different people. It is a chronic propensity of politicians to say things that will be well received, and Roosevelt in particular never overcame his desperate longing to be liked by the people around him.

Nevertheless, Roosevelt envisaged Jewish Palestine as an idealized embodiment of great-power responsibility in the postwar era. At first it was to be himself and Churchill who would preside over the solution, keeping their wartime partnership in business after the war. Later it became the new world order, the future United Nations Organization, that would secure and implement the settlement between the Jews and the Arabs. Nowhere in Roosevelt's record is there any indication that he envisaged the unilateral proclamation of a sovereign Jewish state, such as occurred in May 1948. Indeed, the possibility of such a move would surely have filled him with apprehension. Most other Americans in the early 1940s, moreover, Jews and Gentiles alike, would probably have felt the same.

Roosevelt's Middle Eastern policy implied coexistence between Jews and Arabs. This sounds like the binationalism which became the banner of the State Department and of all who opposed the notion of a Jewish state. But Roosevelt was thinking not of Palestine alone when he thought of Arab-Jewish cooperation. Like the most extreme of Zionists, he thought that Palestine itself should be secure and exclusive for Jewish nationalism. Arab nationalism was to find its full expression in the newly independent Arab states of Syria, Lebanon, Jordan, and Iraq. Together these new nations of the Middle East—the Jewish state and the Arab states—would form a wide binational federation to promote their mutual economic development. They would build cities and highways, their irrigation schemes would shrink the desert and bring food to the people. It would take patience and ingenuity to overcome past generations of bitterness and misunderstanding. It might require an international police force and major-power guarantees to ensure security and mutual confidence. But the people would be fed, and would prosper.

How could such an idealized binationalism be achieved? What could the United States do to promote it? Which hopes were realistic, which dangerous? These are questions that Roosevelt was pondering when his days came to their end and Palestine, along with all the other problems of the world, became the responsibility of others.

7

ON APRIL 11, 1945, the last full day of Roosevelt's life, Allied armies liberated Buchenwald and the meaning of Hitler's "final solution" could no longer be evaded. Without fully comprehending it, and only by macabre default, American Jewry had become the largest Jewish community in the world.

The Nazis obviously understood this demographic shift before anyone else. As early as April 1942, Hitler's propagandists were claiming that "the Jewish question has been solved, except for the five million Jews in the United States." But even less informed observers sensed a significant change in the status of the Jews. A New York Yiddish-language newspaper proclaimed that "the fate of the Jewish homeland will be decided as much in Washington as in London or Jerusalem." And, sitting in London a few months before the attack on Pearl Harbor, the Palestinian labor leader David Ben-Gurion concluded that "whatever the part of America may be in world affairs, in our own affairs she may certainly be decisive."

When war came to Europe, the leadership of American Jewry was confused and impotent. Antisemitism was not without its appeals to "polite" society, and the bigotries of Charles Lindbergh and Father Coughlin were widely heard, if also condemned by the New Deal. Jews felt threatened by the old charge of dual loyalty and sought above all to maintain the positions they had fought for and achieved in American society.

"Those American Jews who are most indifferent or even hostile to Zionism are also, in general, those who are most anxious not to emphasize their own Jewishness," concluded a British diplomatic assessment. "They, therefore, do not take part in public discussion of Jewish affairs, with the result that the Zionists have an influence out of all proportion to their numbers." Still a small minority, Jewish nationalists "remain outside the mainstream of Jewish life and have not reached out beyond a narrow compass," wrote Weizmann in 1941. "The reason is, I think, primarily social. Zionists are recruited chiefly from the lower middle class and to a small extent from the middle classes. The upper middle classes are still either aloof or a minority of them is hostile and ignorant."

This was hardly a wellspring of dynamic leadership. Left to itself, the richest (and soon to be the largest) Jewish community of the world seemed hopelessly inadequate to the tasks ahead. Separately, without any of the plotting that antisemites detected at every turn, Zionist leaders of free Europe and Palestine resolved that American Jewry could not be left to go its own way. From differing origins and political persuasions, employing widely diverse styles of operation, leaders of the world movement for the Jewish homeland descended upon wartime Washington.

"WASHINGTON is not an easy place," wrote Weizmann on a visit early in World War II. "It is a regular whispering gallery, combining all the disadvantages of a great capital and a small village. One has to be meticulously careful in what one says, because rumor and gossip are carried on invisible wings, with . . . lightning rapidity, and in most cases are distorted. Everybody is working there, and the deafening noise caused by the grinding of so many axes is most unpleasant to the ears." New York and Washington became a rehearsal stage for the political feuds of Palestine, and American onlookers were less than edified.

Ben-Gurion had visited the United States several times without ever feeling comfortable. Polish-born, settled in Palestine as a teen-ager, he was becoming a master political strategist as head of the Zionist Socialist labor movement. For nine months, from November 1941 until August 1942, he lingered in the American Jewish community, testing the air for signs of leadership, checking in on contacts made over the years. He saw Brandeis and Stephen Wise, but found more strength and vitality in men like Frankfurter and Ben Cohen, who, alas, were more involved in the New Deal than in Zionism. "There is good will in the United States, but also a lot of caution," he confided to his diary. Ben-Gurion pondered how to translate this vague good will into organizational muscle, something that no home-grown American Zionist had attempted since Brandeis.

Cutting a wider swath was Weizmann, the grand old man of Zionism, mellowed from his earlier clashes with the Brandeisians. By the turn of the 1940s, he had become a figure of veneration in America, even among those who had regarded him before as an interloper. "Quasi-messianic . . . electric," remarked Frankfurter, even as he declined Weizmann's invitation to leave America and settle in Palestine. Weizmann had grown high-handed with his colleagues in the Zionist leadership, and his circle of detractors was growing. "We cannot ignore him, however," said an emissary from Palestine in 1943. "His influence among Jews and Gentiles is strong and his scientific achievements might be able to help us in our aims."

Weizmann and Ben-Gurion were bitter rivals, the elder radiating the cosmopolitan air of the Diaspora, the younger representing the pioneers of Palestine. Against Weizmann's Old World charm and experience, Ben-Gurion was a coarse provincial. Yet the men were still colleagues in the world Zionist movement; and they shared contempt for a third formidable figure of Jewish nationalism who appeared in New York.

Vladimir Jabotinsky had become an outcast from the Zionist mainstream. After their start together in Chelsea, "Jabo" quickly tired of Weizmann's diplomatic airs. He preferred the tactics of militancy, of armed resistance against the Arabs and, eventually, against the British mandatory administration. Breaking away in the 1920s, Jabotinsky's Revisionist Zionism organized its own fighting force in Palestine. The Irgun Zvai Leumi came to remind unsympathetic outsiders of Mussolini's Fascists; Ben-Gurion called the Revisionist leader "Vladimir Hitler." Revisionism and the Irgun made headway among Polish Jewry before the war, and Jabotinsky decided to mobilize the Jews of America. Arriving in February 1940, he established himself as an émigré agitator in two small rooms of a West Side boardinghouse. One weekend in August, he paid an inspection visit to the training camp of his Betar youth movement outside New York City and never returned; aged sixty-one, he died of a heart attack.

A small and seemingly insignificant band of seven zealots remained in New York to carry forward the militancy of their charismatic leader. One of them, Hillel Kook, had appeared quietly in July 1940 to promote the creation of a Jewish army to fight the Nazis and their Arab partisans. A Jewish relief organization at the New York wharves politely asked the lonely thirty-year-old refugee if he needed assistance. He did not, for though he was not prepared to say it in public, Hillel Kook was a well-heeled emissary of the Irgun.

Kook is a name in Jewish Palestine that connotes something like Cabot in New England. Hillel Kook's uncle was the first Chief Rabbi of Palestine; the family tree was adorned with generations of rabbis and scholars of the highest social position. Hillel's interests were more worldly. Captivated by Revisionist activism, he dropped out of Hebrew University in 1937 to go to Poland "for a few weeks" and stayed away from Palestine for eleven years, meeting Jabotinsky and throwing himself into the effort to raise money and weapons for the Irgun. Among his Polish comrades was a zealot named Menachem Begin; Kook thought

Begin a promising young fellow. Irgun missions took Kook to London, then to the United States, where he sat up late nights brainstorming with Jabotinsky just before the leader died.

Literate, engaging, and glib, Kook saw in the wealth and energy of the United States a gold mine for the Irgun. Establishment Zionists, even the breakaway Revisionists, were too prim and hidebound for his tastes. He struck out on his own, launching an audacious program of public fund raising, of big-name committees and newspaper advertisements, to the dismay and fury of the more respectable Zionists, and toward ends that it was prudent never to specify in detail. Consistent with his conspiratorial background, he operated in America under an assumed name. It was as "Peter Bergson" that this scion of the Palestinian aristocracy made his mark in wartime Washington.

WEIZMANN, Ben-Gurion, and Bergson were the stars of the Zionist drama who descended from abroad to activate the Jews of America. With them came a strong supporting cast.

Always at the center of action was the cosmopolitan diplomat of world Zionism, Nahum Goldmann. Russian by origin, Goldmann had been attached to the Berlin Zionist headquarters before World War I; during the war he wrote pro-German propaganda for the Foreign Ministry. Goldmann had delivered his first Zionist speech in 1908, at the age of thirteen, an accomplishment which he remembered principally for the pleasing effect it had on a little girlfriend in the audience. Rising in the Zionist bureaucracy in the interwar decades, he became the Jewish Agency delegate to the League of Nations. In 1943 the Agency transferred Goldmann to the United States, where the feuding between Ben-Gurion and Weizmann was sapping the strength of the American campaign for Jewish nationalism, even diverting support toward the Irgun renegade Peter Bergson.

Goldmann was basically allied to Weizmann, but he also developed an understanding of the American Jewish leaders that transcended factionalism. "You have to speak to American Jews in superlatives before they will listen," he once remarked. "Cool, balanced analysis makes no impression on them, and exaggeration is almost indispensable." Gossip was Goldmann's stock in trade, the more personal and salacious the better. It flowed in a steady stream to his contacts on the diplomatic cocktail circuit, reaching the ears of the most intimate yet independent chronicler of the wartime Zionist drama, a brilliant young Oxford political theorist named Isaiah Berlin.

Latvian-born but on his way up in the British establishment, Berlin was seconded to New York and Washington to analyze the politics of American minority groups. He started producing a regular analysis of the American political scene that became one of Churchill's favorite briefing papers each week. Scattered among his political dispatches to Whitehall were trenchant assessments of American Jewish affairs, in which the British Foreign Office showed far greater and more sophisticated interest than did the Department of State. Berlin's first impressions of American Jewry came from Brandeis. "They won't emigrate in any numbers," the aged jurist told the young diplomat, "but they know that they have got to be a majority somewhere, have a country of their own, if they are to hold their heads up high among other loyal American citizens of recent European origin." Brandeis warned Berlin that American Jews had none of the political zeal of, say, the Roman Catholics, so "the influence they will be able to have on American policy may not be great."

Berlin moved easily through the circles of Jewish officials in the Roosevelt administration, reporting back to London all the while; Frankfurter, Morgenthau, Ben Cohen, Sam Rosenman were all among his political and social friends. For all his integrity as a British civil servant, he never made a secret of his Zionist sympathies and his devotion to Weizmann. He was less friendly with Ben-Gurion and the American critics of the Weizmann circle. And he would have nothing to do with Bergson, that defender and promoter of anti-British terrorism. Thus Berlin's reports to the British Foreign Office were flawed, as he subsequently acknowledged. He seriously underestimated the dynamism and unity which American Jewry was capable of mustering as World War II drew to a close.

The leadership of the community was changing, slowly. Stephen Wise was nearly seventy when the burden of the Holocaust fell upon him. He was already weakened; few knew that he suffered from a blood disease called polycythemia that had been draining his energies for years. Wise had lost the fire that had braced him for political and social combat from the start of the century. Though he continued to move in and out of the White House and other power centers through 1942 and 1943, his reports to his colleagues became vague and garbled. For all his sympathy with Wise's moderation, Berlin reported that the rabbi had gone "a little gaga." Attacked by Bergson and other radical voices, criticized by *The New York Times* and conservative non-Zionist Jews, Wise felt his confidence in the goodwill of his Gentile friends ebbing as well. "I really am inclined to believe that there is a cabal in the State Department deliberately and, I am afraid, effectively working against those Palestinian interests which are precious to some of us," he confided. Even Roosevelt let him down, with his pledges to Ibn Saud: "I worked so hard in all the four campaigns . . . in [his] friendship we all had such implicit faith."

Wise could no longer bring to the Jewish national cause the single-mindedness that the 1940s demanded. After the war's end, with Bergson's anti-British sentiments at fever level, Wise supported an American loan to Britain—in the very week that Whitehall denied him a visa to visit Palestine. Testifying as an elder statesman before an Anglo-American panel in 1946, he was heard with respect. "With his grey mane and strong, worn face, he seemed an aged lion, rousing himself for a heavy effort," reported an observer. " 'A great gentleman' was one British committee member's comment in the hall afterwards." He summoned up the strength early in 1948 to join a fund-raising tour with Golda Meir, and such was the veneration still attached to his name that Mrs. Meir, seeking a code word to report her success in raising 25 million dollars, cabled to Tel Aviv that they had in hand "twenty-five stephens."

Wise never set foot in the state of Israel. His wife of forty-seven years died in November 1947, and shortly thereafter his own illness became critical. He died at the age of seventy-five in New York's Lenox Hill hospital on April 19, 1949.

Stephen Wise's lasting legacy was the personal quality of immense human feeling, "his capacity for sympathy in every case of individual need," in the words of his Christian clergyman friend Reinhold Niebuhr. Enlarging the image that clung to Wise throughout his public career, Niebuhr led the nation in paying tribute to "this touch of lamb in the lion."

No ONE EVER detected a touch of the lamb, or any other gentle quality, in the person of Stephen Wise's final adversary, Abba Hillel Silver of Cleveland. For all the respect and tribute which came to him, Silver remained unloved. "Where Wise was warm and open to the entire world, Silver was cool and closed except to his closest associates," wrote one chronicler. "Where Wise's opponents respected him, some of Silver's allies could not stand him personally." Yet it was Silver, with the toughness of a man who did not care whether he was loved, who brought the Jews of America to a high pitch of discipline and power. It was Silver who founded the Jewish lobby, and made it work.

Abba Hillel Silver was born in Lithuania in 1893, son of a rabbi, one of six children deeply versed in the traditions of scholarship, but lacking aristocratic breeding and means. In June 1902, a thin, dark, curly-haired boy of nine in a little sailor suit was among the human freight disgorged by the S.S. *Köln* on the wharves of New York. With his mother and older brother, Abba moved into the tenement apartment on the Lower East Side that his father had prepared for them. Two years into their new life, Abba and brother Maxwell founded the Dr. Herzl Zion Club in the neighborhood, America's first Hebrew-speaking Zionist youth center, a place where Jewish nationalism and Scripture could be propagated among the new generation in a strange land. The boys' elders chided them for neglecting the spirit of the New World which the immigrant community strove to instill in its young. The Silver boys even used an alien language instead of the English that all the immigrants were struggling to acquire!

Abba headed the group by the year of his Bar Mitzvah; "wholly self-possessed and self-confident, [he] ruled the club with an iron hand," recalled his boyhood friend and lifelong companion, Emanuel Neumann. They went in for political debates and biblical pageants with music, costumes, and paraphernalia. Abba allowed other teenagers to present themselves in leading roles, except when it came to the story of Moses; for that, Silver insisted on playing the title role himself.

Silver went through New York City public schools, then graduated from Hebrew Union College and the University of Cincinnati. After his ordination as a Reform rabbi, his first pulpit was in Wheeling, West Virginia, where he contracted a good marriage with the daughter of one of the community leaders. After only two years he was called to the Temple of Cleveland in 1917; there he remained, spiritual and social leader of one of America's most prosperous Jewish communities, until his death in 1963.

Silver was no Harvard man, but he was captivated by Brandeis. Stephen Wise, nineteen years his senior, took an interest in this promising young rabbi and helped to promote his entrance into the big world of Zionist leadership. Then it all came crashing down with the defeat of the Brandeisian leadership in 1921, and for the next two decades Silver withdrew from national Zionism. Following Wise's lead, he championed labor against capital, but when his New York mentor challenged the rich and influential president of United States Steel in 1921, Silver's zealotry in social causes grew muted.

On strictly Jewish matters, as opposed to social reform, Silver would accept no restraint. To the calls for assimilation to counter outcroppings of antisemitism, Silver took the opposite tack. "We are going to respond to every attack upon our people, to every libel and every slander, by more Jewishness, by more schools and synagogues and by more intensive and loyal work in Palestine," he thundered. To be "more Jewish," rather than less, was the theme of Silver's life struggle in America. A lonely voice at the start, his ethnic and national boldness earned for him prophetic stature.

Silver was an eloquent, humorless orator. "When his eyes flashed anger and his voice seethed with indignation, the opposition generally wilted," recalled an associate. Even Wise, disenchanted with this erratic force from the Midwest, admitted that he began to tremble whenever Silver entered the room. The obscure Jewish revolutionary Menachem Begin of the Irgun invited Silver to his hideout near the Palestinian seashore and wrote: "I am not easily carried away by outstanding personalities, but I must say that at that first meeting Silver made a great impression on me. 'He is a personality,' I told my colleagues."

Silver invariably suffered from comparison, in human terms, with Wise. His was a "talent for making enemies," conceded a Silver partisan. "People were secondary to causes," said another. Nowhere was this attribute clearer than in his reaction to Wise's pleas for refugee resettlement elsewhere than Palestine. The human plight of Hitler's victims was not Silver's interest; "Zionism is not refugeeism," he would argue. His overbearing stiffness brought despair to those around him. Hoping to spruce up his wardrobe, his wife strode into a Cleveland haberdashery and asked for "the loudest black tie in the store." Silver lived and ate extravagantly, dispensing lavish tips to all in sight. A visiting Socialist from Jewish Palestine was shocked to see the rabbi turn first to the stock-market tables as he picked up the morning newspaper. He thrived in the nighttime hours, consuming huge meals when everyone else had long since faded into bed. He loved a particular candy called *taglach*—a weakness shared, as it happened, by Wise, who once quipped as he helped himself to ever more handfuls, "What a pity, Silver likes these too!"

Though he acquired, and nurtured, the label of Republican in domestic politics, Silver had in fact voted for Roosevelt twice, and for Al Smith and Norman Thomas before that. In 1944 he praised the Palestine plank of the Democratic platform as better than the corresponding paragraph of the Republican platform. But against Wise, whose hands were tied in loyalty to "the Boss," Silver saw advantage in befriending Dewey, the Republican challenger, and Silver's fellow Ohioan, conservative Senator Robert A. Taft (who became an eloquent supporter of Zionism). Silver early noticed, and proceeded shrewdly to provoke, the uneasiness that many American Zionists felt about the tactic of deference to Gentile authority, based as it was on a belief that private persuasion among gentlemen of goodwill would serve Jewish interests best. To Silver and his partisans this represented nothing more than age-old Jewish timidity. Wise had seen virtue in being well connected, in having the ear of the mighty. Silver, by contrast, trusted in the good intentions of no one, not those of his own loyalists, certainly not those of any Gentile politician.

Silver made his move back onto the national stage in 1940, calling for a "maximal" Zionist position, a Jewish state covering all of Palestine, sovereign, independent, strong. Established international Zionist leaders tended to be put off by this rabble-rouser from the American Midwest, "the Mufti from Cleveland," as Weizmann called him. "We'll force the President to swallow our demands!" Silver declared. "We are living in a hard and brutal world. . . . The gentle, patient and personal diplomatic approach of yesterday is not entirely adequate for our days. If we speak too softly our voices are likely to be drowned in the cacophony of the world today. . . . Sometimes it is the height of statesmanship to be un-statesmanlike," Silver said. It was this powerful new voice that converted an abstract philanthropic cause into a practical and hard-hitting political machine.

WHATEVER his misgivings about Silver, Weizmann recognized that American Jewry was in trouble. He believed that the antisemitism of the 1930s and early 1940s was partly the Jews' own fault. "Along with a new generation of modest and honest workers, there is a certain part of Jewish bourgeoisie—rich, quasi-powerful, loud, vulgar, pulling a weight far in excess of their numbers, ostentatious," Weizmann wrote. "In the eyes of the Gentiles, they and almost they alone represent Jewry, and this is a grave danger." A reinvigorated national movement of Zionism might be the answer, Weizmann concluded, just like Brandeisian Zionism during the earlier war. But lest American Zionism take an erratic turn, as it did then, Weizmann sought to motivate American Jewry himself. So did Ben-Gurion, acting on behalf of the Palestinian Jews, and Bergson, sniping away on his own initiative.

Laying the personality clashes aside, which was often difficult to do in those early wartime days, the confusion of American Zionists arose from the core issue that had never been resolved under Brandeis or after: in the quest for the survival and enrichment of the Jewish people, is an independent sovereign state necessarily the method "which most promises success"? Public-spirited American Jews had long been troubled by the sorry condition of their brethren in Eastern Europe—long before they knew the worst—and many were genuinely enthusiastic about the growth prospects for the idealistic community in Palestine. But was Jewish sovereignty a desirable goal, with all its political, financial, and military responsibilities? Might it not be wiser simply to press for unlimited

Jewish immigration, developing Jewish cultural and social institutions in Palestine and leaving the responsibility of government and security to an enlightened British, American, or international protectorate? Even if statehood was accepted as the eventual goal, the leadership was still faced with the need to decide whether to press for maximum demands from the beginning or ease toward the national destiny a modest stage at a time.

The issue was joined at the Biltmore Hotel in New York in May 1942, at an extraordinary Zionist conference attended by 586 American delegates, plus Weizmann and Ben-Gurion as honored guests. (Bergson, of course, was beyond the pale of respectable Zionists.) The minimalist position had its roots in American Zionist tradition. It sprang from the mentality of philanthropy, of relief measures for oppressed Jewry that conveyed no awkward political implications. It avoided the old fear of divided national loyalties because the eventual political decisions would be made by the settlers in Palestine, not the Jewish citizens of America— and, if all went well, Jewish immigration would soon produce a Jewish majority in Palestine. It avoided the danger, acutely felt among the upwardly striving Jewish communities of America, that Jews would become less secure with their neighbors by appearing to promote a foreign cause.

But the maximalist position had the virtue of simplicity. National statehood was the desire of every ethnic group, ever since the days of Versailles. Why settle for palliatives and half-measures? To hardheaded delegates at the Biltmore, the caution of the minimalists seemed to be the caution of old men whose lives had been spent under the cloud of discrimination and who had been taught from Jewish infancy not to make trouble. The maximalist spokesmen were a powerful new breed of Jewish hero—Ben-Gurion, whose very life was devoted to the struggle; Silver, whose eloquent voice and determination to be "more Jewish" struck a responsive chord.

The German Army, under Rommel, was bearing down on Alexandria on its way to Palestine as the Biltmore delegates assembled. Telephone calls came to the Jewish leaders from the State Department in Washington, warning of the unrest that would erupt across the Arab world if the Zionists pressed too hard. The British Foreign Secretary, Anthony Eden, warned that the Zionists were assuming heavy risks in pursuing their national aspirations prematurely.

Weizmann had stated his minimalist position in the influential American journal *Foreign Affairs* several months before the Biltmore conference. He proposed an autonomous Jewish Palestine integrated within a Levantine Arab federation, something like the scheme that attracted Roosevelt. But the American Zionist leadership was unimpressed by such

diplomatic subtleties. After just three days of debate the Biltmore conference unanimously adopted a declaration demanding "that Palestine be
established as a Jewish Commonwealth integrated in the structure of the
new democratic world."

The formal deliberations were studded with code words; "commonwealth" grated a little less on the ears of the nervous minimalists than
"sovereign state," but its emotive appeal made up for its vagueness. The
first Jewish Commonwealth had been destroyed by the legions of Babylon
in 586 b.c.; the second fell to Rome in a.d. 70. Now the American
Zionist movement was calling for a Third Commonwealth. All protesta-
tions of purely philanthropic intent cast aside, American Zionism became
a kind of national liberation movement, redress for ancient injustices.

The Biltmore decision came within a week of the first Polish underground report telling of the extermination of Jews by the Nazis. The
delegates at the Biltmore had devoted careful discussion to plans for
absorbing millions of European Jews into Palestine after the war, their
transport, their housing, and their employment. As they debated, no one
seemed to comprehend how few of those millions would still be alive
when the time came.

In the months following the Biltmore conference of May 1942, the
mood of American Jewry began to change. The halting of Rommel's
forces at El Alamein in July eliminated the military threat to Palestine,
yet the news of holocaust in Europe brought a new sense of insecurity.
Isaiah Berlin noted the shift, the growing view, which even assimilated
Jews accepted, "that the condition of the Jews will not be improved by
their good behavior alone, nor by attempting to buy off their enemies;
that a positive policy of some sort is needed, and that a relatively bold
programme on their part to deal with the post-war Jewish situation in
Europe, so far from jeopardizing the position of the Jews in the U.S.,
might, on the contrary, gain them an increased degree of respect." As
assimilated a Jew as Sam Rosenman, at Roosevelt's right hand, was heard
to remark that "everyone is in favor of a Jewish state—we can't keep
out."

But moods rarely reverse themselves overnight. "To our sorrow the
five million American Jews place too much faith in what the neighbors
think, and fear that open admission of their race and open support of the
Zionist movement will render them victims of antisemitic action," reported Moshe Shertok of the Jewish Agency after an inspection tour in
1943. "They have the wrong idea. Antisemitism is getting stronger anyway, a fact which might bring many lost sheep back into our fold; did
not the same thing happen in Germany? Many factors contributed to-

ward the apathy of American Jewry. We ourselves are guilty; we have neglected them for the past 25 years. They have given money for various funds as uncaringly as cows give milk."

The Biltmore conference nevertheless marked a historical turning point. A coup d'état had taken place within Zionism. From this point on, the traditional leadership represented by Weizmann and Wise went into gradual but irreversible decline. In its place emerged the maximalist leadership of Ben-Gurion and Silver, preaching a dynamic approach to the Jewish national fate. The Biltmore declaration was like throwing a snowball into a field of snow, one of the delegates remarked. "It was necessary to continue to roll it to make it larger; the question then was, who was going to roll it?"

Resting at the Catskills resort of Grossinger's after the conference, Weizmann mourned the new mood of militancy. Ben-Gurion "wants to be Bar Kokhba. . . . I don't," he said, referring to the leader of the Jewish independence revolt in A.D. 132. "We've waited so long, fighting for our position, we'll wait a little longer. We don't want bloodshed." To his loyalists, Weizmann tried to play down the importance of the conference. "The Biltmore Declaration is just a resolution, like the hundred and one resolutions usually passed at great meetings in this country." Writing his memoirs five years later, Weizmann managed to cover the period without a single mention of it.

Ben-Gurion determined to be the one to roll the snowball. He turned testy, demanding that the hapless American Zionists make a flat choice between his or Weizmann's leadership. Firing off angry letters, stomping out of closed-door meetings whenever they seemed to be going against him, Ben-Gurion displayed that streak of petulance that would always mar his statesmanship. Many Americans saw in him only another embodiment of the messy Palestinian politics they so sought to avoid, when there was a war to be won, refugees to be succored, lives to be saved.

Isaiah Berlin informed London soon after the Biltmore conference that Silver "is certainly the most effective American Zionist leader at the moment." Silver's first challenge was to sell the new Biltmore program to apathetic American Jews, the vast majority of whom still shunned Zionist affiliation. An American Jewish Conference was called for 1943 to forge a unified position. Dominated by moderate Zionists, the conference succeeded in drawing in some sixty-five other Jewish organizations, including the Jewish Labor Committee on the left and the American Jewish Committee on the right, both of them deeply suspicious of Zionist militancy. The organizers agreed to play down the Biltmore decision; Silver, who would never countenance such a conciliatory tactic, was not given a place on the list of scheduled speakers.

For his part, Wise managed to champion the cause of Zionism without once mentioning the "Jewish commonwealth" as a goal. The omission infuriated Silver. "There was a confrontation between the two in the committee room," recalled Emanuel Neumann. "Silver openly charged Wise with breach of faith and with scuttling the official Zionist position. . . . In my whole Zionist career I have never witnessed such an awesome tongue-lashing as Silver administered to Wise; it was embarrassing to witness." Silver swiftly arranged to address the conference in place of one of the scheduled speakers. Calling for endorsement by all American Jewry of the Biltmore program, he warned, "If we surrender our national and historic claim to Palestine, and rely solely on the refugee philanthropic appeal, we shall lose our case as well as do violence to the historic hopes of our people!" Resounding cheers interrupted Silver repeatedly as his oratory mounted in intensity, shredding the carefully negotiated ground rules for unity. As he concluded, the conference burst into "Hatikvah," the Hebrew anthem of Jewish nationalism.

Hillel Silver had blown the conference wide open, and there was no turning back. In a frenzy of emotion, the American Jewish Conference overwhelmingly endorsed the Biltmore goal of a Jewish commonwealth. Delegates of the American Jewish Committee, led by Joseph Proskauer, walked out of the conference. "Vestigial oligarchs," Silver snorted at the backs of the departing delegates. "Little foxes have been busily at work trying to spoil this vineyard which American Israel has planted. These little foxes should have their little tails scorched!"

With a sense of mass emotions as sure as that deployed by Weizmann against Brandeis two decades before, Silver won for himself a status of leadership in American Zionism that previously Wise had enjoyed alone. Wise did not yield gracefully. "Although Silver could hardly bring himself to believe it," he wrote to the sympathetic Goldmann, "there are still people in and outside of the Zionist movement who, curiously enough, imagine that my name means something in American life. . . . I shall show my fellow Zionists now that I am not to be shelved, I am not to be displaced." Encountering his challenger in the corridor, Wise made one last try. "Rabbi Silver, I am an old man, and have had my moment in the sun," he said. "You are a young man, and will have your proper share of fame. It is not necessary for you to attack me." Silver turned without a word and walked away.

The moderate Zionist establishment was caving in under the "vigorous progress being made by the rebellious Rabbi Silver in stealing from them the leadership of the party," reported the British Embassy. "Their policy of 'go slow and trust the President' seems in imminent danger of shipwreck." The White House despaired at the sudden Zionist turn to militancy. "It was crazy of you Zionists," Judge Rosenman warned Gold-mann, "so long as this administration is in office, to change leadership from a man like Wise, whom the President likes, to a man like Dr. Silver, whom the President dislikes."

But Silver and his followers did not care whether they were "liked" by Roosevelt or anyone else. They held a different kind of asset, a weapon far blunter and, in the end, far more effective than mere entree to the mighty. Silver stated his strategy boldly: "to convert a club of well-intentioned but politically passive Zionist personalities into the nerve center of a revolutionary program with a mass following." The last of those loaded words was the key. No more "quiet diplomacy" in an elitist social setting; Silver called for "loud diplomacy" from the American Jewish masses, as loud and surely targeted as the entire Jewish community of the nation could manage. Thus was born the Jewish lobby.

SILVER ASSIGNED his friend Emanuel Neumann to convert a struggling one-man political action office in Washington into a national apparatus. Known ultimately as the American Zionist Emergency Council (AZEC), its budget rose from $100,000 to over $500,000 after Silver's triumph at the American Jewish Conference. With a disciplined zeal absent since the Brandeis days, the Silver men set about mobilizing American Jewry. They fired off streams of memos to Zionist activists and community leaders across the country. Local emergency committees were to be formed wherever Jews lived, but most particularly in the hometowns—no matter how small—of influential members of Congress.

"The first task will be to make direct contact with your local Con-gressman or Senator," came the instructions from headquarters. Have a luncheon or a dinner at someone's home in his honor. Get someone respectable to pull him aside and brief him privately on the Palestine situation—"Your local Congressman or Senator may be the man who will make a decisive speech on this subject on the floor of Congress—THIS POSSIBILITY MUST NOT BE OVERLOOKED." But DON'T suggest that he intro-duce any resolutions at this time—headquarters will let you know when the time is ripe for that. Silver and his men never wanted to lose opera-tional control of their machine.

By the start of 1944 no less than 200 local emergency committees had been set up, and soon the number doubled. From the Washington office came a barrage of "confidential bulletins," telling the local operatives—fund raisers, Jewish community leaders—how to make their voices heard most effectively. "You must be prepared at quick notice . . . to go into action to organize letter-writing and telegram campaigns." One memo included eighteen sample letters appropriate for the signatures of diverse members of the community—a Christian minister, a naturalized citizen, a Jewish war veteran, a union member, a wife of a serviceman or the parents of a boy overseas. When relevant articles appeared in the public press, favorable or unfavorable to Zionism, the loyalists were supplied with the proper response—letters of commendation or criticism to editors. Local committees received editorial texts that they could rewrite in their own styles and plant in local newspapers. Schedules of visits by Zionist speakers and warnings of lecture tours by anti-Zionists were given wide circulation so that maximum support, or effective opposition, could be set in motion.

From the start, the AZEC tried to reach out beyond the Jewish population. Zionists had long been doubtful about idealistic Christian support for the Jewish national destiny, but Neumann set out to convert this sincere but vague interest into a highly practical operation. The American Palestine Committee, a society of Protestant notables which had languished without direction for years, was revived under secret Zionist sponsorship. The AZEC allotted $50,000 of its own budget to the Christian organization, and the figure grew to $150,000 in the climactic years 1947–48. The interest of the Protestant officers was surely genuine, their atonement for centuries of Christian antisemitism, but the operations of their committee were hardly autonomous. Zionist headquarters thought nothing of placing newspaper advertisements on the clergymen's behalf without bothering to consult them in advance, until one of the committee's leaders meekly asked at least for prior notice before public statements were made in their name.

"In every American community an American Christian Palestine Committee must be immediately organized," came confidential orders from Silver's headquarters.

> Government officials in high places have indicated that strong Christian pressure for a Jewish Commonwealth is needed to spur Federal action on behalf of a Jewish Palestine. Unless the Zionists are first to organize, win and maintain the sympathy and activity of the leaders of American Christendom for our cause, our work will become greatly complicated and an attempt will be made, through clever but insidious and vicious attacks which will be levelled against us, to render our aims suspect. . . . Your first job is to appoint a special chairman. . . . Choose your best representative who can do the job. . . . As soon as we get the name of your chairman, he will be sent a Manual on Organization for American Christian Palestine Committee work.

Church circles were easier for the AZEC to reach than university and intellectual communities. Zionism had never really taken hold on college campuses. Both before and just after World War II, national polls showed far lower pro-Zionist sentiment among Jewish students than among Jewish adults. Reaching out to Gentiles as well, the Emergency Council managed to come up with one petition signed by 150 college presidents and 1,800 faculty members from forty-five states. But as late as 1947, AZEC headquarters complained of its inability to stimulate intellectuals capable of producing articles for "serious" magazines like *Harper's* or *Foreign Affairs*. When something useful did appear, such as the provocative book *Palestine, Land of Promise* by Walter Clay Lowdermilk, the Emergency Council subsidized its broad distribution and it quickly became a best seller.

The largest portion of the Zionist political action budget was assigned to the organization of large rallies and meetings of protest. "It is not difficult to imagine the cumulative effect of a hundred or so mass meetings held simultaneously on one day throughout the United States," local committee heads were told. But again, headquarters warned, don't organize anything on your own—wait for instructions from us.

In skill and effectiveness of political action, the Zionist lobby left the Irish and other nationality groups far behind. Two examples, from 1944 and 1945, show just the kind of impact that Silver's apparatus achieved.

1944: Over 3,000 organizations—labor unions, churches, farm granges, Rotary clubs, none of them Jewish in their orientation—passed pro-Zionist resolutions and sent telegrams to Congress. In Meriden, Connecticut, for example, where the Jewish population numbered no more than 1,500, more than 12,000 letters on Palestine were dispatched to President Roosevelt and the State Department. Similar expressions came to Washington from 200 non-Jewish organizations in Colorado; 60,000 persons in South Bend, Indiana, signed petitions, and from Leominster, Massachusetts, came 1,000 telegrams.

1945: On September 23 the Jewish Agency cabled news of an imminent British move that would be harmful to Zionist interests. The AZEC promptly booked Madison Square Garden for one week later; daily press advertisements and radio spots were ordered, 250,000 notices were mailed out, telephone squads started calling their lists. All this happened the first day. Then telegrams went to the local committees ordering a letter-writing campaign. Mass demonstrations in thirty cities were timed to coincide with the New York rally. Two-thirds of the Senate was approached by constituents in one day, on instruction from the local committees; twenty-seven senators gave speeches about Palestine on the Senate floor in two days, thirty-four more placed their remarks in the

Congressional Record. Two more open-air rallies, one called by the American Christian Palestine Committee, drew hundreds of thousands into New York's Madison Square Park. This all took place in one hectic month, in response to one telegram from the Jewish Agency.

From headquarters came discipline and planning; from the grass roots came enthusiasm. Indeed, AZEC strategists were startled at the spirit their appeals triggered among Americans far from the power centers. Headquarters regularly received pleas from the local committees asking for even greater militancy than Silver and his deputies deemed desirable. For generations, Jewish leaders had shunned political action; Wise had condemned those who "conjured up the spectre of a Jewish vote." Under Silver's leadership, aroused and appalled by the "news from Europe," America's Jews changed. Bernard Baruch, no Zionist but no novice in the use of political power, declared that

> the only thing which will matter in Washington . . . is if the people in the Bronx and Brownsville and Borough Park begin to mutter in their beards, they'll be damned if they continue to cast their votes to a party that breaks its pledges to them. . . . You let me have the Jewish vote of New York and I will bring you the head of Ibn Saud on a platter! The Administration will sell all seven Arab states if it is a question of retaining the support . . . of the Jews of New York alone; never mind the rest of the country.

Silver was not alone in grasping the potential for mass action, from idealistic Christians as well as Jews. Indeed, the hand of the AZEC was repeatedly forced by the brash and unabashed public relations campaigns of the imaginative renegade, Peter Bergson. With Jabotinsky dead and the militant Irgun demoralized in Palestine, Bergson had erected a formidable network of committees. Eri Jabotinsky, son of the leader, wrote a cheerful description of Bergson/Kook's technique to a friend in Palestine (the personal letter was promptly intercepted by British wartime censorship and relayed to proper authorities in Whitehall):

> A circular letter was written to a hundred prominent men whose names were taken out of the *Who's Who,* explaining the necessity to form a Jewish Army and asking them to join the Committee in formation. Ten replied joining the Committee. A second circular letter was sent out to a thousand on stationery bearing the names of the ten who previously had replied 'yes.' The same procedure was repeated several times until today [1943] we

have something like 10,000 names of people who consider themselves prominent on the various committees.

But assembling, and then dropping, names was not Bergson's only technique. As young Jabotinsky described it:

We bought a page in *The New York Times* and advertised the Committee for a Jewish Army just as you would advertise Chevrolet motorcars or Players cigarettes. . . . A coupon under the advertisement asked the public to send in their names and a contribution to cover the expenses. The results were so encouraging that we have since kept up a campaign of full-page advertisements throughout the country. . . . We became the best known Jewish organization among the Gentiles.

Direct-mail was only the beginning for Bergson. His winning personality and sense of good fun brought him into contact with all sorts of otherwise unsympathetic New Yorkers. The playwright Ben Hecht was one of his early converts. Hecht conceived a pageant called *We Will Never Die,* enlisting his friends Billy Rose to produce it, Moss Hart to direct, and Kurt Weill to write the music. Its simple message of Jewish heroism drew in the big dramatic stars—Edward G. Robinson, Paul Muni, and a new young actor named Marlon Brando in the role of the biblical David. It opened in Madison Square Garden in March 1943; the touring company then played to sellout crowds across the country. Eleanor Roosevelt, Chief Justice Harlan F. Stone, and seven other Justices of the Supreme Court saw the show in Washington. The dazzling display touched the American public more than a dozen didactic declarations from the American Zionist Emergency Council.

At times, the AZEC seemed to be expending more of its energies attacking Bergson than supporting Zionism. And across Washington from Silver's headquarters were other Zionist activists who frankly wondered where all the commotion was leading.

WEIZMANN NEVER GAVE UP on quiet diplomacy. While Silver and Bergson were coming on atop the hustings, the veteran Zionist proposed the creation of "an operation similar to what we had in London in the years preceding the Balfour Declaration." He wanted to find a gracious home in Washington to which key people could be invited for man-to-man talk. "The social aspect in Washington is of considerable importance," he wrote his friends. He complained to Isaiah Berlin that the strategy of mass meetings and pageants "might impress the Jews, [but] it would not succeed in moving Washington." Berlin agreed. The Bergson crowd was unspeakable but even Silver, Berlin reported, "believed in confrontation, in forcing the American government to resist Britain, not merely on the White Paper, but on and on, until the Jewish state in the whole of western Palestine came into being. . . . Mobilization of the Jewish masses, however successful, could only be an aid to, never a substitute for, negotiation," Berlin concluded. It was the discreet network of contacts across the power centers of the American government that moderate Zionists like Weizmann and Goldmann worked to establish, while the others flexed their muscles in the public arena.

Weizmann found his setting for convivial, but hardly casual, socializing in the Washington house of Israel M. Sieff, a British clothing magnate temporarily resident in the United States. Sieff was an old-time Zionist, active with Weizmann in the Balfour Declaration days. He understood the Weizmann technique of "tending and watering the ground" of officialdom, almost daily. In October 1942, Sieff invited a little group of well-placed Jewish friends to his home in Washington's Cleveland Park, men like Ben Cohen, then serving on the White House staff; the young economist Robert Nathan, on wartime assignment with American intelligence; David Ginsburg, a lawyer and New Deal bureaucrat. They had several meetings. On occasion David Lilienthal, chairman of the Tennessee Valley Authority, would show up, or the man who would turn out to be the most strategic asset of all, David Niles, shy and self-effacing, a White House staff man.

Initially the Sieff group planned to form itself into a scholarly think tank which would publish monographs of economic and social analysis. Isaiah Berlin agreed to supply academic resource materials. Weizmann, however, saw a more imaginative use for all this talent. "It is better for this new group to remain silent," he wrote Sieff. The little nucleus possessed the entree and the clout to carry the message of Jewish Palestine into the highest policymaking circles—through casual suggestion, indirection, chance remarks among well-placed colleagues in the corridors of power and the salons of social Washington.

The Sieff group was a sophisticated version of Brandeis' Parushim; it would grow into the Zionists' back channel through official Washington in the last years of the Roosevelt administration and the crucial opening years of Harry S Truman's presidency. Its existence was never openly acknowledged—just friends having dinner together—yet the members and their diverse contacts well knew who their colleagues were and who to call when problems arose. Officials outside the circle sensed its existence; among the anti-Zionists of the State Department this amorphous little club aroused all the old fears of an international Zionist conspiracy.

Even after Sieff's return to England after the war, the informal group he founded repeatedly demonstrated its influence.

Bergson played to the galleries, Silver and Ben-Gurion shilled the claques, Weizmann and Goldmann worked backstage, and Berlin wrote the critique. The drama was full of subplots.

Silver and Wise were constantly attacking each other. Bergson could not get past the receptionist at the State Department or the British Embassy. Goldmann represented the Jewish Agency in Washington, the "embassy" of the future Jewish state, and as such could make representations to the State Department only as a foreign national. Silver, representing the Zionists of the United States, could not properly be turned away—except that no American official could sit comfortably in his presence. Goldmann would fume when Silver paid a call on the British ambassador, Lord Halifax, and fail to brief him on the discussion afterward —though, as Berlin remarked, "anyone who knew Lord Halifax could be sure that nothing of the slightest importance could have taken place on a topic that he regarded as at once so unimportant and so unsafe." Sympathetic Americans despaired at the conflicting signals with which they were bombarded; legislators who took stands in response to the arguments from one camp would find the Jewish vote diverted by the champions of another. Diplomats hostile to Zionism were cheered by the disarray.

OFF IN the rehearsal hall of the State Department, the officers of the Near East Division were at work on something that could be called the melodrama of the Joint Non-Statement.

The idea of a declaration to "reverse Balfour" had never really died. With Rommel on the offensive in Egypt and the Zionists at the Biltmore refusing to listen to Foreign Service logic, Murray strode into Secretary Hull's office one morning in June 1942 to complain about the "harmful effects of Zionist agitation on the war effort."

Churchill was hearing the same thing from his diplomats. The British High Commissioner in Palestine was urging on Whitehall a new declaration stating that "His Majesty's Government therefore now declare unequivocally that it is not part of their policy that Palestine should become a Jewish State." Churchill was irate. The Arabs "have been virtually no good to us in the present war," he noted. "They have created no new claims on the Allies should we be victorious." In fact, some 33,000 Jews had enlisted in the British Army, despite the White Paper restraints on Jewish immigration, as compared with only 9,000 Arabs. The leader of the Palestinian Arabs, the Mufti of Jerusalem, was openly supporting the Axis cause.

The war threat eased in October 1942, with the successful Allied counteroffensive at El Alamein. But support for a counter-Balfour declaration came to the State Department from an unexpected source—Rabbi Morris Lazaron, articulate leader of anti-Zionist American Jews, a man who had once declared, "It may be that God Himself has brought us to this place to show us that statehood is not the way." Murray was delighted when he heard these sentiments from a refined American of the Hebrew persuasion, and he supported the rabbi's proposal that Welles should write Lazaron, just the way Balfour had written Rothschild, expressing routine sympathies for Jewish sufferings but referring to Palestine as a symbolic center for Muslims and Christians as well as Jews. Such a letter, Lazaron suggested, would "stop this reckless Zionist agitation."

Once again Welles sat on the anti-Zionist proposal, but he let the fourteen officers of the Near East Division draft contingency statements in coordination with their British colleagues. By June 1943, diplomats in London and Washington had achieved their goal. Agreement was reached that at noon on July 27, 1943, the world would be told that Britain and the United States had "taken note of public discussions and activities of a political nature relating to Palestine and consider that it would be helpful to the war effort if these were to cease."

What happened next was "an absolutely clinical case of how things are done in Washington nowadays," Isaiah Berlin reported. "You may be sure that the Catholic and every other lobby uses precisely the same methods." He told the story in a long dispatch to Whitehall a fortnight later.

Berlin began by noting that it was Goldmann, not one of his own British Embassy colleagues, who first tipped him off "that something 'disagreeable' (he did not know what) was being planned in London. I expressed total (and quite honest) ignorance." Anglo-American negotiations on the statement had proceeded in such secrecy that even a political counselor like Berlin had not been brought into that tight circle. Then word came that an uninvolved Assistant Secretary of State, Dean Acheson, had given a pro-Zionist senator to understand that the subject of Zionist agitation was being discussed at the White House. That chance intelligence raised a red alarm. The senator's Jewish Agency contacts promptly got word to Wise, who as promptly went to see his friend Roosevelt. Berlin continued the saga:

"Wise told his followers that the President had reassured him completely. . . . At first there was much Zionist joy; then . . . the Zionists decided to check up, and after extensive consultations with various Janissaries, Sam Rosenman . . . was persuaded to make a cautious inquiry.

His story . . . blew the lid off in Zionist circles." This, Berlin reported, was just one day before the scheduled publication date of July 27. Wise, Goldmann, and their colleagues started mobilizing all their contacts across the government, the guests at the Sieff house, such dinner companions as Ben Cohen, Felix Frankfurter, Henry Morgenthau, Jr., and the White House staff man David Niles. No one seemed to know quite what was happening, but all agreed that whatever it was, it should be stopped.

On the morning of July 27, with only hours to go before publication of the joint statement, the British Embassy was informed that there would have to be a week's delay. Something had obviously gone wrong, and Berlin scurried around to find out what it was. "The State Department, or someone in it," he learned,

> had suddenly got cold feet about publishing the statement as a purely political document, which would expose them to violent attack by Jews and liberals. . . . Mr. Hull is almost neurotically sensitive to criticism. They therefore wrote to the War Department saying that what they wanted was a specific and clear request from the Army for a statement of this kind on strict security grounds. As the American G2 had been pressing for a damper on Zionist agitation, the soldiers were apparently only too willing to give the green light.

Berlin's information was good as far as it went. For months the Military Intelligence Division of the War Department (G2) had warned that pro-Zionist statements by American politicians "must be stopped at once" or "we most certainly will alienate" the Arabs and thus endanger American forces in the Middle East. But Berlin did not know that Secretary of War Henry L. Stimson harbored a deep distrust of his G2 assessments, recalling their defeatist tone about Britain at the start of the war and their contempt of Churchill as a strategist. When the joint statement came to his desk, Stimson had no qualms about overruling his intelligence officers as "alarmist."

The State Department's wish to involve the War Department "may have been a sound self-protecting move," Berlin reported,

> but with surprising innocence they seemed not to have taken into account the usual Washington factors. . . . Two things happened almost immediately: Morgenthau . . . told [the Zionists] he would do his best to stop it; he added that if HMG are anxious about security in Palestine they must ask USG for more troops, and not seek to deprive U.S. citizens of their constitutional liberties of freedom of speech; never before in the history of the United

States had any such attempt been made to silence a minority of citizens, etc. etc. etc. . . . Meanwhile Herbert Bayard Swope, who is somehow connected with War Department public relations, saw the file in a routine fashion. Swope is a Jewish assimilationist and anti-Zionist, but seems to have reacted rather like Rosenman . . . [and] argued somewhat oddly that if it was indeed true that the Jews in Palestine were straining at the leash and Arab-Jewish riots might break out at any moment, the publication of this document would be the very thing to set them off. In the case, the Jews would inevitably be blamed for the ensuing bloodshed and obstruction of the Allied military effort. The wave of unpopularity would overtake them here and not discriminate between Zionists and non-Zionists. Above all, therefore, things must be kept quiet.

Swope went straight to his longtime mentor, Bernard Baruch. "Baruch agreed that anything said about Jews at the present moment would increase U.S. antisemitism, which was anyhow rising fast, and is worrying people like Baruch intensely," Berlin continued.

Swope then persuaded Under Secretary of War [Robert P.] Patterson, who probably has no views either way, that politically the War Department was 'silly to stick its neck out' quite unnecessarily by accepting responsibility for a dubious move of this kind—the Jews would be very upset, etc., and there would be a political brouhaha of the first order. If the State Department wanted to ask for trouble let them do so without bringing the War Department in. In the meantime Morgenthau seems to have persuaded Stimson of this also, and Baruch had a talk with his old friend Cordell Hull. . . . A pincer movement by Messrs. Baruch and Morgenthau (who don't, in fact, get on with each other at all well) had its effect.

Halifax, the British ambassador, had a chat with Secretary Hull and, as Berlin reported, Hull said "that he had always had his qualms on the advisability of such a statement (I very much doubt this) and, as Stimson would not do his bit of it, he thought it on the whole wiser not to proceed. And that," Isaiah Berlin concluded, "was that." The joint statement was never issued.

The experts in the State Department felt themselves once again outmaneuvered; the political leadership had again intervened. The episode festered, just like Lansing's rebuffs from Wilson and Hugh Gibson's dressing down in Paris. A new generation of American diplomats had what they considered to be good reason to resent Zionist influences, and fully two years later Murray's deputy, Paul H. Alling, would still complain that "a joint American-British statement, the exact text of which had been agreed upon as being in the national interest by the highest political authorities of both countries, was killed by the American Zionist pressure group."

The foreign policy community campaigned against the pressures of the Zionist lobby throughout the government, in the committee rooms of Capitol Hill, in the discreet and clubby study groups of New York's Council on Foreign Relations. The diplomats saw themselves as martyred by domestic politics; the military men worried about the strategic posture of the eastern Mediterranean. And all sides wondered about the future of Middle Eastern oil.

American oil companies saw to it that they were represented by their own personnel in the highest policymaking circles, so that friendly viewpoints could be injected at appropriate moments. Years later a congressional committee uncovered evidence of the oil companies' penetration. Max Thornburg, a vice-president of the Bahrein Petroleum Company, was one of these "moles"; he served in the early war years as a special assistant to Welles, and continued to receive financial retainers from oil interests even while he served on the government payroll. In return, he was adept at devising his own back channels. In letters to his Standard Oil of California superiors, Thornburg regularly reported on policy discussions with officers of the Near East Division, and related how he had spoken for the oil interests in various meetings which he attended as a government staff officer.

Toward the war's end, the diplomats perceived a new threat to America's strategic position in the Middle East. A now embittered Murray seized on every scrap of evidence to argue that "Soviet prestige is already rising in the Arab world like a star in the east," and he urged the American ambassador in Moscow, W. Averell Harriman, to take up the question of future Soviet intentions with Roosevelt. But 1944 was an election year, and none of the experts' strategic calculations could hold the politicians back. In a clear bid for the urban vote, both Republican and Democratic party platforms carried strong pro-Zionist planks on Palestine.

The experts in the State Department were nonplussed. "If we were actually to implement the policy which the Zionists desire, the results would be disastrous," wrote Alling. Breaking through the restraint customary in formal memoranda, the deputy director of the Near East Division poured out his frustrations:

The President's attitude on Palestine makes it difficult for us. The situation is so serious, and the adverse effect upon our long-term position in the Near East so likely, that we should reconsider our entire position, adopt a definite policy on Palestine, and obtain the President's concurrence, with the hope of averting any future misunderstandings as to what our policy actually is.

But the experts stood no chance of getting the President's concurrence to anything at that point. Alling wrote his appeal on April 5, 1945; a week later, Roosevelt was dead.

8

A FEW MINUTES after five on the afternoon of April 12, 1945, just after recessing the Senate for the day, Vice-President Truman received an urgent telephone summons to the White House. Arriving at 5:25, he was ushered directly to Mrs. Roosevelt's study on the second floor. From her he heard the words: "Harry, the President is dead." Ninety minutes later, surrounded by the highest officers of the Roosevelt Cabinet, some of them weeping openly, Truman of Missouri took the oath of office and became the thirty-third President of the United States. The affairs of the nation—and of much of a dazed world—were in the care of an obscure politician of sixty-one who had kicked around all his professional life without convincing anyone outside his most intimate circle that he was a man to be taken seriously in his own right.

For all their differences, Roosevelt and Truman shared one thing—a happy childhood in a nurturing family. The Truman boyhood home was as decent and proper in the setting of the American Midwest as Roosevelt's in the Hudson Valley. Yankee newcomers in search of their fortunes flocked to the boom town of Kansas City, six miles to the west; settled families preferred the peace of the small pioneer community of Independence, where the big north bend of the Missouri connected with the old Sante Fe and Oregon trails.

Truman was actually born in Lamar, down toward the Arkansas line, a market center of 800 where the Ozark farmers would gather every Saturday to stock up on provisions. When he was six years old, his father had prospered enough to move his mule- and horse-trading business to more inviting territory. In 1890 he bought one of the Victorian manses on Crysler Street in Independence, a spacious setting for what Truman always remembered as a thoroughly agreeable childhood. Even poor eyesight could not inhibit the future President's passion for reading. The big print in the family Bible enticed him at the age of five, and by twelve he had read the Scriptures through twice. "The stories in the Bible . . .

were to me stories about real people," Truman recalled in his old age. "I felt I knew some of them better than actual people I knew." His prized boyhood possession was an eight-volume set of 200 biographical essays entitled "Great Men and Famous Women," edited by Charles Francis Horne. Here he learned of heroes and heroines through the ages, from Solomon and David of Israel all the way to Oliver Wendell Holmes and Sarah Bernhardt. The evangelist William E. Blackstone had used the saga of Cyrus and the restoration of the Jews to stir up the enthusiasm of successive Presidents of his day, but young Harry Truman knew the whole story from the books of Isaiah, Ezra, and Daniel, and from "Great Men and Famous Women." He had shuddered at old Nebuchadnezzar's wickedness, and thrilled at the readiness of Cyrus to let the Jewish exiles in Babylon return to Palestine and found their second commonwealth 2,500 years ago.

Truman's passion for biography formed his lifelong preference for real people over abstract ideas. As Roosevelt grew into the family's concept of noblesse oblige, so Truman absorbed from an early age the forceful concept of fair play, the supreme virtue in the small towns of the American Midwest. Your neighbor's opinions were not nearly as important as the fact that he was, and would continue to be, your neighbor. In the big eastern cities, a man could cleave to the like-minded; small-town America offered no such luxury. In the East, public figures could afford to stake out firm positions; in the Midwest, it was more important to be amiable, to be well received by all, to hold strong views, perhaps, but not to let them stand in the way of friendship. Henry Wallace, who had his share of disputes with Truman, gave his amazed impression of the result of this characteristic in the behavior of the man from Missouri. "I suspect there has never been a President who could move two different directions with less time intervening than Truman. He feels completely sincere and earnest at all times and is not disturbed in the slightest by the different directions in which his mind can go almost simultaneously."

ROOSEVELT KNEW the land of the Bible, Truman knew the people. The Jews of the American heartland were part of the life of Independence— it was a Jewish merchant who had sold Truman's father the house on Crysler Street—and for all its gentility, the town was not homogeneous. Besides the Baptists and Presbyterians with whom Truman grew up (including the blond blue-eyed girl named Bess whom he met at Sunday school), there was the Catholic community and the Mormons who called Independence their Zion (until a rebellious faction under Brigham Young headed further west to the Utah Territory).

The Jews did not put themselves forward. "I do not recall that they ever attempted to practice their religion; certainly not in public," wrote a Missouri-bred author, Herbert Asbury. But the state universities and southern schools showed little of the antisemitism then fashionable in the East. "When I was a boy in a midwestern town the few Jews there were regarded as other people, equally respectable and personable . . . ," recalled a contributor to *The Atlantic Monthly*. "Since their standard of character and manners happened to be uncommonly high, they were much looked up to. As for social discrimination against the Jew *qua* Jew, there was none even among us children."

Truman was a twenty-one-year-old bookkeeper in a Kansas City bank when he met a Jew whose friendship would remain important to him— and, in the event, to the Jewish people. Eddie Jacobson was fourteen, a stock boy whose flair for merchandising attracted Truman's notice. Nothing held them together at that juncture, and only the mobilization for a world war threw them back into contact. In the 129th Field Artillery, Truman was a lieutenant and Jacobson a sergeant. Truman promptly put the young man in charge of the battery mess and canteen. Their collaboration brought them distinction in their regiment, and after returning home from the wars in France they formalized their partnership by opening a haberdashery business together.

For all their professional and personal intimacy, Truman never once invited Jacobson and his wife, Bluma, to dinner at the family home. The Wallaces, Bess Truman's family, were "aristocracy in these parts," explained Bluma Jacobson, "and under the circumstances the Trumans couldn't afford to have Jews at their house." Amiability, it seems, had its limits.

The collapse of farm prices in 1921 drove the Truman-Jacobson haberdashery partnership into bankruptcy and, while Jacobson stuck to the only profession he knew, Truman branched out. An insolvent veteran by now aged thirty-eight, he had failed in almost everything he had tried, but he was a joiner and he was amiable, and those were the qualities that counted. Truman helped to organize the American Legion in Missouri; he joined the Masons, the National Guard, and the Farm Bureau. Perhaps, he thought, he would be suited for a minor post in local politics, then in the firm grip of the machine run by boss Tom Pendergast, a man of general benevolence mixed with specific self-interest. Pendergast made a deep impression on Truman; he sprang immediately to mind years later when President Truman met Stalin.

One local group caused problems. The Ku Klux Klan was a civic organization that upwardly mobile young Missouri men found inviting. The Klansmen discovered that Truman's grandfather's name was Solomon—suspiciously Jewish-sounding—but they were willing to overlook this and offered him membership. Truman thought about it, and declined. The Klan, he discovered, believed that some people should be excluded, and that was not amiable. In one of his later political campaigns, Klan opponents seized upon Grandfather Solomon to spread rumors that Truman was partly Jewish. Truman retorted bluntly: "I am not Jewish, but if I were I would not be ashamed of it."

The Jews of Truman's Midwest were not important politically. They never amounted to more than 6 percent of Pendergast's Jackson County electorate. For all their growing social respectability, they held themselves aloof from national and international affairs. As aspiring Americans, they regarded Zionism and such foreign movements with suspicion. It took one of Missouri's senators, Selden P. Spencer (whom Truman would later succeed in office), to tell the Jewish community of Kansas City about the prospects opened up by the Balfour Declaration. The senator advised a skeptical Rabbi Glazer of Kansas City in 1921 that "the people of Israel will get Palestine with or without the consent of our State Department."

In 1922, with machine backing, Truman was elected Jackson County administrator, then lost two years later when the Klan turned against him. This proved to be the only time in his life he lost an election. Restless, nervous about supporting a wife and new baby daughter, the defeated "Judge" Truman enrolled at Kansas City Law School. When the financial strain proved to be too much after only two years, he dropped out and accepted a Pendergast offer to run again for county office. He won the election of 1926 and proceeded to serve for the next eight years as a diligent, strangely independent-minded politician who managed to keep himself aloof from the increasing corruption of the machine.

In 1934 there seemed nothing of the slightest national significance in the political career of Harry S Truman. In that year, however, Pendergast wanted a more pliable man to run Jackson County; perhaps Truman could be sent off to the United States Senate far away. Pendergast saw to it that he won that election.

Truman arrived in Washington in November 1934, an outspoken supporter of the new President Roosevelt and his New Deal. But he found his reception chilly; he was, after all, just the "senator from Pendergast," with neither wealth nor charisma to recommend him, as he made a round of courtesy calls. At the White House, he got no further than Roosevelt's press secretary, and that after a five months' wait. Truman announced his plan to enroll in night classes—a sitting United States senator—at Georgetown Law School, in order to finish the degree work he had been forced to abandon years before. He was determined to keep his feet on the ground, he told the Kansas City Elks Club. "All this precedence and other hooey accorded a Senator isn't very good for the Republic. The association with dressed-up diplomats has turned the heads of more than one Senator, I can tell you." Something about diplomats turned him off from the start.

Truman was named to an obscure subcommittee dealing with interstate commerce. There he met a savvy staff expert named Max Lowenthal, who, impressed with the new senator's confidence in the face of political pressure, offered to introduce him to his revered friend, Supreme Court Justice Brandeis. "I'm not used to meeting people like that," Truman replied, but reluctantly agreed to go along. Brandeis was then over eighty, but had not lost his sharpness of mind or his eagerness to explore the potentialities of promising new people. The feisty junior senator from Missouri hardly fit the pattern of Brandeis' "college men," but there was something attractive about this homespun Farm Bureau politician. After their first meeting, Truman was invited back; they discussed their common interest in protecting the common man against the exploitations of big capital. "The old man would back me into a corner and pay no attention to anybody else while he talked transportation to me," Truman recalled. To Truman, Brandeis was as great a jurist as Oliver Wendell Holmes, known only from boyhood reading, and now here they were in friendly conversation.

It would be tempting to imagine that the subject of Zionism came up as Truman and Brandeis held their spirited conversations in the late 1930s. There is no evidence that it did, and no real reason that it would. The Jewish fate was an enduring interest for Brandeis, but it was not his only interest. For Truman, Zionism was uncharted territory. His thinking about restoring the Jews to Palestine stopped with Nebuchadnezzar and the Emperor Cyrus. "The Hebrews had a republic three or four thousand years ago that was almost ideal in its practical workings," he wrote his schoolgirl daughter, Margaret. "Yet they tired of it and went to a monarchy or totalitarian state. So did Greece, Carthage, Rome. . . . I'm glad you like Ancient History—wish I could study it again with you."

Growing secure in Washington by the late 1930s, Truman heard reports about Jews that no amiable politician believing in fair play could ignore. Hitler's antisemitism was disturbing, but Britain struck him as wrong in the way it handled its mandate over Palestine. Within a week of the 1939 White Paper, Truman spoke on the Senate floor against Whitehall's arbitrary restriction on Jewish immigration. "It made a scrap of paper out of Balfour's promise," he said. "It has just added another to the long list of surrenders to the Axis powers." In 1941, Truman joined the pro-Zionist American Christian Palestine Committee.

That wily entrepreneur Peter Bergson decided to make a special effort to cultivate the midwestern senator. On his own, Bergson had decided to play down the theme of Jewish statehood. He proposed instead as an immediate goal a Jewish Army in Palestine to fight alongside the Allies. Truman disapproved, saying, "I think the best thing for the Jews to do is to go right into our Army as they did in the last war and make the same sort of good soldiers as they did before." Bergson refused to let the matter drop, and paid several calls on Truman to enlist his support. Truman eventually succumbed, and let his name be used by the envoy of the Irgun. He had no interest in the feuds among the Jews—none of Bergson's newspaper advertisements caused any stir in Missouri—but after a year he abruptly withdrew. The reason was not ideological, but simply the sort of personal slight to a friend that Truman inevitably took seriously: Bergson had placed an advertisement critical of a Senate colleague. Despite Bergson's apology, it was the end of Truman's backing of the Irgun.

By 1944, Truman had become more cautious about associating himself with causes that he was not sure he understood. While seventy-seven other senators endorsed the goal of a Jewish commonwealth, Truman held back, exhibiting the same caution as Roosevelt's White House: "My sympathy, of course, is with the Jewish people," he explained, but "a resolution such as this should be very circumspectly handled until we know just exactly where we are going and why. I don't want to throw any bricks to upset the applecart, although when the right time comes I am willing to help make the fight for a Jewish Homeland in Palestine."

"When the right time comes"—the formula Wilson had used nearly three decades before. And, as with Wilson, the "right time" came sooner than anyone expected. For, to the astonishment of the nation, Roosevelt chose the obscure junior senator from Missouri to be his running mate for his fourth, and surely final, campaign for the presidency.

Truman was sworn in as Vice-President of the United States in January 1945, a post he was to hold for only eighty-two days. Even in executive office, he was not taken seriously by the Roosevelt inner circle. He saw the President alone only twice and he was never briefed—let alone consulted—on any of the Chief Executive's planning for the momentous decisions of the postwar world.

But one subject was raised with him, a subject that tantalized Truman. The Middle East was on Roosevelt's mind in those last months after his discouraging meeting with Ibn Saud, and according to Truman, Roo-

sevelt asked him to make a tour of the area, the sort of orientation visit
that Roosevelt himself hoped to make when he retired. The vice-presi-
dential mission had been vaguely planned for April, Truman said later,
the month of Roosevelt's death, and he "regretted immeasurably" that it
never came about. One can wonder what Truman might have done dif-
ferently if, as President, he had approached the Palestine problem from
the experience of an official tour across the Arab world.

THE FACT OF TRUMAN as President of the United States astonished the
Zionists as much as everyone else. "Coming from the Midwest I doubt
whether the President has any connection and relationship to Jews,"
commented Ben-Gurion. "I doubt whether our friends in Washington
will continue to have the same contacts also with the new President."
Weizmann learned that "there has been little contact" with Truman,
though "whatever contact there was, it has been friendly." The archivists
at AZEC pored over their files, but unfortunately found that they had
neglected this obscure Midwesterner.

From their side, the State Department wasted no time in putting the
inexperienced new Chief Executive on notice that Palestine was a diplomatic minefield. Just six days into his presidency, Truman received a
brief memorandum from the Secretary of State. On its face, the communication was innocuous; in the way it was received, it made an impact of
enduring and far-reaching consequence—and not at all along the lines
the diplomats intended.

"My Dear Mr. President," began Secretary Stettinius.

> It is very likely that efforts will be made by some of the Zionist
> leaders to obtain from you at an early date some commitments in
> favor of the Zionist program. . . . The question of Palestine is,
> however, a highly complex one and involves questions which go
> far beyond the plight of the Jews in Europe. If this question shall
> come up, therefore, before you in the form of a request to make a
> public commitment on the matter, I believe you would probably
> want to call for full and detailed information on the subject before
> taking any particular position. . . . There is continual tenseness
> in the situation in the Near East largely as a result of the Palestine
> question and as we have interests in that area which are vital to
> the United States, we feel that this whole subject is one that
> should be handled with the greatest care and with a view to the
> long-range interests of this country.

Perhaps the layers of experts accustomed to drafting messages for presidential attention honestly thought they were being helpful and responsive to the needs of the moment. But they did not yet know Harry Truman. In their patronizing tone, appropriate from a board of senior prefects to a new boy in the lower form, the Palestine experts committed in the first week a miscalculation from which their relations with the President would never recover. "In those days nobody seemed to think I was aware of anything," Truman recalled some twenty-five years later. His memory of that memorandum was still vivid: "a communication from some of the 'striped-pants' boys warning me . . . in effect telling me to watch my step, that I didn't really understand what was going on over there and that I ought to leave it to the 'experts'. . . ."

As a junior senator, Truman had always been suspicious of elegantly dressed diplomats. Closer acquaintance brought no reassurance, at least on the Palestine issue. "I had carefully read the Balfour Declaration," he wrote. "I had familiarized myself with the history of the question of a Jewish homeland and the position of the British and the Arabs. I was skeptical, as I read over the whole record up to date, about some of the views and attitudes assumed by the 'striped-pants boys' in the State Department." Some of them, Truman wrote, were plainly antisemitic.

The new President ignored the State Department's warnings and, just two days later, received a Zionist delegation at the White House. It was a courtesy call, lasting a mere fifteen minutes, but long enough for Truman to reassure the Zionists that he would follow Roosevelt's policy —a dubious reassurance, since neither Truman nor his visitors really knew what that policy was.

With the end of the war in Europe, the forthcoming San Francisco Conference to set up the new United Nations Organization, and, most ominously, the imminence of a new secret atomic weapon of war to be used against Japan, Truman paid no further attention to the "experts' " warnings on Palestine. He routinely signed letters that the State Department put before him, including assurances to Arab leaders which had been prepared for Roosevelt's signature the day he died. Several more memoranda came over from State offering to brief the President on details of Middle East policy, all of which Truman ignored.

Meanwhile Zionist public agitation continued unabated. Under prodding from Rabbi Silver's apparatus, legislatures of 33 states, representing 85 percent of the national population, passed resolutions favoring a Jewish state in Palestine. Governors of 37 states, 54 United States senators, and 250 congressmen signed petitions to the President. Operationally, these were meaningless; they played no role in a specific decision-making process. Psychologically, their effect was cumulative; they set a tone for public discussion.

One friend whom the President could not hold at arm's length as he did the "striped-pants boys," Senator Robert Wagner of New York, urged Truman to discuss Jewish statehood with Churchill and Stalin at Potsdam. And in a pre-summit briefing memorandum, the Zionist leadership made an argument that stayed in Truman's mind. "Granted the determination of the Great Powers and their readiness to use force if necessary," argued this Zionist brief, "the need for its actual employment in implementing a just decision in Palestine will, apart from some minor and sporadic outbreaks, not arise." Perhaps not, but even the suggestion that American military backing might be required to establish the Jewish state did not sit well with Truman in the postwar exhaustion.

Americans—even American Jews—were sending mixed signals to the new President. Judge Proskauer of New York, under whose leadership the American Jewish Committee was firmly resisting Zionism, wrote Truman to argue that a sovereign Jewish state was not the best redress for the tribulations of centuries past. He described his final meeting with Roosevelt back in March, at which the late President "saw in the extreme Zionist agitation grave danger for the world and for Palestine itself." Like Roosevelt, Truman was besieged by conflicting viewpoints without a firm grasp of the facts that would help him make up his mind; as often happens with a preoccupied executive, he tended to believe whoever spoke to him last. This put a premium on regular and frequent access to the President, a luxury enjoyed by neither Zionists nor their adversaries in the Department of State.

Returning home from Potsdam, Truman revealed his concern in an offhand remark at a news conference. Diplomatic efforts with the British and the Arabs were essential, he said, "so that if a [Jewish] state can be set up they may be able to set it up on a peaceful basis—I have no desire to send 500,000 American soldiers there to make peace in Palestine." With that throwaway line, and even the hint of a threatened American military role, Truman tumbled the Zionists into disarray. Rabbi Silver lambasted the President for succumbing to scare talk about an Arab "military menace"; other Zionist officials spread the word that Truman had simply been listening to oil executives out to promote their pro-Arab positions. The Zionists seemed to have forgotten that great-power military commitment, even if only as a deterrent, had been raised in their own presidential brief.

The Near East Division seized upon the news conference remark to work up alarming assessments of the military force that might be required to maintain order in Palestine. Drafting a worst-case scenario, the State

Department got the War Department to say that 400,000 men might be required on an open-ended basis, causing "an indefinite delay in the demobilization of the U.S. Army forces." But other assessments came at the same time. British and American military analysts familiar with the Palestine scene reported that while the Arab Legion of Jordan was a serious military force, the militia of the Jewish community was equally serious and stood fully capable of defending itself against the strongest attack it would be likely to encounter. These assessments were buried; they did not suit diplomats who remained convinced that the specter of a massive American military commitment remained their most powerful rallying cry against Zionism.

A further news conference remark by Truman triggered more serious international complications. In September 1945, he said that he had looked "very carefully" through the correspondence with Ibn Saud and found no commitment from Roosevelt or the United States regarding Palestine and continuing good relations with the Arab world. Truman should have listened to those State Department briefings after all, for the complicated record of the Roosevelt–Ibn Saud exchanges was one of the matters the experts were most eager to put before him. The Arabian King considered the new President's statement a breach of faith; he published the letters he had received from Roosevelt, and Truman had to endure a wave of Zionist complaints about his predecessor's hypocrisy.

This was the moment when Truman began his own file on Palestine, and he kept it for years to come in the right-hand drawer of his desk.

Truman was harassed and worried when he received Rabbis Silver and Wise together on September 29, 1945. "The war is far from over," he told them; negotiations with the Russians were not going well. He complained about all the "ethnic pressure" bearing down on him from Poles, Italians, Jews. The Jews should have patience, he told Silver and Wise.

The White House mailroom reported an increased volume of correspondence concerning Palestine, including many form letters of the kind the Jewish lobby was experienced at stimulating. Truman's mother in Missouri relayed the request of a Jewish friend for favorable attention to the Palestine dilemma. Truman wrote back testily: "There isn't a possibility of my intervening in the matter. These people are the usual European conspirators and they try to approach the President from every angle." He warned his mother: "Don't let anybody talk to you about foreign affairs."

On December 4, 1945, Truman agreed to meet Weizmann for the first time. Ever mindful of approaching authority under the best possible auspices, the elder statesman of Zionism arranged to be escorted to the

White House by the British ambassador, the Earl of Halifax. The meeting was brief, marked by none of the mellow cordiality of their later conversations. Truman interrupted Weizmann's well-rehearsed remarks to say that he did not think the Jewish problem should be viewed in terms of Palestine alone, and he deprecated Weizmann's use of the term "Jewish state" instead of "Palestine state." Truman feared a "theocracy," Halifax reported, and had learned that Zionism stirred doubt among Jewish-Americans who were "not at all keen on the Palestine solution."

For just before Weizmann came in, Truman had received two other Jewish visitors: Lessing J. Rosenwald, president of the anti-Zionist American Council for Judaism, and J. David Stern, publisher of the Philadelphia *Record,* a maverick Zionist. Rosenwald argued that Palestine should "not be a Moslem, Christian, or a Jewish state, but . . . a country in which people of all faiths can play their full and equal part." And Stern was authorized to say as he left the White House that Truman opposed the establishment of Palestine "as a state based on Judaism for the same reason that he would oppose basing it on the Moslem religion or the Baptist denomination. He would throw open Palestine to Jews, Arabs, and Christians alike under a truly democratic government in which all sects would participate."

A few days later, Weizmann tried one further approach to the President. In a seven-page, single-spaced typewritten letter, he fell back on the well-polished persuasion that had so moved Balfour and British statesmen in earlier years. "There never was the intention on the part of those who can speak for the Jews of Palestine and for the overwhelming majority of Jews in the diaspora that Palestine should become a 'religious' or theocratic state," Weizmann pledged. "When we speak of a Jewish state we place no stress on the religion of the individuals who will form the majority of its inhabitants, but we have in mind a secular state based on sound democratic foundations with political machinery and institutions on the pattern of those in the United States and in Western Europe."

As he reached his first Christmas season in the White House, Truman was as perplexed as Roosevelt had been about the Holy Land. He is "greatly disturbed about this thing," said his new Secretary of State, James F. Byrnes, but just as clearly he determined to hold the lines of Palestine policy in his own hands, and not rely on the diplomats. From his first weeks in office, he had viewed the problem through a lens quite different from that of the State Department, different even from that of the American Jewish leaders with their endless feuds and status-seeking. A sovereign state, a "theocratic" state, the Biltmore program—these were abstractions of political theory that troubled Truman but did not really provoke him to action. On his mind was another aspect of the Jewish fate, the human fate of hundreds of thousands of despairing, uprooted people left behind by the Nazis. "My only interest," Truman told an old Senate friend in a moment of candor, "is to find some proper way to take care of these displaced persons, not only because they should be taken care of and are in a pitiful plight, but because it is to our own financial interest to have them taken care of because we are feeding most of them."

Without knowing how closely he was hitting the right chord, Weizmann argued that "Zionism clearly aimed at ending the abnormality of the Jewish people—its homelessness. . . . We believe that a great deal of what is tragic in Jewish history is the result of that homelessness." Give us back our home, Weizmann pleaded.

WHEN ALLIED armies entered the Nazi death camp of Buchenwald, the fact of the Holocaust came home to America. On April 15, four days later, Bergen-Belsen was liberated, then Dachau on April 29. With the American soldiers was CBS correspondent Edward R. Murrow; millions of Americans stared at their radio sets as Murrow's sonorous voice opened his live report from Dachau with the strangely portentous and ominous words: "I pray that you will believe me." The reality discovered by the Western armies in the ruins of the "final solution" defied objective description. Seasoned, toughened war correspondents lost all semblance of self-control as they reported what lay before their eyes.

Starvation and disease were rampant throughout the fallen SS domain. Even after it was liberated, some 13,000 prisoners, mostly Jews, died in Bergen-Belsen. The care of a huge, maltreated population was not a contingency adequately foreseen by the advancing Allied armies. Altogether eight million displaced persons were found in Germany and Nazi-occupied Europe at the end of World War II. Most of them were slave laborers, transported to fuel the Nazi industrial machine; most had their towns and families to which they could return, and so they did in vast numbers. By August five million had gone home, another million by the end of 1945.

But some 50,000 people in this human mass were different. They were Jews, liberated from the concentration camps of Germany and Austria but possessing no homes that awaited their return. A few straggled back in search of their former towns and villages in Poland or Germany; most had no heart even to try. For the Jews of Palestine and the West, this surviving population was accorded the near-mystical title of *Sheerith Haptelah,* the redeeming remnant of European Jewry which deserved the chance to start life anew.

Well before the end of the war, in November 1944, Weizmann had discussed with Churchill a plan to permit some 100,000 immigrants to enter Palestine each year, a figure first mentioned by the American United Palestine Appeal as far back as 1938. It seemed a number plucked from the air, but it soon became the focus of a bitter feud between the American and British governments. Six weeks after VE Day, the Jewish Agency officially demanded that Britain place 100,000 entry permits at its disposal, a request which if granted would effectively countermand the British White Paper policy to assure the Arabs a perpetual majority in Palestine. Non-Zionist Jews, however, were not so ready to grant the Jewish Agency proprietary interest in the survivors of European Jewry. Did anyone know where the survivors themselves wanted to live?

The answer was not as automatic as retrospect—and Zionist faith— now implies. "What if Canada, Australia, South America, England, and the United States were all to open a door to some migration?" asked Morris Ernst, a prominent non-Zionist in New York. "Only a minority of the Jewish DPs would choose Palestine." During the war, in 1943, American intelligence agents reported that German-Jewish refugees who had settled in Palestine after fleeing the Nazis fully intended to return to Germany after the war. The Foreign Secretary of Britain's postwar Labour Party government, Ernest Bevin, asked if it was really right "that the Jews should be driven out of Europe." Even Churchill, whose record of sympathy for Zionism was long-standing and demonstrable, told the House of Commons that "the idea that the Jewish problem could be solved or even helped by a vast dumping of the Jews of Europe into Palestine is really too silly to consume our time in the House this afternoon." And the American State Department continued to warn of Zionist attempts to exploit the human tragedy of Europe's Jews for narrow nationalist ends.

The Jewish survivors of the Holocaust, in short, were a special problem even for sincere and well-meaning policymakers. The *Sheerith Haptelah* was not in itself an edifying body of people, as the American occupation authorities quickly discovered. Most were in pitiful physical, mental and moral condition after the horrors so recently undergone. It was sometimes difficult even for the best-intentioned of outsiders to determine whether this was a responsible body of individuals who had fallen upon hard times or a subhuman mass from which little or no responsible judgments could be expected.

Faced with the news of Buchenwald, Bergen-Belsen, and Dachau, Treasury Secretary Morgenthau urged Truman to raise the problem of the displaced persons before the Cabinet during his first month in office. But the new President had no fondness for Morgenthau, and almost as little interest in anything he proposed as in the advice of the diplomats. Harassed and preoccupied with the war in the Pacific and the burden of deploying an atomic weapon, Truman let Morgenthau's suggestion drop. A short time later, he agreed to a seemingly straightforward proposal from the State Department (he did not know that it was Morgenthau who had put the Department up to the idea) to send an emissary on a fact-finding tour of the DP camps.

Passing over a candidate proposed by Morgenthau's Zionist contacts, the State Department nominated Earl G. Harrison, dean of the University of Pennsylvania Law School, Commissioner of Immigration and Naturalization during World War II, and director of the wartime census of enemy aliens. A proven administrative professional, Harrison had demonstrated experience in politically sensitive situations, and he had no preconceptions about the problems of Jews in Europe or Palestine. From a modest beginning, the Harrison mission in the summer of 1945 had an enduring impact upon Truman's Palestine policy. More than any other single event, it defined the issue for three years to come.

Certain alert Zionists had spotted the potential of the Harrison mission from the start. To Weizmann and his American associate, Meyer W. Weisgal, this objective but idealistic law professor could become an instrument for combining the political aspirations of Zionism with the plight of the surviving Jews of Europe. Weisgal was frequently in touch with Morgenthau. Early in June, just after Truman had dismissed Morgenthau's first suggestion and the Treasury Secretary was raising the DP matter with State Department colleagues, Weisgal reported to Weizmann that Morgenthau had been "very kind and cooperative in a certain important matter he was asked to do." (With censorship and uncertain international mails, indirection was the norm for sensitive correspondence.) Shortly thereafter, Harrison was summoned to Washington for briefings from Morgenthau's associates on the War Refugee Board. On June 21 he accepted the mission "to ascertain the needs of stateless and non-repatriables, particularly Jews, among the displaced persons in Germany."

No one spoke yet of Palestine in this connection. The Near East Division of the State Department was not even invited to meetings concerning the problems of European Jews, for displaced persons and Palestine were still held to be separate and distinct issues. But Weisgal knew otherwise. Recognizing in Harrison a man completely unacquainted with the particular subtleties of this mission, for all his general experience, Weisgal suggested to Morgenthau that the envoy be accompanied by someone "thoroughly steeped in the Jewish situation." He proposed Joseph J. Schwartz, European director of the Joint Distribution Committee, foremost among the voluntary organizations in aiding Jewish homeless. It was an inspired choice. Aside from Schwartz's expertise in refugee matters, his organization had been distinctly non-Zionist, sometimes even anti-Zionist, from the days of its founder, Felix Warburg. A man from "the Joint" could never be suspected of imposing improper Zionist pressure on the fact-finding mission. Yet Weisgal knew his man. Speaking for himself and Weizmann, Weisgal wrote confidentially that "although Dr. Schwartz is on the staff of the JDC, we have absolute faith in his integrity and Zionist convictions."

Harrison was not unaware of the interests converging on him. The head of the War Refugee Board, John Pehle, told him frankly that his investigation had been urged by "political Zionists." While Morgenthau himself was "primarily concerned with the problem of the needs of these displaced people," Pehle said, "the Zionist groups are primarily interested in obtaining information concerning the desire of these people to emigrate from Europe."

Harrison arrived in Europe early in July. The U.S. Third Army was having problems with that subgroup of DPs, the Jews, who defied repatriation procedures. Its commander, General George S. Patton, Jr., had only contempt for this miserable, half-human population left malingering around his occupation zone, and he abruptly issued an order to transfer them to repatriation centers against their will. It seemed to be just another of the "transports" that the Jews had known too well under the Nazis. Harrison heard of it when he first arrived in Munich, and promptly asserted his authority as a presidential envoy to stop the operation. Patton was displeased with Harrison, and Harrison cast a jaundiced eye over the official itinerary that the Third Army had prepared for his inspection tour.

That very first night in Munich, another influence bore down on Harrison, as helpful to the Zionist cause as the appearance of Schwartz as his expert traveling companion, but far less calculated. A young American rabbi named Abraham J. Klausner took it upon himself to call on the presidential emissary, and the two men sat up the night long in earnest discussion.

Klausner was a Jewish chaplain in the American Army. With the German surrender, he had applied for transfer to the Far East but instead, and against his wishes, was ordered to a repatriation center, where it was alleged there were Jews who needed a rabbi. Taking his time to show his annoyance, Klausner spent three days wandering through Bavaria in search of the village of Dachau. In that charnel house of Holocaust, Klausner confronted the destiny of his people. Never much interested in Zionism before, he became a militant devoted to helping the surviving remnant of European Jewry organize itself, undertake self-help programs, and demand a national future that would tell the world, "Never again!"

Klausner heard of Harrison's arrival from a friend in Third Army headquarters and turned up uninvited at the envoy's hotel in Munich. Describing what he himself had seen, he reinforced Harrison's suspicions of the itinerary prepared for him by the Third Army. Klausner took Harrison in hand and showed him the full horrors of the lives of Jewish survivors in Europe. Harrison's notebooks tell the grim story:

> Landsberg. . . . One sees many pathetic malnutrition and psychiatric cases. Many in the camp are wearing prisoner of war (German military) uniforms and they resent it.
>
> Alfondschule, Munich. A very poor school building. . . . There is absolutely no oversight, and the sanitation is awful.
>
> Schleischeim, Munich. The "camp" is a badly bombed building. The food is mainly bread and soup carried around in buckets. Most of the people had gone through four or five camps and expect to be "moved on" soon. Meanwhile, there is nothing for them to do except lie around all day, waiting for bread and soup.
>
> Mauthausen, Linz. Like a maximum security jail on top of a hill, surrounded by a high wall which is heavily guarded. . . . The apathy of the 1,300 residents is shocking. Though they are better housed than in most camps, they seem dazed and hopeless, like prisoners whose spirits have been completely broken.
>
> Celle. A "bad camp," with many Jews living in horse stalls, sick and well together. One inmate told us: "The hardest thing is to look outside the camps and see the Germans so much better off than we are, even the ones that used to be our guards and tormentors. They have better food and better clothes. And they are free."
>
> Bergen-Belsen. We had been repeatedly told that it was useless to visit this place, hitherto one of the most terrible of all the Nazi concentration camps, because "it's all burned down." Nevertheless, we found 14,000 displaced persons there, about half of them Jews. Building No. 1, with the gas chambers and crematoria, had been destroyed. All the rest of Belsen remains much as the Nazis left it. The buildings are substantial but frightfully overcrowded. We were in one loft, 20 by 80 feet, which housed 85 people with all their belongings. Their whole lives—eating, sleeping, bathing, laundry, "recreation"—had to be carried on in that partitionless, dreary space.

Harrison's report to Truman, submitted late in August 1945, conveyed the DP plight in vivid terms. "We appear to be treating the Jews

as the Nazis treated them except that we do not exterminate them,"
Harrison noted (Truman underlined this passage). "They are in concentration camps in large numbers under our military guard instead of S.S.
troops. One is led to wonder whether the German people, seeing this,
are not supposing that we are following or at least condoning Nazi policy." Then Harrison moved beyond administrative and logistical reforms
to make a judgment about the ultimate fate of this problematic populace.
He concluded:

> Palestine is definitely and pre-eminently the first choice. Many
> now have relatives there, while others, having experienced intol-
> erance and persecution in their homelands for years, feel that only
> in Palestine will they be welcomed and find peace and quiet and
> be given an opportunity to live and work. In the case of the Polish
> and the Baltic Jews the desire to go to Palestine is based in a great
> majority of the cases on a love for the country and devotion to the
> Zionist ideal. It is also true, however, that there are many who
> wish to go to Palestine because they realize that their opportunity
> to be admitted into the United States or into some other countries
> in the Western Hemisphere is limited if not impossible.

This was as full an endorsement of the Zionist position as any outside
observer had yet made to Truman. Harrison even cited the figure of
100,000, though at the time of his mission, that exceeded the number of
Jewish DPs under Allied occupation.

Harrison's report created a sensation when Truman made it public in
September, and General Dwight D. Eisenhower, as supreme commander
of the occupation, was hard-pressed to respond to specific criticisms of
administrative failures. But it was Harrison's political conclusions that
made the lasting impact: for the first time and against all the arguments
of Britain and the State Department, Truman was forced to view the
condition of Europe's surviving Jews and the political future of Palestine
as aspects of the same problem.

Harrison was sailing close to the wind in his conclusions. In a confi-
dential report to White House aide David Niles a few months after the
Harrison mission, a senior American relief worker who was a committed
Zionist admitted that Harrison could not possibly have substantiated his
belief that Palestine was the sincere choice of all the *Sheerith Haptelah.*
Zionism was not the only political movement at work among the Jewish
survivors, and among Polish Jews in particular, the anti-Zionist Socialist
Bund was strong in the liberated camps. Since they called for return to
their homes in Poland, the Bundists were not heard among those whom
Harrison met, those who refused repatriation. The politics of the survi-

vors often depended on their origins. In the camps of the American occupation zone, for example, survivors of the Lithuanian ghettos had seized control, and they had been strongly Zionist before the war. At Bergen-Belsen, on the other hand, a struggle was underway between pro- and anti-Zionist factions, and Harrison apparently did not recognize this during his brief visit.

Zionist organizational efforts received a major boost a month after publication of Harrison's report when Ben-Gurion toured the camps; his mere presence on the sordid scene nurtured Zionist hopes among the survivors. But barnstorming was not his total mission. In a series of discreet meetings with his loyalists in Europe that autumn of 1945, the Jewish Agency leader mobilized a network of agents for a massive Jewish migration. Leaving behind the wreckage of the Eastern European ghettos, where the Western occupation forces held no sway, clandestine migrants began the journey to Palestine by moving west into the American occupation zone. Unopposed by the U.S. Army, and sometimes helped along by the open cooperation of the corps of Jewish chaplains, a second wave of DPs swelled the reception centers of the American zone to a population almost double 100,000.

In short, the Harrison report may not have been fully accurate at the time he wrote it, but the dynamics of postwar Europe soon made it true. "It is not safe to make a single simple statement as to the nature of a concentration camp survivor as a human being," David Niles's informant reported. "Many of these people cannot be expected to make normal judgments or moral decisions." But, several months after Harrison and Ben-Gurion had come and gone, this report concluded: "To the extent that . . . personalities are intact and decisions can be made, these Jews want to go to Palestine."

TRUMAN WAS NOT a man to be troubled by subtleties. What he saw in the Harrison report was a moving portrait of human beings, homeless, in desperate need of succor and support. "The misery it depicted could not be allowed to continue," he wrote. If Palestine was what they wanted, and no other country was coming forward with resettlement offers—least of all the United States—then Palestine it must be. Truman sent a copy of the Harrison report to British Prime Minister Clement Attlee, bypassing all the avenues of diplomacy and saying, "The main solution appears to lie in the quick evacuation of as many as possible of the non-repatriable Jews who wish it, to Palestine. If it is to be effective, such action should not be long delayed."

Truman did not bother consulting, or even informing, his State Department about this personal venture into Anglo-American diplomacy. Indeed, just as the President was accepting Harrison's assessments, the Department was preparing a brief opposing the proposal to move 100,000 refugees to Palestine. But as Truman saw it, "the State Department continued to be more concerned about the Arab reaction than the sufferings of the Jews."

At the same time, Truman made no attempt to score political points by informing the American Zionist leaders of his initiative. Instead, he casually told an old Senate crony, Guy Gillette of Iowa, about the letter to Attlee. Gillette promptly informed Peter Bergson, who as promptly leaked word to the press, making it look as though the presidential demarche had resulted from Bergson's own efforts. President for five months and skilled only in the politics of mutual amiability, Truman had not yet perfected Roosevelt's technique for manipulating varied constituencies for maximum advantage. His impulsive and well-intentioned gesture toward the plight of Jews managed to anger not only the British and the diplomats but the official Zionist establishment as well. The latter even sent a delegation to the State Department, of all places, to complain of being left out of presidential decisions before they were announced.

The Near East Division experts could scarcely contain their frustration and their sense of martyrdom. Once the President has decided to "have a go" at Palestine negotiations, wrote one officer, "I see nothing further we can appropriately do for the moment except carry on our current work, answering letters and telegrams, receiving callers, etc., as best we can, pending the time (which will come soon) when the whole thing will be dumped back in our laps."

Across the Atlantic, where the actual decision rested, Attlee was unmoved. "While sympathizing with the views of Mr. Harrison," the Prime Minister replied in a curt telegram to Truman, Britain also had to consider the sensitivities of "ninety million Moslems, who are easily inflamed." In opposition, Attlee and the Labour Party leaders had consistently taken a more pro-Zionist stand than the Conservatives, Churchill excepted. But having taken office themselves after the war, Attlee and Foreign Secretary Bevin fell in line with the pro-Arab views of the diplomatic establishment. Truman's prematurely publicized plea for 100,000 immigration permits threw Britain on the defensive, from which it never escaped during the remaining three years of the Palestine mandate.

Whitehall tried to regain the initiative in November 1945 by proposing an Anglo-American Committee of Inquiry, an attempt to devise a long-term political framework for Palestine and at the same time offer resettlement options to the surviving Jews of Europe. Arguing that such an inquiry was unnecessary, Weizmann wrote Truman that "Palestine, for its size, is probably the most investigated country in the world." Even Rosenman, who had never pressed a Zionist line on either Roosevelt or Truman, told the President, "I certainly do not think you ought to agree to it or have anything to do with it. . . . Apart from any politics, the whole scheme . . . is merely one of temporizing, appeasing and seeking to delay the settlement of the issue." The British Embassy pressed forward with the plan, warning that "the approach of the [Palestine] problem in the United States is being most embarrassing . . . and is embittering relations between the two countries." Privately, Bevin was more outspoken. "I feel that the United States have been thoroughly dishonest in handling this problem," he informed Lord Halifax. "To play on racial feelings for purpose of winning an election is to make farce of their insistence on free elections in other countries."

Truman saw one virtue in the proposed inquiry: the exercise would establish beyond any argument that the fate of Europe's homeless Jews and the political future of Palestine were interlocked. London tried to back away from this line. "For Heaven's sake, stop saying Palestine is the only solution," Halifax pleaded with Byrnes. But in the end the British conceded, and Truman accepted an Anglo-American Committee of Inquiry.

"Zionist political aims have been sacrificed to philanthropy," complained the Jewish Agency, speaking more truth than they knew. For even as Truman was pressing publicly for humanitarian relief measures, he quietly met a group of diplomats posted to Arab capitals and explained his belief that migration to Palestine would relieve the pressure for more extreme political demands. In the face of Zionist pleas for their Biltmore program and the creation of a Jewish state, Truman's patience was fraying at the edges. "It's a very explosive situation we are facing," he wrote an old Senate colleague, "and naturally I regret it very much but I don't think that you or any of the other Senators would be inclined to send a half-dozen divisions to Palestine to maintain a Jewish state. What I am trying to do is to make the whole world safe for the Jews. Therefore, I don't feel like going to war for Palestine."

Even more grating than the Zionist pressures, however, was the antisemitism which Truman detected in the outspoken earthiness of the British Foreign Secretary. Bevin was the sort of man who considered it witty to make a play on the words "prophet" and "profit" in discussing Jews. He provoked a wave of disgust with his warning to the survivors of the Holocaust not "to get too much at the head of the queue" for humanitarian relief. Reviving an old antisemitic theme, he urged agricultural training for European refugees, "so that they would not seek openings in commerce." His undiplomatic outbursts reached their peak in mid-1946 when he said bluntly that Truman and many Americans were agitating for Jewish migration to Palestine only "because they did not want too many of them in New York." Arriving shortly after making that observation, Bevin found New York dock workers flatly unwilling to handle his personal baggage.

Meanwhile the twelve members of the Anglo-American Committee of Inquiry set about their investigation. Two on the American side began to lose credibility as their Zionist ardor became too evident: James G. McDonald, a refugee expert whom the Zionists had proposed for the mission that went instead to Earl Harrison; and a liberal San Francisco Catholic lawyer named Bartley C. Crum. In lengthy hearings in Washington, London, and Jerusalem, the Committee heard recitations from the aged Stephen Wise and Chaim Weizmann, from the more militant Ben-Gurion, from spokesmen of the various Palestinian Arab factions, from British mandatory officers, and, at State Department urgings, from anti-Zionist Jewish spokesmen.

The only really new ground to be covered was in Europe, in the DP camps, where members made diligent efforts to poll the survivors about their wishes for resettlement. British intelligence collected evidence that underground Zionist agents had been roaming the camps one step ahead of the Committee visitors, briefing the refugees to insist upon Palestine as their only chosen destination, a point on which American Jewish relief workers said the DPs needed little persuasion. A poll conducted for the Committee came up with the suspiciously large figure of 96.8 percent of DPs citing Palestine as their first choice. The effect of the camps on the Committee members was as devastating as it had been on Harrison, and Ben-Gurion led a futile effort to press politics over philanthropy with the Committee, arguing that the goal was sovereign statehood, not merely 100,000 new immigrants.

The unanimous report of the Anglo-American Committee of Inquiry, completed on April 20, 1946, confirmed the Zionist fear that philanthropy would win out. It recommended that Palestine be reconstituted as neither a Jewish state nor an Arab state, "that Jew shall not dominate Arab and Arab shall not dominate Jew in Palestine." Instead, the Committee proposed an international trusteeship under the United Nations, to safeguard the Palestinian interests of Jews, Muslims, and Christians alike. A year after his death, the "new formula" toward which Roosevelt had been working became enshrined in official discourse. But the Committee also recommended flatly that "100,000 certificates be authorized immediately for the admission into Palestine of Jews who have been the victims of Nazi and Fascist persecution."

Truman was delighted; the Zionists were horrified. "A shameful document," stormed Ben-Gurion, for it proposed "a British colonial-military state, which was no longer to be a homeland for the Jewish people, and which would never become a Jewish state." But Truman pressed his tactic of emphasizing the 100,000 immigration certificates. "The transference of these unfortunate people should now be accomplished with the greatest dispatch," he declared, and once again Britain was thrown onto the defensive. Addressing the House of Commons on May 1, Bevin and Attlee rejected Truman's proposal and insisted that the immigration recommendation could not be implemented in isolation from the Committee's other proposals. To counter arguments claiming the logistical impossibility of moving 100,000 persons from Europe under chaotic postwar conditions, a compassionate general in the Pentagon named John H. Hilldring launched top-secret contingency planning for a massive transport operation. The Labour government dug in its heels and refused to budge.

For all their disappointment with the Anglo-American Committee report, the Zionists saw their cause rescued by British intransigence. Where a philanthropic, humanitarian operation might well have defused the political demands, its failure only reinforced the pressures of Jewish nationalism.

On February 25, 1947, the British government admitted defeat in Palestine by turning the entire problem over to the United Nations. Even as he tried to lay blame everywhere else, Bevin acknowledged his blunder in refusing to heed the Truman initiatives. "I say this in all seriousness," he told the House of Commons. "If it were only a question of relieving Europe of 100,000 Jews, I believe a settlement could be found. . . . [But] the 100,000 is only a beginning, and the Jewish Agency talks in terms of millions." For once he sounded almost contrite: "If I could get back to the contribution on purely humanitarian grounds of 100,000 into Palestine, and if this political fight for a Jewish state could be put on one side, and we could develop self-government by the people resident in Palestine, without any other political issue, I would be willing to try again."

But that, of course, was just what Truman had been trying to do from the start.

9

HALF OF AMERICA's five million Jews lived in New York, another 35 percent in just nine other large cities across the country. In American life they now aspired to higher education and the professions, no longer toward the mercantile trade that had built the fortunes of earlier generations. Only 18 percent attended synagogue at least once a month, a far lower percentage than that of Christians who went to church, according to a poll conducted by a Jewish publication. Among themselves they pondered the age-old question of identity: What does it mean to be Jewish? Is it our religious "denomination"? Is it our race? Is it our ancient heritage coming back to haunt us? Or to redeem us? Now that the victorious powers of World War II seemed to be taking Jewish nationalism seriously, what exactly was envisaged? Did Zionism mean the creation of a safe haven in which all Jews suffering oppression in alien societies could seek refuge? Or was Bevin right—would the Zionist state be a dumping ground where Christendom could finally rid itself of the Jews?

Isaiah Berlin estimated that no more than half of America's Jews had a strong interest in Zionism. The others "are genuinely opposed to a Jewish state in Palestine," he wrote in one of his last wartime dispatches to the Foreign Office, "and deplore as much as anyone the alleged totalitarian tendencies of the Jewish majority party in Palestine." Ben-Gurion's militancy after his coup at the Biltmore had frightened inheritors of the Brandeis tradition. But Berlin added the perceptive comment that resistance to Zionism, among Jews at any rate, was hesitant and uneasy. Half a population in support was significant, especially compared to far more modest Zionist numbers just a few years earlier. "Solidarity is a source of comfort to unpolitical persons who do not wish to be marked out for attacks in their communities as traitors or appeasers over an issue about which they are none too certain," Berlin concluded.

The year 1945 opened for Jews in "buoyant optimism, that with the destruction of Nazi tyranny, the wishes of the surviving remnant of European Jewry would be given immediate attention, that a removal of Jewish displaced persons to Palestine on a substantial scale would be set in hand, and that plans for a Jewish Commonwealth could revive and ripen in an atmosphere of sympathy and universal approval," the British Embassy reported. Then came the doubts. The governments concerned were not all that sympathetic, while the extent of Nazi terror exceeded the worst fears. America's Jews had a particular reaction to the early evidence of the Holocaust, as a later Israeli historian described it, "a certain reticence in discussing with non-Jews events that appeared both inexplicable and unbelievable." Even British diplomats reported that "it is not difficult to sense the pathological emotions. . . . The memory of a persecution may be as bitter as the persecution itself." American Jews felt their insecurity anew, a "vicarious experience by which resultant mental impressions are notoriously darkened and exaggerated. . . . No imaginative Jew could be blamed for refusing ever to feel safe in Europe again."

One reaction was instinctive and immediate. If conscientious American Jews felt confused about their identity and destiny, one absolutely unambiguous step could assuage all—almost all—doubts. The United Palestine Appeal, later the United Jewish Appeal, had long transcended the political divisions of the community. In 1941 this national charity had raised a respectable $14 million for Jewish relief. By the end of the war, the annual figure reached $35 million. In 1946, with awareness of tragedy and the possibility of redemption in the air, the UJA contributions reached a stunning $101 million, and in the two years following, the figure grew by another 50 percent. UJA receipts were four times more than the entire nation contributed to the American Red Cross; with only occasional Gentile contributors, it came from a minority group of five million, including children.

The Zionists' political machine was in gear, non-Zionists inhibited by the evidence of a genocide that nearly succeeded. And a more discreet but well-orchestrated operation was underway as well. It started at remote border checkpoints in the ruins of Central Europe; it spread to elegant drawing rooms of Uptown Jewry, then to obscure warehouses on the New York and Baltimore waterfronts.

ON JUNE 20, 1945, a brigade of Palestinian Jews in British Army uniforms arrived at a refuge center for the war's displaced persons, survivors of the Holocaust. These Jewish soldiers had faithfully served their British officers during the war; now they were in the service of their own people.

With other cadres of a prewar rescue operation known as Brichah (Hebrew for "flight"), they embarked furtively on a new mission, under the direction of a secretive Palestinian intelligence officer named Shaul Avigur: to draw Europe's surviving Jews to the national homeland. Avigur and his lieutenants decided in July to concentrate Jews in the United States occupation zone of Germany, and there to establish clandestine jumping-off points for Palestine.

By the autumn of 1945, after Earl Harrison had already come and gone, the first hundreds of new refugees were arriving in the American DP camps. In small bands, they would sleep in the forests by day, then hike stealthily with their seasoned escorts through obscure border checkpoints by night. An alert American correspondent, I. F. Stone, found it ironic that "Germany should be the one country in Europe in which the Jewish population was growing constantly." Relief workers struggled to house the newcomers, but every time they thought their job accomplished, more Jews would mysteriously appear at the gates, as many as 1,500 per month. The Joint Distribution Committee anguished about supporting what was obviously an underground operation in violation of regulations, then put up $25 million to do so, more than double what "the Joint" had spent in Palestine since World War I. Nearly every Jewish organization on the Continent found itself, one way or another, caught up in Brichah.

On July 4, 1946, a pogrom broke out against the few hundred Jews who had returned to the Polish town of Kielce; as the news spread, Jewish hopes of returning to normal life in postwar Eastern Europe collapsed. The flow of refugees became a tidal wave. In August, still defensive after Harrison's criticism the year before, the U.S. Army bowed to the inevitable and officially opened the American occupation zone to Jewish refugees from Poland and Czechoslovakia. By September, 90,000 Jews had arrived from Poland, another 25,000 from the Balkans. At the end of 1946 over 250,000 Eastern European Jews were crammed into the DP camps of western Germany.

For the second time in half a century, the flag of the United States served as a magnet for destitute Jews of Russia and the East, and once again not all Americans were happy about it. Senator Tom Connally of Texas called the Army occupation regime "the biggest sucker in the world." A U.S. Army memorandum warned that "every Zionist-indoctrinated Jew who arrives in the American zone is an unconscious asset to Moscow." The flow of the refugees could not be concealed, though American authorities sought refuge in vagueness about the fact that they were heading for Palestine, in defiance of British restrictions. Officially,

the migration was portrayed as a spontaneous expression of human despair. What was carefully concealed was the organization behind it, created by Avigur and his cadres to convert this desperate homeless mass
into the future population of the Jewish state.

It fell to a hapless British general, Sir Frederick Morgan, to blurt out
the truth, which officers on the spot understood but considered it impol-
itic to state. The movement was not at all spontaneous. Morgan had been
Eisenhower's deputy, credited with the formidable logistical buildup for
the Normandy invasion of 1944. He was a respected, if overly blunt,
military professional. In 1946 he was head of refugee relief operations in
Germany. Despite warnings from his political superiors not to mention
the Jewish migration in his public statements, Morgan ad-libbed a few
remarks at a Berlin news conference. So many of the incoming Jewish
refugees were well dressed and well fed, Morgan said, "their pockets
bulging with money," that something other than sheer destitution must
be encouraging their travels.

If he had stopped there, it just might have been all right. But he went
on. "The Jews seem to have an organized plan for becoming a world
force," he said, as if he had just been reading the *Protocols of the Elders
of Zion,* "a weak force numerically, but one which will have a generating
power for getting what they want." And, Morgan said, they have "a
positive plan to get out of Europe."

The antisemitic tone came through far louder than the substance, and
the liberal press of England and America erupted in outrage. Morgan's
remarks were "childish nonsense," said the Manchester *Guardian.* Eddie
Cantor, the beloved comedian from the Lower East Side, took out an
advertisement in *The New York Times* to say, "I thought Hitler was
dead." The World Jewish Congress stated officially that "General Morgan's allegation of a 'secret Jewish force inside Europe aiming at a mass
exodus to Palestine' is . . . fantastically untrue."

For all its antisemitic coloration, Morgan's analysis of the situation
was quite correct. The migration was indeed part of an organized plan,
operating in defiance of civil and military occupation authorities, aimed
at transporting the surviving Jews out of Europe, whether they were in a
condition to want it or not, to Palestine. And though the general public,
including the Zionist faithful, were not privy to Brichah until Israeli
historians began to glorify it many years later, top Zionist leaders understood perfectly well what was happening. Avigur himself, the Brichah
chieftain, was from that elite that managed the affairs of Jewish Palestine
like an extended family; his brother-in-law was the Zionist unofficial
Foreign Minister, Moshe Shertok. That the Zionists of Palestine were

innocent bystanders to a migration in Europe was simply not credible, even if it would have been injudicious for them to admit the facts in public.

Zionist notables in the United States were embarrassed at being caught between the outrage and the fact. Six days after the Morgan blunder hit the press, Stephen Wise invited the Washington representative of Morgan's relief operation to breakfast at the Statler Hotel. If the general would only make a soothing correction of his antisemitic implications, Wise said, the criticism would be halted. Morgan grudgingly obliged.

Remarks like Morgan's, whatever their origin or intent, made a strong impact on America's Jews. Zionist politics were often distasteful to well-heeled Jews nicely settled in American society. But when Gentiles started casting slurs on Jews in general, that was the time for action. The mechanism was in place.

On Sunday, July 1, 1945, at 9:30 a.m., nineteen very wealthy and very concerned American Jews had converged on the penthouse apartment of Rudolf G. Sonneborn on East Fifty-seventh Street in New York City. Apart from the wealth and concern, the main requisite for admission was the ability to keep a secret. Sonneborn himself, a millionaire industrialist, was the epitome of this virtue, modest, neither seeking nor receiving public recognition. Three Palestinian Jews were also at his home that day, the head of the Zionist financial system, the head of the intelligence organization, and David Ben-Gurion.

"Would America take in the refugees?" Ben-Gurion asked. He did not pause for a reply, for he knew the answer and so did the others. Palestine was the only solution, and what were the comfortable Americans prepared to do about it? The meeting went on all day. As Sonneborn recalled it, "We were asked to form ourselves into an . . . American arm of the Haganah," the supply and logistical machinery behind the Jewish defense force in Palestine. "We were given no clue as to what we might be called upon to accomplish, when the call might come, or who would call us. We were simply asked to be prepared and to mobilize like-minded Americans. We were asked to keep the meeting confidential."

And so they did, as secret as Avigur's Brichah in Europe. Every Thursday the most dedicated members of the so-called Sonneborn Institute would meet in a private dining room at New York's Hotel McAlpin. Messages from Tel Aviv were reviewed, the needs of the Palestinian Jewish settlement assessed. These Elders of Zion were not trying to dominate the world, just to secure the tiny plot of desert real estate which history and geography had assigned to the Jews. Their activities were not revealed in newspaper advertisements; they arranged for the purchase of aircraft, of transport ships for smuggling arms and refugees, of jeeps and every other form of war surplus—so superfluous in America, so critical in Palestine. Frequently, to provide facts, would come envoys from the Holy Land—modern *shlichim*. But unlike those messengers of old, these were practical men of affairs. One was an energetic intelligence officer from Vienna named Teddy Kollek, who had fallen in love with the city of Jerusalem and would eventually serve some two decades as its mayor.

Remote and seemingly abandoned warehouses in obscure port blocks of New York and Baltimore would receive unmarked consignments, which would then disappear onto mysterious vessels of unknown origin for unknown destinations. For practical men who tired quickly of the political dialectics of Zionism, this secret effort was a source of deep satisfaction. "Haganah is the biggest romance," said a Philadelphia stalwart of the Sonneborn Institute. "It is the greatest thing certain Jews have had happen to them in this country."

Smuggling and gunrunning could not long escape the attention of the federal government. Under British pressure, in July 1947 the State Department formally asked the Department of Justice for three rulings: against newspaper advertisements soliciting the funds for illegal immigration, against tax deductions for Palestinian-related charitable contributions, and against American involvement in acquiring, outfitting, or manning transport shipping for immigration to Palestine. Attorney General Tom Clark was politically in tune with President Truman; he understood the interactions of law and policy. The Justice Department replied that there might indeed be technical cases against the newspaper advertisements and tax deductions, but to press them would only invite charges of antisemitic discrimination and thus perversely benefit the Jewish national cause. As far as the shipping was concerned, this would be illegal only if the ships in question were to go to war against Britain. "To characterize the ships carrying these hundreds of displaced refugees as vessels of war is to torture the fact," said the Department of Justice.

AN AIR of intrigue hung over these activities of American Jewry in the first postwar years. The general public knew virtually nothing of it. But Americans did know about the Jewish lobby.

For sound and fury, Rabbi Silver's political action machinery was impressive. But just as William E. Blackstone had discovered half a century before, public agitation had to be complemented by a more discreet and carefully directed pressure in the circles of the mighty in order to count. Directives continued to flow from AZEC headquarters; local Jewish communities sent off their telegrams, Christian groups raised their voices (under Zionist instructions), friendly "independent" speakers were encouraged with offers of lucrative lecture tours arranged and paid for by Zionist headquarters.

But what did it all amount to? "A first meeting or petition draws attention by its very novelty; upon repetition it becomes merely monotonous," reported Benjamin Akzin, an iconoclastic member of the Zionists' Washington staff. "Everything has been said many times before, and the press begins to find it boring." Even the fervent campaigns to line up lists of influential senators, congressmen, and public officials in support of the Jewish state had begun to pall. These people are probably "merely desirous of clearing their own record with the substantial portion of Jewish voters," noted this inside observer. "As long as they 'have gone on record' it is thought to be a matter of relative indifference to them whether or not the Palestine policy of our government follows in practice a pro-Zionist pattern." Such comments were not well received at Silver's command center, but struck a responsive chord among members of other Jewish offices in Washington and New York, among the followers of Weizmann, Wise, and the more moderate Zionists who favored the techniques of quiet diplomacy.

San Francisco in June 1945 provided the first tournament ground. No fewer than twenty different Jewish organizations sent representatives to the conference called to found the new United Nations Organization. None of them had any official status; Palestine was not even on the agenda. Some of the Jewish groups were there to argue *against* a Jewish state, on religious or political grounds or both. Goldmann, as Jewish Agency representative in Washington, made no secret of his unease at the role he was called upon to play. Until there was a state, how could the Jewish people claim to be recognized in a political gathering? If a Zionist attempted to speak, whom would an American Jew regard as his spokesman—the Secretary of State, or a self-styled representative of the Jewish people? The old fear of dual loyalties edged toward the surface.

Jews were not alone in forcing relatively parochial concerns upon the global-minded statesmen. Five Arab states had official representatives in San Francisco, along with a host of pro-Arab organizations. British diplomats, conveniently forgetting the pro-Nazi role of prominent Arab nationalists during the war, welcomed them as strategic allies. But this new partnership was not smooth. "The obstreperous activities of the Arab delegations have not . . . much improved their position against the Jews," commented a British Embassy observer from Washington. The Arabs' "tiresome behavior," in fact, probably "boomeranged in favor of the Jews, [because of] the irritation which the reiterated and grandilo-

quent Arab claims produced amongst many of the other countries represented."

Pro-Arab voices in America had long found it difficult to contend on
equal terms with the Jewish lobby in Washington. As Isaiah Berlin had
noted, "There are no Arab senators." In 1945 an official Arab Information Office opened in Washington. "It faces an uphill job," the British
Embassy said. After nearly half a year in operation, its sole visible
achievement was a half-page advertisement in *The New York Times;* the
rival *Herald-Tribune* refused even to carry it. Pro-Arab speakers went
out to college centers, where they were less likely to encounter the hec-
kling common at more public meetings, but even then they tended to feel
like the young Saudi who, as one of the first Arab students to arrive for
study in the United States, detrained at Washington's Union Station only
to find himself swallowed up in a throng of a thousand bearded, black-
coated rabbis on their way to a mass demonstration at the Capitol. Like
him, the Arab spokesmen wondered whether this was really what America was like.

AMERICA, of course, was not like that. For all the excitement that Palestine stirred among American Jews after World War II, the "great mass"
of Americans was not particularly interested. So concluded the British
Embassy. "In the middle west there is some support by non-Jewish
Americans for the Zionist cause because they do not want more Jews in
the United States," reported an embassy dispatch in mid-1947. "In the
south the interest is very small—there was, for example, no editorial on
the subject in New Orleans newspapers over a period of eighteen
months." Polls revealed that fully 46 percent of Americans had not the
slightest idea that Palestine was administered by Britain under a mandate
from the League of Nations. Many assumed that it was already an independent country. Over 60 percent, according to a Gallup poll, were
opposed to any United States intervention to maintain order in Palestine; 72 percent were quite content to let the United Nations handle the
problem.

Within the poll results lurked vestiges of a deeper sentiment. Antisemitism was not openly expressed in America in 1946 and 1947, as the
news of the Holocaust penetrated the popular awareness. A survey by the
Anti-Defamation League of B'nai B'rith covering the year 1946 found
that "organized antisemitism" had decreased throughout the United
States. But Jews were still encountering discrimination in employment
and housing: "more subtle forms" of antisemitism. They eluded precise

measurement, yet they intruded upon the daily life of a Jew in virtually any American community. A Roper poll found that such antisemitism was directly proportional to the concentration of the Jewish population —strongest in the Northeast and Midwest and the large cities, weakest in the Far West, in the South, and in small towns where few Jews had yet settled. Yet "even on the west coast, hostility to the Jews is increasing," reported the British Embassy. Another poll revealed a sobering trend. "Have you heard any criticism or talk against the Jews in the last six months?" was the question. In 1940 the sample replying "yes" was 46 percent; by 1946, after news of the concentration camps and the Holocaust, the number of those claiming to have heard criticism of Jews reached 64 percent. At the same time, the polls revealed that Americans were more kindly disposed toward admitting German immigrants than Jews.

Shocked as they were by the Holocaust, ordinary Americans seemed to have had no notion of the "more subtle" pressures they were imposing on Jews in their midst. Christian missionary societies expressed dismay at the inroads made by Zionism without thinking of themselves as antisemites. "Everyone zealous for Christian missions must feel a veritable heartbreak for the way in which the hasty and ill-advised endorsement of the Zionist program by Congress has nullified the sacrificial labors of generations of missionaries and educators," lamented an elderly Presbyterian veteran of the faculty at the American University of Beirut.

Millar Burrows of Yale, soon to become famous for his analyses of the Dead Sea Scrolls, brought Christian theology into politics. "The central issue between Judaism and Christianity," he declared,

> lies in their answer to the question: What do you think of Christ? The present resurgence of Jewish nationalism is a repetition of the same fatal error that caused Israel's rejection of Jesus. It is the focal point at which Christian opinion, in all brotherly love, should make clear and emphatic its disagreement with the dominant trend in contemporary Judaism. For the authentic, dominating, just now apparently all-conquering devotees of political Zionism we would feel the sorrow that Jesus felt when he wept over Jerusalem.

Unthinkingly, perhaps, conservative Christian voices were contributing to racial prejudice. As the survivors of the Holocaust were struggling to regain their composure as human beings, the *Christian Century* demanded that the Jews decide forthwith "whether they are an integral part of the nation in which they live, or members of a Levantine nation dwelling in exile."

American Christianity did not speak with one voice in making this harsh demand. The fundamentalist heirs of McDonald and Blackstone continued to be active. "The title deeds from the Original Owner of the earth naming the Jews legal owners of Palestine are still extant in millions of Bibles the world around," said the monthly journal of Chicago's Moody Bible Institute. The Baptist *Watchman-Examiner* declared that "Israel cannot be restored except in the divine plan and purpose. If Israel is now being restored, then, as we interpret the Bible, history is rapidly approaching its climax."

Closer to the American mainstream, however, was Reinhold Niebuhr, foremost of the Protestant theologians, whose support for the Jewish state had been eloquently expressed without apology or temerity as far back as 1942. Niebuhr repeatedly argued in terms of the desperate needs of human beings. "It is not pretended that there can be a simply 'just' solution of such a conflict, when competing claims move on such various levels," he said. Other Christian voices were raised on the theme of guilt for what had befallen Jews at the hands of a civilized world. Dorothy Thompson said that "the salvation of the Jews must . . . come in part as an act of repentance from the Christian world."

DURING HIS MONTHS of frustration, Foreign Secretary Bevin echoed what diplomats of Britain and the United States had been saying ever since Roosevelt first took up the Jewish restoration as a cause. Jewish sufferings have created problems, Bevin told Halifax, "which President Truman and others in America have exploited for their own purposes." Palestine had become a matter of domestic politics.

From its earliest days the diplomatic profession was ambivalent about the role of public opinion in the determination of policy. Diplomats "welcomed public interest in foreign affairs," remarked one historian of the Foreign Service, "so long as that interest was remote from action and supportive of professional Foreign Service officers." Another diplomatic historian asserted that the function of the democratic process was simply "to increase popular understanding of the policies pursued by men of authority in political, social and economic life and to secure free popular consent to their decisions." To those who thought this way, the Palestine debate of the 1940s became the classic case of foreign policy determined by politicians pandering for votes. American diplomats who seemed endlessly impressed by demonstrations and editorials in the Arab capitals derided similar expressions in their own country as "playing politics."

Truman's record amply displays the links between politics and policy. In November 1945 he assured a meeting of American ambassadors posted to the Arab world that he would treat the Palestine problem "on a high plane above local political issues." Yet the meeting was put off for four weeks, until after November 6, election day, lest word of it leak out and cost valuable Democratic votes in the New York mayoral election. Announcement of the Anglo-American Committee of Inquiry was held up until after the election—Byrnes admitted as much to Halifax. When that committee opted against a sovereign Jewish state, the New York Democratic chairman wired Truman that "if this plan goes into effect it would be useless for the Democrats to nominate a state ticket for the election this fall."

The most blatant instance of a policy move directly tied to the election calendar came in October 1946. New York Democrats advised the White House that "we need all the help we can get from the Jewish people, who are pretty wrought up over the Palestine question. They think the President could do more." Dewey, the Republican leader, was on the verge of a pro-Zionist declaration—so Rosenman and Niles learned—and unless Truman could pre-empt the play, the Democrats would lose heavily in the New York congressional elections. The result was a presidential statement on October 4, the eve of Yom Kippur, the Jewish Day of Atonement. Truman reiterated his demand for the immediate admission to Palestine of 100,000 Jewish DPs, hinted that the United States would provide economic assistance once a workable political solution had been achieved, and concluded with a palliative: "I cannot believe that the gap between proposals which have been put forward is too great to be bridged by men of reason and goodwill."

Attlee and Bevin received a few hours' advance notice of this statement and erupted in fury; for all its ambiguity, they argued, the statement would upset the delicate diplomacy then underway between Jews and Arabs. In vain, Attlee pleaded for delay. "I shall await with interest to learn what were the imperative reasons which compelled this precipitancy," he cabled sarcastically, as if he were not fully aware of the Democrats' electoral needs.

In his memoirs, Dean Acheson, Truman's most faithful Secretary of State, flatly denied the charges of Bevin and his own diplomatic colleagues that Truman's Palestinian position was based on political opportunism. And, in fact, the Yom Kippur statement is itself the best evidence for Truman's caution, even as he sought to hold the Democrats' longstanding Jewish support. Acheson was its principal drafter. For all the comfort and reassurance which it gave to Jews on the eve of their solemn Holy Day, Truman's message pointedly failed to endorse the Zionist demand for a Jewish state. David Niles, for one, understood the tightwire on which Truman was walking, and with the skilled instincts of the political operator he remarked that everyone would interpret the statement as pro-Zionist anyway. As it happened, Silver did spot the flaw. He denounced Truman's statement as a mere political play for the Jewish vote—just what the diplomats of the State Department and Foreign Office were also saying. But since Silver was himself eagerly campaigning for the Republican Senator Taft, his criticism was put down as a political ploy of his own.

"If you didn't have your fingertips sandpapered to the sensitivities of a matter of this sort," remarked White House aide George Elsey, "it would be easy for domestic political quarrelling to break out in such a fashion that it could have serious international repercussions." Truman held back from the fulsome gestures to Zionist pressure groups that his political advisers urged upon him. He repeatedly refused to meet American Zionist officials, Rabbi Silver above all.

And Truman's personal correspondence was full of careless remarks that would have done him no good if they had got out to places where they could be used against him. "They somehow expect me to fulfill all the prophecies of the prophets," he wrote one friend. "I tell them sometimes that I can no more fulfill all the prophecies of Ezekiel than I can of that other great Jew, Karl Marx." To a New York Democratic party leader, he remarked that "I don't believe there is any possible way of pleasing our Jewish friends." A Cabinet meeting was told: "Jesus Christ couldn't please them when he was here on earth, so how could anyone expect that I would have any luck?" The Jews "aren't going to write the history of the U.S. or my history!" he blurted to James McDonald, who retorted as tactlessly that at least Roosevelt had understood the situation. "I am not Roosevelt," Truman snapped back. "I am not from New York. I am from the Middle West." (Truman later wrote McDonald to apologize.)

"Had it not been for the unwarranted interference of the Zionists, we would have had the [DP] matter settled a year and a half ago," Truman complained to an old Senate friend late in 1947. "I received about 35,000 pieces of mail and propaganda from the Jews in this country while this matter was pending. I put it all in a pile and struck a match to it."

This record is hardly that of a politician determined only to curry favor with the molders of Jewish public opinion.

After the Republican sweep in the 1946 congressional elections, the political pressures on Truman became overwhelming. As he was President and party chief only by default, his grip was weak even among Democrats. Influential party leaders were openly maneuvering to hand the presidential nomination to Eisenhower or Supreme Court Justice William O. Douglas.

In November 1947 two political advisers, James H. Rowe, Jr., and Clark M. Clifford, presented Truman with a state-by-state plan for a campaign strategy. Rowe acknowledged that "Jews hold the key to New York, and the key to the Jewish voters is what the Administration does about Palestine." But New York was probably the only state in which Jews would vote as a bloc. Clifford, a rising young St. Louis lawyer on the White House staff, was sensitive both to Truman's concern about mixing foreign policy and domestic policies and to the subtleties of Zionist sentiments. He added a few key sentences of his own. It is "extremely difficult to decide some of the vexing questions which will arise in the months to come on the basis of political expediency," he wrote. "In the long run there is likely to be greater gain if the Palestine problem is approached on the basis of reaching decisions founded upon intrinsic merit." Clifford knew what Truman wanted to hear, and this is precisely the position the President took in March 1948 when he announced his candidacy for the presidency.

For all the cynicism about Truman's motives, his Palestine record fits the pattern of Presidents before and, to a large extent, after. His instincts, personal and political, were basically sympathetic to the Jewish fate, but he became irritated with the endless maneuvers and ploys practiced upon him from all sides. "I don't even know what the latest plan is," he snapped one day in 1947. "For all his friendship and sympathy," recalled Goldmann, "Truman had indicated several times that he saw no way out and would like to withdraw from the whole thing." Yet compassion was natural to him; in this case it brought political as well as emotional returns, and the contrary arguments of anti-Zionists never could overwhelm his instincts. This was the view constantly and shrewdly pressed upon him by one man who always had the President's ear through the final three years of the drive for the Jewish restoration.

"DAVE NILES was a most secretive individual," recalled George Elsey. He "slunk rather furtively around the corridors of the White House and the Executive Office Building and . . . rarely, if ever, confided to his White House colleagues as to what he said to the President."

Through lifelong shyness as much as anything else, Niles always cultivated an air of mystery. He had served the early New Deal as a faithful but lowly political operator, a protégé of Hopkins and Frankfurter. British analysts, who later had reason to study his record carefully, credited him with extracting half a million dollars from labor leader John L. Lewis for Roosevelt's 1936 campaign. The right-wing opposition singled Niles out as a nefarious eminence behind the New Deal. A Republican congressman from Michigan called him the mastermind of "potentially the greatest, most dangerous and unscrupulous political machine known in all time, in any nation." This awesome and successful conspiracy had actually elected a President of the United States for an unprecedented third term!

Niles lived politics. His job for Roosevelt had been to keep in touch with labor and the ethnic minority groups which supplied the cadres of the New Deal. Truman asked him to stay on, the only administrative assistant to survive the transition from the Roosevelt political family to the Truman White House. Not by design or direction or even, at the start, awareness, Jewish nationalism had as strategically placed an asset as any cause could pray for.

David K. Niles was born in Russian Poland in 1890, one of five children of Sophie and Ascher Neyhus, a tailor. The family immigrated to the *Goldene Medine* in 1891, and Niles (as his name was Anglicized) grew up in the slums of Boston's North End. Yiddish-speaking, poor and plodding, he nevertheless displayed the spunk to be admitted to the distinguished Boston Latin School. Drifting around after high school— college was out of the question for a poor immigrant's son—he found himself involved in ventures with an aggressive cinema producer named Sam Goldwyn; unlike Goldwyn, Niles went broke. Then he came across the congenial Ford Hall Forum, a center of lectures and discussion groups for the Boston intelligentsia. Niles became a hanger-on, inconspicuous at first, eventually indispensable to Massachusetts liberal politics. He was quiet, energetic, and efficient. Others of his upwardly mobile generation found exposure to public affairs at universities; for Niles it came from the radical politics that flowed through the Ford Hall Forum.

He went to Washington during World War I to take a public relations job in the Labor Department which Ford Hall mentors arranged for him. In 1924 the La Follette Progressive Party lured him into the ranks. Two years later it was the civil rights cause célèbre of Nicola Sacco and Bartolomeo Vanzetti that drew his organizational zeal. Gradually the Jewish immigrant's son from the Boston slums found himself acquiring quite a reputation as a master political manipulator—never known to the general public, always in demand among the professionals. In 1928 he headed a committee for Al Smith. There he met an aspiring social worker named Harry Hopkins, who introduced him to the world of the Hyde Park Roosevelts.

No court action ever recorded the change in name from Neyhus to Niles, a lapse that caused Niles no end of grief from his critics. Eventually he had to secure a memorandum from the Assistant Solicitor General of the United States—a member of the White House staff could expect such cooperation—certifying that the change was legal.

The Neyhus family were Orthodox Jews. Aspiring and assimilated, Niles himself displayed no religious or cultural affinity for his heritage. His interest in the Jewish destiny came from an infatuation of his youth that stayed with him to the end of his life. Only a few intimates knew the story:

Niles never married. His friends wondered about the loneliness of his life—he hated parties, he neglected his dress—"No one could ever live with him." Rigid in its routine, his was a slovenly bachelor's life, interrupted only by ad hoc social encounters with other workaholics like his great friend J. Edgar Hoover, head of the Federal Bureau of Investigation. Niles lived at the Carlton Hotel, a couple of blocks from the White House. Every Friday he took the train to New York for an evening at the theater; he was a minor "angel," claiming the hit shows *South Pacific* and *Mr. Roberts* among his modest investments. (Following his experience with Sam Goldwyn, he never talked about the flops.) Then would come a social hour or two with the New York "ethnic" communities—Jews, Italians, whatever—whose political activism consumed his working responsibilities. He listened better than he talked; his sentences would trail off into mutters, leaving companions straining to figure out what he was trying to say.

Saturdays and Sundays he spent in Boston, staying with his sister, holding political meetings over breakfast at the Tremont Hotel, remaining in town just long enough to open the Sunday-evening meeting of the Ford Hall Forum. Proceedings underway, he would duck out to catch the overnight train back to Washington to begin another week of work at the White House.

This was a single-minded devotion to the nuts-and-bolts work of politics. But a few of his bridge-playing cronies knew that there had once been something else, a special woman in his life. She married another man, and for Niles, as he confided in a rare moment of personal disclosure, there was no one else who could measure up. Her name was Justine, a brilliant, restless coed who sampled the intense academic fare of Bryn Mawr, Barnard, and Radcliffe before settling down at Yale Law School. Niles met her at the Ford Hall Forum during her Radcliffe term; her vitality and social activism lit a complementary spark in Niles. Justine joined the labor force of a cotton mill, to help organize the inarticulate workers against the exploitations of management. She walked the picket lines, she harangued her co-workers, and she captivated David Niles.

But there remained always a distance between them. He was a rootless high school graduate from the Boston slums, Justine was the only daughter of one of the most prominent men in American public life, Rabbi Stephen Wise.

Niles had come into contact with Wise at Ford Hall. For political work, a back-room operator like Niles was Wise's type of man. But the social gap was huge; there was no question of personal intimacy in their relationship. Decades later, Justine Wise Polier conceded that Niles had indeed been "very fond" of her, but her father never really took the friendship seriously—nor, for that matter, did Justine. The fact that Niles did take it seriously, and saw that there was no hope of moving it any further, remained his life's sadness. In his White House years, Niles never missed a chance to see or talk with Rabbi Wise. They had all the progressive causes of the 1920s and 1930s in common, their adulation of Roosevelt and the New Deal. From Wise, Niles began to sense something important about being Jewish that he had not known before.

"In a climate saturated by emotion and prejudice," wrote Arthur Koestler, "psychological imponderabilia assume a fateful importance." If ever a national capital was saturated by emotion and prejudice, it was Washington during the Palestine debate of the 1940s. Under both Roosevelt and Truman, the White House contact man with the Jewish community was guided by those "psychological imponderabilia" to seek out and preserve good relations with the Zionist leader Rabbi Wise.

Administrative assistants in the White House are ready prey for conspiracy-hunters. Their importance often appears large as the line blurs between their ideas and those of the Chief Executive. In reality, the functions and responsibilities of staff aides are circumscribed. They screen materials that the executive may need, analyze incoming information, and provide the perspective of alternative viewpoints that he himself has no time to seek out. Like a good lawyer, a good staff aide constantly advises his principal without ever presuming to foreclose options. In the choice of the materials he "sends forward," he can have considerable influence, sometimes without the executive realizing that he is being worked over. But the administrative assistant who consistently presses a personal viewpoint risks the odium of being branded "involved." He drops a notch in his principal's confidence, he loses out in the chain of policymaking—and for a conscientious staff aide this is a fate worse than public humiliation.

As long as Niles was simply maintaining contact with the critical constituencies of organized labor and minority groups, Truman found him the consummate staff man. His dedication to liberal causes ran parallel to Truman's own; there were no grounds for ideological distrust. Then, in 1947 and 1948, as Niles became more and more caught up in

Zionism, Truman gradually distanced himself. He continued to let Niles run interference with the Zionist groups pounding at the White House door—one observer called him a "portable wailing wall." But the policy papers that emerged from Niles's typewriter were received with growing skepticism. Niles was becoming "involved," and so was another staff man, Truman's old friend Max Lowenthal. "Whenever I try to talk to them about Palestine, they soon burst into tears," Truman confided to another aide. "So far I have not known what to do."

Other officers of the Administration were less patient. Secretary of State Byrnes resented Niles's approaches on Palestine questions: "That made me mad, that fellow stopping me when I was so busy," he complained. Secretary of the Navy James V. Forrestal and other anti-Zionists came to regard Niles as dangerous, partisan, and sneaky. The State Department was "seriously embarrassed and handicapped by the activities of Niles at the White House in going directly to the President on matters involving Palestine," Forrestal wrote. For years afterward, diplomats were convinced that Niles had been regularly briefing his Zionist contacts about the most sensitive matters, sometimes telling them about presidential actions even before word had reached the responsible American officials.

One veteran of State Department intrigues, however, saw Niles's activities in a totally different light. This was Ben Cohen, a thoroughly respected public servant who never incurred the suspicions that fell upon his less polished fellow Jew. Cohen scoffed at the charge that Niles improperly leaked information to keep the Zionists informed about the inner deliberations of the Administration. On the contrary, Cohen said, it was only Niles who had the patience to maintain contact with the troublesome Zionists, and therefore it was Niles who brought information to the Administration about the inner deliberations of Zionism. If the State Department was "embarrassed and handicapped" by Niles, it was only because the diplomats and the President were hopelessly at odds over Palestine. The Department would have been relieved to be allowed to pursue its own policies without presidential interference, just as it was in the good old days of the 1920s and 1930s. If it had not been for David Niles, Ben Cohen argued, President Truman might not have known what his own Department of State was doing.

THE STATE DEPARTMENT had lost its atmosphere of clubby comfort under the pressures of world war. Gone were the unruffled policy discussions over pipes and cigars in a semicircle around the Secretary's desk. "Policies," one mournful diplomat remarked, "instead of flowering in the friendly contacts of a qualified few, are almost as devoid of life as the air in which they are made." And worse was ahead. In the spring of 1947, the State Department was moved away from the neighborhood of the White House to a new headquarters, a stark modern building in a swampland corner of Washington known as "Foggy Bottom." The Secretary of State's new fifth-floor office resembled, one early inhabitant remarked, nothing so much as "the anteroom to a Turkish brothel."

In the backwater of the Palestine desk, the old clubbiness survived longer than in the front offices of great-power diplomacy. The cadre of Arabists remained in control; they rotated their trusted colleagues in and out of missions in the Middle East, they wrote their personal letters to each other with their thoughts about policy. They enjoyed the social company of the old hands, veterans of the oil company and missionary communities. In each other's confidence, they found no cause to question long-held assumptions. Only rarely would the experts be brought up short by views contrary to their own. The secretary of a young desk officer, Evan Wilson, looked up at him one day and said, "Mr. Wilson, I don't understand why you let yourself get so bothered about Palestine, when everyone knows it says in the Bible that the Jews are going back there someday!"

Middle Eastern oil had become an issue of high strategy by the end of World War II, for in these lands were two-thirds of the world's proven reserves. The threat of Soviet advances toward the region became ominous in 1945. To no one did the danger appear more acute than the man who succeeded Wallace Murray as the head of the Near East Division just three days after the death of President Roosevelt.

Loy Wesley Henderson came to the problems of Zionism and the Middle East by a circuitous route. He never fit the mold of the classic diplomat, though he rose to the summit of the professional service. Son of a Methodist minister, he was raised on a farm in the foothills of the Ozarks, not eighty-five miles from the town where Harry Truman was born eight years before him. A boyhood injury to his right arm left him ineligible for World War I military service, but alternative duty with the Red Cross took him to western Russia and the Baltic States during the anarchic years of civil war. Here he found a lifelong political passion. He served in various Eastern European diplomatic posts through the 1920s and 1930s, marrying a woman from the Baltic bourgeoisie, becoming chargé d'affaires in Moscow from 1934 to 1938, the era of the purge trials.

Henderson was implacably anti-Soviet, not a helpful posture during the World War II alliance. In 1943, Moscow's ambassador in Washington, Maxim Litvinov, complained to Roosevelt—Henderson was responsible for the Soviet desk in the Department at the time—warning that "as long as Henderson is sitting on these [Soviet] affairs, good relations will be impeded." In the atmosphere of those days, that was the end of Henderson. He still held high career rank, however; the embassy in Iraq needed an ambassador, "and nobody seemed to want it," Henderson recalled. "I took it, and that is how I became involved in the Near East."

World War II Baghdad was a bustling, cosmopolitan crossroads, center of espionage and exotic political rivalries. Iraq, the Arab nationalists, the Jews, Britain and France and their imperial feuds—all this intrigued Henderson, but he never ceased to view all foreign policy through his own prism, the struggle of the West against the menace of Communism. Zionism was but a minor irritant on his world scene, one of the many eccentric tendencies in the Middle East, but one that he reluctantly acknowledged had a certain political importance in the United States.

Unlike his patrician colleagues, Henderson was not motivated by antisemitism. His background was like Truman's in having led him similarly to appreciate the virtue of amiability. "I had no consciousness of Jews one way or the other," he said of his boyhood. "I am certain there must have been Jews among my friends then, but I was not conscious of it. As a religious influence, my father was extremely broad-minded towards non-Methodists."

In maturity, the more he came to know the Arab intelligentsia, the more he sensed what he regarded as the threatening nature of Zionism. A two-hour talk with the Iraqi Foreign Minister in 1944 prompted two long telegrams to the State Department in which Henderson argued the disastrous effects which United States endorsement of Jewish national aspirations would have on the Arabs. Then he apparently had second thoughts. He wrote one of those gentlemanly "Dear Wallace" letters to Murray, acknowledging that "readers of these telegrams are likely to feel that I am rabidly anti-Zionist." Not at all, he argued. "I have no intention of taking sides in the Palestine dispute. I am merely endeavoring truthfully to inform my government what results might be expected in this area from its espousal of the Zionist cause."

When Murray finally retired early in 1945, Henderson was named to succeed him as director of Near Eastern affairs, the ranking State Department expert for the climax of the Jewish restoration.

Henderson had virtually no direct contact with Truman. The man at the White House with whom he dealt on matters of Jewish interest was Niles, and Henderson came to perceive this radical from Boston as the heart of the elusive international Zionist conspiracy. Amiable appearances were always preserved. Henderson would receive Zionists and Arabists alike; his imposing office seemed suitable for a proconsul. A brilliant tiger-skin rug adorned the floor, an eight-foot oil painting of a nineteenth-century Bey of Tunis glared down upon his visitors.

Through the three years that followed, Henderson displayed a sure bureaucratic instinct. He would seize tenaciously on a few points of policy that he considered central; he would never let them drop from discussion, never pass up a chance to reiterate them in memos to the Secretary of State or even the White House. In his definition of the national interest were three basic considerations: Soviet Russian influence must be suspected and countered at every juncture; the goodwill of the Arab world must be preserved at all costs; and the new United Nations Organization must not be allowed to develop a supranational authority which might threaten American freedom of action. If the first of these themes hit responsive chords in Truman's Washington, the latter two made him a target for American liberals from Eleanor Roosevelt to David Niles.

"This man Henderson has a foreign policy of his own," stormed a New York congressman in 1948, "based on such deep-seated prejudices and biases that he functions as a virtual propagandist for feudalism and imperialism in the Middle East." Bartley Crum, who built his membership in the Anglo-American Committee of Inquiry into a national platform for Zionism, publicly named Henderson as an official who was frustrating President Truman's Palestine policies. Only Henderson's resignation, Crum declared, would assure "that the State Department at long last is in accord with the policies of the President."

Niles could afford to observe the accusations and denials from the safe anonymity of a staff position; it was not his style to join a public fray. Working in his own way, closeted in an unmarked second-floor office in the west corridor of the old State Office Building, he planted just the right degree of doubt in a memo to Truman. "Henderson has not yet, in my judgment, satisfactorily answered the charges made against him by Bart Crum. I think that Bart Crum was wrong in making these charges, but I do not think the State Department handled any reply in a way that has removed suspicion from Henderson himself."

With their knives thus unsheathed, the bureaucrats prepared for the battle over Jewish nationalism.

FOR ALL THE ADVANCES made by the Zionists in their public and private endeavors after World War II, there were still many American Jews who would have none of it, perhaps half of them, in Isaiah Berlin's estimate. Some were simply apathetic—about politics, or about being Jewish.

Others were fervent and sincere in believing that the Zionist nation-state was the wrong way for Jews to evolve their identity. The intellectual heirs of I. M. Wise had long dominated some of the most influential and comfortable Jewish communities of America, their new Palestine. "Israel is at home in every free country and should be at home in all lands," declared the Reform movement after the Balfour Declaration. "We . . . do not seek for Israel any national homeland." A Jewish state in Palestine would become an isolated ghetto, said one sober voice at a fund-raising conference in 1937, with a standard of living even lower than that of Polish Jews because of the cost of maintaining a permanent army against hostile Arabs; he was shouted down by the Zionist faithful. As late as 1943, some Reform synagogues around the country denied official position to any member who admitted to Zionist sympathies.

The dilemma of the anti-Zionist Jewish-American found its most powerful expression in the patrician family of Adolph Ochs, owner of *The New York Times.* Ochs had married the daughter of I. M. Wise; their daughter in turn chose for husband, and eventually inheritor of *The Times,* the scion of another Uptown family, Arthur Hays Sulzberger. As a sheltered undergraduate at Columbia, Sulzberger had been shocked and offended when he first encountered Jewish nationalism. "If what you say is so," he told a Zionist classmate, "I will resign from the Jewish people."

Sulzberger's ancestors had come to America in 1695; two were among the Jewish notables who greeted Washington on his visit to Newport in 1790. When the publisher of *The Times* passed through Palestine in 1937 on an inspection tour of the Middle East, he encountered Zionist zealots who presumed to regard him as a "foreigner in America," saying that only in Palestine could he truly belong. "I looked at these Jews and knew it was not so," Sulzberger reported on his return home. "I have travelled pretty well over the face of the earth, but never have I felt so much a foreigner as in this Holy Land. . . . I was a Jew religiously, they racially and nationally." Sulzberger did not shrink from the challenge that less secure Jews chose to evade: "If there was to be any emotional conflict between America as my land and this [Palestine] as my land," he declared, "I must choose America, even if that were to mean that I can no longer be a Jew."

Sulzberger's fear of divided loyalties led him to minimize, if not ultimately deny, his Jewish identity. He was one of those who warned Roosevelt that the appointment of Frankfurter to the Supreme Court might call too much attention to Jews and thus provoke antisemitism. "Jewish-sounding" by-lines of *Times* reporters were regularly disguised under bland initials. Sulzberger helped found the anti-Zionist American Council for Judaism in the early 1940s; Isaiah Berlin called them "an assembly of mice who say that they will bell the Zionist cat." *The Times* often gave as much attention in its news columns to this little splinter group as to all other Jewish organizations combined.

There was, nevertheless, one Zionist, revered but remote from the political mainstream, who could always be heard from in the columns of *The Times*. This was Judah Magnes, a charismatic American rabbi who was so dedicated to the destiny of his people that he had fulfilled the ultimate Zionist commitment: he had moved to Palestine, and from that position of stature he preached a most unorthodox message.

At the turn of the century, Uptown New York Jewry had been ready to adopt the dashing young Magnes as one of its own. Though he was born in San Francisco, his early posts as rabbi were at the fashionable Madison Avenue Synagogue and even Temple Emanu-El, where he married into the family of Louis Marshall. To be sure, he displayed a certain nonconformity from an early age, which only made him more attractive to the Jewish youth of the day. Like many of his well-endowed contemporaries, he threw himself into the social cause of Downtown Jewry; he even took up Zionism, but with a grace and charm that allowed the Uptown aristocracy to forgive this peccadillo. As World War I loomed, his political nonconformism became troublesome. He was an unabashed pacifist, opposed British imperialism as vigorously as German, and even as Brandeis was making Zionism respectable, Magnes was turning against the political ambitions of Jewish nationalism. For Magnes, Zionism meant a spiritual rebirth of the Jewish faith, not just another minority nationality party. He resigned from the American Zionist organization, and in 1922 he turned his back on New York and emigrated to Jerusalem.

He went to become president of the new Hebrew University and there, atop Mount Scopus, emerged as an intellectual and moral presence in the Jewish society of the Mandate. British High Commissioners would take telephone calls from Magnes in a moment, while officials of the Jewish Agency had to wait weeks for an appointment. He had no time for the grubby political maneuvers of Weizmann and Ben-Gurion, and with the outbreak of Arab rioting in 1929, he broke with the intent of the Balfour Declaration. He proposed instead that the Jews relinquish their aim of achieving a majority in Palestine and work side by side with the Arab Palestinians to build a binational state. Felix Warburg sustained him with a large birthday check each year, while the *Christian Century* endorsed his ideals as against the politics of the Zionist mainstream. Ben-Gurion's militancy at the Biltmore was the last straw for this renegade Zionist and his circle of Jerusalem friends. In August 1942, Magnes, Henrietta Szold, American-born founder of Hadassah (the Zionist women's organization), and Martin Buber, the German-Jewish philosopher, formed a political movement called Ihud (Hebrew for "unification"). It was devoted to negotiation and reconciliation with the Arabs of Palestine.

"We think that if the attempt is made to convert Palestine into a Jewish state or an Arab state there will be no peace here," Magnes declared. He favored equal political rights for Arab and Jewish communities, and he opposed the Zionist orientation of the Jewish Agency—for instance, the restrictions on land purchases by Arabs. Magnes' binational vision was similar to Roosevelt's: a large union across Palestine, Transjordan, Syria, and Lebanon in which Jews could immigrate to Palestine without upsetting Arab sensitivities over the whole region. "The Jews have more than a claim upon the world for justice," Magnes declared, but "I am not ready to try to achieve justice to the Jew through injustice to the Arab." On a visit to the United States, Magnes saw the melodramatic Bergson–Ben Hecht pageant with its message of militant nationalism, and commented, "Heaven forbid that we now shackle Judaism and the People of Israel to this madness."

This voice from Jerusalem was immediately attractive to those Americans, Jews and Gentiles, who were seeking an alternative to militant Zionism. When *The New York Times* needed a "reliable" part-time correspondent in Jerusalem, they asked a member of Magnes' staff to report on developments in Jewish Palestine. The numerous pronouncements of the president of the Hebrew University were never overlooked in the columns of the newspaper that Roosevelt, Truman, and all American officialdom turned to first every morning. Wallace Murray in the State Department noted Magnes' activities with approval as early as 1942, though American intelligence analysts dismissed the Ihud group as "old-fashioned liberal Jews." After assuming the leadership of the postwar Near East Division, Loy Henderson was equally impressed with Magnes' "reasonableness," and he made a note to himself that Judah Magnes might be a man who could be helpful someday soon.

AGAINST THE COMBINATION of apathy, *The Times'* anti-Zionism, and Judah Magnes' binationalism, the Zionist leadership regrouped after World War II for the postwar challenge of enlarging its influence among American Jews. The World Zionist Congress convened in Basel, Switzerland, in 1946; the air was heavy with awareness of the Holocaust and the mood was militant. Silver and Ben-Gurion sounded the clarion for what was left of world Jewry. Theirs was the unyielding Biltmore program, the maximalist call for a Jewish commonwealth—now—by force if necessary. From what seemed another era, the seventy-two-year-old Chaim Weizmann rose with a final plea for moderation. "It is all very well to send our boys into the firing line in Palestine from the safety and security of New York and Cleveland!" Weizmann declared in an unmistakable personal swipe at Silver.

The Congress heard the remark in nervous silence, broken finally by a quiet voice uttering the word "Demagogue!" Weizmann looked up in astonishment; frail and nearly blind, he scanned the hall as if seeking out the person who had so offended his presence. "Somebody has called me a demagogue," he said ponderously. "I do not know who. I hope that I never learn the man's name. I a demagogue? I who have borne all the ills and travail of this movement? The person who flung that word in my face ought to know that in every house and stable in Nahalal, in every little workshop in Tel Aviv or Haifa, there is a drop of my blood!" The Congress rose to a standing ovation, to reassure Weizmann. But it was a token tribute to past generations. The militant Ben-Gurion–Silver faction no longer had any use for the moderation of Weizmann or Stephen Wise; both elders were voted out of office, never to return.

In their new militancy, American Zionists ran up against one major and immediate obstacle: the President of the United States would have nothing to do with them. Hillel Silver was not an amiable man, and Truman could not abide him. On July 2, 1946, the rabbi had made the mistake of—literally—pounding on the President's desk, and that was something no one could ever expect an opportunity to do again. From that day until long after the state of Israel was a reality, Truman refused to receive the leader of American Zionism at the White House. And after the way Silver had treated Stephen Wise, he could expect no sympathy from Niles either.

As violence between Arabs and Jews mounted in British Palestine, Truman complained that "Terror and Silver are the contributing causes of some, if not all, of our troubles." Goldmann and his new Jewish Agency colleague in Washington, Eliahu Epstein, did their best to maintain communications with the United States government. Together they tended the groves of officialdom with their proposals and counterproposals, interrogations, maneuvers, interviews, and after-hours socializing— activities that Silver considered namby-pamby and downright un-Jewish. Yet sometimes Silver felt himself left out of the action, and demanded that he be invited to accompany Goldmann on his official errands. Knowing the general attitude toward the rabbi's bombast, the nimble Goldmann fended him off.

Politics of Zionism aside, even non-Zionist Jewish leaders argued that Silver's unyielding militancy was undermining efforts to gain government relief for the homeless Jews of Europe. At the national offices of B'nai B'rith, they pondered ways to penetrate the stone walls around Truman.

The executive vice-president of the fraternal order, Maurice Bisgyer, suddenly remembered something in Truman's past that might work.

BISGYER REACHED for the telephone one morning in the summer of 1947 and called his old friend A. J. Granoff, a lawyer in Kansas City. "A. J.," he began after the usual opening banter, "do you know a man in your city by the name of Jacobs or Jacobstein or Jacoby or something like that, who is in the clothing business and who is a good friend and former business partner of President Truman?" Granoff, as he recalled the moment, allowed himself a gentle grin. "You mean my friend Eddie Jacobson; sure I know him—I ought to, I'm his lawyer!" Not only that, they had been friends ever since the days when they shared car-pool duty at the Kansas City synagogue school of B'nai Yehudah. Worlds apart intellectually, Granoff and Jacobson enjoyed that deep-seated relationship of amiability.

Granoff was a boyhood immigrant from Russia who worked his way through law school to become a respected midwestern attorney. He had long been active in B'nai B'rith, and a telephone call from the national headquarters was nothing extraordinary in his working day; what was unusual was that the subject would be Eddie Jacobson, as unsophisticated in matters Jewish—or almost anything else—as Granoff was erudite. Granoff, in fact, was well ahead of the people in New York. He and other prominent Jews in Kansas City had already realized that Jacobson might be able to provide a valuable channel of access to his old friend the President, and they set about to "educate" the humble haberdasher about the fate of the Jews.

Granoff had become attracted to Zionism through his reading, but he kept quiet about it. Interest in a European conspiracy would not have gone down well at Synagogue B'nai Yehudah, where the revered Rabbi Mayerling professed himself "unalterably opposed" to political Zionism. Never had Granoff and Jacobson talked of the return to Zion. "It would be just like having discussed Greece or Babylonia with him," Granoff recalled. "It never occurred to me, or it never occurred to him." But every Thursday, the two of them would meet, along with other friends, for lunch at a private room in Max Bretton's restaurant, down the street from Eddie's haberdashery at Thirty-ninth and Main. If, as sometimes happened, Jacobson was on his way to Washington, the luncheons would turn into informal prepping sessions about things he might want to bring up with Truman. Then, after lunch, the group would escort Eddie to the downtown airport and wave him off to the White House.

The Jacobson-Truman talks were always off the record, and almost always inconsequential. Jacobson would slip into the White House by a side door, and the meetings would go unlogged in the White House appointment book. But it is evident that on a few particular occasions, contact with the well-briefed Jacobson made an impression on the President of the United States.

Jacobson later emerged as a colorful hero to Israelis, even as others minimized him. For Truman's daughter, Margaret Daniel, the Jacobson stories were "a great deal of myth and emotional exaggeration." But perhaps Margaret shared the scorn of her mother and grandmother for Truman's poker-playing cronies whose social standing did not quite measure up. More weighty was the scorn of Silver and the Zionist leaders. If private little encounters had been so influential, what was left to be said about all the efforts of the Jewish lobby, or of the partisans of Bergson with all his public relations stunts? Jacobson the haberdasher was not of a stature to be recognized by the leadership of American Zionism. For that matter, Jacobson never saw himself as a Zionist. "Never would the Zionists have stooped to the use of the likes of Eddie Jacobson if they had not been totally desperate," said Granoff's son, Loeb, many years later.

But "totally desperate" was a very close description of the American Zionist leadership and the *shlichim* from Palestine in early 1947, as they mobilized for the climax of an ancient epic.

10

ON FEBRUARY 14, 1947, the Jewish restoration was placed in the care of the United Nations. Acknowledging that its mandate had failed to maintain peace between rival Arab and Jewish claimants to Palestine, Britain asked the General Assembly to find a better way—if it could. What Roosevelt had been reaching for in his dying days took shape: the land holy to three of the world's great religions became the first major political test for the new organization of world order.

Whitehall's motive for yielding authority was endlessly debated, but whatever else it may have been, it was not the idealism of Roosevelt. The Labour government clearly expected the General Assembly to fail in its search for a workable political formula and to end up by reconfirming Britain's stewardship over Palestine on more manageable terms. British diplomats calculated (and few rose to challenge the calculation) that Jewish statehood would never muster a two-thirds UN majority and that the renewed mandate would therefore be liberated from the shackles of the Balfour Declaration. Furthermore, Attlee and Bevin delighted in the knowledge that their initiative would force the hand of the United States: once Palestine had become an issue before the General Assembly, Britain would never again be solely responsible for what happened there, the target for any American politician who chose to stand on the sidelines and carp.

The abrupt British move overturned all the diplomacy of the first postwar years, and Zionists and diplomats were alike in their forebodings. "1947 is going to be a bad year in Palestine and the Middle East," Under Secretary of State Dean Acheson warned Henderson, "with increasing violence and grave danger to our interests." Retired but still involved, Weizmann mourned that "so far nothing has come from America's side which would justify greater hopes in the future." The new forum of the United Nations offered "a great chance if it is properly prepared and handled," Weizmann wrote, "but it is also the last chance." The veteran of Zionist diplomacy was deeply skeptical about the ability of his successors, militants like Silver and Ben-Gurion, to shepherd the cause through the legislative subtleties of an untested fifty-seven-nation parliament. "There is no appeal from this tribunal," he warned them.

In that spring of 1947, the United Nations had not yet moved into its skyscraper home in Manhattan. Instead, delegates from around the world convened upon the suburban flatlands of Flushing Meadow, Queens, about a half-hour drive from midtown. In plenary session, the General Assembly gathered in a converted skating rink, built for the New York World's Fair of 1939; smaller committee meetings were held in the clutter of a remodeled factory, formerly the home of the Sperry Gyroscope Company, in the Long Island bedroom community buoyantly named Lake Success.

With the move to this new setting, the Zionists had to regroup their diplomatic forces—and fast. Brushing Weizmann's reservations aside, Silver asserted his right to lead the Zionist delegation to Lake Success. But Ben-Gurion and the Jewish Agency leaders in Palestine made the case that they, after all, were the people most directly affected. Moshe Shertok, the Agency's unofficial Foreign Minister, proposed that Weizmann himself should be called back into action in consideration of his vast diplomatic experience and stature. But Silver, as newly elected head of the World Zionist Organization, pulled rank, and with all the organizational and financial muscle of American Jews behind him could not be denied the role of official spokesman for Zionism in the assembly of nations. In this capacity he dominated the press conference and lecture circuit, but a little team of Zionist professionals arrived in New York to deal with the quiet diplomacy of the corridors and committee rooms.

Goldmann was among them. He had lost ground during the factional disputes at Basel in December, but he could never stay away from a mission of quiet diplomacy, and working with him was the young up-and-coming Walter Eytan, later founder and director general of the Israeli Foreign Ministry. There was David Horowitz, a brilliant and articulate young economist whose powers of persuasion were not limited to the balance sheets. He became governor of the Bank of Israel. And there was a plump and arrogant young English scholar, Major Aubrey (he later Hebraicized his name to Abba) Eban.

The General Assembly devised its approach in the spring of 1947. It established the United Nations Special Committee on Palestine (UNSCOP), bestowing upon it "the widest powers to ascertain and record facts, and to investigate all questions and issues relevant to the problem of Palestine." It was to report back to the General Assembly in the autumn, with its findings to serve as starting point for a general debate and vote. Britain declared its intention to remain sternly aloof from the General Assembly's considerations, and the United States tried to take the same position, at least in the opening stages. But American diplomats went so far as to insist that no great power—least of all the Soviet Union —be represented on UNSCOP. The idea was that Palestine should be a test of international responsibility, not power politics, and the eleven delegates named to the committee came from countries far removed from Middle East power struggles.

UNSCOP took its work and responsibility seriously. The members toured Palestine and sought to learn for themselves why the Arabs opposed Jewish immigration. They visited DP camps in Europe to verify Zionist claims that the refugees truly sought emigration to Palestine. They held hearings in Jerusalem; Palestinian Arab nationalists refused to appear before them, but all other voices were heard—the Jewish Agency, the Franciscans and Anglicans representing the Christian communities. Six different organizations testified on behalf of world Jewry, representing cultural, religious, and decidedly anti-Zionist views.

Weizmann was summoned from retirement to speak—to the discomfiture of Ben-Gurion and his Jewish Agency colleagues, who feared his stubborn moderation. The old chemist-diplomat was nearly blind by this time; the text of his prepared statement had been printed for him in letters nearly an inch high. As he lowered himself into the chair at the witness table he knocked the dozens of pages of text onto the floor in hopeless disarray. Without a moment's hesitation, ignoring the now useless text, he delivered as eloquent a plea for the Jewish state as any that could have been written for him.

Events had as much impact on UNSCOP as testimony. The day the diplomats arrived in Palestine, British administrators sentenced five members of the Jewish underground to death. The resentment and dismay of Jews in Palestine colored the committee's entire tour. And worse was to come.

The Sonneborn Institute of New York had bought a battered old Chesapeake Bay ferryboat, refitted her to hold 4,500 DPs for the Mediterranean crossing to Palestine, and named her *Exodus-1947*. The British blockade fleet spotted the vessel and resolved to make an example of it in order to discourage the illegal immigration. British seamen boarded the *Exodus* off the Palestine coast, interned the passengers, and, as the world press sent out lurid daily dispatches describing their misery, transported the refugees back to Germany. If ever a show of force was counterproductive, it was this one. A watching public in a dozen countries, including people who had no particular interest in Jews or in Palestine, could scarcely avoid sympathizing with the *Exodus* passengers, Jews tragically returned by force to barbed-wire encampments in Germany. The *Exodus* returnees arrived at the same time as the UNSCOP members; visiting the internment centers, the UN investigators judged the frustrated refugees "the best possible evidence we can have" for the necessity of increased Jewish immigration to Palestine.

UNSCOP had a large staff, but one aide was particularly influential among the committee members, an American Negro named Ralph Bunche. Bunche organized the committee's travels and the testimony which would be presented; he prepared the agendas, assembled the working papers, made sure that the members were properly briefed. At the news of the execution of five Palestinian Jews, Bunche took it upon himself to arrange for UNSCOP to meet the hunted chieftain of the Jewish underground army, Menachem Begin, in his hideout near the Mediterranean seashore. Changing cars several times en route to avoid detection, Bunche brought along two particularly discreet committee members to hear Begin's passionate appeals for national redemption.

Bunche was moved by his exposure to the Jewish plight. After hearing Weizmann, he confessed that his own feelings as a Negro had been awakened in "emotional identity." As he was leaving Begin's hideout, the no longer completely dispassionate diplomat said something that the future Prime Minister of Israel never forgot: "I can understand you. I am also a member of a persecuted minority." Richard Crossman of Britain asked jocularly at one point if Bunche's exposure to the Jews had made him antisemitic "yet." Bunche replied without humor, "That would be impossible." Caught up short, Crossman turned equally serious. "Why?" "Because I've been a Negro for forty-two years. . . . I know the flavor of racial prejudice and racial persecution. A wise Negro can never be an antisemite," Bunche said.

At the start of their three-month investigation, no more than three of the eleven UNSCOP members had been sympathetic to the Jews' desire for their own state. When they were finished, the split was quite different. Unanimously, the committee voted that Britain's thirty years of mandate over Palestine should be ended. A minority of the group opted for the formula favored by the earlier Anglo-American Committee of Inquiry: a unitary federal Palestine with Arab and Jewish communities sharing power. But a majority proposed instead that Palestine should be partitioned into separate Arab and Jewish states.

The two proposals set forth in the UNSCOP report eloquently defined the Palestine dilemma in 1947; both positions were actually written by the same draftsman, Ralph Bunche. Representatives of seven countries

—Canada, Czechoslovakia, Guatemala, the Netherlands, Peru, Sweden, and Uruguay—voted for partition, with an economic union, between an Arab and a Jewish state.

> The basic premise is that the claims to Palestine of the Arabs and Jews, both possessing validity, are irreconcilable. . . . Regardless of the historical origins of the conflict, the rights and wrongs of the promises and counter-promises, . . . there are now in Palestine some 650,000 Jews and some 1,200,000 Arabs who are dissimilar in their ways of living and, for the time being, separated by political interests which render difficult full and effective political cooperation among them. Only by means of partition can these conflicting national aspirations find substantial expression and qualify both peoples to take their places as independent nations.

A special provision was made for the holy city of Jerusalem (encompassing nearby Bethlehem) to be administered by the United Nations as an international zone.

In contrast, the three nations in the minority—India, Iran, and Yugoslavia (Australia abstained from both recommendations)—stated the same premises and came to opposite conclusions: "Palestine is the common country of both indigenous Arabs and Jews; both these people have had an historic association with it and . . . both play vital roles in the economic and cultural life of the country. . . . The objective of a federal state solution would be to give the most feasible recognition to the nationalistic aspirations of both Arabs and Jews and to merge them into a single loyalty and patriotism, which would find expression in an independent Palestine." Partition, the minority argued, "is impracticable, unworkable, and could not possibly provide for two reasonably viable states."

The rhetoric of both sides was compelling; Bunche had done his staff work well (though he conceded he felt like a "ghost-writing harlot" doing so). But behind the rhetoric were practical political interests. For the Arabs and their sympathizers, the unitary state of Palestine was clearly preferable; they were the majority and, with continued limits on immigration, they would remain the majority. Partition, by contrast, would give the Zionists a state of their own, inadequate in size, to be sure, but a homeland for national survival.

THE PARTITION OF the Holy Land, the notion that the Jews should share the divine inheritance with another people, had no place in the prophecy of Pastor McDonald or Mordecai Noah, or even in Franklin D. Roosevelt's declaration that "Palestine should be for the Jews." But the idea did occur to a few timorous Zionists in the 1930s, as they saw the intensity of Arab passions and the difficulties involved in realizing the promise of Balfour. Reluctant to give away too much too soon, they were hesitant to promote the idea.

In January 1937, as a British Royal Commission heard testimony in Jerusalem, a professor of colonial history at Oxford named Reginald Coupland suddenly injected a novel idea. "Might it not be a final and peaceful settlement to terminate the mandate by agreement and split Palestine into two halves, the plain being an independent Jewish state . . . and the rest of Palestine, plus Trans-Jordania, being an independent Arab state?" Weizmann was the witness to whom the question was put. He was too shrewd a negotiator to agree on the spot—"It is cutting the child in two," he protested—but once out of the hearing room his excitement overflowed. With Coupland's casual suggestion, he raved to an aide, "the Jewish state was at hand."

Other Zionists were dubious. The right-wing followers of Vladimir Ze'ev Jabotinsky were outraged at being asked to part with any of the ancestral land. Even moderates like Stephen Wise argued that ancestral Palestine had already been partitioned in 1922, when Britain bestowed the land across the Jordan on the Arab Hashemite family. But Weizmann's loyalists argued that the Jews should be willing to settle for a city-state of Tel Aviv, just to establish the principle of the homeland.

The Royal Commission headed by Lord Peel formally proposed partition in July 1937, and a furor erupted among the Jewish settlers in Palestine. "Someday my son will ask me by what right I gave up most of the country," argued the American immigrant from Milwaukee Golda Meir, "and I won't know how to answer him." But Ben-Gurion reluctantly admitted that the future potential of half a state was better than nothing, and when a Zionist world congress convened in Zurich in August 1937, he defended the proposition for an entire week. By a narrow majority, the assembled Zionists voted to open negotiations with Britain toward dividing Palestine into separate Jewish and Arab states. It would be a start. "If partition is accepted and goes through," said a pro-Zionist member of the House of Commons, "I hope that the Jews will treat it merely as a stepping-off ground for further advance."

Other governments watched the British strategy with interest, none so much as Nazi Germany. "The formation of a Jewish state or a Jewish-led political structure under British Mandate is not in Germany's interest," Foreign Minister Konstantin von Neurath advised his diplomatic missions, "since a [Jewish] Palestinian state would not absorb world Jewry but would create an additional position of power under international law for international Jewry, somewhat like the Vatican State for political Catholicism or Moscow for the Comintern. . . . Germany therefore has an interest in strengthening the Arab world as a counterweight against such a possible increase in power for world Jewry." In Washington, the State Department maintained a firm lack of concern, for Palestine was Britain's problem.

The Arabs rejected the whole idea. No Arab lands should be abandoned to the intruding Jews, they argued, for the Zionists would regard a sliver of a state as no more than a toehold. The Peel Commission proposal was withdrawn, and the pendulum in Whitehall swung toward the Arab demand to restrict Jewish immigration, culminating in the White Paper of 1939.

The idea of partition lay dormant through the early 1940s. At the Biltmore, Ben-Gurion spoke of an undivided Palestine, for there was no point in conceding anything at that stage. Weizmann, however, kept his private hopes alive. "He cannot forget his partition plan," Shertok reported to a Zionist meeting in 1943. "If we were given any part of Palestine for a Jewish state, I think he would accept it." Shertok was right. In a remarkably frank interview with one of Churchill's private secretaries in October 1944, Weizmann made explicit the theory of the toehold which the Arabs so feared. The British official jotted down Weizmann's remarks:

> He made it clear that he did not regard it as impossible to devise some form of partition which would be acceptable and frankly gave his reason as being that it was possible to take two bites at the cherry. So long as sufficient elbow room was given at the start, he did not see why all the burden should fall on the present generation and why one could not look to the possibility of future expansion by some means or other.

And he made the point directly in a letter to Welles:

> Our heritage in Palestine was cut down to the bone when Transjordan was separated in 1922. What is left is clearly a unit, and further partition of it would deprive the settlement of finality.

With the shock of Roosevelt's death, the disclosures of the Holocaust, and the despair of the survivors in the DP camps, nothing was to be gained by presenting subtle political formulas for Palestine. By the late summer of 1946, however, perhaps the time was at hand to resume talk of partition. Goldmann was one who thought so, and he flew to Washington to test the atmosphere. His inquiries stirred guarded interest at both

White House and State Department, since the unitary state proposed by the Anglo-American Committee of Inquiry was going nowhere. But United States policy was still to leave such matters to the British.

Then came the move to the General Assembly, and the UNSCOP majority recommendation. "We could urge more ideal solutions. . . . We could point to more logical plans," commented the *Christian Science Monitor*. "But the best present hope is not in some other plan; it is in perfecting this one—which carries the indispensable sanction of careful and impartial study by a United Nations agency."

THE UNITED STATES could no longer leave all political questions about the Holy Land to Britain. Senior officials, who had previously ignored the matter, began to realize that Palestine might require a certain amount of personal attention in the months to come. One such was the hard-driving Secretary of the Navy, James V. Forrestal. Palestine had no place on his personal agenda before the United Nations became involved. Truman had at least read history and savored the ancient drama of the Jews' yearning to return to their homeland; Forrestal's only perspective on the Middle East had been the Navy's need for secure sources of oil, and what did Palestine have to do with that?

Dutifully, he decided to learn something more about the situation; he asked a staff aide for a briefing paper about the Balfour Declaration and everything that had happened since. Obviously there were many books on the subject, he noted, but he just wanted a quick fill-in. The result was a six-page memorandum from a rear admiral in the office of the Chief of Naval Operations. It told the story of Zionism from the beginning, encompassing the struggles of generations in statements such as "There is a wide divergence of opinion on the problem of Palestine among both Zionists and Arabs." Forrestal now felt ready to stake out a firm position, one of unswerving hostility to Zionism. Over the months to come, his would be one of the strongest voices arguing that the Jewish restoration would pose a deadly threat to the security and strategy interests of the United States in the Middle East.

At least one small government office needed no crash briefings on Palestine. Henderson and his Near East Division were not accustomed to being accorded high-level attention, and when it fell upon them they were a little skittish. Niles at the White House had long been undermining them with his innuendos, and Bartley Crum of California had followed up his public tirades against Henderson with a book of memoirs about his brief experience in diplomacy as a member of the Anglo-American Committee of Inquiry. Its title, *Behind the Silken Curtain,* conveyed an air of mystery and intrigue, and it hit the *New York Times* best-seller list as soon as it came out.

The central perception behind the diplomats' silken curtain in mid-1947 was that whatever happened, whatever UNSCOP and then the General Assembly decided about Palestine, the United States should not be out in front—neither in proposing a solution nor in assuming responsibility for sustaining one. "If the plan finally adopted should be considered as primarily an American plan," Henderson argued, "or as a plan decided upon as a result of American pressure, we should probably be held primarily responsible for the administration and enforcement."

Henderson visited United Nations headquarters to get a personal sense of the situation, and returned "with the strong conviction that the Department is in for very serious pressure from Jewish quarters in the United States." Faced with such a prospect, he moved to ensure that the lines of policy direction and communication would be tamper-proof. He proposed that the United States delegation to the forthcoming General Assembly include one adviser solely responsible for Palestine, with a separate staff and reporting directly to Washington—insulated, in short, from the contentious politics of New York and the Assembly floor. His candidate for this sensitive post was George Wadsworth, ambassador to Iraq, a true diplomatic professional, trusted Arabist, and firm anti-Zionist—just Henderson's type of man. But Niles was ever alert over at the White House, and when he saw routine State Department traffic about Wadsworth, he spotted Henderson's proposal for the bureaucratic power play that it was.

On July 29, 1947, Niles sent Truman a carefully drafted memorandum assessing the Palestine strategy for the forthcoming General Assembly. Here was the "involved" staff man at work, nudging his principal's thought processes along with innuendo but without overt partisanship. "As you may recall," Niles began, "there was much unfavorable comment last April from certain sources about the alleged failure of the United States delegation . . . to carry out your policy on Palestine." The opening line set Truman's attitudes clearly in place: American Zionists had been upset at United States aloofness over UNSCOP; Niles phrased this in terms of "failing to carry out Truman's policy," whereas, in truth, Truman really had no policy at that point and the diplomats were just showing prudent reserve.

"Perhaps by taking some steps, we can anticipate and thus avoid more such criticism before, during and after the Fall session. It might become very damaging in those areas that gave us trouble last November." Translation: here is the way to avoid losing more of the Jewish vote. "I understand that the key advisors on Palestine . . . will be Loy Henderson and George Wadsworth. Because both are widely regarded as unsympathetic to the Jewish viewpoint, much resentment will be engendered when their appointment is announced and later. Moreover, on the basis of their past behavior and attitudes, I frankly doubt that they will vigorously carry out your policy. But your administration, not they, will be held responsible." Between politicians nothing could be clearer than that. "I believe that it is most important that at least one of the advisors be a vigorous and well informed individual in whom you, the members of the United States delegation, and American Jewry have complete confidence. There is only one person I know who would fill the bill completely. . . ." With the nomination of his own candidate, in sum, Niles moved to short-circuit Henderson's attempt to pack the delegation.

Niles's candidate, Major General John H. Hilldring, had been a tough infantry officer who affected the gruff air of "just a simple soldier." But he was also an assiduous administrator, and had been assigned oversight of the DP problem in occupied Europe after the uproar of the Harrison report. When the occupation regime passed to civilian control, Hilldring left the Pentagon to become Assistant Secretary of State for the Occupied Areas. Hilldring had no interest in Zionism, but he knew the survivors of the Holocaust and he grew to appreciate their aspirations to Zion. Niles urged Truman, "as a matter of urgency," to name him to the United States delegation to the General Assembly "to insure that your viewpoint is effectively expressed."

Truman accepted Niles's recommendation, and the Henderson power play collapsed. With Hilldring on board, wrote the astute journalist I. F. Stone, Truman had safeguarded his Palestine policy "against sabotage by the State Department bureaucracy." For the climactic weeks of autumn 1947, it was Hilldring—not Henderson or any of the professional diplomats—who controlled policy for Palestine in the United States delegation to the United Nations, and he acted with the authority of the White House behind him.

Hilldring had no interest in personal publicity. He wrote no books or articles about himself, withdrew to private life in 1948, and lived on until 1974 in relative obscurity as others around him were hailed for their parts in the drama of the Jewish restoration. It fell to his aide and longtime friend, Herbert Fierst, to declare after his death, "If not for General Hilldring, there might not have been a State of Israel."

THE REAL QUESTION awaited an answer. Would the United States vote for the partition of Palestine or not? The issue engaged public-minded citizens across America of all creeds and persuasions, visionaries and reactionaries, liberals, conservatives, Jews, guilt-ridden Christians, anti-semites, missionaries, oil men, DPs, propagandists, the President, the State Department, the Pentagon, and the political pros.

One person held a particular place in the public mind and in Truman's own estimation. Eleanor Roosevelt had acquired unique political and moral stature; in her own right she was a member of the United States delegation to the General Assembly. When she wrote the President in support of partition and Jewish statehood, Truman replied with tact and respect, but no conviction. "I fear very much that the Jews are like all underdogs. When they get on top they are just as intolerant and as cruel as the people were to them when they were underneath. I regret this situation very much because my sympathy has always been on their side," Truman wrote.

The late President's widow had long since overcome the snobbishness of her patrician upbringing, and had come to see the Jewish destiny as a great humanitarian challenge. Even more, Palestine was to her the acid test of the United Nations itself. In those early years of idealism and adventure, any step that would strengthen the foundations of a new world order could command widespread support in the United States, whatever might be the merits of the issue at hand. By a majority vote, a United Nations committee had recommended the partition of Palestine. American support for this verdict, Mrs. Roosevelt declared, would "strengthen the United Nations in the mind of the American people."

To Henderson and other hard-line diplomats in Washington, a strengthened United Nations was just what they did not want to promote —yet another reason to be skeptical about the UNSCOP partition plan. The very week of UNSCOP's creation, moreover, the Truman Doctrine was implemented to protect Greece and Turkey from Communist aggression. Stalin's Russia was no longer a wartime ally, but seemed a real threat to peace. How would the Soviet Union try to exploit the Palestine confrontation?

Since the 1920s, Soviet spokesmen had been criticizing Zionism as another outcropping of bourgeois imperialism. Britain, the United States, and the Jewish Agency were as one in assuming that the Russians would oppose any plan to create a Jewish state. On May 10, 1947, the American chargé d'affaires in Moscow, Elbridge Durbrow, cabled that Soviet policy would be "opposition to formation in all or part of Palestine of Jewish state, which USSR would regard as Zionist tool of west, inevitably hostile to Soviet Union."

Just four days later the young spokesman for the Soviet Union, Andrei Gromyko, stepped to the podium of the General Assembly and exploded all the diplomats' calculations. The Soviet Union understood "the legitimate rights of the Jewish people," as well as those of the Arab population, Gromyko said. An "independent, dual, democratic, homogeneous Arab-Jewish state" in Palestine would be the best means of securing those rights, but if that were to prove impossible of realization, then partition into separate Arab and Jewish states could certainly be a reasonable fallback position.

"This was a windfall," wrote a Jewish Agency observer, Abba Eban. "At one stroke we had to revise all our predictions about the possible outcome of a United Nations discussion." So did the British, who had never imagined the possibility of Soviet support for a Jewish state. Durbrow in Moscow and his colleagues in the State Department pondered for thirteen days and concluded that the Gromyko statement was a ruse, a tactical maneuver to gain points with liberal and Jewish intellectuals in the West, while preserving their own freedom of action. For all the Kremlin's interest in the Arab and Muslim world, a dynamic Zionist state would be more likely to reject British influence than a weaker state dominated by the Arabs. Any step that would remove a Western bridgehead in the Middle East would be a plus for Moscow, and whatever would take its place would be open to manipulation and exploitation. Finally, the Russians could not have failed to note that militant Zionism was driving a wedge between Britain and the United States, and with their own designs building up on Eastern Europe, Germany, and Berlin, dissension in the West would be helpful.

With suspicion but intense curiosity, American diplomats watched as Jewish Agency delegates held lengthy discussions with the Russians at their mission at Park Avenue and Sixty-eighth Street in Manhattan. In these discussions, intended to confirm Moscow's support for each detail of a future partition accord, Rabbi Silver took part—somehow his style of bombast and desk-pounding was not offensive to the diplomats of the Soviet Union. Indeed, ever alert for ways to needle Washington officialdom, Silver haughtily refused to hold official discussions with any of the big powers, unless his newfound Soviet comrades were included.

The confidential minutes of the Jewish Agency Executive Committee reveal the excitement over the Soviet attitude as the UN deliberations were heading toward the final vote. "This Russian business is quite extraordinary; historically, it is quite fantastic," exclaimed the normally pedantic Shertok. "It is nothing short of an ideological revolution that these people have undergone. . . . It is a complete reorientation on the basic issue of the Zionist, of the Jewish state. . . . They accepted the idea of a provisional Jewish government right away. . . . They accepted the idea that the Jewish Agency will become the parent body of the government." Winding up his breathless report to his colleagues, Shertok said, "It was fantastic. . . . First of all, . . . they offered wine, and then Stein [one of the Soviet diplomats] said, 'Gentlemen, what are you waiting for, an official invitation for a toast?' We drank an ordinary 'Le Chaim,' then on the second round Tsarapkin [the chief Soviet delegate] raised his glass and said, 'Let's drink for the Jewish State!' "

Shertok and his colleagues reported to the Americans after every meeting with the Russians, but the State Department experts could never be sure that they were being told everything. "The American government is not going to support the establishment of a Jewish state unless it is sure that such a state will be an asset to her interests, and not a liability," said Archibald Roosevelt, soon to be posted to the embassy in Beirut. He reminded an acquaintance in the Jewish Agency of the nagging suspicion that Communist infiltrators were among refugees moving to Palestine from Europe. Another Roosevelt cousin, Kermit, whose years of intelligence operations in the Middle East tied him closely to the Arab cause, worked out what was to become the standard explanation for the Soviet position. The idea that a Jewish state would be hostile to the Soviet Union was merely disinformation, he declared, cleverly planted over the years and accepted by gullible Americans. In reality, Kermit Roosevelt argued, the partition of Palestine would aid the Soviet drive to the warm waters of the Mediterranean. The Russians "would gain a military foothold in the Middle East, on the assumptions that partition must be imposed by force and that force used for this purpose by the UN must involve Russian participation." And most important, he concluded, partition would "insure chaos and confusion in the Middle East."

The experts' reading of the linkage between Bolshevism and Zionism remained as subjective in 1947 as it had been in 1917. When the Russians appeared to oppose the creation of a Jewish state, that was supposed to be cover for their long-standing strategy of introducing fifth columnists and underground agents through the flow of refugees from Europe. Then, when the Russians switched to endorse the Jewish state, that was supposedly proof that Moscow saw Zionism as wholly congenial with the idea of world revolution.

IN THE AUTUMN of 1947, when the matter of the Jewish restoration came up for decision, Washington was caught between opposing pressures: idealism for the UN, guilt for the Holocaust, even religious zeal for the realization of ancient prophecy worked on one side; on the other were the negative strategic arguments, the fear of losing secure fuel sources, the traditional diplomatic sympathy for the Arab world. And the wily

Soviet ally/adversary—which was it?—kept sending mixed signals in Europe and the Middle East.

Once an official United Nations body had endorsed partition, even non-Zionist American Jews could rally around the principle of a Jewish state without endangering their loyalty to the United States. To doubters like Judge Joseph Proskauer, head of the American Jewish Committee, this internationally approved plan served as a belated solution to the plight of the homeless Jews remaining in Europe. Militant Zionists, of course, were less than enthusiastic about the offer of only half a state, and on the extremist flanks Irgun leaders—Bergson in America, Begin in Palestine—condemned the readiness of the Zionist moderates to consider giving up any part of the Jewish patrimony.

The diplomats in the Near East Division objected to partition for opposite reasons. In a top-secret letter to the new Secretary of State, George C. Marshall, Loy Henderson conveyed the views "of nearly every member of the Foreign Service or of the Department who has worked to any appreciable extent on Near Eastern problems." United States national interests would not be served, Henderson argued, by "any kind of a plan at this time for the partitioning of Palestine or for the setting up of a Jewish state in Palestine."

The American delegation to the UN—including even the two members most sympathetic to Zionism, General Hilldring and Eleanor Roosevelt—voiced nervousness about the responsibility that the United States would incur by endorsing partition, against Arab and British opposition. On the other hand, the United States certainly did not want to weaken the United Nations. Arab representatives were in the meantime bearing down with threats about turning to the Soviet Union if the United States let them down, threats so bold and unsubtle that even anti-Zionist State Department officers could be heard muttering about "blackmail." Marshall met the assembled Arab ambassadors at a luncheon on September 23 and firmly warned them that the United States would not consent to "throw the UNSCOP report out of the window." The wiser course, he argued, "was to dignify the proceedings of the United Nations by paying tribute to the UNSCOP effort and by accepting the UNSCOP report as a working basis."

Next day the decision was made formal, to accept the UNSCOP majority report in principle—about as lukewarm an endorsement of partition as diplomatic ingenuity could fashion. On October 11, when its turn came to speak before the General Assembly, the United States declared for partition. The Soviet Union followed two days later. It was the first major political test of the new organization, and the two rival superpowers were on the same side.

Then began the legislative process. The UNSCOP formula had to be converted into a detailed and sweeping constitutional document. Diplomats from half a hundred countries parsed every passage and nuance in tedious committee deliberations, Zionist sympathizers seeking to maximize the gains for the Jewish state, opponents determined to preserve all they could for the Arabs of Palestine. The lobbying, persuasion, haggling were intense. Formal deliberations took place in the old skating rink at Lake Success; other meetings, some announced, some secret, convened at hotels, restaurants, and diplomatic missions across New York City. The shiny black limousines sped back and forth across the East River day after day.

Among the first-class passengers arriving on the *Queen Mary* early in October was a dignified and stately relic from the old Zionist battles. Ailing but determined to miss nothing, Chaim Weizmann returned to New York. Even his rivals in Zionism conceded that the old man might still have some useful influence. A report spelling out the UN state of play was handed to him on the deck—details of the wavering delegates, the buttonholing, the diverse pressures at work in New York and Washington. "Pendulum swings back and forth," Weizmann was advised, and he set to work straightaway to gain access to the one man of importance who so far refused to listen to Zionist entreaties.

The President of the United States had reached his limit of amiability, even of civility. But here was a distinguished old man, the scientist who had served the Allies well in two world wars, a man who had known Balfour, who would surely belong in a new edition of "Great Men and Famous Women"—such a man could not be denied access to Harry Truman's White House, and Weizmann knew it. The meeting took weeks to arrange, but on November 18 Weizmann boarded the overnight train to Washington. His former adversary and present disciple, Justice Felix Frankfurter, was waiting for him at Union Station. They drove together to a suite at the Shoreham Hotel. At noon, Weizmann met Truman for an off-the-record interview that lasted a scant fifteen minutes.

Weizmann saw this as the wrong moment for generalities, however glowing, or for old grievances, however much he felt that Truman had wronged the Zionists. Instead, he concentrated on a single point, one that was even then under discussion at Lake Success: a proposal, which the United States seemed likely to support, to detach the wide desert wastes of the Negev from the Jewish state proposed by UNSCOP and assign it instead to the Arab Palestinian state. Truman listened politely to the worldly old gentleman holding forth about the desert that could bloom as the rose, the symbolism of a stretch of wasteland as remote from the plains of Missouri as could be found on the globe. "It's the first time in my life," Weizmann said, "that I have met a President who can read and understand maps!" (typical disingenuous flattery, for the old Zionist had gone over many maps with Roosevelt, the amateur geographer).

Truman had not followed the maneuvers at Lake Success closely. The Negev for the Jews or for the Arabs meant nothing to him. On the spot, he decided that the old man's arguments were convincing and that he, Truman of Missouri, would let the Jews have their Negev. There ensued, over the next three hours, one of those comically crossed signals that give diplomats nightmares—and change the map of the world.

Under Secretary of State Robert A. Lovett had kept on top of the UN discussions and, with Henderson's concurrence, had decided that the Arab nationalists would consider accepting partition only if they got the Negev. At 1 p.m., Lovett telephoned his instructions to Hilldring and the chief American delegate, Herschel Johnson, to prepare them for a 3 p.m. consultation with the Jewish Agency delegation. Lovett knew that the President had just seen Weizmann, but it never occurred to him to consider that any technical or operational matter might have come up. Nor did Truman, careless as always about things that got diplomats so excited, see any need for urgency in telling his State Department of the promise he had just made to his visitor.

Weizmann himself was not so naïve about the workings of bureaucracy. He promptly telephoned word of his talk to the Jewish Agency delegates at Lake Success, so that they would know about Truman's promise before the 3 p.m. meeting with the Americans.

Diplomats of the two sides arrived at the delegates' lounge on schedule. Johnson was ready, on Lovett's instructions, to announce that the United States favored changing the UNSCOP recommendation and assigning the Negev to the Arab state. Shertok and the Jewish Agency aides expected, on the basis of their report from Weizmann, to hear that the United States would propose no change in the UNSCOP map. The delegates arranged themselves casually around a little table, exchanging the obligatory small talk, sorting out the correct assignments of coffee black, with cream, with sugar, with cream and sugar. Then Johnson started to deliver his message.

In midsentence a page summoned him to the telephone. Johnson dispatched Hilldring to take the call and resumed his statement. Hilldring reappeared to whisper that the President himself was holding the line from Washington. "Ambassador Johnson leapt to the telephone booth like a startled and portly reindeer," recalled Eban. He was absent for twenty minutes. Shertok scribbled a little note to one of the junior Americans: "I am surprised you people are taking such a strong stand on this." Johnson returned and slowly reseated himself among the now empty coffee cups. "What I really wanted to say to you," he declared carefully, "was that we have no changes in the map you suggest." The Negev was for the Jews.

No record exists of exactly what Truman said to Johnson a few minutes after 3 p.m. on November 19, 1947. It was something about doing nothing to "upset the applecart," and all the hapless ambassador at the end of the line could assume was that the President wanted him to leave everything just the way it was. Only three hours later did Lovett finally get through to Truman and learn firsthand how the President had overruled the State Department once again.

A GUN-SHY AMERICAN delegation at Lake Success discovered that it was following two different—and contradictory—lines of instructions. From the State Department, from Lovett and Henderson, came orders that the American role in the partition debate should be passive: the United States would support partition, but it would not attempt to influence others. From the White House, from Niles through Hilldring, the signals made plain that American diplomacy should be more active, that influence should be mobilized to line up votes for partition.

Vote-counting in the United Nations was not a well-developed art in 1947, when the General Assembly was only two years old. But the delegation of the Jewish Agency could not afford to leave anything to chance. While Shertok and Silver made their public pronouncements, Eytan, Eban, Horowitz, and the others were keeping book on all delegates' inclinations, political and personal.

"Here was the Jewish people at the threshold of its greatest transition," Eban wrote, "and yet there was a danger that everything would be lost through utterly marginal circumstances in countries ostensibly external to the issue." To whom would the Liberian delegates really listen? Could anyone reach the Philippines delegation via friends in Manila? How was Haiti leaning on Tuesday? Accosting delegates at every turn, in the lounges at Lake Success, in the diplomatic dining rooms of Manhattan, the Jewish Agency teams deployed all the techniques of persuasion that Weizmann himself had perfected in Balfour's London a generation before. Their arguments were tailored to the interests and emotions of each particular interlocutor. To the diplomats from the Netherlands, the representatives from Jewish Palestine stressed economic development, praised Dutch efforts at reclamation at home. "We propose to conquer the wilderness in the same way you conquered the ocean," argued Horowitz. To the Ethiopians, by contrast, the Zionist team stressed ancient

history, the Queen of Sheba, the ties of Ethiopia with the land of Israel
in biblical days.

UN membership stood at 57. Britain, fearful that the General Assembly might come up with some solution after all, announced that it would
oppose partition. The United States and the Soviet Union, for their quite
different reasons, supported the creation of separate Jewish and Arab
states. The two other big powers, France and China, remained impon-
derables.

Solid against partition were five Arab states: Saudi Arabia, Syria,
Iraq, Lebanon, and Egypt. Aligned with them were states with large
Muslim populations: Iran, Pakistan, Afghanistan. Yugoslavia leaned toward the Arab view—influenced by its own multi-ethnic experience, it
had voted with the UNSCOP minority—but lobby conversations gave hints
that if theirs proved to be the deciding vote, Belgrade's delegates could
change. India was a special case: In view of its own Muslim population
of 30 million, its urge to identify with the Arab cause was strong. So also
was a reluctance to accept partition as a solution for anything, given the
partitioning of their own land and the creation of Pakistan. Yet India's
chief delegate, Mrs. Vijaya Pandit, sister of the Prime Minister, seemed
deeply sympathetic to the Jewish representatives, with whom she held
long and intense consultations. The seventeen non-white member states
of the UN formed a bloc feared by the Jewish Agency; decisions might
well be made along racial lines. China, for instance, "wobbled all over,"
noted one of the Zionist lobbyists, torn between considerations of racial
independence and economic and diplomatic reliance on the United
States.

Europeans displayed a worried inability to choose between Jewish
destiny and Arab oil. Jewish nationalists had strong supporters in the
delegations of Sweden and Iceland, while the Danes tended to follow
Britain. Belgium, the Netherlands, and Luxembourg looked nervously
back and forth between Britain and ambivalent France.

The greatest challenge for the Jewish lobbyists at Lake Success was
the bloc of Latin American states, which totaled one-third of the UN
membership. Niles had noted the importance of this bloc long before.
Urging that the United States support UN membership for Franco's
Spain, thus shocking his liberal friends, Niles argued, "Letting Spain
into the UN means nothing, but if we support it, that will assure us of
eleven votes for partition." An indefatigable Zionist promoter named
Moshe Tov was persuaded to abandon his medical practice in Argentina
to fly to New York. With his wide contacts in Latin society, Tov sought
to break through the Catholic fear of finding Christian holy places under

the temporal control of Jews. The Jewish Agency's political map of Latin America became a crosshatch of conflicting pressures. Cuba and Colombia leaned to the Arabs, partly owing to diverse political ambitions among individual delegates. Uruguay and Guatemala favored partition; Arab lobbyists were working hard here. The delegations of Chile, Costa Rica, Ecuador, Honduras, and Paraguay continued to be battlefields of competing viewpoints.

From the earliest days of the General Assembly, political professionals assumed that the Soviet Union and the United States each controlled a bloc. The Communist governments of Eastern Europe, including the Ukraine and Byelorussia, were faithful followers of any lead from Moscow. It was widely assumed that the same was true of the Latin Americans and the lead from Washington. But, acting under State Department instructions, the American delegation provided no lead. After all, as Forrestal argued, "proselytizing for votes and support would add to the already serious alienation of Arabian goodwill."

For once the State Department position did not upset Truman, and Niles's "involved" opposition could be disregarded. The President approved the vote for the UNSCOP report "because it was a majority report, but we were in no sense of the word to coerce other delegations to follow our lead." Long afterward, in his memoirs, Truman still fumed at the pressure tactics of the Zionists. "I do not think I ever had as much pressure and propaganda aimed at the White House as I had in this instance," he wrote. "The persistence of a few of the extreme Zionist leaders—actuated by political motives and engaging in political threats—disturbed and annoyed me." The upshot was that the so-called American bloc, the Latin American members of the United Nations, received no policy direction from Washington in the crucial weeks of November leading up to the final vote.

Partition would require the support of two-thirds of those voting to pass; if all fifty-seven members voted, twenty negative votes could scuttle the whole effort. But some of the uninterested or overly confused delegations would presumably abstain, and the arithmetic would become complicated. Jewish Agency strategists calculated that any fifteen governments anywhere in the world could defeat the Jewish restoration. On preliminary ballots, Arab opponents of partition had registered a solid thirteen votes. It was too close to let anyone relax.

On Wednesday, November 26, the day before Thanksgiving, pro-partition forces were desperate. It looked as though fifteen, and possibly sixteen, member states were prepared to vote against them, and the final tally could come at any moment. This was a time for parliamentary artifice. Pro-partition Latin Americans rose to deliver lengthy speeches which they knew would delay proceedings; Arab spokesmen, not quite comprehending the trap into which they were falling, felt called upon to deliver impassioned replies at equal length. As the day before the American holiday wore on, Hilldring persuaded his delegation that a recess might properly be called until Friday, thus gaining two more days for a last-ditch effort.

For the next forty-eight hours, at the UN and in the capitals of the wavering member states, no possible line of access and influence was ignored. "The fighting spirit rose in us again," Horowitz recalled.

> We met at the Agency offices and consulted on ways and means to turn the wheel of events once more. . . . The telephones rang madly. Cablegrams sped to all parts of the world. People were dragged from their beds at midnight and sent on peculiar errands. And, wonder of it all, not an influential Jew, Zionist or non-Zionist, refused to give us assistance at any time. Everyone pulled his weight, little or great, in the despairing effort to balance the scales to our favor.

In near-panic unseemly for a proper diplomat, Lovett called Truman's private secretary to complain that "our case is being seriously impeded by high pressure being exerted by Jewish agencies. There have been indications of bribes and threats by these groups." Another American diplomat, Llewellyn E. Thompson, Jr., learned from the pro-Arab Cuban ambassador, Guillermo Belt, that "one Latin American delegate had changed his vote to support partition in return for $75,000 in cash and that another Latin American delegate, I believe the Costa Rican, had refused a forty-thousand-dollar offer but . . . subsequently had been ordered by his government to support partition. It was Mr. Belt's belief that some member of the delegate's government had accepted the bribe." Truman himself, pressured not only by Zionists but also by old colleagues in Congress, finally told Niles that he would be willing to have a little United States influence exerted where it might do some good. Two weeks before, at a Cabinet meeting, there had been discussion about which delegations might be swayed by United States pressure.

Four countries were the target of the most intense pressure over that Thanksgiving holiday. Haiti, the Philippines, Liberia, and Greece had all announced opposition to partition on Wednesday. Each of them was susceptible, in one way or another, to American influence. If just three could be persuaded to change their votes—and everything else held firm —partition would carry.

The Philippines had switched back and forth in the preliminary jousting. Advised by Niles of the desperate situation, Frankfurter rounded up fellow jurist Frank Murphy and together they paid a call on the Philippine ambassador in Washington. Ambassadors from small countries were not accustomed to receiving visits from Justices of the U.S. Supreme Court. Ten senators (more signed on later) sent the President of the Philippines what he called a "high-pressure telegram" warning of the adverse effect that a vote against partition would have on Philippine-American relations; in particular, there was that matter of a financial aid package, just then pending in Congress . . .

The Zionists learned from a retired governor-general of the Philippines that an American civil servant named Julius Edelstein happened to be a personal friend of the Philippine President. Edelstein was at that moment in England. He was located through the American Embassy; a middle-of-the-night telephone call roused him in his hotel and, after sleepy protest, he agreed to telephone Manila, awakening his friend, the President, from his afternoon siesta. The Philippines changed its vote.

Liberia was one of those wavering states eager to know what the United States expected of it. Through official channels, the State Department and the UN delegation, they got the official word that no American persuasion was being exerted. If the matter was that unimportant, Liberian delegates felt comfortable about withholding their support for partition of Palestine, which really did not matter one way or another to them. But once Niles had swung into action over Thanksgiving, enlisting the help of his friend from the Weizmann-Sieff discussion groups, Robert Nathan, an economist who knew Liberia, things were bound to change. Nathan promptly called the Liberian delegate in New York to warn that unless he voted for partition, former Secretary of State Stettinius would have to call *his* friend, Harvey S. Firestone, Jr., head of the tire and rubber company that dominated the Liberian economy. As it happened, Stettinius went even higher, calling Liberian President Tubman himself to explain his interest. Liberia changed its vote.

That Wednesday before Thanksgiving, Haiti had also come out against partition, yet the Haitian chief delegate had said that he would vote for it. Who was really in charge of the Haitian vote? Goldmann called an old friend, former Assistant Secretary of State Adolf A. Berle, who in turn sent a cable to the President of Haiti, Dumarsais Estimé. Then Niles mobilized some businessmen friends with good Haitian contacts to find out what was going on. The local business community got the word to the American consul in Haiti, Robert H. McBride, who reportedly let President Estimé know that the White House wanted him, "for his own good," to change his country's vote. Estimé assured Berle by return cable that he had changed his mind and would send instructions to his UN delegation. Haiti voted for partition.

Only with Greece did the effort fail. Greece was badly in need of UN votes for aid and survival in 1947, and such support could come either from the United States bloc or from the Arab bloc. For Greek purposes, it did not matter which. From the American delegation came no hint that a vote for partition would ensure United States sympathies or guarantee continuing massive American aid. From the Islamic bloc, however, came assurances of at least a dozen votes for aid when their turn came on the agenda—that is, if they voted against partition. The case was compelling. Niles called a Boston friend of his named Tom Pappas, a politically astute American businessman, who lined up friends like Spyros Skouras, the motion-picture executive. Telegrams went off to the Greek Prime Minister reminding him how much the Greeks owed to the American Jewish community. "When starvation and terrorism under Nazi occupation seemed about to crush the life of Greece, good friends helped me . . . to bring aid to Greece by lifting the blockade at that very critical hour. . . . Now these very friends have asked me to appeal to Your Excellency." More cables turned the screws even tighter. But Greece voted against partition.

The other undecided votes were harder to deal with. Siam seemed inclined to abstain, which would help in the rush for two-thirds of those voting. In the event, a coup d'état in Bangkok occurred at the critical moment and the Siamese delegate left New York without voting.

France was an enigma from the start, torn by competing interests. Still mortified by the loss of its own Middle Eastern colonies after World War II, the French could hardly summon up much sympathy for the British plight in Palestine. The Jewish cause was a significant and emotionally charged issue in France; so was the maintenance of credentials among the Arabs of French North Africa; and so was the need for American sympathy—and financial support—for economic recovery. The French were approachable on a number of levels. One was through the revered old political lion Léon Blum, retired Prime Minister and a Jew, to whom his old friend Chaim Weizmann sent a telegram asking, "Does France wish to be absent from a moment unfading in the memory of man?" Blum made some telephone calls. Bernard Baruch in New York had excellent contacts among his fellow financiers on the Bourse. No Zionist, he nevertheless was caught up in the fervor of the Jewish moment and had a talk with Niles. One talk led to another, and Baruch ended up by telling the French delegate to his face that a French vote against partition would mean the end of all American aid to France. France voted for partition.

It had been an intense forty-eight hours. Parliamentary procedures consumed the time, and it was not until Saturday, November 29, shortly after 5 p.m., that the General Assembly finally acted. The vote of 56 members of the United Nations (Siam absent) divided along these lines: abstentions, 10; against partition, the hard core of 13; for partition, a carrying vote of 33 (2 more than necessary), including the United States and the Soviet Union. Britain's three decades of mandate over the Holy Land were ended. The Palestinian Arabs were offered a state of their own—but they did not want it. International recognition was accorded the Jewish homeland in Palestine, as Balfour had promised thirty years before.

11

WHEN A long-anticipated moment finally arrives, people often act in unexpected ways.

"One by one we left the hall and drifted into the lobby. . . . I glanced at Silver and saw what I had never seen before—he wept." Thus Rabbi Silver's loyal friend Harold Manson recalled the scene at the United Nations, late on November 29, 1947.

Shertok, Tov, Eban and his wife, Suzy, the team from the Jewish Agency, stepped into a limousine together. For weeks and months past, their lives had been swallowed up in continual persuasion. This evening, the four sat through the forty-five-minute journey back to Manhattan in total silence.

Weizmann, who had thrived through three decades of courtesy calls and working meetings with the mighty, was too exhausted to move from his New York hotel suite. Instead, the mighty and the faithful called on him spontaneously as they heard the news, in small groups which swelled to dozens and then scores. Eventually they persuaded him to rise from his bed and appear at a joyous Zionist rally at Madison Square Garden. As he addressed the throng, the worldly, cosmopolitan statesman from the Russian Pale lapsed into Yiddish.

Hilldring, his mission for Truman and Niles completed, turned to a young American Foreign Service officer in the limousine taking them back to Manhattan and said, "Okay, now it's up to you people at State to straighten all this out."

A forty-nine-year-old woman sat in a kitchen in Jerusalem, her ear pressed against an old radio set, chain-smoking as she kept a running tally of the UN vote on a notepad. Her kitchen table, littered with chipped china coffee cups, had been and would be the setting for great decisions about the Jewish destiny. On this night in Jerusalem, Golda Meir chose to sit at her kitchen table alone.

Yigal Yadin, distinguished archaeologist and military strategist for the Haganah, pursued his dual life. As archaeologist, that morning he had advised his father about ongoing haggling with an antiquities merchant in Arab Bethlehem to acquire the first of what the world would soon know as the Dead Sea Scrolls. By evening he was with his Haganah colleagues for war.

The father of the Haganah, Yitzhak Sadeh, sat with thirty or so of his fellow officers in Jerusalem, all of them fugitives from the British administration. They, too, had followed the voting at the United Nations. "If the vote is positive, the Arabs will make war on us," he said. "And if the vote is negative, then it is we who will make war on the Arabs."

In America and in Palestine there was rejoicing. But there were Zionists who did not rejoice, notably Begin and his underground partisans. The Irgun commander issued an Order of the Day: "The Homeland has not been liberated, but mutilated. . . . Eretz Israel will be restored to the people of Israel. All of it. And forever." An announcer for one of the underground radio stations stood on a rooftop in Tel Aviv that night of November 29, looking at the celebrating throngs below, and despaired over partition: "A Jewish state without Jerusalem, without Hebron and Bethlehem, without the Gilead or the Bashan or the lands beyond the Jordan." That, in the lifetime of Begin and his followers, would have to be corrected.

Truman was satisfied with the outcome, and mused about the grandeurs of the Near East in the days of Nebuchadnezzar and Cyrus the Great, when the Jews were permitted to return to their Promised Land. "I have my doubt as to whether it will be put into effect," he had written a friend before the vote; afterward, he wrote that maybe partition "could open the way for peaceful collaboration between the Arabs and Jews."

To be sure, more mundane considerations also entered into Truman's satisfaction. Congressman Emanuel Celler of New York, one of the Zionists' most persistent lobbyists on Capitol Hill, thanked the President for his "effective work" in rounding up the necessary votes. Just to make sure that Truman grasped the obvious as the 1948 election approached, Celler added, "I shall make it my business to emphasize the wonderful work you did when I address New York audiences as well as other audiences in various parts of the country."

Happy to accept the political bonus, Truman nevertheless rejected suggestions that he had done anything so cynical as to bring influence to bear on sovereign members of the United Nations. And his annoyance at Jewish pressure showed no signs of abating. "The vote in the United Nations is only the beginning and the Jews must now display tolerance and consideration for the other people in Palestine with whom they will necessarily have to be neighbors," he wrote Henry Morgenthau, Jr. In the Mideast, no less than the Midwest, Truman believed that people should be amiable.

AFTER THE NIGHT of rejoicing came the morning of reality. The UN had spoken, but then what? A vote recorded an idea, but nothing had actually happened. On the day following the UN decision, Arab forces launched concerted attacks on Jewish concentrations; the Haganah counterattacked and strengthened its own position. At the State Department, the experts took a jaundiced view of the goings-on in New York, and continued to argue "the manifest impossibility of implementing the partition of Palestine."

Even before the partition vote, Henderson had begun preparations for retrieving the situation. On November 10, in a low-key memorandum, he had proposed an embargo on arms shipments to Palestine and neighboring states, designed to ensure that the United States would not be drawn into the inevitable Arab-Jewish war. This suggestion was routinely cleared through State Department channels. It seemed a reasonable enough precaution, and no one thought it sufficiently important to discuss with the White House—or so they later explained. On December 5, 1947, the United States banned all military shipments to the area.

Here was a classic instance of bureaucracy going its own way, without technical impropriety, unrestrained by any superior authority. Niles, for one, would have opposed the embargo vigorously had he known of it, for beneath its reasonable surface it was grossly one-sided. The Arab armies could get most of what they needed through their supply contracts with Britain. The Jewish forces had no such secure channels. Their sources of arms and matériel were, first and foremost, the network of the Sonneborn Institute of New York. When these secretive and practical-minded Jews realized that they were being cut off, or at least forced into greater illegality than they had known before, it was too late. The embargo was in effect, and to reverse it would create a political furor.

Harassed by his Zionist contacts, Niles summoned Henderson for one of their rare face-to-face meetings. As Henderson recalled it, Niles asked what would happen if a vessel carrying arms were discovered about to leave from Philadelphia or Baltimore or some other American port. "Would you have to report it to the Department of Justice?" An astonished Henderson replied that he would, of course, report it. Niles muttered that Henderson would "get hell" if he interfered with a matter that was so important to the President's relations with the Jewish community.

The next step in the bureaucratic counterattack came with a call by the National Security Council for a fundamental policy review of the problems of Palestine as they related to the security interests of the United States. All the relevant departments of government were invited to submit their views, comprehensive and thorough, staffed in depth.

The first of the State Department heavyweights reported on January 19, 1948: George F. Kennan, head of State's newly created Policy Planning Staff. "US prestige in the Moslem world has suffered a severe blow, and US strategic interests in the Mediterranean and Near East have been seriously prejudiced," Kennan concluded. "Our vital interests in those areas will continue to be adversely affected to the extent that we continue to support partition." The Policy Planning Staff recommended that no further initiatives be undertaken to bring about partition, that the arms embargo be maintained, that "we should endeavor as far as possible to spread responsibility for the future handling of this question, and to divest ourselves of the imputation of international leadership in the search for a solution." The whole matter should be reopened at the General Assembly, and the United States should press for an international trusteeship over a federated Palestine. Instead of a Jewish state and an Arab state, which would be bound to go to war and demand outside military support, something like the old British mandate should be renewed under more modern auspices.

Kennan's views went the rounds, with each appropriate division adding its embellishments, and by the time the agreed-upon State Department text went to the White House, it had become a stern warning:

> We are deeply involved . . . in a situation which has no direct relation to our national security, and where the motives of our involvement lie solely in past commitments of dubious wisdom and in our attachment to the UN itself. . . . If we do not effect a fairly radical reversal of the trend of our policy to date, we will end up either in the position of being ourselves militarily responsible for the protection of the Jewish population in Palestine against the declared hostility of the Arab world, or of sharing that responsibility with the Russians and thus assisting at their installation as one of the military powers of the area. In either case, the clarity and efficiency of a sound national policy for that area will be shattered.

This was the weighty language of statecraft, the considered assessments of dozens, perhaps hundreds, of responsible officials bringing all their resources to bear. Whatever Truman may have thought of "striped-pants boys" personally, no Chief Executive could treat this kind of pronouncement lightly.

But Kennan, Henderson, and the experts at State were only the beginning. A new agency set up to coordinate all American intelligence services, the Central Intelligence Agency, weighed in with an estimate that had the color of objectivity, since the intelligence community had until now taken little part in the Palestine debate. Its findings were clear-cut:

> It is apparent that the partition of Palestine . . . cannot be implemented. The Arabs will use force to oppose the establishment of a Jewish state and to this end are training troops in Palestine and other Arab states. Moreover, the United Kingdom has stated repeatedly that it will take no part in implementing a UN decision not acceptable to both Jews and Arabs. . . . Even among Jews there is dissatisfaction over the partition plan.

Then, from the new Department of Defense and the Joint Chiefs of Staff, messages reached Truman's desk warning that the United States might be drawn into the conflict. Even if that didn't happen, a Jewish state would surely be a potential outpost of Soviet Communism. As late as March 16, 1948, the Joint Chiefs of Staff believed that the dominant Labor Party of the Jewish Agency "stems from the Soviet Union and its satellite states and has strong bonds of kinship in those regions, and ideologically is much closer to the Soviet Union than to the United States."

FACING THE PROSPECT of a difficult presidential election campaign, Truman had chosen a universally respected man to preside over foreign policy. Years before, Senator Truman had called General George C. Marshall "the greatest living American"—and this when Roosevelt was still alive. "Wherever this man goes he inspires reverence," said Roosevelt's secretary William Hassett, "may God spare him." The Senate confirmed Marshall as Secretary of State in January 1947. No hearings were called, no recorded vote was taken; the committee meeting to pass on his nomination lasted all of twenty minutes. An army officer his entire adult life, Chief of Staff during World War II, Marshall held himself aloof from politics; he refused to vote, believing even that modest political act improper for a serving officer. He called no man by his first name; no one ever called him "George." He once described himself to Truman as a man of no feelings, "except a few which I reserve for Mrs. Marshall."

But Marshall was accustomed to taking orders from his commander in chief. Senator Connally of Texas, veteran of the Foreign Relations Committee, wrote that the general always "tried to find out what the President wanted, and then do it." Marshall felt comfortable dealing with the problems of postwar Europe, but when it came to Palestine he was unsure of himself, and unsure about the political considerations weighing on the President. On the rare occasions when he did venture an opinion on such unfamiliar matters, he spoke from a position wonderfully removed from the fray. Early in April 1948, for instance, he sent an urgent "eyes only" advisory to his under secretary suggesting that the Palestine meanderings in the United Nations were casting doubt on the American commitment to world order. "We must do something behind the scenes at Lake Success and elsewhere to get ourselves properly understood," Marshall cabled. This kind of Olympian instruction from the Secretary of State left the working diplomats somewhat bemused.

Marshall relegated working responsibility for Palestine policy to Under Secretary Robert A. Lovett, a Republican investment banker from Wall Street, a man of keener political interests than the general. He had served as Assistant Secretary of War during World War II, and for all his hardheaded dedication to an orderly staff system, he knew that it was the President's opinions that mattered. In the wake of the partition vote, neither he nor Marshall was eager to press a barrage of bureaucratic criticism upon the President. No such reticence troubled another formidable presence in the Truman administration, the man charged with the direction of the newly unified defense establishment.

James V. Forrestal had taken up the anti-Zionist cause as a personal crusade. His concern was the security of Middle Eastern oil supplies and the strategic posture of the United States against the rising threat of Soviet Russia; the Jewish fate was irrelevant in this world view. His ties with big oil companies were close, dating from his days as a partner in the New York investment banking firm of Dillon, Read, which had financed major Middle Eastern oil ventures.

Shortly before the partition decision, the Democratic National Chairman had confronted Forrestal with the judgment that two or three pivotal states would be lost without the Jewish vote. "I said I would rather lose those states in a national election than run the risks which I felt might develop in our handling of the Palestine question," he confided to his diary. He found it "a most disastrous and regrettable fact that the foreign policy of this country was determined by the contributions a particular bloc of special interests might make to the party funds." Forrestal made it his quixotic mission to see that Palestine played no part in domestic politics during the winter of 1947–48.

Franklin D. Roosevelt, Jr., called on him in February to urge that he play down his opposition to Zionism, lest he hurt the President's reelection campaign. Forrestal replied that instead of worrying about "losing" New York, Pennsylvania, and California to those well-known special interests, "it was about time that somebody should pay some consideration to whether we might not lose the United States." Bernard Baruch took him to lunch that same day, and the same issue came up.

> He took the line of advising me not to be active in this particular matter and that I was already identified, to a degree that was not in my own interests, with opposition to the United Nations policy on Palestine. He said he himself did not approve of the Zionists' actions, but in the next breath said that the Democratic Party could only lose by trying to get our government's policy reversed, and said that it was a most inequitable thing to let the British arm the Arabs and for us not to furnish similar equipment to the Jews.

Forrestal began seeing the age-old conspiracy at work. The sincerity of his dedication to the national interest has never been questioned. But in light of his subsequent mental illness, which led to his suicide, psychologists have carefully probed the roots of his anti-Zionism.

Forrestal shared the Dutchess County background of the Hyde Park Roosevelts, and his professional life had been spent amid the genteel antisemitism of Wall Street and the New York and Washington clubland. The Department of the Navy, in which he held his first high government office, was notorious for a service promotion policy that kept the higher ranks out of bounds to Jews. Forrestal himself thought of Jews as "different," recalled a Wall Street friend. "I remember an occasion when I was involved in his presence in an argument with a Jewish friend. At one point I got overheated and I said something like 'you son-of-a-bitch.' Jim was shocked that I could talk that way to someone who was Jewish. He himself was always very reserved with people who were Jews. I think there was something about them he couldn't understand, or maybe didn't like." Yet Baruch was a genuine friend, and there were other Jews among his intimates.

On advice from all sides, Forrestal finally dropped his campaign against Zionism. Later in 1948, once the Jewish state was a reality, he telephoned the ambassador of Israel to convey his good wishes and acknowledge that his forebodings had been ill founded. But his paranoia was advancing, and a few months later he was expressing belief that a "conspiracy of Communists, Jews and persons in the White House were out to get me, and succeeded." That came the day after his resignation as Secretary of Defense on March 29, 1949. "Bob, they're after me," he told Lovett, an old colleague from Wall Street days. "Forget it, Jim, we all get those threats," Lovett replied.

During sessions of intensive therapy at Walter Reed Hospital, he revealed suspicions that he had been systematically "shadowed" through the winter of 1947–48 by "Zionist agents." Were these the rantings of a guilt-ridden paranoid? Years afterward, Israeli intelligence officers familiar with the period expressed total confidence that no agent of the Haganah or any other official body could conceivably have been assigned to the relatively minor job of shadowing a high American official, for all his anti-Zionist leanings. But in the inquests on his death, a Forrestal aide testified that he had, in fact, been "shadowed" by a photographer on speculative assignment from some Zionist organization who hoped to get a picture of the Secretary of Defense or one of his aides walking into the embassy of an Arab state. Nothing had come of the assignment.

Forrestal was found dead in May 1949, below the open window of his Georgetown home, aged fifty-seven. He was diagnosed a victim of involutional melancholia.

MAD OR SANE, in the winter of 1947–48 Forrestal was not alone among Americans in wondering whether the ancestral yearnings for a Jewish state could be accommodated within the national interests of the United States on the brink of cold war. Polls of the population revealed a pattern of divided opinion.

Back in 1944, the goal of a Jewish state had commanded the sympathies of about one-third of American Christians, according to polls of religious groups across the country. One-quarter, approximately, took the Arab side in opposing such a state. By February 1948, when the Palestine issue had dominated the front pages for months, sympathy for both sides had declined and the percentage of "no opinion" had increased to half the populace. But then came an interesting change. In March the question was put: "If Jews independently set up a Jewish state anyhow," should the United States support them? Fully 50 percent of Protestants and 44 percent of Catholics said yes; only 10 percent of Protestants and 14 percent of Catholics gave an unqualified no; and only 19 percent of both groups offered no opinion. Americans were clearly not averse to a Zionist preemptive move. They "tend to see the partisans of a Jewish state as following in the footsteps of the United States founding fathers," reported a British diplomat with atavistic scorn, "and the Arabs as the modern equivalent of George III."

The mail received at the White House was strongly pro-Zionist—Silver's organization saw to that—and its geographical origins reflected the regions where the Jewish community was concentrated: the Middle Atlantic States were the most concerned, New England next. From the Midwest, with its large Protestant population, came vigorous pro-partition letters and telegrams, but the impetus was world order, not the Jewish restoration. "Our only hope for world peace lies in the survival of the United Nations. The reversal of the Palestine decision would mean the end of that hope," wrote the idealistic young mayor of Minneapolis, Hubert H. Humphrey.

An older and more insidious sentiment was also at work. It could not be discussed in polite society, but it found its way indirectly into the opinion polls. *Fortune* magazine found in 1947 that one-third of Americans questioned believed that Jews wielded "too much" economic power; one-fifth said that the Jews' political influence was excessive as well.

Joseph and Stewart Alsop, at the peak of their influence as purveyors of strategic thinking to American newspaper readers, conveyed warnings of renewed antisemitism:

> Any honest man, who faces all the facts of American life, good and bad . . . knows that the most sordid of all these facts is the presence in this country of a considerable strain of racial hatred. . . . It is doubtful whether the Congress would agree to a Palestine expedition, even in obedience to the United Nations. But a mere serious proposal to send troops, let alone the actual sending of them, would fan the flames of racial hatred in a dangerous and terrible manner. This is the real reason why the second alternative of American military intervention . . . is as unthinkable as the first alternative of letting the Palestine bloodbath run its cruel course.

Gloom hung over the marble halls of New York's Council on Foreign Relations, where the establishment of diplomatic experts held their discussions behind closed doors on the pressing matters of the day. Colonel Hoskins, now the elder statesman among the specialists, dropped in at one such meeting fresh from an inspection tour of the Arab capitals and declared the Middle East to present the "most depressing picture" he had ever seen. The Jewish state that seemed about to emerge might well seek aid from the Soviet Union, and everyone knew what that would mean to the strategic posture of the West. Arnold Toynbee came to the Council from England to give the broad historical perspective, and declared the partition of Palestine to be "the *reductio ad absurdum* of territorial nationality." His counterproposal: "a despotic government over Palestine by a third party, for the indefinite future." Since Britain had clearly botched the job, the United States was in Toynbee's view the ideal candidate for despot. He added that an absolute prerequisite for effective rule would be a firm and final halt to all Jewish immigration for generations to come.

Public discussion dealt less with the mounting terrorism in Palestine than with the perceived incompetencies of the Truman administration in facing this agonizing test of foreign policy. Walter Lippmann thought it "preposterous" that Britain and the United States could not impose peace upon Arabs and Jews, for "among the really difficult problems of the world, . . . [their conflict was] one of the simplest and most manageable." *Time* magazine declared that "Harry Truman's comic opera performance had done little credit to the greatest power in the world." It was a season for jokes about "Harry the Horse," the small-town politician who happened to succeed to the seat of Franklin D. Roosevelt and now presumed to offer himself for the presidency on his own hapless record. Sulzberger's *New York Times,* where editorial comment on Jewish issues was restrained in the extreme, nevertheless called Truman's policies "a series of moves which had seldom been matched for ineptness in the handling of any international issue by an American administration," a point of view echoed by such disparate publications as the Baltimore *Sun* and *PM,* the liberal New York daily.

Truman liked to think that he was ignoring all the attacks mounted against him by Zionists during the winter of 1947–48, but he was not. His fighting spirit rose to the surface in offhand remarks. An old Senate colleague reported that Truman had brushed aside the whole matter of the Jewish vote in a testy private conversation: "I don't know about that [the Jewish vote], I think a candidate on an antisemitic platform might sweep the country."

AMERICAN ZIONISTS were nonplussed by the turn of events. On the day after the partition vote, a few euphoric Zionist officials believed—just like Brandeis after the Balfour Declaration—that since the job was now done it might be possible to disband the Zionist lobby. Over the winter, their mood changed. "The Jews are worried and gloomy," reported the British Embassy. Rabbi Silver's confidence in mass agitation was revealing itself as misplaced, while the public relations ventures of the Irgun renegade Peter Bergson were even more tired. The Zionist leadership hardly knew where in the government to turn, either to spot the source of trouble or to neutralize it.

On Tuesday evening, February 3, a small, informal group of influential American Jews met with some emissaries from Palestine over dinner at the home of Washington lawyer David Ginsburg. Silver was not invited; this was not an occasion for posturing or proclamations. Rather, this discreet group of the faithful pondered ways to penetrate the American policymaking machinery, to find where the new resistance to Zionist aspirations was coming from, where the doubts and inhibitions could be isolated and neutralized, so that the momentum of the previous November could once again move events.

Niles, the obvious starting point, was on medical leave for a few weeks. Ben Cohen, back in private life after serving as Counselor of the State Department, dropped in at Ginsburg's house that evening. Also on hand were Robert Nathan, Oscar Gass, Richard Gilbert, loyal second- and third-level members of the New Deal establishment. Speaking for the Jews of Palestine were Shertok and Eliahu Epstein, Washington representative of the Jewish Agency (he adopted the Hebraic surname Elath when he became Israel's first ambassador to the United States).

Like all the best occasions in the Weizmann tradition, the dinner at the Ginsburgs' was a "purely social" affair—but during three hours of talk decisions were made. Two specific avenues would be pursued. First, a concerted effort would be made to convey the merits of the Zionist cause, especially its compatibility—against all the arguments of Forrestal and the strategists—with American national interests. Second, "responsible figures in both political parties" would be led to understand "that it would be most unwise, from a strictly electioneering point of view, to jettison the United Nations decision." Specifically:

- General William Donovan, retired head of wartime intelligence, would be prodded to discuss Palestine with Marshall at State and other old friends at the Pentagon.
- Eleanor Roosevelt would be asked to call on Truman and Marshall.
- Ralph Davis of the American Independent Oil Company, one of the few oil executives who gave the Zionists a hearing, would be encouraged to press for Cabinet-level attention to the matter.
- Isaiah Berlin should be invited back from Oxford to work his infectious powers of persuasion through his many official contacts.
- Ginsburg and Aubrey (Abba) Eban would draft a letter to Truman, and solicit influential Americans—Baruch, Sumner Welles, John Foster Dulles, and Henry Stimson were among the names mentioned—to sign it.
- Urgent efforts would be made to get Weizmann in to see the President and Marshall again.

That was the avenue of persuasion. On the political front, the channels of influence were mapped to policymakers in both parties:

- Cohen agreed to work on the influential Republican chairman of the Senate Foreign Relations Committee, Arthur Vandenberg of Michigan.
- Ginsburg would get in touch with his friends at the Democratic National Committee.
- Epstein would help the retired Sumner Welles back into public prominence to argue his increasingly pro-Zionist views.
- Harriman, who had exchanged his diplomatic career for the political life, would be asked to lend an encouraging hand, along with two emerging Democratic figures from Illinois, Paul Douglas and Adlai Stevenson. The Republican leaders Thomas Dewey and Robert Taft would also be approached. There was no telling in that election year of 1948 who might be in a position to help the Zionist cause.

In the days following the February 3 meeting, Jewish Agency communications buzzed in frenzied effort. Weizmann had returned to London after the partition vote and was packing files and furniture for the final move to his retirement home in Palestine. But shortly before the Ginsburg dinner, he had received a telephone call from New York in which there was guarded talk of the "weather" in the States; "extremely cold, both indoors and outside," Weizmann was told. Could the Great Persuader return to the scene immediately? It took him no more than thirty minutes to reverse all his plans, and he arrived back on February 4. He promptly swung into his old, well-rehearsed routine of letters and telephone calls; just as promptly he succumbed to a chill and had to be put to bed for a few valuable days.

Lengthy memoranda arguing the Zionist case were fired off to Donovan, Welles, and others, expressing hope that these statesmen on the fringes of policymaking Washington would raise the arguments with old friends in officialdom. "Our difficulty," a Zionist official informed Welles, is "that we have no access to those people in the administration whose minds are sufficiently open and whose knowledge sufficiently wide to be in a position to argue out this question."

In feverish weeks of probing and prodding, of accosting and arguing, the Zionist brain trust gained only the vaguest idea of the bureaucratic machinery they were up against, of the National Security Council assessments, the Policy Planning Staff, CIA, and Joint Chiefs of Staff papers which built such formidable cases against them. But they were well informed about the action in one key quarter—the propaganda and pressure from American oil interests who spoke on behalf of Arab nationalism in the best Washington circles.

Early in 1948 the Arab League had decided to deny pipeline rights to American companies unless Washington's support for partition were withdrawn. The message had its impact. American interests controlled some 42 percent of Middle Eastern oil reserves, but without pipelines the asset could not be cashed in. Pursuing the campaign initiated at the Ginsburg dinner, Epstein arranged a social meeting with Max Ball, director of the Oil and Gas Division of the Department of the Interior. Ball had a nagging admiration for Zionist spunk, but he warned that America faced a shortage of gasoline supplies in the coming summer, and everyone knew how the American public would react to that! He tried to explain to Epstein how the oil men really felt about the situation: "These people are not guided by any kind of antisemitism, but they know that at present the tense situation in the Middle East necessitates their being very careful with regard to Arab sensibility." After several weeks of investigation, Epstein concluded that "the oil aspect has been magnified and exploited by the State Department, in order to justify some of their political policies in the Middle East, out of proportion to the actual situation and desires of the companies themselves."

In general, the Zionists found little reason to be encouraged. On March 6 a telegram went from the Jewish Agency's Washington office to Ben-Gurion in Tel Aviv. It reported the opinions of three men whom Ben-Gurion would hear with respect: Frankfurter, Rosenman, and Cohen. "They appraise situation as extremely serious in view of strong opposition," the cable said. In their view, the only way to bring the half-century of Zionist efforts to a successful outcome would be for the Palestine Jews themselves to take unilateral action as the British pulled out. They should declare a provisional government, establish a Jewish army and administration over whatever of Palestine was under Jewish control —in effect "enforce partition by our own means."

This was bold advice. Arab and Jewish militias were fighting it out in almost daily skirmishes and terrorist attacks; the hapless British administrators were stymied in their efforts to keep the peace. As it seemed to many observers, in fact, the British were only trying to keep their own installations intact until their departure on May 15. What would happen then? The Americans advised Ben-Gurion that only a fait accompli would bring the American government along. And, the polls showed, the broad American public regarded the possibility of a Jewish state with more interest than alarm.

WHAT THE JEWISH AGENCY—as well as Ben-Gurion, Frankfurter, Rosenman, and Cohen—did not know was that the carefully planned Zionist pressure campaign was working in Washington. The first indications of this appeared in a five-page memorandum that reached Truman's desk on March 6, the very day that the Jewish Agency telegram went off to Tel Aviv.

With Niles on sick leave, the problem of holding the Jewish vote in line passed to his superior on the White House staff, the brilliant, elegant, and street-smart Missourian Clark M. Clifford. Clifford had come to the White House in 1946 as an officer in the U.S. Navy; his title was Assistant Naval Aide to the President, one of those traditional posts that brought useful people to the staff without clearly defined functions. He quickly found his niche in the speech-writing section under Rosenman. Like Rosenman, Clifford had a good sense of what words could do; his training was legal, but his instincts were political. He moreover possessed an incisive, analytical mind with a knack for getting to the heart of a new subject and presenting it in a form most useful to a busy Chief Executive. When Rosenman retired as Special Counsel to the President, the forty-one-year-old Clifford easily took over.

Clifford knew next to nothing about Jews or Palestine. But he knew American politics. He grew out of the fair-play ethic of the Midwest, and he understood the humanitarian impulses that moved the American public and especially the American President. Clifford found in Niles a natural partner who blended progressive ideals with pragmatism in politics. In Niles's absence during the crucial weeks of February and March, Clifford sought the aid of Max Lowenthal, a kindred political spirit, who took over Niles's staff work temporarily. It was the sort of family arrangement that politicians rely upon: Truman and Lowenthal were old friends, Truman trusted Clifford, Clifford trusted Lowenthal. It was all so much more human than the ponderous, shapeless bureaucratic documents that kept thudding upon the Chief Executive's desk.

On March 6, Clifford submitted his "heart of the matter" memo on Palestine policy. It was a welcome change from the bundles of paper emitted by the executive agencies. "The policy of the United States must be to support the United Nations settlement of the Palestine issue," Clifford began. "This government urged partition upon the United Nations in the first place and it is unthinkable that it should fail to back up that decision in every possible way."

Then followed a step-by-step proposal of how the United States should respond to the tactical decisions:

- Pressure should be exerted upon Britain and the Arabs for partition; if that failed, the Arabs should be branded as aggressors and the American arms embargo, which inhibited only the Jewish militia, should be lifted.

- No American troops should be involved in any international army to implement partition; but a volunteer expeditionary force should be considered, and the United States "should assume its part of the cost of recruiting, arming, and maintaining this international security force." Americans should not be penalized if they chose to go to Palestine to defend partition, Clifford argued; "American citizens were not barred from joining the British Air Force or the Chinese Flying Tigers in the last war."
- The Holy City of Jerusalem needed special attention, Clifford warned Truman. But his concern was not the old one that had haunted Christendom for centuries, that the holy places would be controlled by Jews; Clifford worried rather that Christian holy places would fall under the control of "fanatical Moslems."

Two days later, Clifford sent in another memo to the President. Either the Special Counsel had preferred not to combine two aspects of the issue in a single communication or, more likely, Truman had asked him to pursue the point when they talked during those two days. Oil shortages, war in the Middle East, Communist expansionism, these problems had been analyzed. The new—or rather not yet fully discussed— facet of the Palestine question was its bearing on the immediate domestic political situation. The fact was that Truman had never been *elected* President. Many Democrats were continuing to urge that a more popular candidate be chosen in his place. On March 8, 1948, Truman faced this rebellion head on. He announced that he would offer himself for the presidency; he may have become President by chance, but now he was ready to run on his own.

In this mood he sought high-toned political position papers on which he could stand. Clifford obliged, and Palestine was one of the central issues. "At the outset, let me say that the Palestine problem should not be approached as a Jewish question, or an Arab question, or a United Nations question," he began his second memo. "The sole question is what is best for the United States of America." Clifford knew what Truman was hearing from Forrestal and Lovett, and he knew that his chief was sensitive to charges of political opportunism in foreign policy. Pouring it on a little thick, the presidential aide declared: "One's judgment in advising as to what is best for America must in no sense be influenced by the election this fall. I know only too well that you would not hesitate to follow a course of action that makes certain the defeat of the Democratic Party if you thought such action were best for America. What I say is, therefore, completely uninfluenced by election considerations." This is what Truman preferred to hear, as Clifford well knew.

"Your active support of partition was in complete harmony with the policy of the United States," Clifford assured the President. "Had you failed to support partition, you would have been departing from an established American policy and justifiably subject to criticism." Then, another sensitive point: "partition is the only course of action with respect to Palestine that will strengthen our position vis-à-vis Russia," Clifford argued. A stand for the partition of Palestine was a stand for the United Nations. A doubting public could see that the United States still believed in the world organization.

Clifford had answers to each of the bureaucrats' objections. The Arab oil threats are empty, he argued, for "the fact of the matter is that the Arab states must have oil royalties or go broke. . . . Their need of the United States is greater than our need of them." As for partition not working, "This comes from those who never wanted partition to succeed, and who have been determined to sabotage it." By drawing back at this stage, "The United States appears in the ridiculous role of trembling before threats of a few nomadic desert tribes. This has done us irreparable damage. Why should Russia or Yugoslavia or any other nation treat us with anything but contempt in light of our shilly-shallying appeasement of the Arabs?" Clifford noted "a complete lack of confidence in our foreign policy . . . shared by Democrats, Republicans, young people and old people. There is a definite feeling that . . . the United States, instead of furnishing leadership in world affairs, is drifting helplessly." The way to begin to change this impression would be to "promptly and vigorously support the United Nations actions regarding Palestine." Only thus could America's reliability and leadership be confirmed; only thus could Soviet Russia be prevented from exploiting Middle East tensions; only thus could full-scale war between Jews and Arabs be averted when Britain's Palestine mandate terminated on May 15, just two months hence.

Clifford's intervention was a virtuoso act of bureaucratic combat. But where did this Missouri lawyer, with no background in the Middle East, acquire the information—and the confidence—to press such a controversial and forthright position against all the experts? It takes little effort to show that the arguments Clifford put before Truman early in March closely paralleled the lines of "rational persuasion" adopted by Ginsburg's dinner guests the evening of February 3. When Eliahu Elath, one of those present, published his memoirs thirty-one years later, he confirmed that this was no coincidence. Niles had told his Zionist friends to focus on Clifford; in Niles's absence, a natural avenue to Clifford was his pro-tem aide, Lowenthal, whom the Ginsburg group had no difficulty in reaching. The evidence is circumstantial, though convincing, of a most effective back channel at work.

Clifford's memos reached Truman at a time when the President was eager for fresh advice and guidance. Niles and Lowenthal had grown a bit too "involved" to be fully relied upon—they "burst into tears." Tru-man had confided in one trusted troubleshooter and old friend, a mid-western lawyer named Oscar R. Ewing, who had proceeded to make an independent legal study. In his disinterested view, the Zionist position was sound in international law. Now from Clifford came ringing endorse-ment of the Zionist position in terms of domestic politics and foreign policy as well—and Clifford was never the sort to burst into tears.

THE PRESIDENT began to show confidence in his instincts on Palestine, but the operations of government were not immediately responsive to executive instinct. Truman gave routine and perfunctory approval to statements drafted for Warren Austin, the United States ambassador to the United Nations, to deliver in the Security Council during debate on steps to be taken following British withdrawal on May 15.

The campaign of the Jewish lobby likewise continued on its own momentum. Silver, in a total misreading of how decisions were actually made, boasted at one Zionist strategy meeting that his machinery had "flooded the White House with 100,000 telegrams in order to save the Negev." (Irrelevant, to his way of thinking, was the brief meeting be-tween Truman and Weizmann that actually produced the Negev deci-sion.) Some of the lobbying efforts were so crude as to backfire. A Brooklyn rabbi placed a flier on the desks of all the children in a New York public school, with sample telegrams to the President, instructing them to have their parents send them off. As chance would have it, one child's father worked for the Arabian American Oil Company, and he sent the flier straight to the company's vice-president, who sent it on to Henderson at the State Department, saying simply, "I thought you would be interested." In obvious delight, Henderson dispatched it to the White House, where an aide unsympathetic to the Zionists saw that Truman read it.

Silver gloried in reports of angry White House reactions. "It shows we're getting under their skin!" he declared; smelling a Republican vic-tory in 1948, he announced that "What Truman says or does does not mean a damn thing." Other Zionists did not share Silver's confidence, most notably Weizmann, who, recovered from his chill, was trying desperately to reach Truman again. Even Eddie Jacobson found his old friend's office door barred, though he had at least the gesture of a personal apology from Truman, vacationing in Key West at the end of February. The schedule was just too crowded to fit Weizmann in; "there wasn't anything he could say to me that I didn't already know, anyway," Truman wrote. Jacobson bided his time.

The next two weeks were crammed with grim developments, not only for Palestine. Czechoslovakia passed under Communist domination; the blockade of Berlin by Soviet Russia signaled the final collapse of the wartime alliance. Truman returned to Washington, refreshed from the Florida sun, overburdened with the possibility of war. Jacobson flew to the capital and walked into the White House without an appointment on Saturday morning, March 13. Truman's appointments secretary, Matthew Connelly, pleaded with him not to raise the issue of Palestine. Jacobson replied, "That's what I came to Washington for." Connelly could not forbid entry to as old a friend as Truman had.

"When I entered the President's office, I noticed with pleasure that he looked well, that his trip to Florida did him much good," Jacobson recalled.

> For a few minutes we discussed our families, my business. . . . I then brought up the Palestine subject. He immediately became tense in appearance, abrupt in speech and very bitter in the words he was throwing my way. In all the years of our friendship he never talked to me in this manner. . . . I argued with him from every possible angle, reminding him of his feelings for Dr. Weizmann which he often expressed to me, telling him that I could not understand why he wouldn't see him; [I] told him that Dr. Weizmann, an old and sick man, had made his long journey to the United States especially to see the President. . . .
>
> The President remained immovable. He replied how disrespectful and how mean certain Jewish leaders had been to him. I suddenly found myself thinking that my dear friend, the President of the United States, was at that moment as close to being an antisemite as a man could possibly be, and I was shocked that some of our own Jewish leaders should be responsible for Mr. Truman's attitude. I happened to rest my eyes on a beautiful model of a statue of Andrew Jackson. . . . I then found myself saying this to the President, almost word for word: "Harry, all your life you have had a hero. You are probably the best read man in America on the life of Andrew Jackson. . . . Well, Harry, I too

have a hero, a man I never met but who is, I think, the greatest Jew who ever lived. I too have studied his past and I agree with you, as you have often told me, that he is a gentleman and a great statesman as well. I am talking about Chaim Weizmann. . . . Now you refuse to see him because you were insulted by some of our American Jewish leaders. . . . It doesn't sound like you, Harry."

Truman started drumming on his desk with his fingers. As Jacobson paused, he abruptly swung around in his swivel chair and stared out into the Rose Garden. "I knew the sign," Jacobson recounted. "I knew that he was changing his mind. I don't know how many seconds passed in silence but it seemed like centuries. All of a sudden he swiveled himself around again, looked me straight in the eyes and said, 'You win, you bald-headed sonuvabitch, I will see him.' " To Jacobson, they were "the most endearing words I have ever heard from his lips."

The bald-headed haberdasher from Kansas City walked out of the White House, wandered into a nearby hotel bar, and for the first time in his life, drank a double bourbon all by himself.

"The clouds suddenly broke," Vera Weizmann noted in her diary. Her husband once again took the overnight train from New York to Washington, incognito, and on March 18 spent forty-five minutes alone with Truman. The meeting was held in total secrecy, not only without public announcement but without even notice to the Department of State. Truman could have saved himself much grief later if he had only trusted his diplomats enough to inform them that he had decided to receive Weizmann.

What was actually said at the meeting is of small importance. Indeed, if the words exchanged represented Eddie Jacobson's greatest service to Zionism, then historians would have grounds for deflating a myth. Even as he drank his double bourbon, Eddie should have admitted to himself that he had cheated a little. The fact is, he knew next to nothing about Weizmann. His briefings from Granoff had not gone into much detail; there was no way that the chemist from Pinsk could have been a "lifelong hero" to the notions salesman from Kansas City.

Weizmann conveyed no new information to Truman on March 18; no bargain was struck between statesmen. All that happened was the creation of mutual trust between two men, a mood of mellow responsibility, a mood that would have a decisive effect on the President of the United States when the crisis erupted not twenty-four hours later.

.   .   .

TRUMAN TOOK his wife, Bess, and daughter, Margaret, to a concert of the Don Cossack Choir at Constitution Hall that evening. During the intermission he ducked out to give a routine appeal for the War Savings Bonds at a rally a few blocks away, then returned for the remainder of the concert.

On Friday, March 19, he told his morning staff meeting that he was thinking of a cross-country campaign tour during the summer, to end up in California just before the Republican convention. He busied himself with problems created by a strike of government service employees, then examined plans to reorganize the Air Force and to establish the Franklin D. Roosevelt Memorial Foundation. Palestine, the Jews, the United Nations—all were far from his mind.

Up at Lake Success, the American representative, Warren Austin, prepared to deliver a major policy statement. He had every reason to believe that he was acting with the full authority of the President. Eleven days earlier, on the presidential yacht between Key West and St. Croix, Truman had given routine approval to the Palestine position paper submitted by the State Department. The Department proposed that, if partition turned out to be unworkable, the United States should accept an international trusteeship to enforce peace between Jews and Arabs. It was a hypothetical position, as Truman saw it; he told one friend on that vacation trip that he had not given up on partition, despite the experts' advice. Neither Niles nor Lowenthal nor even Clifford had been on hand to alert the President to the possible dangers in the State Department recommendation. Moreover, Truman himself had sent specific instructions a week or so earlier: "nothing should be presented to the Security Council that could be interpreted as a recession on our part from the position we took in the General Assembly"—that is, in favor of partition. But he approved the hypothetical position paper and thought nothing more about it.

Henderson and the Department experts, of course, were promoting the trusteeship plan, for they had believed from the start that partition would prove unworkable. On March 16 Austin was instructed to turn to the alternative position paper. Two days later, Truman met Weizmann and assured him of America's reliability in support of partition. But the State Department knew nothing of that meeting, and Truman knew nothing of the messages passing from the Department to the UN delegation in New York.

On March 19, Austin sought recognition in the Security Council to declare that so far as the United States was concerned, partition was no longer a viable option, and therefore his government favored international trusteeship over Palestine. Once again, an international bombshell:

the United States had defected from the majority decision of the United Nations. "Initial comment on the change in American policy towards Palestine may be summed up in the remark of one commentator who said simply, 'I am ashamed of us,' " reported an astonished analyst at the British Embassy. "Comparisons with the fate of the League of Nations are frequently mentioned." American press comment was scathing, about both trusteeship and Truman. The Baltimore *Sun* speculated that the Arabs had forced a reversal of American policy as the price for a truce. Why did the Truman administration press so hard four months ago for a policy which it now declared unworkable? asked *Time* magazine. Why had it waited so long "to take a step it now insisted was necessary for the nation's security"? "Almost every major paper in the country has commented on recent developments concerning Palestine," acknowledged the State Department's press office. "Ineptness," "weakness," "vacillating," seemed to be the words most frequently used. The Australian Foreign Minister declared that the United Nations had been "undermined by intrigues directed against the Jewish people." Secretary-General Trygve Lie was so upset with the Americans that he prepared his resignation; so did Eleanor Roosevelt, a member of the United States delegation.

The Arabs of Palestine and the neighboring states were elated. The "valiant defense" of their homeland had forced the United States to back down, declared the Prime Minister of Egypt. From Tel Aviv came the angry response of Ben-Gurion: "It is we who will decide the fate of Palestine. We cannot agree to any sort of trusteeship, permanent or temporary—the Jewish state exists because we defend it." Four days later, the Jewish Agency leadership formally announced that it would establish a provisional Jewish government by May 16, 1948.

In all the uproar, none was the fury to match that of the President of the United States.

12

TRUMAN WOKE up on Saturday, March 20, 1948, to banner headlines: "Reversal of United States Policy on Palestine" . . . "Ineptitude" . . . "Weakness" . . . "The League of Nations" . . . "Loss of American Prestige." It was the first the President knew of the statement at the UN. "The State Department pulled the rug from under me today," Truman wrote in his diary. "Isn't that hell? I am now in the position of a liar and a doublecrosser. I've never felt so low in my life. There are people on the third and fourth levels of the State Department who have always wanted to cut my throat. They've succeeded in doing it."

His staff dissuaded him from calling an urgent Cabinet meeting, for that would only have compounded the impression of an administration in disarray. But he ordered Clifford to drop everything that Saturday morning and find out exactly what had happened. It was "the most embarrassing position of his presidential career," wrote press secretary Charles Ross. It was also the inevitable consequence of Truman's trying to run the presidency on the basis of the casual goodwill that had served him as a Kansas City judge.

Whatever else they do, bureaucrats know how to cover their tracks. All hands immediately exhibited to Clifford the specificity of their instructions, their understandings, their attempts to be responsive to the pressing needs of the situation. And Truman had, after all, approved the fatal position paper. Admittedly, no one had bothered to tell him when the fallback position would be assumed—but then Truman had never bothered to tell anyone about the assurances he was giving to the Zionists. Where was the staff man who was supposed to be on top of all this? Where was David Niles?

Recovering from his heart ailment, Niles returned quickly to Washington to help Clifford, Lowenthal, Oscar Ewing, and a handful of other advisers "salvage what we could from an impossible situation," Ross wrote. Marshall was ordered to familiarize himself with the problem and give a press conference to explain it away. The professional diplomats of half a dozen countries listened, and shook their heads in incredulity.

Truman was not concerned with that. The anguish he felt had nothing to do with the diplomats—rather, it was that he had unwittingly misled a kindly old gentleman who had sat in his office just one day before the bomb burst.

That same Saturday morning, as Clifford set out on his face-saving inquiry, who should call at the White House but Judge Sam Rosenman, arriving for one of his regular off-the-record meetings to talk politics. The old Roosevelt loyalist had no official position in the Truman White House by this time, but he was happy to be of help in thinking out the coming campaign. On this day, Truman had something more specific to ask of him: Did Rosenman know how to get in touch with "the little doctor"? Could he let him know that the President meant every word he had said two days before, that the partition of Palestine had his fullest support? And further, would Weizmann please accept Truman's word that, at the time they spoke, the President did not know of the statement that was about to be delivered at the United Nations? Rosenman had not expected such a mission, but he promptly carried it out.

When Weizmann had first heard the news, just a day after speaking with the President, he was "nonplussed and indignant," Vera Weizmann wrote in her diary. Then came the second thoughts, and the message from Rosenman, and the old man regained both his composure and his sense of where things might be moving. He took pains to inform an anguished Eddie Jacobson, and other inquirers as well, that his confidence in President Truman remained undiminished. Weizmann was too old and jaded to be moved by the passions that captured all around him, by the fury of Silver and his forces crying "betrayal," by the posturing of the administration loyalists insisting that nothing, really, had changed. Weizmann was thinking of the life-and-death situation facing the Jewish community in Palestine. War was raging, survival was a matter of morning to night; who cared what the diplomats were saying in Washington and New York?

Weizmann fully shared the belief of his Zionist heirs in Palestine that events, not words, would determine the fate of the Jewish restoration. Since the Jews of Palestine were themselves about to proclaim the long-awaited Jewish state, and defend it with their lives, the real issue was not partition or trusteeship or mandate, it was whether the United States would recognize the Jewish state once the Jews themselves brought it into being.

It was to this goal, American recognition, that Weizmann now directed his efforts. Over the next few weeks, he and Rosenman held discreet discussions, and Rosenman talked of the recognition problem with Truman. On April 23, the eve of Passover, Weizmann received an urgent request for a meeting with the judge in New York. Both men were aged and infirm; immobilized by a leg ailment, Rosenman literally could not move from his chair. Would Weizmann be willing to call upon him at his suite at the Essex House Hotel, on Central Park South? Weizmann had agreed to celebrate the traditional Seder that night with his friends Siegfried and Lola Kramarsky. He stopped off at the Essex House first and spent an hour alone with Rosenman. When he finally appeared at the Seder, he seemed withdrawn and lost in contemplation. At the break in the festive service, before the recitation of the second half of the Haggadah, he left without giving a clue to the source of his preoccupation.

What had happened? Long after the trusteeship proposal had been explained away, Truman had told Rosenman he still had Weizmann "on my conscience." Would the judge once again approach the little doctor and tell him, in the highest secrecy, that if a Jewish state were declared, and if the United Nations remained stalled in its drive to establish a trusteeship, the President of the United States would recognize the new state immediately? Truman laid down one further condition, according to Weizmann's later report. At no time during the period to come would he deal with any of the other Zionist leaders who so enraged his sense of propriety. Weizmann, Jacobson's "hero," would be his sole point of contact with the Jewish destiny.

Going off to his Seder that night, the veteran of the Balfour Declaration well understood the need for secrecy. If he gave the slightest hint of this promise, if he conveyed any reassurance to any of the Zionist factions agitating in Palestine, Europe, and the United States, the confidence would be broken and the assurance rendered worthless. Through the agonizing pressures of the next three weeks, Weizmann kept his silence.

The move was typical of Truman, a statement of personal integrity and intent, uncluttered by bureaucratic options and provisos. It was the word of one amiable citizen to another, one from Independence, the other from Pinsk. Yet it was as binding as an act of state. Truman never notified the State Department of his promise. But Clifford sensed the intent of the Chief Executive, and so did other members of the White House staff. As events rushed toward their climax, they acted accordingly.

THE PUBLIC MOOD was disturbed; nothing of these private discussions, obviously, was known to an electorate troubled by other foreign crises. Even as he secretly met Weizmann the month before, Truman had stood before an emergency joint session of Congress to propose measures of mobilization that would place the nation close to a war footing once again. The Soviet menace in Central Europe was sweeping all other foreign policy considerations aside.

Popular support for the partition of Palestine and the aspirations of Zionism was widespread but not fervent. Uncertainty on the issue prevailed across the United States, even among American Jews, many of whom still found the notion of a Jewish political entity deeply disturbing to their own sense of identity. If a Jewish government in Palestine and the government of the United States started pulling in opposite directions, with which side should the Jews of America identify? Until March 1948 the choice could be avoided; the goals of Zionism and the policies of American Presidents seemed identical. But when the government retreated from partition and lent support to trusteeship, the comforting pattern was broken. Soviet moves made the situation even more frightening, raising the fear that the settlers in Palestine might seek aid from the Soviet Union. "Such action would create a terribly difficult position," warned one strategist for the American Jewish Committee. "It would be imperative for American Jews and American Jewish organizations to speak out at once and unequivocally in support of American policy"— even if this meant opposing the policies of a Jewish government.

Other American Jews managed to defer consideration of such dire eventualities in favor of immediate problems. Some 650,000 Jews were holding on in Palestine, intent on declaring their sovereignty whether the international community liked it or not. They hoped for political support, but what they desperately needed first was something more tangible: weapons, and money to buy weapons, for their daily life struggle against the million Arabs of Palestine.

Arab Palestinian militias delivered crippling blows to the Haganah during March 1948, even as the diplomats were bartering away partition in New York. They blocked the Tel Aviv–Jerusalem highway, bombed the Jewish Agency headquarters, and captured arms and armored vehicles in an ambush near Bethlehem. As full-scale war became ever more likely, the arms-supply operation started by the Sonneborn Institute increased in scope and boldness.

Amateur radio operators made informal contact between the eastern seaboard of America and Europe and the Mediterranean, to provide a rapid communications network. A Jewish-owned yacht moored in Hewlett Harbor, just outside New York City limits off Long Island, secreted a powerful radio transmitter through which instructions and advisories could be passed to Tel Aviv. Sealed boxes of "farm equipment" and "industrial goods" continued to pile up in the dockside warehouses. Outsiders began noticing things, and some could not help admiring what they saw. To New York's Mayor William O'Dwyer, it summoned up memories of the Irish campaigns of an earlier day. An arms cache was discovered on West Twenty-eighth Street, and lawyer Paul O'Dwyer managed to get everyone involved acquitted. As far away as Kansas City, local Jews persuaded returning soldiers to hand over weapons and equipment; oiled and packed, they were sent off to an address in New York.

The Federal Bureau of Investigation was charged with enforcing Henderson's embargo on arms shipments to Palestine. But the FBI was headed by J. Edgar Hoover, a man of diverse interests and with friends in high places with whom he exchanged favors. One of his friends was his fellow Washington bachelor David Niles; another was economist Robert Nathan. Men like Niles and Nathan and David Ginsburg knew as much about the arms traffic to Jewish Palestine as they chose to, and if any trouble arose they knew where to turn. Awkward situations arose and were dealt with, while in the carpeted halls diplomats continued to shuffle their option papers. One example conveys the situation:

A young Palestinian messenger carrying mortar-making machinery from Canada to the port of New York was stopped at the Vermont border. He panicked and telephoned the highest contact in his notebook, industrialist Abraham Feinberg, one of the Sonneborn stalwarts. It was 4 A.M. Feinberg called Nathan in Washington, who waited until dawn before getting in touch with Hoover. At a moment like this, candor was imperative. Nathan told Hoover that a secret operation was underway, not damaging to the United States. "It is not straight up and aboveboard," he said, but if it were exposed, "some prominent people and some important organizations could be hurt." Hoover asked if it involved weapons to be used in the United States. No. Would they be used against the United States? No. The FBI chief absorbed this information and terminated the conversation. The apprehended messenger was released on a minor charge, the Sonneborn executives paid a $1,500 fine, and a few days later a consignment of "textile machinery" departed New York Harbor.

HUDDLED ON THE TERRACED and rocky hillsides of Judea that spring of 1948, as for a thousand seasons before, the Arab village of Deir Yassin was asleep. Two or three hundred residents, shepherds, their women, their children, lived as their parents and grandparents and their grandparents had done. This was the traditional Palestine that the "intruding" Jews threatened to upset with their European ways, their commerce and their aspirations to nationalism.

Deir Yassin lay astride the approaches to Jerusalem. On April 9, 1948, Irgun irregulars attacked the village, slaughtered more than two hundred Arab men, women, and children and threw their mutilated bodies down the village well. The Haganah repudiated the deed, but Menachem Begin, the underground Irgun commander, stood by his men. For the Arab Palestinians, Deir Yassin was the fatal symbol. Street vendors peddled photographs of the victims through the streets of Jerusalem's Arab quarters; radios and word-of-mouth networks spread news of what the Arab populace could expect from Zionism triumphant. Palestinian Arabs who could manage it fled to neighboring countries, expecting soon to return home behind victorious Arab armies. Jacques de Reynier, the Swiss representative of the International Red Cross, described the scene at the Arab city of Jaffa: "Everyone was consumed with terror. . . . In the hospitals, the drivers of cars and ambulances took their vehicles, assembled their families, and fled. . . . Many of the ill, nurses, even physicians, departed the hospital wearing the clothes they had on. . . . For all of them the one obsession was to escape at any cost."

It was almost as Roosevelt had fantasized; Palestine was being left for the Jews, there were no Arabs remaining—or rather, just a fraction of their previous majority. Looking back on it, Weizmann called the flight of the Arab Palestinians nothing short of a miracle, the latest of the many that had protected the children of Israel since Genesis, "a miraculous simplification of Israel's tasks." Had they been driven out by a deliberate Jewish offensive? Or did they flee their Palestinian homes voluntarily? The ideological issue would be thrashed over for decades to come. What mattered in April and May of 1948 was that the Jewish settlers found at least 200,000 fewer Arabs to trouble them as they set about establishing their sovereign homeland. And simultaneously with the restoration of the Jews came a new diaspora, as Palestinians flooded into neighboring Arab lands without a livelihood or a welcome.

WASHINGTON WAS in customary turmoil that spring of 1948. After the Austin trusteeship speech, Henderson assured friends that no matter what the White House had to say, the retreat from partition was in accord with American national interests. The United States had supported partition in the first place only because "we had been misled by propaganda that all talk about violent resistance by the Arabs was just mere bluff. Since then, we have come to realize that it is not so."

The White House could hardly agree. In fact, once Clifford had set to work repairing the public damage, a first priority was to make certain that the third- and fourth-ranking people at State would not be in a position to pull the rug out from under the President again. At Niles's suggestion, Truman named the reliable Hilldring Special Assistant to the Secretary of State for Palestine Affairs. Weizmann telephoned Hilldring no fewer than six times to persuade him to accept. "His appointment was made in the face of bitter opposition by our enemies in the [State] Department," wrote a Jewish Agency observer. "Hilldring's responsibility will be to both the President and the Secretary of State and he will rank superior to Loy Henderson."

Henderson first learned of this upstaging move from a radio newscast, and was "upset and bewildered," reported a British contact. American diplomats at the UN also despaired "since they suffered last autumn under Hilldring's authoritarian and entirely pro-Jewish policy." Hilldring was by now worn out physically, and he never took up the new position. But the message that the President had wanted him—and the policy implications of that message—was not lost on Marshall and Lovett in April 1948.

State Department policy, however, remained locked in its old mold. Lovett warned Zionist petitioners that American financial support might well be withheld from Jewish Palestine if they insisted on their scheme to proclaim themselves a sovereign government. The Department feared that Jews and Arabs would each proclaim Palestine as "their" state and compete for recognition from other governments, establishing competing lines to outside arms suppliers to support their inevitable warfare.

In desperation, Henderson conceived a plan to inject "moderate and temperate" views into the deadlocked Arab-Jewish debate. Early in April he dispatched two secret telegrams, one to his old friend Azzam Pasha, Secretary-General of the Arab League, expressing the hope that this distinguished Arab spokesman could fly to the United States immediately. Then he sent the same message to a Zionist notable of unquestioned moral and political stature, the one prophetic figure who he knew could be relied upon to oppose the rush to statehood: Judah Magnes.

Azzam Pasha temporized and eventually declined the bait, but the president of the Hebrew University was interested. "For more than a generation I have been pleading for peace and conciliation," Magnes told an associate. "How can I not go? This is the moment I have been preparing for all these years." Then seventy-one years old, Magnes was anguished at the loss of idealism among his fellow Zionists; the new generation seemed to be mere political agitators and warriors, no longer prophets and visionaries. "I fear greatly for what will happen to this blossoming community here," he wrote Governor Herbert Lehman of New York. "During 25 years it was possible to build up the beginnings of a true and beautiful Jewish life. It is in my opinion a great misfortune that since the adoption of the Biltmore Program in 1942 the minds and hearts of the Jewish people have been bedevilled by the mirage of a Jewish state."

Henderson knew his man. And he knew how this charismatic old-time Zionist luminary, expressing such unorthodox "anti-Zionist" views in the last month of the British Mandate, would confound American public and Jewish opinion. But it was essential to be discreet. Magnes naïvely suggested that he would be more heeded in America if he came as an official guest of the State Department, a suggestion to which Henderson replied in haste: absolutely not. The Department's role in a Magnes mission should not be revealed; he should come only at the invitation of members of the American Jewish community. Magnes promptly fell in line and, through State Department communications, cabled his loyal New York contact, Maurice Hexter, to suggest that an ad hoc committee of Jewish notables be set up to break Jewish Agency discipline and invite him. Lessing Rosenwald and other anti-Zionist Jewish spokesmen promptly obliged, agreeing as well to underwrite the cost of Judah Magnes' last tilt at American public opinion.

He arrived in New York on April 21, 1948. Hexter had arranged suitable quarters, medical attention, a salt-free diet, and a special bed for him. Four days later he told assembled American Jewish leaders that a Jewish state in 1948 was impractical, that Arab numbers and resources would surely win out. Asked what would happen if Ben-Gurion and the other "extremists" went ahead and declared a state anyway, Magnes replied confidently that it would have no standing, that only Russia, among the outside powers, would recognize it, and that warfare would ensue for a generation to come. He hit with passion at the theme that had guided his independent diplomacy for the decade past. "Given another thirty years of upbuilding, together with compassionate immigration, Palestine can be ours—not by force of arms, not by force of statehood, not by conflict—but ours with cooperation."

Marshall and even Truman received this strange prophet from Palestine, so different from other Zionists whom they refused to meet. Magnes urged not only that the United States withdraw support from the idea of a Jewish state, from the principle of partition, but that it take the positive step of imposing financial sanctions against the Jews of Palestine. Although past financial support had produced farms, universities, and hospitals, Magnes argued, now the dollars sent to the Jewish community were being used solely for war, "which eats up everything." Marshall told Magnes that his "was the most straightforward account on Palestine" that he had ever heard. Henderson's little stratagem seemed to have succeeded well.

But with the Jewish community and the general public, Magnes' welcome was mixed. One member of the Jewish Agency Executive Council in New York informed his colleagues that he had spoken with the controversial visitor; "several members objected to any contact with Dr. Magnes," reported the minutes of the meeting. Magnes' public statements picked up some support among non-establishment Jews, including Albert Einstein and the spiritual leader of German Jewry during the dark Nazi years, Rabbi Leo Baeck. They jointly urged "Jews in the United States and Palestine not to permit themselves to be driven into a mood of despair or false heroism, which might lead to suicidal measures." As news of his remarks reached the Jewish community in Palestine, Magnes began receiving assassination threats, of which the State Department took note and precaution.

By and large, Judah Magnes' plea to the American conscience came too late; opinions were already fixed. While to the diplomats he spoke with the voice of reason, to the masses his words fell into a void. His mission was one of no fewer than twenty-six initiatives taken by the State Department in those final weeks before the scheduled British withdrawal on May 15. Less dramatic were the ones launched at the United Nations, where formulas of trusteeship had evolved into simpler calls for temporary truce, to give the international peacemakers more time. Militias of Jews and Arabs were clashing in ever heavier combat across Palestine; armies of the Arab states were deployed on every hand, ready to invade the minute the British left.

The head of the State Department's UN Office, Dean Rusk, conceived a bold scheme to force Jewish and Arab leaders in Palestine to sit down together around a conference table. Since Shertok and other influential Jewish Agency leaders were still at Lake Success, he offered Truman's presidential aircraft to carry them directly to the conference site. (Lovett had to reassure Truman that it need not be his own plane—"any good C-54 would do.") But even as he lobbied for this and other temporizing moves, Rusk was losing any illusions he may have had about further options. "I think if we start taking up any of these things, the only possible way would be to extend the [British] mandate," he told a colleague in New York. "The caboose has gone by, and they would have to start a new train here. . . . I hope by early afternoon we can give you the green light to go full speed ahead at a snail's pace."

THE JEWISH AGENCY Executive Council was torn by doubt and indecision that first week of May 1948. It was not just the presence of Magnes and the anti-Zionist American Jews that caused the problem; it was not even Bergson and his publicists, who had cut loose from Begin's Irgun and established themselves in Washington with an "embassy" of the Hebrew Liberation Movement. The fundamental question for the mainstream Zionist leadership was whether—when the British pulled out and the long-awaited moment actually came—to declare the Jewish state unilaterally or to agree to a delay in hopes that the diplomats at the UN could work out a more peaceful transition. Goldmann urged caution. Shertok was ambivalent. Silver would not listen to anything that smacked of moderation. Ben-Gurion understood better than any the enormity of the risk, for he and his colleagues in Palestine were fighting the Arabs every day. And his own "extremists," Begin and the perpetrators of Deir Yassin, announced that if the Zionist establishment did not declare the state, they would do it themselves.

Through the night of May 3–4, Rusk's proposals for a presidential aircraft and a last-ditch conference came in for heated discussion among the Jewish Agency leaders in New York. Shertok and Goldmann argued strongly for considering the plan, even though that would delay the proclamation of Jewish statehood scheduled for May 15. Silver and his partisans would have none of it, and they prevailed. With only Shertok and Goldmann dissenting, the Agency executive voted to reject Rusk's proposal, and the American mission to the UN was so informed at eight-thirty the next morning. Concealing his own doubts, Shertok firmly conveyed the majority view that "we cannot accept the offer; it is far too spectacular; it involves a moral responsibility which we cannot engage to keep up."

Amid the turmoil one man held aloof, ill but not forgotten. Weizmann had been the voice of moderation against "extremists" from the early years of international Zionism. He had long since lost all executive authority, but everyone, Zionist and diplomat alike, was curious to learn where he stood at the moment of decision for the Jewish national cause.

Austin and a few key aides from the UN mission paid him a formal call (since they were all living at the Waldorf-Astoria Hotel, this meant descending five floors in the elevator). Surely, Austin believed, Weizmann was experienced enough in diplomacy to see the wisdom in delaying the proclamation of the Jewish state for just ten days while a last-minute diplomatic effort was allowed to unfold. And perhaps he could exert personal influence on the younger generation of Zionist leaders. To the Americans' surprise, the Zionist elder gave them no satisfaction. With a vehemence they could not understand, he defended the decision of the Jewish Agency. He even seemed to think that Washington and other

capitals would accord official recognition to the Jewish state. His confidence almost suggested that he knew something about American policy
that they did not.

With his hesitating Zionist colleagues, Weizmann was also inexplicably uncompromising. He urged the ambivalent Shertok to resist all the
lures of a truce or any form of trusteeship—anything, in fact, that would
interrupt the present momentum. Sending word to his old adversary
Ben-Gurion, Weizmann told Shertok, "Moshe, don't let them weaken,
don't let them swerve, don't let them spoil the victory. The Jewish state,
nothing less." As Shertok was leaving to join his colleagues in Palestine,
Weizmann had him paged at the airport and on the telephone he repeated
his message: "Proclaim the Jewish state, now or never!" Shertok, like
Austin, was mystified by the old man's vehemence.

Ben-Gurion had already decided that he needed Weizmann's counsel
—the step about to be taken in the name of the Jewish people was too
risky to be handicapped by animosities of earlier days. Not yet in receipt
of Shertok's message, Ben-Gurion asked Meyer Weisgal to find out
whether Weizmann really approved the unilateral proclamation of the
state. On the transatlantic telephone, through the eavesdropping of half
a dozen interested parties, Weizmann replied to Weisgal in Yiddish,
"What are they waiting for?" Weisgal promptly called Ben-Gurion: "The
answer is yes."

Weizmann never revealed the promise from Truman that allowed him
to be so assured. But word of Truman's intent began filtering out through
other channels. Bartley Crum had occasion to see the President early in
May, and he asked Truman how he would react if the Jews went ahead
and proclaimed their state. Crum eagerly reported to his Zionist friends
that Truman had replied unhesitatingly, "I would recognize the state, of
course." Welcome news, but could Crum be believed? His enthusiasm
often exceeded the facts. Besides, what was an offhand comment by the
man who happened to be the President worth, when a whole array of
diplomats and generals and other advisers were lined up against Jewish
statehood?

Shertok requested a final meeting with Marshall before leaving for
Palestine, and the American diplomats saw one last opportunity to delay
the inevitable. "The fact that Mr. Moshe Shertok wishes to see you
before his departure for Jerusalem is of considerable significance," Rusk
informed the Secretary. "There is a bitter debate going on within the
Jewish Agency . . ." On short notice, Marshall agreed to receive Shertok
after lunch on Saturday, May 8; Shertok's plane was due to leave Washington at 3:45 P.M. Time was short, the moment decisive, yet personal
affairs put matters of state in their place; Marshall was late for the meet-

ing, detained at the White House at a festive birthday luncheon for Truman.

Lovett and Rusk began the conversation in the Secretary's absence. They lambasted the British for the mess they had made in their last days in Palestine, and Shertok offered his latest intelligence about Arab military moves. At 2:20, Marshall appeared, and gestured for the meeting to continue while he collected his thoughts. Actually, everyone knew that once Shertok got started it was difficult to stop him. His first meeting with Marshall months before had lasted twenty-one minutes; Shertok consumed twenty minutes, Marshall spoke for one. This time it was a little different. Marshall affected intense, though silent, interest as Shertok and Lovett exchanged the legalistic parries by which diplomats suppose they influence the course of events, then the general roused himself to intervene.

By that time the hour was 3:25. Rusk quietly telephoned the airport to say that the 3:45 commercial flight would have to be delayed on whatever pretext; Marshall signaled an aide to have his personal driver stand by to convey Shertok directly to the plane. The Secretary promised to be brief. He directed attention to a map of Palestine on his office wall. "Here you are surrounded by Arabs," he began, his hand placed on the Negev. "And here, in the Galilee, you are surrounded by other Arabs. You have Arab states all around you and your backs are to the sea." This was the weathered voice of military experience. "Believe me, I am talking about things which I know," Marshall continued, and none in the room could challenge him. "You are sitting there in the coastal plains of Palestine while the Arabs hold the mountain ridges. I know you have some arms and your Haganah, but the Arabs have regular armies. They are well trained and they have heavy arms. How can you hope to hold out?"

Shertok was shaken by this straight talk, for he had himself suffered doubts about the military prospects. Marshall "could not help thinking about his experience in China," Shertok later reported.

The analogy was striking. He had almost succeeded in arranging for a truce for a certain period, . . . but at that time the Government forces had just scored a success in the field and they were afraid that they would lose more than they would gain by the truce. Then the same thing happened on the other side and they too had the same fear. As a result the truce did not come off.

"He himself was a military man," Shertok went on,

but he wanted to warn us against relying on the advice of our military people. . . . Flushed by victory, their counsel was liable to be misleading. If we succeed, well and good. He would be quite happy; he wished us well. But what if we failed? He did not want to put any pressure on us. It was our responsibility and it was for us to face it. We were completely free to take our decision, but he hoped we do so in full realization of the very grave risks involved. . . .

"By the time he finished, all possible time limits had been exhausted," Shertok concluded. The "Foreign Minister" of the Jewish Agency could make only a quick parting statement. If the Jews in Palestine chose to act "contrary to what [Marshall] thought was right, it would not be because they would not heed his advice." Then he left for the airport in Marshall's limousine. Lovett drafted a quick cable to London to report Shertok's latest intelligence about Arab military moves.

ON MONDAY, Crum managed to see Truman again and word came back to the Zionists that their eager friend was "fairly optimistic." Clifford's office was producing memos warning against unquestioning acceptance of State Department worries. Indeed, recognition of the Jewish state, one memo insisted, "might bring our country a useful ally and supporter, diminish violence, help the United Nations." These documents are unsigned; they are written in the style of Niles and Lowenthal.

During his final session with Shertok, Lovett had made veiled reference to an option the Department was considering: an attempt to turn American public opinion against the Zionists by means of a documented record of Jewish pressure tactics, of the many irregularities noted—and overlooked—on the wharves of the Atlantic seaports. He made the threat explicit to Goldmann on May 11, pointing to a dossier on his desk and saying, "You see those files? That is all evidence of the violent, ruthless pressures exerted on the American government, mostly by American Jews. I wonder to whom they feel they owe their primary loyalty." Goldmann was shaken as he left Lovett. He telephoned Lowenthal at the White House, who promptly wrote a memo to Clifford telling what the State Department was up to. "Clark," he penciled at the bottom, "please do not let anyone else read this dynamite."

Lovett touched all bases, asking the State Department's Legal Adviser, Ernest Gross, for an opinion about recognition of a Jewish state, should it be declared. Gross, an impeccably objective international lawyer, obliged with a treatise explicating the conditions under which recognition of a successor state might be legal.

By May 12, the issue could be avoided no longer. In three days the

British would abandon their Palestine mandate, the Zionists would declare their own state in accordance with the UN partition plan, and the
Arab armies would invade to crush Jewish nationalism and declare Palestine an undivided Arab state. What was the United States going to do?

Truman, of course, had already made a promise to recognize the
Jewish state, and if he really wanted to insist on it, he could impose that
decision upon his administration. But no Chief Executive can afford to
disregard the considered recommendations of his expert advisers, particularly advisers of the stature of General Marshall, most of all in an
election year, when the pressures against his candidacy were intense and
a single defection of prominence could be fatal.

Rusk showed his sensitivity to the political process when a colleague
at the UN asked him about the United States position:

> What is likely to come out from down here, particularly across
> the way [the White House], is the idea that something has hap-
> pened in fact over there [in Palestine]. It is not according to plan
> but nevertheless there is a community in existence over there
> running its own affairs. Now that community apparently is going
> to get an open shot at establishing itself. We have told them that
> if they get in trouble, don't come to us for help in a military sense.
> Nevertheless, I don't think the boss [Truman] will ever put him-
> self in a position of opposing that effort when it might be that the
> US opposition would be the only thing that would prevent it from
> succeeding.

Truman went to a Sigmund Romberg concert the evening of May 11.
First thing the next morning, his staff meeting opened with a consideration of a dispute between the White House and the State Department
about an exchange with Soviet Foreign Minister Molotov. The White
House attitude was unfriendly—both to Molotov and to State. Clifford
seized this moment to report on Palestine. He called the State Department's position nothing short of "incredible." What with partition and
trusteeships and truces, all the diplomats had succeeded in doing was to
"embarrass the President." Truman concurred, according to notes taken
at the meeting.

The mood of the morning patterns the mind for the day. At four that
afternoon, Wednesday, May 12, Truman's calendar provided for a meeting with the Secretary of State to decide the course of Palestine policy.
Interested members of both the White House staff and the Department
of State would participate. When the policymakers gathered in Truman's
office, the President deferentially placed Marshall alone on his right,
while the others arranged themselves on his left. Clifford, Niles, and

Matthew Connelly represented the White House staff, Lovett and two officials from the UN Office and the Near East Division came from State. Such was the personal tension by this time that the presence of the chief of the Near East Division, Loy Henderson, was not deemed advisable.

Neither in poker nor in politics was it Truman's style to tip his hand at the start of play. Clifford was alone in the knowledge that his purpose in calling the meeting was to engage the bureaucracy in the decision that he, as President, had already made—to recognize the Jewish state. Truman opened blandly, asking what was likely to happen in Palestine when the British withdrew forty-eight hours hence. Lovett swung into a briefing on the latest intelligence. Marshall let his deputy clear away the details, then reported the stern advice he had given to Shertok the previous Saturday. Lovett resumed, describing Rusk's maneuvering at the UN. Everyone agreed that the British had played a "lamentable, if not altogether duplicitous, role in the Palestine situation." On that point, and that alone, everyone at the meeting could agree. "The President then invited Mr. Clark Clifford to make a statement," wrote the note takers.

This was Clifford's moment. When the meeting was being scheduled a day or two before, Truman told his counsel, "I want you to get ready for this as if you were presenting a case to the Supreme Court. You will be addressing all of us present, of course, but the person I really want you to convince is Marshall." Although Marshall and Lovett had remained seated during their remarks, Clifford rose to his feet like a young attorney before the bar. Briefings from Niles and even Ben Cohen, summoned into temporary duty, had prepared him well, but his heaviest artillery was his knowledge that he would be stating the position that Truman had already accepted.

All the agitation at the UN, he began, was impractical; the State Department was ignoring reality in imagining that a truce between Arab and Jewish armies could still be arranged. He reminded the meeting that Rusk had told another group at the White House that a truce could be negotiated in just two weeks—yet that was six weeks ago and the truce was still nowhere in sight. American policy should move beyond contrived trusteeships, truces, or extended mandates, Clifford argued. The President should give prompt recognition to the inevitable Jewish state and, to gain maximum political and diplomatic advantage, that recognition should come immediately, before the Soviet Union could do the same. Finally, Clifford offered a draft statement for Truman to make at a news conference the next day announcing his intention to recognize both the Jewish state and an Arab state in Palestine, if and when they were declared.

After fifteen minutes, the presidential counsel sat down, and the meeting turned to the State Department team for a response. Lovett jumped to the attack on all points: "Premature recognition" would be injurious to the diplomacy underway to avoid all-out war. It would be "buying a pig in a poke," for how did anyone know what kind of state the Jews would establish? He pulled from his briefing papers a series of intelligence reports about Soviet agents dispatched to Palestine under cover of Jewish migration from the Black Sea areas. The policy recommended by Clifford "was a very transparent attempt to win the Jewish vote," whereas in his judgment it would lose more votes than it would gain.

That was Lovett's view, and Clifford considered it "preposterous," but this was not the moment to engage in rhetorical combat. The man who counted, Marshall, was ready to speak. Immediately afterwards, the Secretary dictated from memory what he had said:

> I remarked to the President that, speaking objectively, I could not help but think that the suggestions made by Mr. Clifford were wrong. I thought that to adopt these suggestions would have precisely the opposite effect from that intended. . . . The transparent dodge to win a few votes would not in fact achieve this purpose. The great dignity of the office of President would be seriously diminished. The counsel offered by Mr. Clifford was based on domestic political considerations, while the problem which confronted us was international.

Indeed, "unless politics were involved," Marshall said, "Mr. Clifford would not even be at this meeting"—to say nothing of Niles, whom the Secretary did not deign to notice.

Truman would not countenance charges of political opportunism, not even from Marshall. "Mr. Clifford is here at my personal request," he replied icily, "since it seems sensible to air both sides of the question." Clifford felt Marshall glaring silently at him. The meeting was turning out worse than anticipated. Truman reverted to banter to try to soften the atmosphere. "Well, General," he said, "it sounds to me as if even you might vote against me in November if I go ahead to recognize." George C. Marshall was not a man to banter. "Yes, Mr. President, if I were to vote at all, I might do just that."

That was a low blow. In jest, perhaps, or possibly in all seriousness, Marshall was threatening to break politically with Truman. This was not what the underdog from Missouri needed in May 1948, two months before a Democratic convention he did not yet control, six months before a presidential election in which he looked like a sure loser. Clifford was incensed at Marshall; "he said it all in a righteous, goddamned Baptist tone," he wrote later.

Nothing more could be accomplished in such circumstances, and Truman ended the meeting. He authorized the State Department to continue the diplomatic efforts at the UN, and he put aside the draft statement which Clifford had prepared for the next day's news conference. But he gave the departing officials no further clue about what he would do on May 15. Clifford lingered behind as the others filed out of the Oval Office. "I'm sorry, Clark," said Truman quietly. "I hope you understand." "That's all right, Mr. President; this isn't the first time I've lost a case." But Truman kept his options open. Let everyone sleep on it, he told Clifford, and then "we will get into it again."

Direct confrontation was not Marshall's style, certainly not confrontation with his commander in chief, and on an issue which he so little understood. The Secretary was still bruised by the unseemly public misunderstandings after the trusteeship episode in March and he was comfortable leaving the whole matter to Lovett, who also had some doubts. It apparently dawned on the under secretary that Clifford had been speaking with unusual authority. Lovett had faithfully argued the State Department's case against Clifford, but ever since the appointment of Hilldring a few weeks before, there had been grounds for wondering whether, so far as the President was concerned, their case, and not Clifford's, might already be lost. Lovett telephoned Clifford the next morning to convey his uneasiness over the way the meeting had gone. He and the others at State would be talking it all out among themselves that day, he said. Perhaps it would be a good idea if the two of them, just Lovett and Clifford, had a private little lunch on Friday.

Truman maintained a holding pattern at his Thursday news conference. When a reporter asked what he intended to do about the imminent declaration of a Jewish state, he said simply, "I will cross that bridge when I get to it."

Both Clifford and Lovett saw the bridge in front of them when they sat down to lunch at the 1925 F Street Club at noon on Friday. Clifford made it as easy as he could for the Secretary of State. There would be no need for Marshall to give the President a formal retraction of his Wednesday advice; indeed, Clifford assured Lovett that Truman had been very much impressed by the Department's arguments against recognition in advance of the Jewish state's proclamation, and had followed that advice by making no move at his news conference. By 6 P.M. Friday (midnight in Tel Aviv), however, the circumstances would be different. "There would be no government or authority of any kind in Palestine," Clifford said. "Title would be lying about for anybody to seize and a number of people had advised the President that this should not be permitted." A Jewish state would be declared, its boundaries defined, the composition of its provisional government announced—it would no longer be "a pig in a poke," but a tangible reality.

Lovett listened in ever fuller understanding of the imminence of the act. The question was no longer whether to recognize the Jewish state, but how soon. Lovett regrouped his arguments to urge only against "indecent haste." Even a day's delay would help the diplomats prepare the ground. Clifford agreed that key officials should be forewarned—but he would not agree to a delay of even twenty-four hours. Advisory cables must go out immediately. Timing was "of the greatest possible importance to the President from a domestic point of view," he said; "the President was under unbearable pressure to recognize the Jewish state promptly." Lovett remembered the words, and put them down in a formal memo for the Department's files. They became the authoritative basis of the diplomats' case that Truman had acted only to grab the Jewish vote.

"My protests against the precipitate action and warnings as to consequences with the Arab world appear to have been outweighed by considerations unknown to me," Lovett wrote archly, "but I can only conclude that the President's political advisers, having failed last Wednesday afternoon to make the President a father of the new state, have determined at least to make him the midwife."

A YEAR or so after the Jewish state came into being, its Chief Rabbi paid an official call on Truman. To Niles's discomfort—"I thought he was overdoing things"—the Israeli dignitary blessed the President with the words: "God put you in your mother's womb so you would be the instrument to bring about Israel's rebirth after two thousand years." Niles's embarrassment turned to amazement as he looked at Truman and saw that "tears were running down his cheeks." Ben-Gurion recounted a similar experience after meeting Truman in New York. "His eyes were still wet when he bade me goodbye," the Israeli Prime Minister wrote. "I tried to hold him for a few minutes until he had become more composed, for I recalled that the hotel corridors were full of waiting journalists and photographers." And when Eddie Jacobson introduced the President to some Jewish scholars as "the man who helped create the State of Israel," Truman let his love of ancient history go to his head. "What do you mean, 'helped create'? I am Cyrus, I am Cyrus!"

The actual record of those spring days of 1948 does not enhance Truman's place on Israel's scrolls of honor. One of the ironies of the

Jewish restoration, as it came about in fact, is the way the credit has been apportioned between Roosevelt and Truman. Roosevelt's sorry record in refusing to face the Holocaust has blotted out memory of his radical vision for a Jewish Palestine. As for Truman, as he himself admitted sheepishly years later: "Those Israelites have placed me on a pedestal alongside of Moses." But except for occasional musings about Cyrus and the Near East of the Bible, Truman never showed great interest in the Jewish restoration. The notion of a Jewish state held no romance for him; the Zionist politicians agitating for that dream were, to him, nothing short of repugnant.

On Israel's first day of existence in the modern world, May 15, 1948, Truman wrote a letter to Weizmann, the only Zionist leader who seems to have really touched the President. Surely this was a natural opportunity for any expression of historical sentiment or appreciation which Truman might have felt. There was none. He told Weizmann simply that "I sincerely hope that the Palestine situation will eventually work out on an equitable and peaceful basis." Four months later, Truman still displayed no sympathetic feelings for the Jewish restoration being realized amid war and disruption. "I hope that peace will come to Palestine," he wrote Weizmann in September 1948, not even using the word "Israel," "and that we will eventually be able to work out proper location of all those Jews who suffered so much during the war." These letters were typewritten, presumably drafted by a correspondence secretary. But Truman signed them, without adding any of the handwritten messages through which he carried on unguarded personal correspondence on matters of real import to him.

From his first days in office, he had regarded the problem of Palestine as a matter of finding homes for miserable people ravaged by war, not as any political revolution or act of statecraft following two thousand years of exile. All the various diplomatic formulas of those years were to him no more than legalistic double-talk that kept the striped-pants boys busy. As late as March 1948 he could refer blithely to the Anglo-American Committee report and the UNSCOP proposal in the same breath, ignoring the fact that these international bodies had come to quite opposite political conclusions.

"My soul [sic] objective in the Palestine procedure has been to prevent bloodshed," he wrote on May 18, 1948, two days after the new state of Israel had been invaded by surrounding Arab armies. "The way things look today we apparently have not been very successful." Even after he had incurred the wrath of his foreign policy advisers by recognizing Israel, he still saw the restoration of the Jews as nothing more than "the Palestine procedure."

Most revealing of all was the letter Truman wrote on the very day of Israel's rebirth to Bartley Crum, energetic Gentile custodian of the Zionists' back channels. "I think the report of the British American Commission on Palestine [*sic*] was the correct solution," Truman wrote, "and, I think, eventually we are going to get it worked out just that way." But the Anglo-American Committee of Inquiry had rejected partition; instead of a Jewish state and an Arab state, it advocated an imposed unitary state of rival and incompatible communities—just what the State Department had attempted to bring about against Truman's wishes. Here indeed is the Truman described by Henry Wallace, a man whose mind could move off in at least two different directions with little time intervening and no loss of sincerity.

TWO LITTLE BANDS of policy managers were at work in Washington during the last hours before the proclamation of Jewish statehood. Lovett and Henderson dispatched top secret advisory cables to American missions around the Arab world, hoping to limit the damage they anticipated. The other group was at work with Clifford at the White House. Niles and Lowenthal were on the job officially, and for extra help they called in such other members of the political family as David Ginsburg and the venerable Ben Cohen, who was destined to play the most ironic role of all on that final day.

These political aides left the final maneuvering at the United Nations and in the diplomatic community to the State Department. Their mission was to prepare the United States' act of recognition. The first step was to lay to rest the "pig in a poke" argument which had carried the day at the unpleasant Wednesday meeting. Recognition should come only in response to an official request from a sympathetic new government of the Jewish state. But there could be no official lines of communication with a government that did not yet exist. Ginsburg took it upon himself Thursday to invent some. He called Weizmann in New York, asking that a formal request for recognition be submitted. Weizmann's longtime aide and secretary, Josef Cohn, carried the letter of request to Washington by the overnight train.

But Weizmann held no official position, and Shertok, the man who would become Foreign Minister, was in Palestine. Eliahu Epstein, however, was the Jewish Agency representative in Washington (he would become the ambassador) and he was in the closest touch with both State and the White House. Clifford and Henderson each telephoned Epstein on Friday to ascertain the boundaries that the new state would claim. Clifford also wanted to know the precise hour at which the proclamation of independence would become effective, and further, whether the government to be installed would be described as "provisional." To be absolutely proper, he asked for a request for recognition more official than Weizmann's letter.

Epstein had no instructions from Palestine, but he acted without hesitation on his own responsibility. All he needed was help in the formal drafting of such a weighty message. For guidance in procedure, he thought of an American friend now returned to private life but experienced in the workings of the American government: Ben Cohen. They started drafting the letter together, but promptly faced an awkward problem: the Jewish Agency office in Washington had not yet been told what the name of the new state would be—Judea? Israel? The proclamation of independence had gone through several drafts. They settled for reference simply to "the Jewish state," and Epstein's press aide, Harry Zinder, jumped into a taxi to deliver the letter to Clifford's office. Moments after he left, word came on the shortwave radio that the state was to be called Israel. Epstein sent another aide in his own car to intercept Zinder's taxi, and two blocks from the White House gate, sitting in the car, Zinder inserted the name "Israel" with a ball-point pen on the neatly typed letter to the government of the United States.

Alerted that the official request was on its way, Clifford's staff started drafting the reply, the official announcement of recognition. Niles and Clifford parsed the formal phrases but, for a final check, they asked a former colleague with greater experience in drafting documents of state to read through it. Thus it was that Ben Cohen helped draft both sides of the exchange that confirmed the Jewish restoration, the request for recognition and the American response. Decades later, Cohen took the remembered irony in stride. "I guess I was always in the middle of complicated things," he said.

Proclamation of the Jewish state of Israel was to come into effect at 6 P.M., Washington time, May 14, 1948. At 5:40, Clifford called Lovett to say that the White House would announce recognition within a few minutes. Then he called Rusk to get the word to Austin at the UN. "But this cuts across what our delegation has been trying to accomplish in the General Assembly," Rusk protested. With no time to waste, Clifford replied, "This is what the President wishes you to do." Rusk's telephone call pulled America's chief delegate off the floor of the General Assembly. Austin listened in silence to the information that Rusk so brusquely gave him. He decided he could not return to the debate. Without informing anyone of the news just delivered to him, he walked to his limousine and went home.

Toward six every afternoon, the Washington press corps confidently expects word that "the lid is on," that there will be no more news from officialdom, that they are free to go home without worrying about missing anything. Great was the annoyance on May 14 when the White House press office refused to lower the lid. Moments before six, Clifford walked into the office of press secretary Charles Ross and handed him a statement to read to the reporters. It took a few minutes to assemble everyone in the press room. At 6:11, the White House announced:

> This government has been informed that a Jewish state has been proclaimed in Palestine, and recognition has been requested by the provisional government thereof.
> The United States recognizes the provisional government as the de facto authority of the new State of Israel.

A moment later the telephone rang on Niles's desk. "Dave, I want you to know that I've just announced recognition." It was the President's cheerful voice. "You're the first person I called, because I knew how much this would mean to you."

In New York, Weizmann was entertaining friends at tea. His political aide, Ivor Linton, burst into the room. Weizmann spoke before he could say a word: "President Truman has recognized our state." "How could you know?" asked Linton. "You don't have a radio." In full serenity, Weizmann replied, "I saw it in your face."

Traffic came to a halt in front of the Jewish Agency offices on Sixty-sixth Street. With a grin as broad as a teen-age boy could ever manage, Chaim Shertok, son of the man just named Foreign Minister of the Jewish state, unfurled the blue and white flag of Israel.

Lessing J. Rosenwald, president of the anti-Zionist American Council for Judaism, issued a statement to ease the anxieties of his membership. The new Jewish state "can have no claim upon the national attachments of those of Jewish faith who are citizens of other lands."

The Jewish Agency office in Washington was suddenly the Embassy of Israel. Amid the throngs of well-wishers who paid spontaneous calls of congratulations that evening were the veteran of the Roosevelt years, Sumner Welles, and Mrs. Woodrow Wilson, widow of the President who had placed the Jewish restoration on the agenda of American diplomacy.

Lovett rushed from the State Department to join the festive mood of the White House staff. With the deft footwork of one destined for ever higher political office,* the man who had pressed the State Department's

* He eventually became Truman's Secretary of Defense.

arguments through all the final debates congratulated the President on his decision and said blandly, referring to his now disowned diplomatic colleagues, "They almost put it over on you!"

About 10 P.M., a telegram arrived at the White House from Kansas City. Eddie Jacobson sent his old friend the message: "Thanks and God bless you."

The Jews of the United States were far more numerous than those of Israel. In between was another community of Jews, a restive human population whose presence and need had provided the final impetus for the restoration of their nation.

Chaplain Oscar M. Lifshutz, U.S. Army, was about to begin his Sabbath services for the refugees at the Riedenberg DP camp, near Salz-burg, on Saturday morning, May 15. Unannounced, up drove a jeep from Army headquarters, bringing a senior staff officer, a Colonel Long. "Chaplain," the colonel began, "I'm a Protestant, but I feel that I too have given a helping hand in bringing these children of Israel to freedom. I want to be able to tell my children how I once helped a people to find their home." At the colonel's gesture, two American MPs advanced to the flagpole, lowered the American flag, folded it into the regulation triangle, saluted, and handed it to their colonel. Long marched over to the leader of the Jewish camp inmates, saluted, and handed him the flag. "We want you to remember us," he said.

Unable to speak, the Jewish survivor took the flag and signaled to a fellow inmate who had a large bundle under his arm. It was a homemade flag of Israel. Two DPs fixed the new flag to the halyard and pulled it to the top of the flagpole. Refugees and American soldiers sang together the Jewish anthem, "Hatikvah," and "America the Beautiful."

In the 172nd year of its existence, the American republic was the first of the world's nations to recognize the sovereignty of the Jews, restored in their homeland.

EPILOGUE

Aᴍᴇʀɪᴄᴀ's ᴅɪᴘʟᴏᴍᴀᴄʏ for the Holy Land lay in shambles. Only one point was clear: all the months of jostling, for truce, trusteeship, or binational power-sharing, became irrelevant. Guatemala, Uruguay, and Nicaragua quickly followed the United States in recognizing Israel. On May 17, the Soviet Union extended recognition, followed by Poland, Czechoslovakia, and Yugoslavia. Next came South Africa under General Smuts, last surviving member of the British War Cabinet that had approved the Balfour Declaration three decades before.

But the generals moved faster than the diplomats. Arab armies entered Palestine before dawn on Israel's first day, advancing to Ramallah, Nablus, Latrun, and south of the Sea of Galilee. The Egyptians advanced into Gaza. The Haganah, now the army of Israel, fought back, launching an offensive to capture Jaffa and Acre on the Mediterranean coast. Most of all, the Haganah fought to open the road from the coast to besieged Jerusalem.

In Washington, Marshall remained unimpressed by the military actions. "The present evident aggressive tendencies of the Israeli government to capitalize to the limit on military advantages, real and anticipated, is bound to have unfortunate results," Marshall advised, "where a more conservative course can well lead to a settlement advantageous to that government." The Israelis went on fighting.

One of the neighboring Arab leaders was tempted to make peace. The Hashemite King Abdullah of Transjordan had met secretly with Golda Meir of the Jewish Agency in November 1947, at the guest house of a power station on the Jordan River frontier. The two agreed to live with, and exploit, the UN partition plan: the Jews would have their sector, Abdullah would take on the assigned Arab lands for his own kingdom, and neither would breach the partition line against the other. Such private deals collapsed in the bellicosity of May, but once military stalemate took hold in 1949, King Abdullah set about renewing his arrangements with the Israelis, speaking this time with Lieutenant Colonel Moshe Dayan, the Israeli commander in divided Jerusalem. In March 1950 they concluded a secret draft treaty of peace between Israel and Jordan. The secret could not be kept for long, and the treaty was never implemented. Sixteen months later, as Abdullah was at prayer at the Mosque of Omar in Arab Jerusalem, an assassin shot him dead. Twenty-six years would pass before another neighboring Arab leader ventured upon the path to peace with the Zionists.

AMERICAN POLITICIANS and historians have charged Truman with crude political pandering in his recognition of Israel on May 14, 1948. Was politics a factor? "Of course it was," acknowledged Clifford many years later. "Political considerations are present in every important decision that a President makes." But Clifford insisted that Palestine and the Jewish vote were neither compelling nor decisive. The question of Palestine lurked on the margins of the 1948 campaign to the very end, but faced with Zionist entreaties and threats, Truman remained as stubborn as always. Some 65 percent of America's Jews lived in the three large states of New York, Pennsylvania, and Illinois, with 110 electoral votes among them. Truman lost all three—and won the election.

There were really several issues that concerned America's Jews, not one. The first had to do with the way Truman actually recognized Israel: what he accorded on May 14 was de facto recognition of a living reality, not the de jure recognition that would acknowledge legal legitimacy. After their first expressions of gratitude, Rabbi Silver and his political organizers grasped the halfhearted nature of Truman's action. Ignoring their demands, Truman insisted that de jure recognition could come to Israel only after elections in the new state and the installation of something more than a provisional government. Not until January 1949 did that come about—and only then, when it no longer had real bearing on American domestic politics, did Truman upgrade the level of diplomatic recognition.

Of more tangible importance was the embargo on American arms shipments to Palestine. This remained in effect even against the sovereign Jewish state. Through all the fighting of Israel's first months, the months of America's election campaign, Truman refused to lift the restrictions that Henderson had pushed through.

In spite of Zionist pressure, he let the diplomats pursue their quest for compromise between warring Arabs and Israelis. A United Nations mediator, Count Folke Bernadotte of Sweden, proposed new boundaries which would once again turn the Negev over to the Arabs. Marshall

promptly accepted the Bernadotte plan; American Zionists protested another "betrayal of American policy." Bernadotte was assassinated by Israeli irregulars in September. Truman refused all demands that he
repudiate Marshall and the Bernadotte plan.

As late as October, on the whistle-stop tour of America that reversed
his electoral fortunes, Truman resisted the blandishments of Weizmann
and Jacobson to make political capital of his Palestine decisions. Only
when his Republican opponent, Dewey of New York, accused him of
betraying pledges to Israel did Truman declare his full support for the
Jewish state—as the United Nations, not the Israelis, had defined it.

By election day, Israel had become too confusing a problem for the
general American electorate to take sides. Truman's own interest had
waned—as far as he was concerned, the problem of the homeless refugees
had been solved.

THE STATE DEPARTMENT regrouped to recover from the collapse of its
Palestine policy. Three of those who figured in the events of May survived untouched; Marshall, Lovett, and Rusk, who continued his jour-
neyman's work in the Department and eventually became Secretary of
State under President John F. Kennedy.

Henderson was vulnerable, for on Palestine he had declared himself
and lost. Once before, this able professional had fallen afoul of the political leaders, when Roosevelt exiled him for his unfashionable anti-Com-
munism. In July 1948, Henderson was transferred from the Near East
Division to become ambassador to India. His diplomatic career eventually resumed its ascent, and before his retirement, he had served in the
most senior posts open to a Foreign Service officer. The State Department named the imposing meeting room in its new headquarters overlooking the Lincoln Memorial the Loy W. Henderson Conference Room.
Later Secretaries of State into the 1980s would hold periodic meetings to
reassure American Jewish leaders about support for Israel, and they
would meet in the Henderson room. Neither officials nor visitors noted
the irony; Henderson's role with Palestine and Israel had been forgotten.

David Niles, nemesis of the State Department, thrived into the second Truman administration, maneuvering through the sensitive missions
and minority politics that had been his life since the early New Deal. The
leaders of Israel regularly invited him to visit the homeland to which he
had devoted so much effort, but he never made it. His name came up
during an investigation into the financial scandals that hit the Truman
White House in 1950; the "five-percenters" on the staff were sprucing up
their bank accounts in the course of official business. Niles was never

shown to have made money—the slovenly bachelor had no interest in it —but he had once spent a free vacation in a fancy resort. He resigned and went home to Massachusetts. Few people knew it, but David Niles had cancer. Alone during his last months as all through his adult life, he died in May 1951.

The experts' worst fears about the consequences of the Jewish state never materialized.

Granted their sovereignty, the Jews did not defile the Christian holy places. No American or other foreign troops ever had to be dispatched to defend Israel; on the contrary, Israel eventually became a military power in the region in its own right. The Israelis obtained their aircraft, weapons, ammunition, and spare parts despite the American embargo; Communist Czechoslovakia, in fact, served as Israel's first major source of military matériel.

And even then the new state exhibited no sympathies with Communism. All those Bolshevik agents supposed to have been smuggled into the Jewish state—if any existed—did not make their mark on policy. For the first couple of years, the Jewish state tried to avoid ties with either East or West, but then the outbreak of the Korean War in 1950 changed all that. Israel dropped the pretense of neutrality and solidly aligned itself with the West.

The Israelis soon became a strategic asset to their new allies in a special way. From the earliest days, the leaders of the Haganah intelligence organizations maintained extensive networks inside Eastern Europe and the Soviet Union. Offers to exchange intelligence were considered and reluctantly rejected by the appropriate United States officials, but habits of under-the-table cooperation developed, and the American intelligence community grew to be more sympathetic to the Jewish state than either the State Department or the Pentagon.

Israel's economy posed even greater problems than had been anticipated. With destitute immigrants pouring in, not only from the DP camps of Europe but from the more backward Jewish societies of North Africa, of Yemen and the rest of the Middle East, the demands of assimilating a disparate population and building a viable economy challenged development experts. Teams of economists from America and Europe repeatedly analyzed Israel's needs and declared the situation to be hopeless. Two consultants to the United States Treasury displeased Zionist planners by concluding that the Israelis would have to subsist largely on figs and olives, just as the Arabs had during the British mandate.

The American foreign aid program provided more than $1 billion in grants, loans, and technical assistance teams during the 1950s; in 1962

Israel ceased to meet the criteria of an underdeveloped country. Striking progress was made in developing export industries. Eventually fashionable breakfast tables in Paris and Rome would be decorated with flowers cut the day before in Israel. Citrus growers supplied canneries in Europe and even North America; Israel became the largest exporter of polished diamonds in the world. Stylish bathing suits and other specialty clothing captured the fancy of the smartest couturiers. Small arms and weaponry went to armies and police forces throughout the Third World.

A major irritant was the economic embargo imposed upon the Jewish state by the Arab League in 1951. In principle, the Arab world refused to do business with any foreign firm that also did business with Israel; telephone connections and postal exchanges were barred, transport companies, banks, and many industrial investors were forced to choose between two markets. Israelis drank Coca-Cola; Arabs drank Pepsi-Cola. Carelessly applied and full of loopholes, the boycott reached absurd extremes: Cairo canceled a performance by Helen Hayes when the traveling company was booked into Tel Aviv as well. Movies distributed by Republic Pictures were barred in some of the Arab countries because one of its principal stockholders had been a chairman of the United Jewish Welfare Fund. Yet when real economic interests were involved, the boycott was ignored; Conrad Hilton managed to build modern new hotels in Cairo and Tel Aviv at the same time.

ISRAEL FADED from America's public agenda. In the early 1950s President Eisenhower was able to address even Jewish audiences without once mentioning the state of Israel. The Korean War, the end of Stalinism, and the rise of a new Communist menace on the Chinese mainland all provoked greater public passions.

The year 1956 brought the last burst of colonialism in the Middle East, when the British and French, reacting against the militant Egyptian nationalism of Gamal Abdel Nasser, sent troops to occupy the Suez Canal. Seizing the opportunity to demolish Nasser's military bases in the Sinai, Israel secretly colluded with the European powers and launched a swift military operation. In 100 hours at the end of October, Israeli parachute and tank units overran the entire Sinai and stood on the eastern bank of the Canal. Eisenhower and Secretary of State John Foster Dulles regarded the European allies' action as a betrayal of alliance solidarity. But despite the general anger, policy lines were far from clear. In one strategy meeting at the height of the tension, Dulles asked the representative of the Joint Chiefs of Staff if America's Mediterranean fleet was properly deployed in case the United States was drawn into the conflict. "Yes, sir," he was advised, "but you haven't told us which side we are on."

For the Europeans the Suez campaign was unmitigated disaster, and Israel's gains were short-lived. The United States asked the United Nations Security Council to consider ordering a cutoff of military, economic, and financial assistance to Israel, and after four months of painful negotiations Dulles threatened full-scale economic sanctions if Israel failed to comply with a General Assembly demand for withdrawal of all invading troops from Egyptian territory.

Before the Suez debacle, American public opinion polls found five critics of Egypt for every two critics of Israel; after the war, the ratio became three to two. With only nine years of sovereign existence behind it, the Jewish state had neither the resources nor the gumption to resist this frightening decline in United States sympathy. Israel withdrew from all points in the Sinai in March 1957. To a new generation of Israelis, withdrawal from occupied territories became a code phrase for diplomatic humiliation.

THE CREATION of the new state in 1948 had an immediate, profound, and confusing impact on the Jews of America.

For a few key people, the proclamation of Israel's independence brought an instant—and not altogether pleasant—redefinition of roles. Rabbi Silver had savored his stature as an international spokesman of Zionism, dominating the lecture circuits as head of the American section of the Jewish Agency. Suddenly, on May 15, Ben-Gurion, Shertok, and the other leaders in Palestine gained the status of ministers of a sovereign state, leaving Silver little more than a difficult provincial rabbi. He jockeyed to retain some of his former political standing, leading an alarmed Ben-Gurion to worry that he might abandon his Cleveland power base, immigrate to Israel, and run for Prime Minister.

But Silver's dictatorial style was no longer acceptable among Jewish community leaders across the United States. Once the statehood crisis was passed, even some of his colleagues in the central leadership felt free to criticize him. In 1949, Ben-Gurion himself moved to help reform the American Zionist organization, shifting power from Silver's staff to the local organizations. Silver was outmaneuvered and went home to his own community affairs in Cleveland. Like other American Jewish leaders, he continued to raise funds for the Jewish state, but his impact on policy faded. He died in 1963.

Weizmann was in an even more ambiguous position, for he was old and tired when Israel came into being, yet also deeply conscious of his image as a prophet who had carried Zionism through the twentieth century to the moment of redemption. He had moved his life to Palestine, to Israel. But Ben-Gurion and the other pioneers of the Jewish state forgot to leave a space for his signature on the Scroll of Independence, a slight which he considered deliberate. Within days amends were made; he was named President of Israel. Weizmann was welcomed in Washington as a state visitor before the month of May 1948 was out—and before he had actually set foot on the sovereign territory of his own land. No longer forced to slip unnoticed through the East Gate of the White House, this time he arrived in parade up Pennsylvania Avenue. But once he had been established in his presidential villa in Israel, he was ignored by Ben-Gurion and the active politicians. Embittered, languishing in honorific oblivion, he died on November 9, 1952, a few days before his seventy-eighth birthday.

As he brought the leadership of American Jewry to his side, Ben-Gurion delivered a stirring call to American Jewish youth to immigrate to their new homeland. The elders of the Jewish establishment were shocked; this violated the old understanding that the state would serve the needs of downtrodden Jews living under oppression, but had no personal claims to make on the secure Jews of America. In the summer of 1950 the president of the American Jewish Committee, Jacob Blaustein, set out to define the formal relationship between Israel and American Jewry.

Ben-Gurion, never known for his tolerance in the best of circumstances, was thoroughly impatient with the emissaries from America. To him they seemed spineless and cowardly. After long bargaining sessions, however, he realized that a certain political advantage might be gained from humoring the Americans' inexplicable loyalty to their adopted country. The deal was struck: Israelis would not interfere with American Jewish affairs, Americans would not engage in Israeli politics—unless, of course, they uprooted themselves and moved to Israel. America's Jews "have only one political attachment, and that is to the United States of America," Ben-Gurion acknowledged. Israel "in no way presumes to represent or speak in the name of the Jews who are citizens of any other country . . . [Israelis] have no desire and no intention to interfere in any way with the internal affairs of Jewish communities abroad."

The Ben-Gurion–Blaustein compact became the formal definition of Israel's relations with American Jewry. But the sticky question of encouraging Americans to immigrate could not easily be put aside.

Over the years, North American Jews had not responded well to the Zionists' call for immigration. Some 3,000 may have gone in the mid-

1920s. Between 1936 and 1945, just 500 Americans and Canadians made the move; of the half-million Jewish immigrants who settled in Palestine before 1948, no more than 2 percent came from North America.

With restoration and statehood, committed Israelis asked, what excuse would Americans have to hold back? Ben-Gurion reopened the question at the Twenty-third World Zionist Congress in July 1951. A fierce ideological battle ensued, reminiscent of the Brandeis-Weizmann conflict, in which opposing definitions of Zionism were exposed in stark relief.

How could a man claim to be a good Jew, asked the Ben-Gurion partisans, if he deliberately chose to live in the despised exile, estranged from the restored Jewish state? The response was angry and swift. Who are you in Israel, a motley minority of world Jewry who chose to live in the deserts because you had nothing to lose, to tell us that we are not secure and fulfilled in our adopted land? We will support you, as we always have, with our prayers, our energies, and our wealth, but you have no right to ask us to abandon our particular and proud heritage as Americans. So said spokesmen from the United States.

The Eastern European zealots could not let go. After two years of bitter exchanges, Ben-Gurion demanded the "duty of personal immigration" from anyone who claimed to support Zionism. An American businessman who had committed untold energies to campaigns to raise money for the Jewish state proudly told the Prime Minister, "This is my fourteenth trip to Israel!" Ben-Gurion turned away in disgust, saying, "I would be more impressed if you had only come once—and stayed." An American writer, Meyer Levin, wrote a devastating satire called "After All I Did for Israel," telling of the American Jew who had poured himself into fund raising and community political action for Israel, only to find his own children proposing to leave home and try living there! Polls of American Jewry through the 1950s and early 1960s revealed nearly unanimous support for Israel—94 percent of adults, in one study—but no more than 4 percent ready to emigrate. In 1956 the grand total of American emigrants to the Jewish homeland was 187 persons.

Americans who heeded the call and settled in Israel were received as coolly as Brandeis' idealists had been in the 1920s. They were dubbed "Anglo-Saxons" by the Israeli populace, a gratuitous slur against Jews who had deliberately given up Anglo-Saxon society. Israelis tended to consider the North Americans spoiled, condescending, and, of course, wealthy beyond imagination. For their part, American Jews found Israeli society coarse and rude. (Perhaps with justice: as late as 1965, personnel of a large Israeli enterprise were polled about their contacts with the public. Sixty percent said they were not accustomed to offering a greeting to a visitor or returning a greeting offered to them; still more acknowledged that they did not believe in offering a visitor a chair, finding it perfectly correct to let the visitor stand before the desk of authority.)

Israeli statisticians proudly and publicly noted all those Jews who immigrated, but became awkwardly mute when asked how many subsequently went back to their previous homes in disillusionment. An officer of the Association of Americans and Canadians in Israel estimated in 1959 that of 35,000 North Americans who had moved to Israel, no more than 6,000 remained.

But American Jews took comfort in the fact that the old dilemma of divided loyalties had not turned out to be as formidable as previous generations had feared. The Ben-Gurion–Blaustein compact provided the legal formula; in everyday terms, the Brandeisian concept prevailed; multiple loyalties were perfectly acceptable, as long as they were not brought into conflict. There was, after all, little danger that the United States and Israel would ever be at war. Interest in Israel brought civic awareness, and civic awareness made for good citizenship. Israel came to be regarded as an "insurance policy," a safe haven for Jews worried about renewed antisemitism.

Less openly discussed at first was the fact that most of those Americans who chose to settle in the Jewish state went to great lengths to retain their United States citizenship and passports—another "insurance policy," in case wars or economic distress made their lives in Israel unbearable. By 1982 the unspoken had become the subject of satire: a popular revue on the Tel Aviv stage instructed native-born Israelis how to apply for an American visa, just in case. Emigration out of the Jewish state, noted one Israeli commentator, was like sex in Victorian England: often thought about, seldom discussed in polite company.

Freed from the obligation to emigrate, and confident that their political loyalties would not be questioned, American Jews now embraced the cause of Israel with a devotion that belied the insecurity of their skeptical parents and grandparents who had seen Zionism as a threat. Giving money to Israel continued the tradition of *halukkah,* a way to assert Jewish identity without interfering with daily life in a non-Jewish society. "Special Emergency Fund" drives, which helped pay for the first months of combat against the Arabs and establishing the state, soon became annual events as ingenious fund-raisers generated regular "emergencies."

Over the first two decades, 60 percent of Israel's balance-of-payments deficit was met by contributions from American Jewry, far exceeding the next most important source of foreign funds, the $1.73 billion in reparations from the government of West Germany to survivors of the Holocaust. United States economic aid ranked only third.

.   .   .

BEYOND THE POLITICS and the economics, the emotions of the Jewish restoration transformed the self-image of America's Jews, just as Noah and Dembitz, Kallen and Brandeis had anticipated. Indeed, considered in the context of modern intellectual history, Zionism is unique among radical ideologies. Among all the movements to spring out of Europe's discontent at the turn of the century, it arguably succeeded beyond all others. Arising in a quixotic minority fringe of a dispersed and despairing people, it managed to capture the imagination and loyalty of virtually its entire natural constituency. So overwhelming was this identification that the term "Zionist" fell out of favor. "We are all Zionists now," said American businessmen when demonstrating their loyalty to Israel, thus dismissing half a century of anguished Jewish political debate.

The sensitivities of generations were compressed into a simple, seemingly insignificant moment in April 1971, when Iphigene Ochs Sulzberger, daughter, widow, and mother of publishers of *The New York Times,* arrived in Jerusalem. She was a frisky seventy-nine years of age and brought two granddaughters with her for what she fancied would be a pleasant holiday jaunt. She had scarcely disembarked when she learned of the ideological meaning which Israelis were reading into her visit. The widow of Arthur Hays Sulzberger and the granddaughter of I. M. Wise was up to the challenge.

"We were always very much aware of our Judaism, as Americans," she told Israeli diplomatic reporter Ari Rath in an interview. "In the twenties I opposed a Jewish state. In the thirties, with the advent of Hitler, it seemed a good thing to have another haven for refugees. We support you as another nation. We are Americans of the Jewish faith, and you are Israelis. There are millions of Irish people in the States who were happy to see an independent Irish Republic, but would never want to live there. I think you should realize this is the view of a large segment of American Jewry."

Prime Minister Golda Meir heard of Mrs. Sulzberger's visit and promptly invited her over for coffee with some friends. The two elderly ladies knew each other only from the newspapers, but it was clearly an occasion for the good china; they sat in the living room, not around the kitchen table. Mrs. Meir ignored security guards to open the front door of the official residence herself; the leader of the Jewish state and the heiress to the anti-Zionist line of American Jewry started to shake hands, then they looked up as one grandmother to another and they hugged each other for a long time.

THE MODERN JEWISH homeland entered a golden age in 1967. Neither the early Zionists nor their early American supporters anticipated that it would be as soldiers, and not as dreamers, that Jews would capture the imagination of the Gentile world.

Perhaps they should have. Within Jewish tradition is a symbolism that in some ways echoes the contrasting values of Athens and Sparta. Over the centuries of exile and yearning the ancient academic community of Jabneh, a short way inland from Palestine's Mediterranean coast, symbolized spiritual and intellectual glory. During the same long years, overlooking the barren Judean cliffs and bleak waters of the Dead Sea, the ruined fortress of Masada embodied the heroism of Jewish patriots who fought to the death against Rome in A.D. 73. After 1967, when modern Israel astonished the world with its martial prowess, Jabneh was swallowed up in the industrial suburbs of Tel Aviv; Masada became a national shrine.

Politically, economically, even socially, Israel was in distress as its twentieth anniversary approached. In 1966, more Jews left the state than arrived. Israel spent 11 percent of its official budget on defense, much more if hidden costs were included. The military budget had soared sixteenfold since 1952.

Political scandals and infighting were sapping the confidence of the ruling Labor Party. An alarming social gap had opened between the cultivated European Jews who dominated public affairs—taking their dominance for granted—and the poorer immigrants from North Africa and surrounding Arab lands who were only patronized by the power structure.

At 7:10 A.M. on June 5, 1967, Israel bombarded the airports and aerial staging areas of Nasser's Egypt. In 170 minutes, 300 of Egypt's 340 combat planes were destroyed. Israel's ground forces moved across the Sinai Peninsula with a swiftness that left the chancelleries of the world aghast. More Israeli troops attacked Syrian defenses on the Heights of Golan, overlooking the farming communities around the Sea of Galilee. Learning of the air raids against Egypt, but not of their stunning success, King Hussein of Jordan ordered his army into combat, as he had refrained from doing in 1956. It was a serious mistake; Israeli troops forced the Jordanians out of the lands on the west bank of the Jordan River and then out of Arab Jerusalem, parts of Palestine that successive partition plans had denied to the Jewish state.

Back in the early 1940s, Chaim Weizmann had decided that future

Jewish generations could be trusted to regain their people's territorial patrimony; on that assumption he was ready to accept partition as an interim step. In the Six Day War of 1967, his confidence was borne out. Some of the Zionist "extremists," that faction led by the former underground fighter Menachem Begin, were still not satisfied; they argued that since the Jews' biblical ancestors had also occupied the lands beyond the Jordan, they too were part of the patrimony. But Israelis and their American supporters did not take Begin seriously in the late 1960s and early 1970s. He had languished as an opposition politician for so long; there was no need to listen to his extravagant claims.

When the fighting ended, Israeli armed forces were in possession of the Sinai Desert, the sliver of land atop the Golan, and the entire west bank of the Jordan. The world was impressed. Immigrants poured in. Nearly 10,000 Americans dropped what they were doing (dropping as well their frustrations with America's tedious war in Vietnam) to rush to the aid of the Jewish state. Nearly half stayed on after the Six Day War, seeking in the Jewish homeland the answer to their search for meaning in life. Symphonic conductor Zubin Mehta canceled all engagements and flew to Israel to lead whatever ensembles he could put together for the morale of troops and home front. He was subsequently named musical director of the Israel Philharmonic Orchestra. In Moscow one day during the war, a Soviet Armenian journalist came into my office, grinning from ear to ear, and told how a Soviet Jew had approached him on the subway that morning and muttered under his breath, "We're really thumping them, aren't we!" "Excuse me," my friend replied, "I am Armenian." "That's all right," said the stranger, "you can do the same to the Turks!"

Objections to Israel's action were also heard. Henry P. Van Dusen, one of America's most prominent Protestant clergymen, compared the military sweep to the Nazi blitzkrieg against Western Europe in 1940, "aiming not at victory but at annihilation." Among the displaced Arab Palestinians were many Christians, products of generations of missionary effort. "How can a Christian applaud the murder of a brother Christian by Zionist Jews?" asked another churchman, former moderator of the United Presbyterian Church.

From the beginning of their national awareness, the Arab Palestinians had been cursed with political leaders who were shortsighted, opportunistic, and only too willing to serve as pawns for the rival Arab governments around them. The Arab governments suffered defeat in 1967, and from that debacle came a national force of disenfranchised Arab Palestinians. It grew into a moral, political, and, eventually, military diaspora that stirred the conscience of the outside world almost as much as had the plight of the Jews of a previous generation.

The symbolism of Jabneh did not disappear altogether; some in Israel wondered aloud if military success was really the key to national survival and security. "It was not for this that we have prayed two thousand years," mourned Yaakov Talmon, an admired Israeli scholar. Moderate politicians remembered Marshall's somber advice to Shertok in those last tense pre-statehood days. Marshall had been wrong in the near term, of course; the Israeli settlers had managed to hold out against numerically superior Arabs, and by 1967 even to expand their positions dramatically. But his skepticism about heeding the generals in political decisions still rang true: "Flushed by victory, their counsel was liable to be misleading," Marshall had said. In history, as Isaiah Berlin reminded a generation of Oxford students, neither Masada nor Sparta ultimately prevailed.

The awakening came on the holy day of Yom Kippur, October 6, 1973. Israel's air force was by then the sixth largest in the world; its tank corps ranked third. But measures of preparedness and intelligence had grown lax. Massed Egyptian forces totaling more than 600,000 men, with tanks, heavy artillery, and SAM missile batteries, opened fire across the Suez Canal, and by nightfall an Egyptian bridgehead with fully 30,000 infantrymen had been established in the Israeli-occupied Sinai. In the north, Syrian armored divisions smashed through Israeli settlements on the Golan Heights. It was Israel's War of the Day of Atonement, and this fourth full-scale campaign threw the country's military and political leaders into confusion.

On October 15, after nine days of threatening Egyptian advances, Israeli forces under the burly paratroop commander Ariel Sharon counterattacked, managing their own crossing of Suez into the Egyptian heartland. For nine more days the battles raged, until a ceasefire finally took hold on October 24. The war had come to stalemate, with Egyptians holding positions in the Israeli-occupied Sinai and Israelis entrenched on the far bank of the Canal inside Egypt.

Once again the American Secretary of State intervened, not with advice but mediation. The shuttle diplomacy of Henry A. Kissinger over the next twenty-three months first untangled the two armies on terms that allowed both sides to claim satisfaction, then moved to line up formal separation-of-forces agreements. Israel and its Arab neighbors were exhausted militarily and politically. The moment was at hand in the late 1970s for the most dramatic initiative for peace the Middle East had yet known, and it took the diplomats totally by surprise.

A NEW BREED of diplomat had taken charge in the 1970s. No longer was the Near East Division a backwater of the State Department; its officers were among the most dynamic and competent—and politically sensitive —of any in the Foreign Service. They enjoyed an access to the White House that few others in the Department could claim. They had freed themselves from the bigotries of earlier generations; propagandists occasionally dusted off the old image of "State Department Arabists"—or even antisemites—but the descriptions no longer fit. A few American diplomats even learned to speak Hebrew.

The European empires had lost their credibility in the Suez crisis and France's Algerian struggle. The Soviet Union made repeated attempts to establish a strategic foothold with one or another Arab regime—Egypt, Syria, Iraq, even the incipient Palestine Liberation Organization. Repeatedly, expectations of both sides exceeded either side's capabilities. Americans, by contrast, quietly built up stature as the only outsiders who could deal with both sides to real effect.

Starting in 1967, United States diplomacy toward Arabs and Israelis was premised upon a simple bargain: peace for territory. Israel was to return Arab lands occupied in the Six Day War; Arabs were to recognize the Jewish state and make peace. The bargain was codified in Security Council Resolution 242 on November 22, 1967, and fleshed out in plans outlined by Secretary of State William P. Rogers in 1971 and President Ronald Reagan in 1982.

It seemed a reasonable enough transaction in Washington, but for the peoples of the area the simple bargain was flawed from the start. The diplomats were asking for more than marginal concessions; they were demanding the fruits of decades of conflict. Israelis, having once planted themselves on patrimonial lands denied them by diplomatic maneuvers and partition plans, would not easily relinquish what they had gained— perhaps the Sinai and even the Golan could be bargained away, but not the west bank provinces of Judea and Samaria, and certainly not Jerusalem. The Arabs, having resisted from the start of the century any form of Zionist presence, could not find "making peace" an easy step to take; they considered the occupied territories to be theirs, and resented being asked to pay a price to regain them. Israelis could never be brought to say how much territory they would abandon; Arabs could never be brought to state how much peace they would grant.

Each side blamed the United States for the recalcitrance of its adversary—and used the United States for its own enrichment. Israelis questioned America's reliability as a diplomatic partner, but readily accepted $2 billion and more each year after 1977 in military and economic aid. Arab oil producers blamed the United States for supporting Israel in 1973 and imposed an embargo on oil exports—then they reopened the oil pipelines at, eventually, five times the price charged before. The United States held the carrot and the stick; the initiative for resolving tensions between Arabs and Israelis always fell to Washington—or so it seemed.

ANWAR EL-SADAT, a minor military conspirator, had ruled Egypt since September 1970, when he succeeded to the presidency upon the sudden death of Nasser. The onlooking world was slow to size up this man, but at least one Israeli had an idea right at the start.

Ben-Gurion had withdrawn from politics by 1970, but he stayed alert to the changing fortunes of Arabs and Jews. He, rare among Israelis by that time, accepted the principle of trading territories for peace. Early in October, I paid a call on him at his Negev kibbutz for a perspective on Sadat's sudden accession. The veteran of Jewish wars and politics was mellow in retirement, and he was strangely optimistic about the transition in the land of his enemy. "I cannot believe that responsible people inside Egypt do not believe that they must have a new government, with the main tasks to be improving the position of the Egyptian people," Ben-Gurion said. "It's impossible that a man who thinks about his people should not see that this is his problem. Therefore I think that peace may come." The old prophet never knew the prescience of his words. He died of a cerebral hemorrhage on December 1, 1973, at the age of eighty-seven.

The Yom Kippur War and the Kissinger shuttles had drained generals and diplomats of ideas. President Jimmy Carter was working for a full-scale Geneva conference to negotiate a comprehensive Middle East settlement, but the obstacles were mounting faster than the opportunities. In October 1977, Carter wrote Sadat a letter in longhand, asking him to take some dramatic step to cut through the impasse. Even as he wrote the letter, Carter admitted that he did not know exactly what to expect—but perhaps Sadat would have an idea. Within three weeks the President of Egypt announced that he would personally fly to Jerusalem to talk with the leaders of Israel, for the purpose of making peace.

Thus impulsively, Sadat of Egypt became the first Arab leader to offer the Jewish state a public hand of recognition. Carter threw the prestige of his presidency on the line, inviting the leaders of Egypt and Israel for a marathon negotiation at Camp David, Maryland, and in 1979 the Jewish state sealed a treaty of peace with its most powerful neighbor. Israel returned the entire Sinai Peninsula to Egypt.

Two years later, the fate of Abdullah befell Sadat. The Egyptian

President succumbed to an assassin's bullet. The peace he had made survived him, but it was a separate peace. For years to come, no other Arab leaders dared to follow Sadat to Jerusalem.

A FEW MONTHS before Sadat made his move, the Labor Party of Israel fell from power. The political movement built by Ben-Gurion had succumbed to overconfidence. After three decades of one-party dominance Israel needed a revolution, as its intellectuals used to say, and in 1977 they got one.

The new Prime Minister was the perennial opposition leader, Menachem Begin. Leader of the old Irgun underground army, long sought by the British as a terrorist, Begin had steadily advocated the hard line in political and diplomatic dealings with the surrounding Arabs. He was never reconciled to the principle of partitioning Palestine; he never compromised his conviction that from the Mediterranean to the River Jordan, and even beyond, the land of Israel belonged rightfully to the Jews.

Before taking office, Begin regularly dismissed warnings that his policies would set Israel on a collision course with the United States. American Jews could always make their influence felt, he would argue, to keep officials in Washington faithful to Israel. But with Begin as Prime Minister, American Jews faced an unprecedented situation. His ideology was not popular in the United States; his right-wing political faction had little organizational backing among American Jewish communities. From the Biltmore conference onwards, American Jewry had identified with the movement of Ben-Gurion and Labor, which had come to seem over the decades almost synonymous with Israel itself. All of a sudden, the Jewish homeland had passed into the control of the "extremists," the men of the Irgun against whom so much energy had been spent in the rivalries of the 1940s. Singly and in discreet delegations, influential Americans tried to warn Begin that the power of the Jewish lobby in Washington was not as great as he supposed, and the devotion of American Jews to Israel did not constitute blind endorsement of everything the Israeli leaders decided to do.

Begin dismissed the warnings, went his own way, and carried the fractious Israeli Parliament with him, winning a second national election in 1981. The American Jews' "insurance policy" looked less and less attractive, and the number of Israelis moving to the United States in search of jobs and comfort far exceeded the number of Americans emigrating to Israel in search of their Jewish identity.

On Israel's tenth birthday, in 1958, the American historian Henry

Steele Commager had paid tribute at a New York rally. He spoke of the differing qualities of nationalism embodied in Israel and in the neighboring Arab states. While Jewish nationalism was "benign" and devoted to peace, Commager declared, the nationalism of the surrounding lands was committed to "chauvinism, militarism, and territorial and cultural imperialism."

Twenty-five years later, it was not clear that the historian's distinctions could be so readily drawn.

THE "RESTORATION OF THE JEWS" had been a beacon of inspiration to the pious Christians of early America, as it had been to Jewry through their centuries of dispersion. An ancient dream realized in the fifth decade of the twentieth century, restoration in their Holy Land brought national redemption to a people "scattered and trodden down," as Pastor McDonald and the others had prophesied. But its promise always contained the seeds of disillusionment.

The Puritans sought the ingathering of the Jews to signal a state of grace for all mankind. John Adams hoped that, once restored to their patrimony, the Jews might even become good Unitarian Christians. William E. Blackstone, the evangelist, despaired at the atheism of the early Zionists. Arthur James Balfour, the diplomat of empire, blandly assumed that the restoration of the Jewish homeland could come about without prejudicing "the civil and religious rights of existing non-Jewish communities in Palestine." President Franklin D. Roosevelt was probably the last of the great statesmen who honestly believed that the Jews could be awarded their homeland in full justice. President Truman supposed that the essential problem was solved once refugees were given a home. The saga is a record of forlorn hopes.

But disillusionment is hardly the whole story of Israel in the mind of America. Mordecai Noah's belief was justified, that restoration would allow his people to prove their prowess in agriculture, against the land-grabbing prejudices of medieval Christendom—agriculture, after all, is what the early books of the Bible were all about. A century later Brandeis discovered the instincts of group responsibility which had held the Jews together through their dispersion; he argued that political restoration could overcome what Jefferson had called "the prejudices still scowling on your section of our religion."

For a time the promise prevailed. With the Holocaust and the emergence of Israel, the scourge of antisemitism faded in America. A poll in 1962 pulled out an old question and asked if the Jews posed a threat to

America; only 1 percent replied yes. No more than 3 percent said they would dislike having a Jewish family live next door. Discriminatory quotas in colleges and clubs all but disappeared.

Then, gradually, the rise of Jewish ethnic pride presented new targets for bigotry; centuries of myth do not vanish in a generation. Incidents of antisemitism began rising again in America in the late 1960s, no longer as an ideological or religious crusade but as an expression of social and economic frustration. American Jews had prospered, and antisemitism took hold among the disadvantaged of the urban ghettos who felt exploited by Jewish merchants and landlords, the teachers in their children's schools. On the global scene, "anti-Zionism" became a rallying cry when antisemitism could not be admitted; here it was Israel's very success as a military force that led to political hostility.

As Masada gained over Jabneh, the self-image of many Israelis became one of "fundamental pessimism and ruthlessness," wrote Israeli novelist Amos Oz in 1982; their heroes displayed "cynical treatment of all ideals except heroic patriotism." American liberals who had promoted the creation of Israel, Jews as well as Gentiles, began pulling back. Israel became a cause attractive to conservatives, impressive as a military bastion against international Communism and anarchy.

But something more fundamental than the *realpolitik* of the day has long defined America's awareness of Israel. For all the high hopes that were bound to be dashed, the wishful thinking which no reality could ever embody, Israel has succeeded in its primary mission: providing a home and a refuge for those of its people in need. American diplomacy has consistently honored that success. No American administration ever seriously entertained the possibility of reversing the decisions of 1947 and 1948, which established the Jewish state in law and sovereignty. Calls by Palestinian Arabs in the 1970s for a binational state of all Palestine—the formula rejected in 1947—continue to fall on deaf ears in Washington and across the United States.

For, liking it or not, Americans who are willing to look see something of themselves in Israel. Even as they go their own way, in pursuit of their own national interests, Americans and Israelis are bonded together like no two other sovereign peoples. As the Judaic heritage flowed through the minds of America's early settlers and helped to shape the new American republic, so Israel restored adopted the vision and the values of the American dream. Each, the United States and Israel, grafted the heritage of the other onto itself.

NOTES ON SOURCES
INDEX

NOTES ON SOURCES

A COMPREHENSIVE bibliography of the range of topics covered in this narrative would easily double the size of the book. It would also be out of date by the time it appeared, so rich is the flow of new research and inquiry. Instead, therefore, for the main topics of each chapter I list important archives and secondary works that I found most useful. Quotations not specifically attributed may be found readily in one or more of these sources; I give specific citations here for more obscure quotations.

Prologue

Three published collections of documents are invaluable for the early history of Jews in America, from the time of Stuyvesant onwards: Morris U. Schappes, *A Documentary History of the Jews in the United States, 1654–1875* (New York: Schocken Books, 1971); Joseph L. Blau and Salo W. Baron, *The Jews of the United States, 1790–1840: A Documentary History* (New York: Columbia University Press, 1963); Arnold A. Rogow, *The Jew in a Gentile World* (New York: Macmillan, 1961).

For discussion of the Puritans and other early American attitudes, see Moshe Davis (ed.), *Israel: Its Role in Civilization* (New York: Jewish Theological Seminary of America and Harper & Bros., 1956). Professor Davis, a man of immense energy, also inspired the massive publication project *America–Holy Land Studies* (New York: Arno Press), reproducing scores of long-out-of-print documents, sermons, and monographs which modern researchers have only begun to tap. The *American Jewish Historical Quarterly* for September 1972 contains the full report of an interesting colloquium, "America and the Holy Land," and Davis edited a further volume, *With Eyes Toward Zion* (New York: Arno Press, 1977). Two general works were helpful: Michael N. Dobkowski, *The Tarnished Dream* (Westport, Conn.: Greenwood Press, 1979), and Louis Harop, *The Image of the Jew in American Literature* (Philadelphia: Jewish Publication Society of America, 1974). For any topic relating to Jews, a good place to start is the monumental *Encyclopedia Judaica,* published in Jerusalem in 1972, a magnificent work of sensitive scholarship.

Pastor John McDonald's vision is one of the long-overlooked works rediscovered in the America–Holy Land series; I also found an original copy of his pamphlet deep inside the New York Public Library. The Presbyterian Historical

Society in Philadelphia, the Presbytery of Albany, and the Albany Institute of History and Art were all helpful in trying to locate more material. For a thorough analysis of *Niles' Weekly Register,* see Isaac M. Fein, *"Niles' Weekly Register* on the Jews," *Publication of the American Jewish Historical Society,* September 1960.

The saga of Mordecai Noah presents a fascinating case of scholarly "investigative reporting." Two young graduate students separately began unraveling the story of his dismissal by the State Department: Esther Cember, whose unpublished 1968 master's thesis, *Mordecai Manuel Noah, American Diplomat in Barbary, 1813–1815: A Reappraisal,* is available at the Butler Library, Columbia University; and Jonathan D. Sarna at Yale, who read Cember's work, conducted his own prodigious research, and wrote a full-length biography, *Jacksonian Jew* (New York: Holmes & Meier, 1981), incorporating careful reference to all previously published works and much newly analyzed material. Dr. Sarna was as generous a scholar as one could ever encounter, sharing his manuscript with me before publication and guiding my own research; he may not agree with every detail of the story that I have pieced together, but I am deeply in debt to him.

pp. 4–6　*The Puritans and Ezra Stiles:* see Arthur A. Chiel, "Ezra Stiles and the Jews: A Study in Ambivalence," in *A Bicentennial Festschrift for Jacob Rader Marcus* (New York: American Jewish Historical Society and Ktav Publishing House, 1976), pp. 63–76; Eugene R. Fingerhut, "Were the Massachusetts Puritans Hebraic?" *New England Quarterly,* December 1967.

5　*Great Seal imagery:* John Adams to his wife, August 14, 1776, in *Letters of John Adams* (Boston, 1841), Vol. I, p. 150.

5　*"Not a Christian nation":* quoted in Carey McWilliams, *A Mask for Privilege* (Boston: Little, Brown, 1948), p. 51.

6　*"Ethics . . . little understood":* quoted in Jonathan D. Sarna, "Antisemitism and American History," *Commentary,* March 1981, p. 44.

7　*"Nearer the mind":* quoted in Howard Mosley Sachar, *The Course of Modern Jewish History* (New York: Delta Books, 1958), p. 162.

7　*Conversion impulse:* see Blau and Baron, *op. cit.,* Vol. III, and two monographs by Jonathan D. Sarna: "The American Jewish Response to Nineteenth-Century Christian Missions," *Journal of American History,* June 1981, and "The Impact of the American Revolution on American Jews," *Modern Judaism,* Vol. I (1981).

8　*Napoleon and English restorationists:* see Barbara W. Tuchman, *Bible and Sword* (New York: New York University Press, 1956), pp. 97, 105.

9　*Missionaries and fundamentalism:* see *Holy Land Missions and Missionaries* (New York: Arno Press, 1977), pp. 12, 32; also two monographs by David A. Rausch: "Protofundamentalism's Attitudes Toward Zion, 1878–1918," *Jewish Social Studies,* Spring 1981, and "Arno C. Gaebelein (1861–1945): Fundamentalist Protestant Zionist," *American Jewish History,* December 1978. Two broad surveys provide the context: Timothy P. Weber, *Living in the Shadow of the Second Coming* (New York: Oxford University Press, 1979), and Ernest R.

Sandeen, *The Roots of Fundamentalism* (Chicago: University of Chicago Press, 1970).

11–12 *The* shadarim *and Leeser:* Salo W. and Jeannette M. Baron, "Palestinian Messengers in America, 1849–79," *Jewish Social Studies,* 1943, pp. 115–62, 225–92; also *Brandeis Avukah Annual* (Boston, 1932); also Maxine S. Seller, "Isaac Leeser's Views on the Restoration of a Jewish Palestine," *American Jewish Historical Quarterly,* September 1968.

13 *Israeli poll, 1970: American Jewish Historical Quarterly,* March 1978, p. 260.

16 *Noah to Secretary of State, 1811:* National Archives, Manuscript Division, M438 Madison Administration, January 7, 1811, Noah to Robert Smith.

Chapter 1

The full record both of the Damascus Affair and of General Grant's Order No. 11 is to be found in Schappes and in Blau and Baron, cited above. Travel literature and romantic attitudes toward the Holy Land are fully discussed in the *Encyclopedia Judaica* and the general works by Davis, Harop, and Dobkowski, cited above. See also David H. Finnie, *Pioneers East* (Cambridge: Harvard University Press, 1967). Too late to have guided my own researches is a highly readable survey, with a helpful bibliography: Neil Asher Silberman, *Digging for God and Country* (New York: Alfred A. Knopf, 1982).

The modern literature on I. M. Wise is thin, presumably because present-day scholars find him such an unsympathetic character. The basic full-length biography, striving to be kind but confronting the problems squarely, is James G. Heller, *Isaac M. Wise, His Life, Work and Thought* (New York: Union of American Hebrew Congregations, 1965). One modern scholar, Lucy S. Dawidowicz, produced a sprightly and interesting essay, "When Reform Was Young," reprinted in her collection *The Jewish Presence* (New York: Harcourt Brace Jovanovich, 1978). See also David Polish, *Renew Our Days* (Jerusalem: World Zionist Organization–The Zionist Library, 1976), for a heroic attempt to explain to a modern generation the anti-Zionism of the early Reform movement. Finally, Wise's own body of writings is easily available in research libraries, in the microfilm collections of his journal, the *American Israelite.*

The great Russian immigration to the United States is the subject of a vast and growing literature. A good starting place is Melvin I. Urofsky, *American Zionism from Herzl to the Holocaust* (Garden City, N.Y.: Anchor Press/Doubleday, 1975 and subsequent reprints). This work and others by Urofsky are lucid and comprehensive for the entire American Jewish experience with Zionism. The flavor of the Lower East Side is beautifully conveyed in Irving Howe, *World of Our Fathers* (New York: Simon & Schuster, 1976).

For the story of "the Reverend" Blackstone, see Yona Malachy, *American Fundamentalism and Israel* (Jerusalem: Institute of Contemporary Jewry, Hebrew University, 1978); Hertzel Fishman, *American Protestantism and a Jewish State* (Detroit: Wayne State University Press, 1973); and the works of Weber and Sandeen cited above (Prologue).

Invaluable for the entire period up to the 1940s are two authoritative surveys, sadly out of print: Samuel Halperin, *The Political World of American Zionism*

(Detroit: Wayne State University Press, 1961), and Frank E. Manuel, *The Realities of American-Palestine Relations* (Washington, D.C.: Public Affairs Press, 1949). The best tribute to the usefulness of these books, if not to the conscience of graduate students, is the fact that both are inexplicably "lost" from the shelves of several research libraries I visited. After years of frustration, I finally found a copy of Manuel in a secondhand-book stall on the sidewalk one day while I was waiting for a bus near Columbia University ($4.50!); I have yet to lay my hands on Halperin for my own library.

pp. 24–5 *The elder Brandeis to his fiancée:* quoted in Sachar, *op. cit.* (Prologue), p. 167.

  25 *"150 rebels . . . and 4 Jews":* quoted in Simon Wolf, *The Presidents I Have Known from 1860–1918* (Washington, D.C.: Press of Byron S. Adams, 1918), p. 8.

  25–6 *Lincoln and Monk:* The only source I have found for this strange, but not implausible, encounter is Richard S. Lambert, *For the Time Is at Hand* (London: Andrew Melrose, Ltd., 1947), a biography of Monk written from his own diaries and papers.

  27 *The Mark Twain quotations:* Daniel Morley McKeithan (ed.), *Traveling with the Innocents Abroad* (Norman: University of Oklahoma Press, 1958), p. 250.

  32 *"Here are his true relatives":* quoted in *American Jewish History,* March 1982, p. 404.

  32 *Wise on Rumanian Jews: American Israelite,* April 15, 1887.

  34 *Reaction to Herzl's death:* quoted in Leonard Stein, *The Balfour Declaration* (New York: Simon & Schuster, 1961), p. 188.

  38–9 *Roosevelt and Schiff:* Josephus Daniels, *The Wilson Era: Years of War and After* (Chapel Hill: University of North Carolina Press, 1946), Vol. II, p. 216.

  40 *"It will be impossible":* J. Augustus Johnson, "The Colonization of Palestine," *The Century,* Vol. II (1882), p. 296.

  41 *"degraded and undesirable persons":* The Executive Documents of the House of Representatives for the 53rd Congress, House Document, Vol. I, p. 535; for Merrill and Adee, see Manuel, *op. cit.*

Chapter 2

The literature on Brandeis and Zionism is, of course, enormous. The issues surrounding his "conversion" are illuminated by the following monographs: Yonathan Shapiro, "American Jews in Politics: The Case of Louis D. Brandeis," *American Jewish Historical Quarterly,* December 1965; Ben Halpern, "Brandeis' Way to Zionism," *Midstream,* October 1971; Stuart M. Geller, "Why Did Louis D. Brandeis Choose Zionism?" *American Jewish Historical Quarterly,* June 1973; Sarah Schmidt, "The Zionist Conversion of Louis D. Brandeis," *Jewish Social Studies,* January 1975; Allon Gal, "In Search of a New Zion: New Light on Brandeis' Road to Zionism," *American Jewish History,* September 1978. There are others, but these convey the essence of the dispute.

The basic, authorized biography of Brandeis is Alpheus Thomas Mason, *Brandeis: A Free Man's Life* (New York: Viking Press, 1946), fine for the overall context but weak on his Jewish and Zionist interests. A generation later, Urofsky's several works cited below are essential. Two other books examine Brandeis' political action in a new light but do not change the picture of his Zionism: Michael E. Parrish, *Felix Frankfurter and His Times* (New York: The Free Press, 1982), and Bruce Allen Murphy, *The Brandeis/Frankfurter Connection* (New York: Oxford University Press, 1982). A modern Israeli perspective is found in Evyatar Friesel, "Brandeis' Role in American Zionism Historically Reconsidered," *American Jewish History,* September 1979. The story of the Parushim is told in Sarah Schmidt, "The Parushim: A Secret Episode in American Zionist History," *American Jewish Historical Quarterly,* December 1975.

Two basic books tell the story of the Balfour Declaration: Leonard Stein, *The Balfour Declaration* (New York: Simon & Schuster, 1961), seemed definitive until Isaiah Friedman, *The Question of Palestine, 1914–1918* (New York: Schocken Books, 1973), added important new evidence. For the American involvement, see also Richard Ned Lebow, "Woodrow Wilson and the Balfour Declaration," *Journal of Modern History,* December 1968; Herbert Parzen, "Brandeis and the Balfour Declaration," *Herzl Yearbook* Vol. V (New York: Herzl Press, 1963); Selig Adler, "The Palestine Question in the Wilson Era," *Jewish Social Studies,* October 1948.

On the role of the American diplomatic service, the already cited works of Davis (Prologue) and Manuel (Ch. 1) are essential, along with Phillip J. Baram, *The Department of State in the Middle East, 1919–1945* (Philadelphia: University of Pennsylvania Press, 1978).

For the Morgenthau mission, see *Foreign Relations of the United States (FRUS), The Lansing Papers, 1914–1920,* Vol. II; Richard Ned Lebow, "The Morgenthau Peace Mission of 1917," *Jewish Social Studies,* October 1970; William Yale, "Ambassador Henry Morgenthau's Special Mission of 1917," *World Politics,* April 1949. Wilson's general attitudes are explored in Joseph L. Grabill, "Cleveland H. Dodge, Woodrow Wilson, and the Near East," *Journal of Presbyterian History,* Winter 1970; also Joseph P. O'Grady (ed.), *The Immigrants' Influence on Wilson's Peace Policies* (Lexington: University Press of Kentucky, 1967).

p. 53 *"A Moses, a Jefferson, a Lincoln":* Irma L. Lindheim, *Parallel Quest* (New York: Thomas Yoseloff, 1962), p. 85.

56 *"A desire to 'help others' ":* Emanuel Neumann, *In the Arena* (New York: Herzl Press, 1976), pp. 63–64.

58 *Washington before World War I:* see the oral history of Felix Frankfurter in the Butler Library, Columbia University, Vol. II, pp. 196–97.

58 *"Great is diplomacy!":* John A. DeNovo, *American Interests and Policies in the Middle East, 1900–1939* (Minneapolis: University of Minnesota Press, 1963), p. 97.

60 *The map of the Near East:* Ronald Steel, *Walter Lippmann and the American Century* (Boston: Little, Brown, 1980), p. 130.

61 *Morgenthau's land-buying:* Barbara W. Tuchman, *Practicing History* (New York: Alfred A. Knopf, 1981), p. 213.

62 *"Who* are *all these people?"*: Chaim Weizmann, *Trial and Error* (New York: Schocken Books, 1949, 1966), p. 263.

66 *"God sent him here"*: Public Record Office (PRO), London, FO800/84.

67 *"When he takes up a new subject"*: PRO, FO371/2151; I am grateful to my friend Stephen A. Oxman for locating this and the previous quotation.

67 *"The son of the manse"*: Joseph L. Grabill, *Protestant Diplomacy and the Near East* (Minneapolis: University of Minnesota Press, 1971), p. 178.

69–70 *Lansing's letter: FRUS, Lansing Papers,* Vol. II, p. 71.

Chapter 3

Brandeisian Zionism has come under more sympathetic scrutiny from American scholars after some years of neglect. See Ben Halpern, "The Americanization of Zionism, 1880–1930," *American Jewish History,* September 1979; Sarah Schmidt, "Toward the Pittsburgh Program: Horace M. Kallen, Philosopher of an American Zionism," in Melvin I. Urofsky (ed.), *Essays in American Zionism* (New York: Herzl Press, 1978); Urofsky led a symposium on the subject, published in *American Jewish Historical Quarterly,* March 1974; the trail-blazing work is Judd L. Teller, "America's Two Zionist Traditions," *Commentary,* October 1955.

For the clash with Weizmann, see Esther L. Panitz, " 'Washington versus Pinsk': The Brandeis-Weizmann Dispute," in Urofsky, *Essays,* cited above; Howard L. Adelson, "Ideology and Practice in American Zionism: An Overview," in *ibid.*; Esther L. Panitz, "Louis Dembitz Brandeis and the Cleveland Conference," in *American Jewish Historical Quarterly,* December 1975; George L. Berlin, "The Brandeis-Weizmann Dispute," *American Jewish Historical Quarterly,* September 1970.

Weizmann's life and career form a central theme in all the histories of Zionism and the memoirs of all in his circle. Basic references include his own memoirs, *Trial and Error,* first published in 1949, reprinted by Schocken Books (New York, 1966), with an introduction by Abba Eban, and it is a classic example of a personal story remembered just the way the author wanted to remember it. Slightly more detached, but just as loving, is *Chaim Weizmann: A Biography by Several Hands,* edited by Meyer W. Weisgal and Joel Carmichael (New York: Atheneum, 1963). New anecdotes and gossip appear in his widow's memoir: Vera Weizmann, *The Impossible Takes Longer* (New York: Harper & Row, 1967).

The literature on Versailles seems unending. For the sideshow of Zionism, the memoirs of the participants and Grabill, *Protestant Diplomacy,* cited above (Ch. 2), are useful beginnings. The basic and sympathetic text for the King-Crane Commission is Harry N. Howard, *The King-Crane Commission* (Beirut: Khayats, 1963); also Ray Stannard Baker, *Woodrow Wilson and World Settlement* (Garden City, N.Y.: Doubleday, Page, 1923), Vol. II, Ch. 34. See also Manuel, *op. cit.* (Ch. 1), which tells the story of William Yale.

p. 72 *Reaction to Balfour:* Charles Israel Goldblatt, "The Impact of the Balfour Declaration in America," *American Jewish Historical Quarterly,* June 1968.

76 *"A hundred shades and inflexions"*: Sir Charles Webster, quoted in Friedman, *op. cit.* (Ch. 2), pp. 283–84.

77 *"By ingenious political action"*: *Brandeis on Zionism* (Washington, D.C.: Zionist Organization of America, 1942), p. 117.

80 *"Thirsting for his words"*: quoted in Melvin I. Urofsky, *A Mind of One Piece* (New York: Charles Scribner's Sons, 1971), pp. 112–13.

81 *"Where Western science and technology"*: Edgar E. Siskin, "Mr. Justice Brandeis: A Rabbi's Recollection," *American Jewish Archives,* November 1966.

81 *Tea and watercress sandwiches:* I am grateful to Virginia Durr for her recollections of these occasions.

81–2 *Weizmann's call of reconciliation:* Neumann, *op. cit.* (Ch. 2), p. 163.

82 *Ben-Gurion tribute to Brandeis:* Central Zionist Archives (CZA), Jerusalem, Z4/14632, October 21, 1941.

83 *Page on Zionism:* Burton J. Hendrick, *The Life and Letters of Walter H. Page* (Garden City, N.Y.: Doubleday, Page, 1925), Vol. II, pp. 349–51.

84 *Appropriate stationery:* William Phillips' oral history, Butler Library, Columbia University, p. 69.

84 *The FDR desk:* William R. Emerson, director of the Franklin D. Roosevelt Library at Hyde Park, kindly researched this matter for me and reported his findings in a letter dated May 22, 1980.

87 *Lansing on Faisal:* quoted in Manuel, *op. cit.* (Ch. 1), p. 227.

91 *Balfour's memorandum:* reprinted in J. C. Hurewitz (ed.), *The Middle East and North Africa in World Politics* (New Haven: Yale University Press, 1979), Vol. II, pp. 189–90.

Chapter 4

The Hugh Gibson experience is told in letters filed in the Gibson Collection, Hoover Institution Archives, Stanford, Calif., containers nos. 5, 6, and 7. See also Martin Weil, *A Pretty Good Club* (New York: W. W. Norton, 1978); Robert D. Schulzinger, *The Making of the Diplomatic Mind* (Middletown, Conn.: Wesleyan University Press, 1975); Charles Reznikoff (ed.), *Louis Marshall, Champion of Liberty* (Philadelphia: The Jewish Publication Society of America, 1957), pp. 601–11.

A good survey of Henry Ford and the interbellum antisemitism is Leo P. Ribuffo, "Henry Ford and 'The International Jew,' " *American Jewish History,* June 1980. See also Dobkowski, *op. cit.* (Prologue), and *The Atlantic Monthly,* July 1921 and August 1922, an article by Paul Scott Mowrer and reply by William Yale. *Fortune* published an important survey called "Jews in America" in February 1936.

The story of Abraham Cahan is related in Albert Waldinger, "Abraham Cahan and Palestine," *Jewish Social Studies,* Winter–Spring 1977. For the odyssey of Felix Warburg, see Jerome M. Kutnick, "Felix M. Warburg and the Jewish Agency," in Urofsky, *Essays, op. cit.* (ch. 3).

Stephen Wise is another interesting test of biographical objectivity. Revered in the first years after his death, he became irrelevant to the next generation, perhaps even distasteful as the reports of his caution in facing the Holocaust became common knowledge: retrospective moral judgments are as cruel as they are unfair. A modern attempt to put Wise in perspective came from the indefatigable Urofsky, *A Voice That Spoke for Justice,* State University of New York Press, Albany, 1982. Unfortunately for me, it came too late to save me months of research, but its conclusions are not too different from mine. The basic references are the autobiography, *Challenging Years* (New York: G. P. Putnam's Sons, 1949); the revealing collection edited by Justine Wise Polier and James Waterman Wise, *The Personal Letters of Stephen Wise* (Boston: Beacon Press, 1956); and the sympathetic memoir of Carl Hermann Voss, *Rabbi and Minister* (Cleveland: World Publishing Company, 1964). See also Voss's paper, "The Lion and the Lamb—An Evaluation of the Life and Work of Stephen S. Wise," in *American Jewish Archives,* April 1969. For the rest, Wise figures prominently in all the standard surveys of American Zionism.

The "rescue and resettlement" drama is similarly plagued with emotion, guilt, and attempts at self-justification, such that objectivity is still beyond reach. One courageous historian willing to ask the awkward questions has been Henry L. Feingold of the City University of New York: "Roosevelt and the Holocaust: Reflections on New Deal Humanitarianism," *Judaism,* Summer 1969; *The Politics of Rescue* (New Brunswick, N.J.: Rutgers University Press, 1970); and "Who Shall Bear Guilt for the Holocaust? The Human Dilemma," *American Jewish History,* March 1979. A moderate attempt to dull the accusations of revisionists is Marie Syrkin, "What American Jews Did During the Holocaust," *Midstream,* October 1982.

p. 95 *Major Hollyday's report:* Gibson Collection, quoted in Weil, *op. cit.,* pp. 277–78.

95 *"The Pole hates the Jew":* Zosa Szajkowski, "The Consul and the Immigrant: A Case of Bureaucratic Bias," *Jewish Social Studies,* January 1974, p. 5.

96 *"The Christian mind":* quoted in Fishman, *op. cit.* (Ch. 1), p. 37.

97 *Niebuhr: The Nation,* Feb. 21, 1942, p. 215.

97 *"You should try to ameliorate":* William E. Dodd, Jr., and Martha Dodd (eds.), *Ambassador Dodd's Diary, 1933–1938* (New York: Harcourt, Brace, 1941), pp. 10–11; see also Shlomo Shafir, "American Jewish Leaders and the Emerging Nazi Threat (1928–January, 1933)," *American Jewish Archives,* November 1979.

98 *"The Jew was not the cause":* The Atlantic Monthly, February 1938, p. 242.

98 *"They know the 'ropes' ":* Robert S. Allen and William V. Shannon, *The Truman Merry-Go-Round* (New York: Vanguard Press, 1950), pp. 407–8.

99–100 *American interests in Palestine:* see previously cited works by Manuel (Ch. 1), Baram (Ch. 2), and DeNovo (Ch. 2).

102 *"Americans are supposed to be missionaries":* CZA, S25/585, Agronsky to Kisch.

102 *"Take away the money":* Blanche Dugdale, *Buffy* (London: Vallentine, Mitchell, 1973), p. 10.

105 *Wise with the schoolchildren:* Tuchman, *Practicing History,* cited above (Ch. 2), p. 214; she was one of the children involved.

107–8 *"Even if the Hitlerites":* Zosa Szajkowski, "Relief for German Jewry: Problems of American Involvement," *American Jewish Historical Quarterly,* December 1972, pp. 112–14, 136.

111 *Japanese approach to Wise:* Marvin Tokayer and Mary Swartz, *The Fugu Plan* (New York: Paddington Press, 1979), pp. 72–77.

Chapter 5

Roosevelt's attitudes toward Jews have to be pieced together from snippets and anecdotes scattered throughout the standard biographies, memoirs, and accounts of conversations, as well as the numerous personal collections of papers at the Franklin D. Roosevelt Library, Hyde Park, N.Y. Good places to start are the two biographies by Joseph P. Lash: *Eleanor and Franklin* (New York: W. W. Norton, 1971), and *Eleanor: The Years Alone* (New York: W. W. Norton, 1972). Dr. Emerson at Hyde Park called my special attention to Rexford Tugwell, *In Search of Roosevelt* (Cambridge: Harvard University Press, 1972), and George Martin, *Madame Secretary* (New York: Houghton Mifflin, 1976). The overall diplomatic context is well conveyed in Robert Dallek, *Franklin D. Roosevelt and American Foreign Policy* (New York: Oxford University Press, 1979).

Policy toward the Jews of Europe facing extermination is carefully explored in three comprehensive studies: Feingold, *The Politics of Rescue,* cited above (ch. 4); David S. Wyman, *Paper Walls* (Amherst: University of Massachusetts Press, 1968); and the first exposé, Arthur D. Morse, *While Six Million Died* (New York: Random House, 1967). The Breckenridge Long diaries are extensively quoted and quotable; they are held in the Manuscript Division of the Library of Congress. See also Selig Adler, "The United States and the Holocaust," *American Jewish Historical Quarterly,* September 1974.

New research has accumulated on how the news of the "final solution" reached the outside world. See, in particular: Walter Laqueur, *The Terrible Secret* (Boston: Little, Brown, 1980); Alex Grobman, "What Did They Know? The American Jewish Press and the Holocaust," *American Jewish History,* March 1979; Yehuda Bauer, "When Did They Know?" *Midstream,* April 1968. Much useful documentation is found in Bernard Wasserstein, *Britain and the Jews of Europe, 1939–1945* (London: Institute of Jewish Affairs, and Oxford: Clarendon Press, 1979). Two interesting interpretations are: Yehuda Bauer, *The Holocaust in Historical Perspective* (Seattle: University of Washington Press, 1978), and Evyatar Friesel, "The Holocaust and the Birth of Israel," *Wiener Library Bulletin,* Vol. XXXII, 1979.

Other specialized aspects are explored in: Michael Mashberg, "Documents Concerning the American State Department and the Stateless European Jews, 1942–1944," *Jewish Social Studies,* Winter–Spring 1977; John Morton Blum, *From the Morgenthau Diaries,* Vol. III: *Years of War, 1941–45* (Boston: Houghton Mifflin, 1967). The Morgenthau diaries were excerpted in *Collier's* magazine, the section on the Holocaust appearing in the issue of November 1, 1947; Shlomo Shafir, "American Diplomats in Berlin (1933–1939) and Their Attitude to the Nazi Persecution of the Jews," *Yad Vashem Studies* (Jerusalem), Vol. IX (1973), and "George S. Messersmith: An Anti-Nazi Diplomat's View of the German-Jewish Crisis," *Jewish Social Studies,* January 1973; John P. Willson, "Carlton

J. H. Hayes, Spain, and the Refugee Crisis, 1942–1945," *American Jewish Historical Quarterly,* December 1972; Haim Genizi, "James G. McDonald: High Commissioner for Refugees, 1933–1935," *Wiener Library Bulletin,* Vol. XXX, 1977; David Brody, "American Jewry, the Refugees and Immigration Restriction (1932–1942)," in Abraham J. Karp (ed.), *The Jewish Experience in America,* Vol. V (New York: Ktav Publishing House, 1969).

p. 113 *The two Niles quotes:* Samuel Halperin and Irvin Oder, "The United States in Search of a Policy: Franklin D. Roosevelt and Palestine," *Review of Politics,* Vol. XXIV (1962), pp. 327–28, and Alfred Steinberg, *The Man from Missouri* (New York: G. P. Putnam's Sons, 1962), p. 304.

113 *Baruch:* quoted in Joseph B. Schechtman, *The United States and the Jewish State Movement* (New York: Herzl Press, Thomas Yoseloff, 1966), p. 116; Cordell Hull, *Memoirs* (New York: Macmillan, 1948), Vol. II, p. 1536.

114 *Roosevelt and the DAR:* Nathan Miller, *The Roosevelt Chronicles* (Garden City, N.Y.: Doubleday, 1979), p. 2; the sophomore essay, *ibid.,* p. 45.

116 *Phrase suggested by Wise:* FDRL, President's Personal File (PPF), 3292.

116 *"Imagine what Goebbels would pay":* Nahum Goldmann, *The Jewish Paradox* (New York: Grosset & Dunlap, 1978), p. 156.

120 *"I hope you're not helping Jews":* quoted in Robert Bendiner, *The Riddle of the State Department* (New York: Farrar and Rinehart, 1942), pp. 100–1; see also Wyman, *op. cit.*

121 *"A little close to the wind":* quoted in Nicholas Bethell, *The Palestine Triangle* (New York: G. P. Putnam's Sons, 1979), p. 114.

121 *"The candle-flame for the moth":* quoted in Wasserstein, *op. cit.,* p. 51.

122 *The Mann broadcast:* see Thomas Mann, *Listen, Germany!* (New York: Alfred A. Knopf, 1943), pp. 69 ff.

122 *"That's the way it was":* Katia Mann, *Unwritten Memoirs* (New York: Alfred A. Knopf, 1975), p. 114.

123–6 The main points of the Riegner episode are related, first, in Morse, *op. cit.,* and further discussed and analyzed in Walter Laqueur, "The Mysterious Messenger and the Final Solution," *Commentary,* March 1980. Dr. Riegner discussed these accounts with me in an interview on May 16, 1980, in New York, still refusing after nearly forty years to disclose the name of his original informant who, he said, is no longer alive. "I promised I would not reveal his name, and I won't," he said, adding his speculation that the surviving family may fear neo-Nazi recrimination. Riegner is still at this writing active as the Secretary-General of the World Jewish Congress and has a long record of distinguished service over the years after his crucial role in 1942: "I do know how to do things other than send telegrams," he remarked wryly.

125 *Telegram's receipt in New York:* see Rabbi Irving Miller's oral history at the Ben-Gurion Archives, Sde Boker, Israel.

126 *"There were many things happening":* Alvin Rosenfeld, in *The Impact of the Holocaust on Judaism in America: A Colloquium at The American University,* March 23, 1980, p. 93.

127 *Weizmann, March 1, 1943:* see PRO, FO371/35042.

127 *Morgenthau denied access to telegram:* see *Collier's,* November 1, 1947.

129 *"America was a place of refuge":* ibid.

130 *"Some very wonderful high land":* quoted in Blum, *op. cit.,* p. 207.

130 *"It does not stimulate my imagination":* FDR Library, President's Secretary's File (PSF) Box 64.

131 *"In that magnificent hall":* Golda Meir, *My Life* (New York: G. P. Putnam's Sons, 1975), p. 158.

131 *Isaiah Bowman's views:* quoted in Urofsky, *Essays,* cited above (ch. 3), pp. 219–20.

131 *Roosevelt at Casablanca:* FRUS, *Casablanca Conference,* pp. 608–9; see also Wasserstein, *op. cit.,* p. 207.

132 *Karski to Roosevelt:* Jan Ciechanowski, *Defeat in Victory* (Garden City, N.Y.: Doubleday, 1947), p. 182; see also Karski in the American University colloquium, cited above.

132 *Karski to Frankfurter: ibid.,* p. 34.

Chapter 6

Roosevelt's views about the political future of Palestine are even more difficult to discern than his personal attitudes toward Jews, but a clear pattern emerges when the broad range of possible sources is tallied up. This has never been done before, to my knowledge, and it will be interesting to watch as researchers uncover additional remarks and comments to refine the composite picture presented here.

Basic evidence is in the archives at the FDR Library (FDRL), both the President's own files and the many collections of papers of persons around him with whom he discussed Palestine. As each documentary collection was opened for inspection, diligent scholars updated the public record. Among the most important analytical works are: Halperin and Oder, *op. cit.* (Ch. 5), which drew from both the FDRL and the CZA. Two papers by Herbert Parzen combed the records of the American Zionist Emergency Council and the State Department files for the period: "American Zionism and the Quest for a Jewish State, 1939–43," *Herzl Year Book,* Vol. IV (New York: Herzl Press, 1961–62), and "The Roosevelt Palestine Policy, 1943–1945," *American Jewish Archives,* April 1974. A distinguished scholar, Selig Adler, distilled years of research in three important papers: "United States Policy on Palestine in the FDR Era," submitted to a colloquium on America and the Holy Land and published in *American Jewish Historical Quarterly,* September 1972; "Franklin D. Roosevelt and Zionism—the Wartime Record," *Judaism,* Summer 1972; and "The Roosevelt Administration and Zionism: The Pre-War Years, 1933–1939," in Urofsky, *Essays,* cited above (ch. 3). Of crucial importance is *The Diaries of Edward R. Stettinius, Jr., 1943–1946* (New York: New Viewpoints, 1975).

A good brief survey of the wartime diplomacy is Michael J. Cohen, "American Influence on British Policy in the Middle East During World War Two: First Attempts at Coordinating Allied Policy on Palestine," *American Jewish Historical Quarterly,* September 1977. Basic text for the Roosevelt–Ibn Saud meeting is the pamphlet by William A. Eddy, *F.D.R. Meets Ibn Saud* (New York: American Friends of the Middle East, Inc., 1954).

p. 134 *FDR and British policy:* Selig Adler, in Urofsky, *Essays,* see also *Roosevelt & Frankfurter: Their Correspondence* (Boston: Little, Brown, 1967), p. 463.

134–5 *The President's file:* FDRL, President's Secretary's File (PSF), Palestine, Box 64.

135 *"Not often marked with excitement":* quoted in Evan M. Wilson, "The Palestine Papers, 1943–1947," *Journal of Palestine Studies,* Summer 1973, p. 35; for attitudes of the Department, see Phillip J. Baram, "A Tradition of Anti-Zionism: The Department of State's Middle-Managers," in Urofsky, *Essays,* as well as Baram's longer study, cited above in the introductory note to Chapter 2.

135 *"Distinct Bolshevik tendencies":* Weizmann to Frankfurter, June 21, 1941, p. 4, in Israel State Archives (ISA), File 7, Box 2270.

136 *Welles blocked Murray's recommendations:* PRO, FO371/35041, November 1943.

136 *Cohen's "radical solution":* National Archives RG59, Notter File, Box 56, P. Document 66 (Palestine), September 4, 1942.

137 *Kirk's recommendations:* Shechtman, *op. cit.* (Ch. 5), pp. 55–56; *FRUS, 1941,* Vol. III, pp. 610–16.

137–8 *FDR and White Paper:* Wasserstein, *op. cit.* (Ch. 5), pp. 24–25; *FRUS, 1939,* Vol. IV, pp. 748–58.

138–9 *FDR plan to transfer Arabs:* Goldmann to Weizmann, June 20, 1939, in CZA, S25/237b.

139 *"A little baksheesh":* Note of Conversation, CZA, Z4/15463.

139–40 *FDR 1942 comments:* ISA, 7-2270; *Roosevelt & Frankfurter,* cited above, p. 667; *FRUS, 1942,* Vol. IV, pp. 543–44; FDRL, President's Personal File (PPF), 8084.

140 *"What I think I will do":* Blum, *Morgenthau Diaries,* cited above (ch. 5), p. 208.

140 *"Police the world," with Churchill:* William D. Hassett, *Off the Record with FDR* (New Brunswick, N.J.: Rutgers University Press, 1958, pp. 166, 152.

140 *"You and I are strong enough":* FDRL, PPF 8857.

141 *Churchill in Cairo:* Wasserstein, *op. cit.,* pp. 32–33; *FRUS, 1943,* Vol. IV, p. 780.

141 *FDR to Peabody:* Thomas H. Greer, *What Roosevelt Thought: The Social and Political Ideas of Franklin D. Roosevelt* (East Lansing: Michigan State University Press, 1958), p. 167.

141 *FDR discounts negative views:* PRO, FO371/35041, p. 156.

141 *Background on Hoskins:* see Grabill, *Protestant Diplomacy,* cited above (Ch. 2), p. 162; R. Harris Smith, *OSS* (Berkeley: University of California Press, 1972), p. 124; *FRUS, 1942,* Vol. IV, p. 28; Parzen, in *American Jewish Archives,* p. 37, cited above.

142 *St. John Philby saga:* related in Weisgal, Morgenthau letters, November 13, 1943, in FDRL, PSF-Palestine; Philby to Weizmann and Weizmann to Welles, December 7, 1943, in CZA, Z4/15463.

143 *Hoskins ignorant of Philby approach:* Evan M. Wilson, *Decision on Palestine* (Stanford, Calif.: Hoover Institution Press, 1979), p. 189.

143 *FDR talk with Wise: FRUS, 1943,* Vol. IV, p. 812; see also FDRL, PSF-Palestine.

144 *Hoskins' report: FRUS, 1943,* Vol. IV, pp. 811–14.

144 *Department's response: ibid.,* pp. 815–21.

145 *FDR and Meyer:* CZA, Z5/388, October 29, 1943; also PRO, FO371/35041, p. 3.

146 *"While freely admitting":* Hull, *Memoirs,* cited above (Ch. 5), Vol. II, pp. 1535–36.

146 *FDR's doubts: FRUS, 1945,* Vol. VIII, pp. 690–91; Morris L. Ernst, *So Far So Good* (New York: Harper & Bros., 1948), p. 172; James MacGregor Burns, *Roosevelt: The Soldier of Freedom* (New York: Harcourt Brace Jovanovich, 1970), p. 442; William Leahy, *I Was There* (New York: Whittlesey House, 1950).

146–7 *FDR and Rosenman:* CZA, Z5/388; Hassett, *op. cit.,* pp. 209–10.

147 *FDR and Stettinius:* Stettinius, *op. cit.,* p. 170.

148 *December 23 meeting: FRUS, 1944,* Vol. V, pp. 655–57.

148 *Harriman and Landis memos: FRUS, 1944,* Vol. V, pp. 646–49, and *FRUS, ibid., 1945,* Vol. VIII, p. 682.

148 *FDR and Wise:* Halperin and Oder, *op. cit.,* p. 337.

149 *FDR's plan with Ibn Saud:* Stettinius, *op. cit.,* p. 211.

150 *Zionist memo:* ISA, 3-2268.

150 *"Roosevelt said to some of us":* Harry S Truman Library (HSTL), OF204, Niles to the President, May 27, 1946.

150 *"I assure Your Majesty": FRUS, 1943,* Vol. IV, p. 787.

150 *FDR's thank-you note:* FDRL, PPF 7960–Ibn Saud.

150 *Landis on Ibn Saud: FRUS, 1945,* Vol. VIII, pp. 680–81.

150 *"Churchill was better informed":* Leahy, *op. cit.,* p. 295.

151 *FDR at Yalta:* Robert E. Sherwood, *Roosevelt and Hopkins* (New York: Harper & Bros., 1948), pp. 871–72; Charles E. Bohlen, *Witness to History, 1929–1969* (New York: W. W. Norton, 1973), p. 203.

152 *"I had an exceedingly pleasant":* James F. Byrnes, *All in One Lifetime* (New York: Harper & Bros., 1958), p. 242.

152 *"The Arabs and the Jews": FRUS, 1945,* Vol. VIII, pp. 2–3.

153 *"Decreasing the desert": Chaim Weizmann: A Biography,* cited above (Ch. 3), p. 277.

153 *FDR to Baruch and Hopkins:* Schechtman, *op. cit.,* p. 110, and Sherwood, *op. cit.,* pp. 871–82.

154 *"Some formula, not yet discovered":* Edward R. Stettinius, *Roosevelt and the Russians* (Garden City, N.Y.: Doubleday, 1949), pp. 289–90, cited in Halperin and Oder, *op. cit.,* p. 338.

154 *"The President seemed placid and frail":* Winston S. Churchill, *Triumph and Tragedy* (Boston: Houghton Mifflin, 1953), p. 397.

154 *"Roosevelt put his hand":* PRO, FO371/45400, p. 5.

154 *"There was nothing I could do":* PRO, FO371/45398, p. 2.

155 *"Joe, you know":* Joseph M. Proskauer, *A Segment of My Times* (New York: Farrar, Straus, 1950), pp. 69–70.

155 *FDR with Hoskins: FRUS, 1945,* Vol. VIII, pp. 690–91.

155 *FDR and the UN: ibid.;* PRO, FO371/45398, p. 3.

156 *"I think Eleanor and I":* Martin, *op. cit.* (Ch. 5), p. 89.

156 *"A typical State Department letter":* Hassett, *op. cit.,* p. 335.

157 *FDR on ultimately overruling the Arabs:* PRO, FO371/45398, pp. 2–3.

Chapter 7

Far and away the best chronicler of the drama of the Zionists in wartime Washington is Isaiah Berlin, political officer at the British Embassy, who interspersed his detailed dispatches on American politics with a series of chatty and well-informed reports on American Jewish affairs. Buried within the tattered dossiers of the British Foreign Office at the Public Record Office, Kew Gardens, London, these have been largely overlooked by researchers since they were opened for inspection in the 1970s. They are peripheral to the main interplay of American politics, and are thus ignored in the otherwise fascinating collection of his reports edited by H. G. Nicholas, *Washington Despatches, 1941–1945* (Chicago: University of Chicago Press, 1981). Though he rapidly moved on to deeper matters in the British intellectual establishment, Berlin allowed himself a retrospective look at his wartime interests in an important lecture, "Zionist Politics in Wartime Washington: A Fragment of Personal Reminiscence," delivered at the Hebrew University of Jerusalem on October 2, 1972, and privately printed. Professor Berlin subsequently replied to a few of my direct inquiries in a four-page letter —terseness was never his style, in talking or writing—which begins by saying that he really has nothing of interest to add, the sure tipoff that interesting tidbits are coming after all.

The Biltmore conference and other aspects of the Zionist experience are well surveyed in Urofsky's two histories, the first cited above in the introductory note to Chapter 1 and *We Are One!* (Garden City, N.Y.: Anchor Press/Doubleday, 1978). See also Nahum Goldmann, *Autobiography* (New York: Holt, Rinehart and Winston, 1969); his second thoughts, in *The Jewish Paradox,* cited above (Ch. 5); and his oral history, which I consulted at the Center for European Studies at Harvard. Less-known aspects of the period are explored in David H. Shpiro, "The Political Background of the 1942 Biltmore Resolution," Isaac Neustadt-Noy, "Toward Unity: Zionist and Non-Zionist Cooperation, 1941–1942," and Melvin I. Urofsky, "Rifts in the Movement: Zionist Fissures, 1942–1945," all in Urofsky, *Essays,* cited above (Ch. 3).

Abba Hillel Silver has yet to be honored with a proper biography. A few of his closest associates have provided their reminiscences: Neumann, *op cit.* (ch. 2); Leon I. Feuer, "Abba Hillel Silver: A Personal Memoir," *American Jewish Archives,* November 1967; Harold F. Manson, "Abba Hillel Silver: An Appreciation," in Daniel Jeremy Silver (ed.), *In the Time of the Harvest: Essays in Honor of Abba Hillel Silver* (New York: Macmillan, 1963). See also Abraham J. Feldman, "Abba Hillel Silver," *American Jewish Historical Quarterly,* June 1965, and Aaron Berman, "Abba Hillel Silver, Zionism and the Rescue of the European Jews," *Working Papers II,* Center for Israel and Jewish Studies, Columbia University, Spring 1979. Scholars were long refused access to Silver's personal papers, but some of their flavor shows through in Zvi Ganin, *Truman, American Jewry, and Israel, 1945–1948* (New York: Holmes & Meier, 1979).

The organization of the "Jewish lobby" is well described in Leon I. Feuer, "The Birth of the Jewish Lobby: A Reminiscence," *American Jewish Archives,* November 1976; Doreen Bierbrier, "The American Zionist Emergency Council: An Analysis of a Pressure Group," *American Jewish Historical Quarterly,* September 1970. Bierbrier had impressive access to the confidential records of the American Zionist Emergency Council, and after publication of her revealing paper the Zionist Organization in New York became more chary about opening these records to researchers. Many of the same materials, however, are readily available in the Central Zionist Archives in Jerusalem, where I consulted them. For a more disinterested political scientist's assessment, see Earl D. Huff, "A Study of a Successful Interest Group: The American Zionist Movement," *The Western Political Quarterly,* Vol. XXV (1972). A later account is in I. L. Kenen, *Israel's Defense Line* (Buffalo, N.Y.: Prometheus Books, 1981).

p. 159 *"Jewish question . . . solved":* Grobman, *op. cit.* (Ch. 5), p. 347.

159 *"The fate of the Jewish homeland":* PRO, FO371/32860, February 6, 1942, p. 2.

159 *Ben-Gurion memo:* CZA, Z4/14632, p. 28.

159–60 *British and Weizmann assessments:* PRO, FO371/32680; ISA, 7-2270, June 21, 1941.

160 *"Washington is not an easy place":* Weizmann to Namier, June 27, 1942, Ben-Gurion Archives, Sde Boker, Israel.

160 *"Quasi-messianic":* Joseph P. Lash, *From the Diaries of Felix Frankfurter* (New York: W. W. Norton, 1975), pp. 22, 26–27.

161 *"We cannot ignore him":* PRO, FO371/35035, p. 106.

161 Hillel Kook (Peter Bergson): Much of my information on the exploits of the Bergson group came from a long interview with Bergson in New York on September 20, 1978. One of his associates, Dr. Samuel Merlin, possesses vast documentation on the movement at his research center in New York, the Institute for Mediterranean Affairs; other relevant archives are to be found in the Jabotinsky Institute in Tel Aviv and the Sterling Library, Yale University. Bergson testimony before Executive Sessions of Congress is reprinted in the 1976 Historical Series of the House of Representatives, Committee on International Relations, *Problems of World War II and Its Aftermath,* Part 2. A sympathetic contemporary account is Ben Hecht, *A Child of the Century* (New York: Simon & Schuster, 1954); see also Isaac Zaar, *Rescue and Liberation* (New York: Bloch Publishing Co., 1954); J. Bowyer

Bell, *Terror Out of Zion* (New York: St. Martin's Press, 1977). The first attempt of a new generation of scholars to analyze the movement, against the generally contemptuous accounts of the mainstream Zionist histories, is Monty Noam Penkower, "In Dramatic Dissent: The Bergson Boys," *American Jewish History,* March 1981.

p. 162 *"You have to speak . . . in superlatives":* Goldmann, *Autobiography,* cited above, p. 195.

163 *Berlin on Brandeis:* "Zionist Politics," p. 12.

163 *"A little gaga":* PRO, FO371/31379, p. 55; also PRO, FO371/35039, September 23, 1943.

164 *"A great gentleman":* Voss, *Rabbi and Minister, op. cit.* (Ch. 4), p. 325.

164 *"Where Wise was warm":* Urofsky, *Essays,* pp. 200–1; see also Benjamin Akzin, oral history, p. 9, Ben-Gurion Archives, Sde Boker.

166 *"I am not easily carried away":* Menachem Begin, *The Revolt* (Jerusalem: Steimatzky's Agency Limited, 1951).

166 *"What a pity":* story told to me by Dr. Abram Sachar and his son, Howard Morley Sachar.

167 *"Height of statesmanship":* quoted in Ganin, *op. cit.,* p. 38.

167 *Weizmann on American Jewry:* Lash, *Frankfurter,* p. 166; also ISA, 7-2270.

168 *Weizmann's minimalism: Foreign Affairs,* January 1942.

169 *Berlin after Biltmore:* PRO FO371/35031, January 21, 1943.

169 *"To our sorrow":* PRO, FO371/35035, May 19, 1943.

170 *"Just a resolution":* Meyer Weisgal, *So Far* (New York: Random House, 1971), pp. 173–74; see also Ganin, *op. cit.,* p. 8; Urofsky, *We Are One!,* pp. 82–83.

170 *Ben-Gurion's petulance:* The Ben-Gurion archives at Sde Boker contain dozens of his angry letters to all sides.

170 *Berlin on Silver:* PRO, FO371/31379 and 35042, p. 3.

171 *"An awesome tongue-lashing":* Neumann, *op. cit.,* p. 192.

171 *American Jewish Conference:* comprehensive report in PRO, FO371/35039, September 23, 1943.

171 *"Little foxes":* quoted in Bierbrier, *op. cit.,* p. 101.

171 *"Their policy of 'go slow' ":* PRO, FO371/40130, March 31, 1944.

172 *"It was crazy":* CZA, Z5/388, April 27, 1944.

173 *Christian activities:* One of the churchmen involved gives an interesting, if somewhat defensive, account in Carl Hermann Voss, "The American Christian Palestine Committee," in Urofsky, *Essays (op. cit.).*

174 *Reports of 1944 and 1945:* quoted in Bierbrier, *op. cit.,* pp. 91, 98–99.

175 *"Bronx and Brownsville":* quoted in Ganin, *op. cit.,* p. 101.

175–6 *Eri Jabotinsky's letters:* PRO, FO371/40129.

176–7 *Weizmann and the Sieff group:* see ISA, 7-2270; CZA, Z5/641, Weizmann to Sieff, November 8, 1943; Berlin, "Zionist Politics," pp. 55–56.

178 *Revival of the "reverse Balfour":* FRUS, 1942, Vol. IV, pp. 538–39.

178 *Churchill on the Arabs:* quoted in Martin Gilbert, *Exile and Return* (Philadelphia: J. B. Lippincott, 1978), pp. 261–62.

179 *Rabbi Lazaron:* Adler in Urofsky, *Essays*, p. 141; see also Monty N. Penkower, "The Joint Anglo-American Statement on Palestine," in *ibid.*, p. 237; Baram, *The Department of State* cited above (Ch. 2), pp. 263, 268.

179–80 *Berlin dispatch on the "Joint Non-Statement":* PRO, FO371/35037; see also Penkower, *op. cit.*

182 *Alling's complaint:* FRUS, 1945, Vol. VIII, pp. 698–703.

182 *Thornburg: Investigation of the National Defense Program*, 80th Congress, 2nd session, Report 440, Part 5, pp. 26–29.

Chapter 8

The availability, finally, of the three massive collections of official archives—American, British, and Israeli (Jewish Agency)—opens the way for a fundamental reappraisal of the role of Harry S Truman in the drama of the Jewish restoration, 1945 to 1948. Triangulation and comparison of the three provide the basis for the climax of this narrative, in this chapter and the four following.

The British records, the papers of the Foreign Office and the Cabinet, are now available for inspection at the efficient Public Record Office, Kew Gardens, London, and are invaluable. The Zionist perspective must be sought in three locations, which sometimes duplicate but more often complement each other: the library of the Zionist Organization of America (Zionist Archives) in New York, the Central Zionist Archives (CZA) at the headquarters of the Jewish Agency in Jerusalem, and the Israel State Archives in the Kirya, Jerusalem. The United States record is contained at the National Archives, Washington, D.C., Diplomatic and Modern Military branches, and the Harry S Truman Library in Independence, Missouri. Both these American sources need to be consulted, though the most important documents have been published in the annual volumes of the exemplary series *Foreign Relations of the United States* (FRUS), available at all serious research libraries.

The latest and best overall record of the first Truman administration is Robert J. Donovan, *Conflict and Crisis* (New York: W. W. Norton, 1977), which draws from all previously available materials. Chapters 34 and 39 are excellent beginnings of the story, from the official Washington perspective. The President's daughter's loving portrait, Margaret Truman, *Harry S. Truman* (New York: William Morrow, 1973), contains material not available elsewhere; and the retrospective oral history, Merle Miller, *Plain Speaking* (New York: G. P. Putnam's Sons, 1974), is also enlightening. Truman's own memoirs, the two volumes *Year of Decisions* and *Years of Trial and Hope* (Garden City, N.Y.: Doubleday, 1955 and 1956), have to be consulted, though they suffer from the inevitable desire of key players to remember their roles and attitudes just the way they want to remember them. More contemporary biographies, by Steinberg and Daniels, cited below, are still useful.

For the milieu of Independence and the Midwest background, I drew particular benefit from interviews with Irving Levitas, one of the Granoff-Jacobson circle, now in Yonkers, N.Y., and Loeb Granoff, A. J.'s son, in Kansas City. I hope they both accept the interpretations I have built on what they told me; obviously, they are not to be held responsible for my judgments. Frank J. Adler was also most generous with his time in Independence.

Truman and the problem of Palestine is the subject of several scholarly works, each written tentatively—since the full documentation was not available to authors—and inclining toward a particular judgment. The best statement of the view that Truman acted only as a cynical political pragmatist, to further his own fortunes in the 1948 elections, is John Snetsinger, *Truman, the Jewish Vote, and the Creation of Israel* (Stanford, Calif.: Hoover Institution Press, 1974), a view to which Clark Clifford took angry exception, as will be cited below. A more measured and better-documented statement of the professional diplomats' perspective is Wilson, *op. cit.* (Ch. 6). Early assessments from a more Zionist perspective, though trying not to grind ideological axes, are Schechtman, *op. cit.* (Ch. 5), and Herbert Parzen, "President Truman and the Palestine Quandary: His Initial Experience, April–December 1945," *Jewish Social Studies,* January 1973. Finally, there are scholarly works which support the view that Truman acted for more idealistic reasons than the critics perceive. First, and impressive considering the lack of official documentation at the time he was researching the problem, is Ian J. Bickerton, "President Truman's Recognition of Israel," *American Jewish Historical Quarterly,* December 1968, a work which Margaret Truman Daniel and others cite for their own accounts. With a better access to archives is Ganin, *op. cit.* (ch. 7). Another Israeli scholar, Amizur Elan, brought a disciplined scrutiny to the materials available; his doctoral dissertation for St. Anthony's College, Oxford, was completed in the trenches along the Suez Canal during Israel's War of Attrition with Egypt in 1970, and has yet to be published; he was kind enough, however, to discuss the problems with me on a warm evening at his home at Kibbutz Lahav in the Negev.

The liberation of the death camps and the political implications that followed are related in Yehuda Bauer, *Flight and Rescue: Brichah* (New York: Random House, 1970); Herbert Agar, *The Saving Remnant* (New York: Viking Press, 1960); and Leo W. Schwarz, *The Redeemers* (New York: Farrar, Straus and Young, 1953). Especially helpful is Leonard Dinnerstein, "The U.S. Army and the Jews," *American Jewish History,* March 1979. The most recent account of these developments is by Abram L. Sachar, *The Redemption of the Unwanted* (New York: St. Martin's/Marek, 1983), which, I am sorry to say, was not available to me as I conducted my own research.

Earl Harrison's mission to Europe in the summer of 1945 is one of the great unresearched turning points in the whole drama. I was unable to locate any unpublished personal papers he may have left behind. The files of the War Refugee Board at the FDRL are revealing, as are the CZA. The Department of State *Bulletin* reproduced all the public documents; and an interesting personal story is told in Abraham J. Klausner, "A Jewish Chaplain in Dachau," reproduced in *American Jewish Memoirs: Oral Documentation* (Jerusalem: Institute of Contemporary Jewry, Hebrew University, 1980).

p. 185 *"Great Men and Famous Women":* My edition is from Selmar Hess, Publishers, about 1894, in eight volumes, but I cannot be sure that was the same edition that the young Truman read.

185 *Wallace on Truman:* John Morton Blum, *The Price of Vision* (Boston: Houghton Mifflin, 1973), pp. 602–3.

185–6 *Jews in the Midwest:* Herbert Asbury, *Up from Methodism* (New York: Alfred A. Knopf, 1926), p. 26; I am grateful to my friend Richard Bulliet for calling this to my attention. See also Albert Jay Nock, "The Jewish Problem in America," *The Atlantic Monthly,* June 1941, pp. 699–700.

186 *"Aristocracy in these parts":* Miller, *op. cit.,* p. 106.

187 *"I am not Jewish":* Steinberg, *op. cit.* (Ch. 5), p. 224.

187 *"With or without the consent":* Frank J. Adler, *Roots in a Moving Stream* (Kansas City, Mo.: The Temple, Congregation B'nai Jehudah, 1972), p. 202.

188 *"All this . . . hooey":* Steinberg, *op. cit.,* p. 123.

188 *Truman and Brandeis:* Jonathan Daniels, *The Man of Independence* (Philadelphia: J. B. Lippincott Co., 1950), pp. 184–86.

189–90 *Truman's proposed tour of the Middle East: FRUS, 1945,* Vol. VIII, p. 18.

190 *Department of State memo to Truman: ibid.,* pp. 704–5.

192 *Zionist memo for Potsdam:* ISA, 3-2268.

192 *Reaction to Truman press conference:* CZA, Z5/386; PRO, FO371/45400, Tandy dispatch, p. 23.

193 *Strength of the Jewish militia:* Herbert Feis, *The Birth of Israel: The Tousled Diplomatic Bed* (New York: W. W. Norton, 1969); also Allen H. Podet, "Anti-Zionism in a Key United States Diplomat," *American Jewish Archives,* November 1978, p. 175.

193 *Truman's Palestine file:* A. J. Granoff, oral history, HSTL, p. 82.

193 *Truman to his mother:* Margaret Truman, *op. cit.,* p. 326.

193–4 *Truman's first meeting with Weizmann:* PRO, FO371/45403, p. 61.

194 *Other meetings on his "Jewish day": ibid.,* pp. 80–81; Ganin, *op. cit.,* pp. 46–47.

194 *Weizmann to Truman:* CZA, Z4/15364.

195 *"My only interest":* HSTL, OF204 Misc., letter to George, October 17, 1946.

195 *Murrow at Dachau:* I am grateful to my friend and mentor Drew Middleton for helping me understand the mood of these days.

196 *American intelligence reports:* National Archives, RG226, Records of the Office of Strategic Services, 39006, pp. 1–2.

196 *Bevin and Churchill:* PRO, FO371/45403, p. 27; Gilbert, *op. cit.* (Ch. 7), p. 290.

197–8 *Weisgal and Schwartz:* FDRL, WRB, Box 9, June 27, 1945; also Herbert Fierst, oral history, Hebrew University, p. 29.

198 *"We have absolute faith":* CZA, Z5/967, June 28, 1945.

198 *Pehle to Harrison:* FDRL, WRB, June 12, 1945.

198–9 *Klausner and Harrison:* Bauer, *op. cit.,* and Klausner, *op. cit.*

199 *Harrison's notebooks:* I could find these only as published in *Survey Graphic,* December 1945, pp. 469–73.

200 *Report to Niles:* found in Niles Papers, Brandeis University, n5.195; I am grateful to the chancellor of Brandeis, Dr. Abram Sachar, for granting me access to these papers.

202 *Anger at Truman initiative:* CZA, Z5/1204, September 18, 1945.

203–4 *"Openings in commerce":* quoted in Gilbert, *op. cit.,* p. 275.

205 *Transports for the 100,000: Near East Report,* January 30, 1974, p. 19; see also newly declassified files in National Archives, RG319, Records of the Army Staff, P&O 383.6 TS (case #7 only).

Chapter 9

The Brichah operation is fully described in the works of Bauer, Agar, Schwarz, and Dinnerstein, cited above (Ch. 8). The most interesting account of the Sonneborn Institute is Leonard Slater, *The Pledge* (New York: Simon & Schuster, 1970).

David Niles has proved as elusive to history as he was to his contemporaries. His style was secretive and only rarely did he commit his thoughts and activities to writing. What papers he left behind are tightly held by his executor, Dr. Abram Sachar at Brandeis University, who allowed me a brief inspection of the files relating to Palestine; they consist almost entirely of notes and memos he received, rather than materials he originated. Dr. Sachar was willing to spend several hours with me talking about Niles, though his own research was not yet completed. I did have access, however, to the undergraduate history honors thesis of his son at Harvard in 1959, which uses the Niles papers extensively: David B. Sachar, "David K. Niles and United States Policy Toward Palestine," Harvard University Library, HU 92.59.765. See also the one major contemporary profile of Niles: Alfred Steinberg, "Mr. Truman's Mystery Man," *The Saturday Evening Post,* December 24, 1949. I am particularly grateful to Justine Wise Polier for sharing some of her memories of Niles with me.

Background on Loy Henderson is more plentiful, and I benefited from an hour-long meeting with him at his home in Washington in 1978, early in my research for this book. My friend William Quandt provided me a copy of his notes of his earlier interview with Mr. Henderson, covering some of the same ground. Most important of all, however, is the massive, two-volume oral history which Mr. Henderson gave to the HSTL. The best analysis of Henderson on Palestine is Podet, *op. cit.* (Ch. 8).

Judah Magnes is virtually a non-person to modern Zionist scholarship, though an American-born professor at the Hebrew University, Arthur A. Goren, has published a valuable collection of Magnes's writings: *Dissenter in Zion* (Cambridge: Harvard University Press, 1982). Dr. Goren was kind enough to share with me some of his conclusions about Magnes's role in Zionism. Otherwise, the only biography available, written shortly after his death by a longtime friend, is Norman Bentwich, *For Zion's Sake* (Philadelphia: Jewish Publication Society of America, 1954). Background on Arthur Hays Sulzberger can be found in the various books about *The New York Times,* but the McDonald Papers at the Lehman Library, Columbia University, contain important unpublished materials about his attitudes toward Palestine and Zionism. The best sources for Eddie Jacobson's story, aside from the general works on Truman, are his own papers and the oral history of A. J. Granoff, both at the HSTL. A useful analysis of all the materials is in Chapter 9 of Frank J. Adler, *op. cit.* (Ch. 8).

p. 206 *Berlin on American Jews:* PRO, FO371/40131.

206-7 *"Buoyant optimism . . . the pathological emotions":* PRO, FO371/ 52568, March 12, 1946.

207 *"A certain reticence":* Evyatar Friesel, "The Holocaust and the Birth of Israel," *The Wiener Library Bulletin,* Vol. XXXII (1979).

207 *UJA contributions:* Urofsky, *We Are One!,* cited above (Ch. 7), p. 125.

208 *I. F. Stone observations:* I. F. Stone, *Underground to Palestine* (New York: Pantheon, 1946, 1978), pp. 5, 20.

208 *"The biggest sucker":* quoted in Raul Hilberg, *The Destruction of the European Jews* (Chicago: Quadrangle, 1961), p. 730.

209 *The Morgan incident: ibid.,* pp. 729–30; also Bauer, *op. cit.,* and Schwarz, *op. cit.*; *The New York Times,* January 3, 1946; Sir Robert G. A. Jackson, oral history, Lehman Library, Columbia University; CZA, Z5/860; PRO, FO371/52568, p. 4.

209 *"General Morgan's allegation":* CZA, Z5/860, January 3, 1946.

210 *Sonneborn's account:* Slater, *op. cit.,* p. 27.

211 *"To characterize the ships":* Miriam Joyce Haron, "United States–British Collaboration on Illegal Immigration to Palestine, 1945–1947," *Jewish Social Studies,* Spring 1980, pp. 178–79; also PRO, FO371/ 61756, p. 5.

211-12 *Jewish lobby:* CZA, Z5/1204; CZA, Z5/1175, September 13, 1945; ISA, 13-2266.

212 *San Francisco conference:* PRO, FO371/45398, April 4, 1945; PRO, FO371/45399, June 23, 1945; Eliahu Elath, *Zionism at the UN* (Philadelphia: Jewish Publication Society of America, 1976), pp. 14–15, 165–69.

213 *Arabs in America:* PRO, FO371/52568, p. 6.

213 *American mood:* PRO, FO371/61756, p. 6.

214 *"Everyone zealous":* quoted in Urofsky, *We Are One!,* p. 123.

214 *Millar Burrows: ibid.,* p. 124.

214 *Christian Century:* quoted in Fishman, *op. cit.* (Ch. 1), p. 36.

215 *"The title deeds":* quoted in William L. Burton, "Protestant America and the Rebirth of Israel," *Jewish Social Studies,* October 1964, pp. 204–5.

215 *Niebuhr and Thompson:* Urofsky, *Essays,* cited above (Ch. 3), p. 247;

Louis L. Gerson, *The Hyphenate in Recent American Politics and Diplomacy* (Lawrence: University of Kansas Press, 1964), p. 154.

215 *"Welcomed public interest":* Robert D. Schulzinger, *The Making of the Diplomatic Mind* (Middletown, Conn.: Wesleyan University Press, 1975), p. 140.

215 *"To increase popular understanding":* H. Bradford Westerfield, *Foreign Policy and Party Politics* (New Haven: Yale University Press, 1955), p. 3.

216 *"On a high plane":* FRUS, 1945, Vol. VIII, pp. 13–18, 777.

216 *New York Democratic chairman:* HSTL, OF204 Misc., August 2, 1946; see also Jean M. Caldwell, "Zionist Pressure Groups and the Palestine Policy of the Truman Administration," unpublished master's thesis, University of Kansas, 1961, p. 53.

216 *Yom Kippur statement:* FRUS, 1946, Vol. VII, pp. 703–5.

216 *Acheson denial:* Dean Acheson, *Present at the Creation* (New York: W. W. Norton, 1969), p. 169.

217 *"Your fingertips sandpapered":* HSTL, Elsey oral history, p. 85.

217 *Truman's remarks:* From sundry correspondence and notes of meetings, these remarks are most conveniently cited in Michael J. Cohen, "Truman, the Holocaust and the Establishment of the State of Israel," *Jerusalem Quarterly,* Spring 1982; see also Donovan, *op. cit.* (Ch. 8), pp. 319, 326; Ganin, *op. cit.* (Ch. 7), p. 81.

218 *Clifford memo:* Gregory William Sand, "Clifford and Truman: A Study in Foreign Policy and National Security, 1945–1949," doctoral dissertation, St. Louis University, 1973, pp. 223–24; also Irwin Ross, *The Loneliest Campaign* (New York: New American Library, 1968), pp. 21–26.

218 *"For all his friendship":* Goldmann, *Autobiography,* cited above (Ch. 7), p. 230.

218 *"A most secretive individual":* HSTL, Elsey oral history, p. 330.

219 *"Potentially the greatest":* Congressional Record, House, April 1, 1943, p. 2818.

220 *The woman in Niles's life:* see Goldmann, oral history, Harvard University, no. 14, July 29, 1975, pp. 5–6.

221 *"Psychological imponderabilia":* Arthur Koestler, *Promise and Fulfilment* (New York: Macmillan, 1949), p. 20.

221–2 *Niles and Truman:* Jack Redding, *Inside the Democratic Party* (Indianapolis: Bobbs-Merrill, 1958), p. 203; Allen and Shannon, *op. cit.* (Ch. 4), p. 75; Ganin, *op. cit.,* p. 157.

222 *Criticism of Niles:* FRUS, 1945, Vol. VIII, p. 780; HSTL, Henderson oral history, pp. 110–12; Walter Millis (ed.), *The Forrestal Diaries* (New York: Viking Press, 1951), pp. 346–47, 360–61.

222 *Ben Cohen's view:* expressed to me in an interview in Washington on October 23, 1978.

222–3 *Mood at State:* Henry S. Villard, *Affairs at State* (New York: Thomas Y. Crowell, 1965), p. 20, and his review "The Riddle of Mr. Bendiner," *American Foreign Service Journal,* October 1942; also Allen and Shannon, *op. cit.,* pp. 393–406.

223 *"Mr. Wilson, I don't understand":* Wilson, *op. cit.* (Ch. 6), p. 5.

224–5 *Henderson reports: FRUS, 1944,* Vol. V, pp. 626–29, 631–33.

225 *"This man Henderson": Congressional Record,* House, January 26, 1948, pp. 557–61.

226 *"Israel is at home":* Naomi Wiener Cohen, "The Reaction of Reform Judaism in America to Political Zionism," *Publication of the American Jewish Historical Society,* June 1951, pp. 383–84; Sam C. Chinitz, "The Jewish Agency and the Jewish Community in the United States," unpublished master's thesis, Columbia University, 1959, pp. 168–70.

226 *"I will resign":* Neumann, *op. cit.* (Ch. 2), p. 30.

226 *Sulzberger after returning from Palestine:* Lehman Library, Columbia University, McDonald papers, President's Advisory Commission, Palestine—Partition, May 22, 1937.

226–7 *"An assembly of mice":* PRO, FO371/35031, January 21, 1943, p. 3; PRO, FO371/35039, September 23, 1943, p. 4.

227–8 *Magnes:* Urofsky, *Essays,* pp. 127–29; Bentwich, *op. cit.,* pp. 252–53, 261, 188, 240.

228 *Reaction to Magnes:* OSS report, found in PRO, FO371/41702, p. 6; PRO, FO371/45398, April 4, 1945; *FRUS, 1942,* Vol. IV, pp. 555–56.

228–9 *The Basel conference:* Abba Eban, *An Autobiography* (New York: Random House, 1977), pp. 68–70.

229 *Truman and Silver:* HSTL, OF204, Palestine and Misc., May 1, 1946, November 18, 1946, May 13, 1947; PRO, FO371/52568, March 12, 1946; Ganin, *op. cit.,* pp. 25, 74–75, 94–109.

231 *"A great deal of myth":* Margaret Truman, *op. cit.* (Ch. 8), p. 423.

Chapter 10

The Jewish restoration before the United Nations is the subject of a rich official literature and scores of memoirs—few of them, it need hardly be said, sympathetic to the British or Arab Palestinian position. Important new sources became available in 1979 when the government of Israel produced a published edition of its early archives, following the pattern of the United States *FRUS* series. Drawn from the collections of the Israel State Archives and the Central Zionist Archives, the first volume of this undertaking, *Political and Diplomatic Documents, Dec. 1947–May 1948 (PDD)* (Jerusalem 1979), sets a high standard of comprehensiveness and interest. A companion volume summarizes Hebrew documents in English. Despite the indicated dates, this collection contains important material about the earlier UN period which allows all the previously published memoirs and accounts to be studied in a new light.

One of the early accounts of the UN experience stands up even now among the best: David Horowitz, *State in the Making* (New York: Alfred A. Knopf, 1953). Two other memoirs by participants are Jorge Garciá-Granados, *The Birth of Israel* (New York: Alfred A. Knopf, 1948), and the more comprehensive account by Elath, *op. cit.* (Ch. 9).

Among the secondary works, and holding up remarkably well after three decades, is J. C. Hurewitz, *The Struggle for Palestine* (1950) (reissue; New York: Schocken Books, 1976). Evan M. Wilson's *Decision on Palestine,* cited above (Ch. 6), is comprehensive from the United States perspective and contains a helpful bibliographical essay pointing to other sources. Other previously cited surveys, particularly Donovan (Ch. 8), Ganin (Ch. 7), Urofsky, *We Are One!* (Ch. 7), all contain useful material culled from the wealth of accumulated documentation.

p. 232 *Acheson's warning: FRUS, 1947,* Vol. V, p. 1048.

232–3 *Weizmann's:* quoted in Ganin, *op. cit.,* p. 122.

234 *Weizmann's text in disarray:* Bernard Postal and Henry W. Levy, *And the Hills Shouted for Joy* (New York: David McKay, 1973), p. 100.

234–5 Exodus *incident:* A good summary account is in Urofsky, *We Are One!,* pp. 136–38.

235 *Bunche's role:* A full account of the secret meeting is found in Begin, *op. cit.* (Ch. 7), pp. 297–301; see also Horowitz, *op. cit.,* pp. 159–60, 177, 204. I am particularly indebted to my friend, and Bunche's biographer, Brian Urquhart, for sensitive guidance on this part of the story.

235 *No more than three out of eleven: PDD,* p. 4.

235–6 The actual UNSCOP report of 1947 makes illuminating reading from more than three decades of retrospect; it was commercially printed as *Report on Palestine* (New York: Somerset Books, 1947).

236–7 The background on partition is conveniently described in Howard M. Sachar, *A History of Israel* (New York: Alfred A. Knopf, 1976), pp. 203 ff.; see also Wasserstein, *op. cit.* (Ch. 5), pp. 13–14.

237 *"Someday my son":* Meir, *op. cit.* (Ch. 5), p. 157.

237 *"If partition is accepted":* quoted in Bethell, *op. cit.* (Ch. 5), p. 32.

237–8 *Von Neurath comment:* Aaron S. Klieman, "In the Public Domain: The Controversy over Partition for Palestine," *Jewish Social Studies,* Spring 1980, pp. 159–60.

238 *"He cannot forget":* PRO, FO371/35035, p. 106.

238 *"Two bites at the cherry":* PRO, PREM 4/52/3/410, cited in Wasserstein, *op. cit.,* p. 336.

238 *Weizmann to Welles:* CZA, Z4/15463, December 7, 1943.

239 *Briefing paper for Forrestal:* National Archives, RG428, General Records of the Department of the Navy, Forrestal papers, Wooldridge to Forrestal, July 3, 1947.

240 *Henderson's advice: FRUS, 1947,* Vol. V, pp. 1120–23; see also Ganin, *op. cit.,* p. 126.

240–1 *Niles memo:* HSTL, OF204, Palestine, July 29, 1947.

241 *Stone and Fierst on Hilldring:* quoted in Frank J. Adler, "Review Essay," *American Jewish Historical Quarterly,* June 1973, p. 417; *Near East Report,* January 30, 1974.

242 *Truman to Eleanor Roosevelt:* Donovan, *op. cit.,* p. 325; Ganin, *op. cit.,* p. 129.

242–3 *Durbrow cable and subsequent analysis: FRUS, 1947,* Vol. V, pp. 1081, 1088–89.

243 *Eban on Gromyko's statement:* Eban, *Autobiography,* cited above (Ch. 9), p. 75.

243 *Silver and the Russians:* Neumann, *op. cit.* (Ch. 2), p. 249.

243–4 *"This Russian business":* ISA, 44-2266.

244 *Archibald Roosevelt:* ISA, 6-2270.

244 *Kermit Roosevelt:* see his article "The Partition of Palestine," *The Middle East Journal,* January 1948, pp. 7–8.

245 *Henderson's advice and Marshall's decision: FRUS, 1947,* Vol. V, pp. 1153–62.

245 *Arab "blackmail": ibid.,* p. 1175.

246 *"Pendulum swings back and forth":* quoted in Ganin, *op. cit.,* p. 138.

246–7 *"First time in my life":* Vera Weizmann, *op. cit.* (Ch. 3), p. 219.

247–8 *The Herschel Johnson mix-up: FRUS, 1947,* Vol. V, pp. 1269–72; Eban, *Autobiography,* pp. 94–95; the atmosphere was nicely re-created for me by one of the young American diplomats in attendance, Frazier Wilkins, in an interview in Washington on March 3, 1978. Donovan, *op. cit.,* pp. 327–28, and more particularly Ganin, *op. cit.,* pp. 138–41, try sorting out the confusion.

248 *Vote-counting at the UN:* The entire sequence that follows is reconstructed from numerous sources. Most important is Document No. 1 in *PDD,* pp. 3–15, a long confidential report from a member of the Jewish Agency delegation, Michael Comay, to a Zionist friend in South Africa, written just a few days after the vote. Horowitz, Garciá-Granados, Neumann, and Eban, *Autobiography,* all cited above, also contain vital pieces of the picture from active participants; Ganin, Donovan, and Wilson pull together the official sources and reports of observers that were available at the times they did their research.

249 *"Letting Spain into the UN":* related to me by Abram Sachar, one of Niles's closest friends, in an interview in New York, May 8, 1979.

250 *"Proselytizing for votes":* Forrestal Diaries, cited above (Ch. 9), p. 345.

251 *"Bribes and threats":* Donovan, *op. cit.,* pp. 329–31, 455, records the sources of these stories in the State Department files at the National Archives—not the published *FRUS* volumes.

252 *The Philippines and Edelstein: FRUS, 1947,* Vol. V, pp. 1305–7; Neumann, *op. cit.,* pp. 251–53; David B. Sachar, *op. cit.* (Ch. 9), pp. 72–73.

252 *Liberia:* David B. Sachar, *op. cit.,* p. 72.

252 *Haiti: FRUS, 1947,* Vol. V, p. 1309; Donovan, *op. cit.,* p. 330; Garciá-Granados, *op. cit.,* pp. 264–65.

253 *Greece: FRUS, 1947,* Vol. V, p. 1307; David B. Sachar, *op. cit.,* p. 71.

Chapter 11

To sort out the climactic reversals of the next five months, I took as a base the careful researches of Ganin, Bickerton, Wilson, Donovan, and Urofsky, all cited above (Chs. 7–9), and concentrated my own efforts on the new *PDD* collection and the Foreign Office files in the Public Record Office, London—sources not available to these previous analysts. With the Israeli and British records in hand, it was then possible to examine the various collections in the HSTL and the *FRUS* documents with fresh perspective. Quotations in this chapter and the next that are not specifically attributed below can be found in one or more of the previous studies, but particularly including an earlier version of Ganin's chapter which includes some useful documentary material that did not survive into his book: Zvi Ganin, "The Limits of American Jewish Political Power: America's Retreat from Partition, November 1947–March 1948," *Jewish Social Studies,* Winter–Spring 1977; see also Michael J. Cohen, "Truman and the State Department: The Palestine Trusteeship Proposal, March 1948," *Jewish Social Studies,* Spring 1981.

Basic sources for Forrestal are Arnold A. Rogow, *James Forrestal* (New York: Macmillan, 1963), and *Forrestal Diaries,* cited above (Ch. 9). The February 3 meeting and its aftermath are carefully detailed in *PDD.*

pp. 255–6 *Various reactions to partition:* Manson, *op. cit.* (Ch. 7), p. 23; Eban, *Autobiography,* cited above (Ch. 9), p. 99; interview with Frazier Wilkins; Jacques Derogy and Hesi Carmel, *The Untold History of Israel* (New York: Grove Press, 1979), p. 74; Postal and Levy, *op. cit.* (Ch. 10), p. 107; Urofsky, *We Are One!,* p. 146; Begin, *op. cit.* (Ch. 7), p. 335; Bell, *op. cit.* (Ch. 7), p. 314.

256–7 *Truman's reaction:* HST memoirs, cited above (Ch. 8), Vol. II, p. 184; HSTL, OF204, Palestine, November 19, 1947; *ibid.,* Misc., December 2, 1947.

257 *Arms embargo:* An excellent study is Shlomo Slonim, "The 1948 American Embargo on Arms to Palestine," *Political Science Quarterly,* Fall 1979.

257–8 *State Department policy review: FRUS, 1948,* Vol. V, pp. 545–62, 655–57.

259 *CIA review: ibid.,* pp. 666–75.

259 *Joint Chiefs review:* newly declassified documents in the National Archives, Modern Military Branch, RG319, P&O 091 Palestine, TS Sect. I, Part I.

259 *Comments on Marshall:* Hassett, *op. cit.* (Ch. 6), p. 249; Norman A. Graebner (ed.), *An Uncertain Tradition* (New York: McGraw-Hill, 1961), pp. 247–48.

259 *"Except a few":* HST memoirs, Vol. II, p. 137.

259 *"What the President wanted":* Graebner, *op. cit.,* p. 265.

260 *"We must do something":* National Archives, Diplomatic Branch, 501.BB Palestine/4-348.

261 *"I remember an occasion":* Rogow, *op. cit.,* pp. 191–92.

261 *"Forget it, Jim":* interview with James Rowe, Washington, February 17, 1978.

262 *Polls:* Alfred O. Hero, Jr., *American Religious Groups View Foreign Policy* (Durham, N.C.: Duke University Press, 1973), pp. 360-61.

262 *"Equivalent of George III":* PRO, FO371/68650, May 24, 1948.

263 *Humphrey comment:* Bickerton, *op. cit.* (Ch. 8), pp. 215, 236.

263 *Council on Foreign Relations:* Archives of the Council on Foreign Relations, Digest of Discussion, April 20, 1948, Study Group on "The Near and Middle East," Vol. XXVII-A.

264 *Lippmann's comment:* Steel, *op. cit.* (Ch. 2), pp. 453–54.

264 *"On an antisemitic platform":* Ganin, *op. cit.* (Ch. 7), p. 182.

264 *Zionist mood:* ISA, 9-2266; PRO, FO371/68630, February 21, 1948.

264–5 *February 3 meeting:* described in *PDD*, no. 173.

265 Niles's absence during these crucial weeks has been little noted; in an interview in Jerusalem on July 8, 1980, Eliahu Elath (Epstein) told me of his illness.

266 *Weizmann's return: ibid.,* no. 183; Vera Weizmann, *op. cit.* (Ch. 3), p. 221.

266 *"Our difficulty":* PDD, no. 179.

267 *Epstein and the oil men: ibid.,* nos. 210 and 281.

267 *March 6 telegram: ibid.,* no. 257.

268 *Background on Clifford:* Allen and Shannon, *op. cit.* (Ch. 4), pp. 26–27, 48; Donovan, *op. cit.* (Ch. 8), p. 380.

268–9 *Clifford's first memo:* FRUS, *1948,* Vol. V, pp. 687–89.

269–70 *Clifford's second memo: ibid.,* pp. 690–96.

270—1 *Clifford and "rational persuasion":* Elath interview, cited above.

271 *Public-school flier:* HSTL, OF204, Misc., March 17, 1948.

272 *Truman to Jacobson: ibid.,* February 27, 1948.

272–3 *Truman meeting with Jacobson:* Truman gives his own brief account in his memoirs, Vol. II, p. 189; Jacobson, obviously savoring his moment, wrote a long personal account with Granoff's help on March 27, 1952, on file in the HSTL.

274 *White House atmosphere:* HSTL, Eben A. Ayers diary, p. 44; for Truman's views in the crucial days before the trusteeship statement, *PDD*, no. 269, conveys important insights based on a conversation Truman had aboard the yacht with William Hillman, Washington bureau chief for *Collier's* magazine.

275 *Reaction to trusteeship:* PRO, FO371/68648, March 22, 1948; National Archives, Department of State, Office of Public Affairs, "U.S. Opinion on Recent U.S. Policy Statements Concerning Palestine," April 2, 1948; *ibid.,* Diplomatic Branch, 501.BB Palestine/4-948, 4-1348; Schechtman, *op. cit.* (Ch. 5), p. 277.

Chapter 12

A colorful account of these days based on Clark Clifford's papers and numerous interviews is Dan Kurzman, *Genesis 1948* (New York: World Publishing Company, 1970). Such are the dangers of oral history, however, that many of the specific facts have to be cross-checked. (In the files of the HSTL, Clifford papers, is a useful set of questions posed by Owen S. Stratton of Wellesley College, April 9, 1960, which have helped guide later researchers through the massive documentation.

The May 12 White House meeting remains controversial. From all sides come charges that the official record, reprinted in *FRUS, 1948,* Vol. V, pp. 972–76, carries terseness to the point of distortion. One of the junior participants in the back of the room, Frazier Wilkins, told me that he protested to the drafter of the memo, his State Department colleague Robert McClintock, immediately upon seeing his official account the next day; a particular point of contention is the Marshall "threat," which, Wilkins insists, was delivered in banter and not the weighty tones of the memo. Among harried executives, however, banter is often a pleasant guise for messages too serious to be stated directly. The heaviest onslaught against the "official" version is the paper which Clark Clifford delivered to the American Historical Association in December 1976, subsequently published with a revealing interview in *American Heritage,* April 1977, an account presumably triggered by the "revisionist" scholarship of John Snetsinger. In the National Archives, Diplomatic Branch, 501.BB Palestine/3-2248, is an interesting memorandum of a conversation on June 20, 1974, between Clifford and the director of the Historical Branch of the State Department about identification of authorship of certain unsigned papers, an example of the historical sleuthing which goes into the preparation of the *FRUS* volumes.

Alongside Kurzman, the readable account of Postal and Levy, *op. cit.* (Ch. 10), is interesting for its anecdotes and personal reminiscences of many who are no longer clear of memory.

p. 276 *"Most embarrassing position":* HSTL, Charles G. Ross papers, "Notes re Palestine etc.," March 29, 1948.

276 *The bureaucrats' response: FRUS, 1948,* Vol. V, pp. 751–55.

277 *Rosenman's role:* see an interesting description in *PDD,* no. 263.

277–8 *Weizmann-Rosenman talks: ibid.,* no. 452.

278 *Weizmann's Seder:* see Eban's account in *Chaim Weizmann: A Biography,* cited above (Ch. 3), pp. 308–11.

279 *American Jewish Committee deliberations:* Ganin, *op. cit.* (Ch. 7), p. 172.

280 *J. Edgar Hoover's involvement:* see Abraham Feinberg, "The Anatomy of a Commitment," *Rehovot,* Spring 1974.

280–1 *Deir Yassin:* see Wilson, *op. cit.* (Ch. 6), p. 140; Sachar, *History,* cited above (Ch. 10), p. 334; *FRUS, 1948,* Vol. V, p. 817.

281 *"We had been misled": PDD,* no. 290.

282 *Hilldring and the State Department: PDD,* no. 446; PRO, FO371/68649, May 2, 1948; Vera Weizmann, *op. cit.* (Ch. 3), p. 230.

282 *Henderson's invitations: FRUS, 1948,* Vol. V, pp. 811–12.

282 *"How can I not go?":* Bentwich, *op. cit.* (Ch. 9), p. 298.

282–3 *"I fear greatly":* Lehman Library, Columbia University, Lehman papers, Magnes file, February 6, 1948.

283–4 *Magnes' visit:* National Archives, Diplomatic Branch, UNA Palestine, April 13, 1948; *ibid.,* 501.BB Palestine/5-1048; *FRUS, 1948,* Vol. V, pp. 901–4; ISA, 29-2271; PRO, FO371/68649, p. 81; Bentwich, *op. cit.,* pp. 299–305.

284 *Rusk's scheme: FRUS, 1948,* Vol. V, p. 969.

285 *Zionist reaction to Rusk proposal: PDD,* no. 477; ISA, 29-2271; Bell, *op. cit.* (Ch. 7), p. 311.

286 *Weizmann and Ben-Gurion:* Vera Weizmann, *op. cit.,* pp. 230–32; Neumann, *op. cit.* (Ch. 2), p. 258; Eban, *Autobiography,* cited above (Ch. 9), p. 111; Zeev Sheref, *Three Days* (London: W. H. Allen, 1962).

286 *"There is a bitter debate": FRUS, 1948,* Vol. V, pp. 930–35.

286–8 *Marshall-Shertok meeting: ibid.,* pp. 940–41; *PDD,* no. 483; Sharett's version in his memoirs was published only in Hebrew, but this passage (pp. 226–28) was translated for the State Department records and filed in the National Archives, Diplomatic Branch, 867N.01/5-848.

288 *White House memos:* HSTL, Clifford papers, see Stratton memo, nos. 10, 11.

288 *Goldmann and Lovett: PDD,* no. 483; Kurzman, *op. cit.,* pp. 212–13.

288 *Gross memo: FRUS, 1948,* Vol. V, pp. 959–65.

289 *"What is likely to come out": ibid.,* pp. 965–69.

289 *Truman, the evening of May 11:* HSTL, Eben A. Ayers diary, p. 97.

290 *"I want you to get ready":* Clifford, *American Heritage,* April 1977, p. 8.

292 *Lovett's doubts: ibid.;* HSTL, Ross notes, cited above, p. 6.

292–3 *Lovett-Clifford luncheon: FRUS, 1948,* Vol. V, pp. 1005–7.

293 *Truman and Ben-Gurion:* Steinberg, *op. cit.* (Ch. 5), p. 308.

293 *"I am Cyrus":* Moshe Davis, "Reflections on Harry S. Truman and the State of Israel," in *Harry S. Truman and the Founding of Israel* (Jerusalem: Hebrew University, 1978).

294 *"Those Israelites":* Robert Ferrill (ed.), *Off the Record: The Private Papers of Harry S. Truman* (New York: Harper & Row, 1980), p. 402.

294–5 *Truman letters:* HSTL, OF204d, Misc., May 15, 1948, September 10, 1948; HSTL, OF204, Misc., March 6, 1948, May 18, 1948.

295 *Weizmann's letter:* Vera Weizmann, *op. cit.,* p. 233.

296 *Epstein's letter:* Postal and Levy, *op. cit.,* pp. 333–36.

296 *"I guess I was always":* Cohen interview, cited above (Ch. 9).

297 *"You're the first person":* David B. Sachar, *op. cit.* (Ch. 9), p. 1.

297 *"How could you know?":* Vera Weizmann, *op. cit.,* p. 234.

298 *"They almost put it over":* HST memoirs, cited above (Ch. 8), Vol. II, p. 194.

298 *Scene at the DP camp:* Postal and Levy, *op. cit.,* pp. 368–69.

Epilogue

p. 299 *"The present . . . aggressive tendencies":* Lehman Library, Columbia University, McDonald papers, General Correspondence, Marshall, George C., August 31, 1948.

302 *U.S. Treasury analysts:* Eli Ginzberg, *Israel and American Jews: The Economic Connection,* prepared for the Task Force on American Jewish–Israel Community Relationship, Jerusalem, January 1977, pp. 1–2.

308 *Iphigene Sulzberger to Rath: The Jerusalem Post Magazine,* May 14, 1971.

314–15 *Commager tribute:* Kenen, *op. cit.* (Ch. 7), p. 142.

INDEX

Ball, Max, 267
Bank of Israel, 233
Barton, James, 83
Baruch, Bernard, 110, 113, 175, 181, 253
Beam, Jacob D., 117
Beecher, Henry Ward, 5
Begin, Menachem, 76 n., 161–2, 166, 235, 256, 281, 285, 310; as Prime Minister, 314–15
Behind the Silken Curtain (Crum), 240
Behrman, S. N., 33
Belt, Guillermo, 251
Ben-Gurion, David, 81, 102, 159, 160, 168, 201, 210, 293; and Biltmore Declaration, 170; death of, 313; and declaration of Israel, 286; opposes trusteeship, 275; post-1948 stature of, 305–6, 313; telegram from American Jews, 267; vs. Weizmann, 161, 162, 170; Zionism of, 170, 206, 228
Ben-Gurion–Blaustein compact, 305–7
Bergen-Belsen, 195, 199, 201
Bergson, Peter (Hillel Kook), 161–2, 163, 164, 175–6, 177, 178, 189, 202, 264, 285
Berlin, Irving, 33
Berlin, Isaiah, 162–3, 169, 170, 177, 179–81, 206, 225, 265, 311
Bernadotte, Count Folke, 300–1
Bethlehem, 27, 236
Bevin, Ernest, 196, 203–4, 205, 215, 232
Biltmore conference (1942), 168–72, 227, 228
Bisgyer, Maurice, 230
Blackstone, William Eugene, 35–8, 42, 67, 91, 117, 185, 211, 215
Blackstone Memorial, 37, 40, 41
Blaine, James G., 39
Blaustein, Jacob, 305–7
Bliss, Howard, 85–6, 87, 89
Blum, Léon, 253
B'nai B'rith, 43, 213, 229–30
Bolshevik Revolution, 72
Bolshevism, 302; and Zionism, 72, 82, 97, 118, 244; *see also* Communism

Brandeis, Louis Dembitz, 25, chapters 2 and 3, 94, 101, 104, 107, 137–8, 165, 188; on Arab question, 81; and Balfour Declaration, 62–5, 67, 72; "conversion" of, 48–51; old age and death of, 81–2; Supreme Court appointment of, 57; vs. Weizmann, 74–80; Zionism of, 48–58, 63, 73, 74, 77–81
Brazil, 3, 4
Brichah operation, 208–11
Britain, 54, 58, 59, 84, 89; *see also* British Middle East policy
British Jewry, 63
British Middle East policy: Balfour Declaration, 60–5, 67, 68–9, 77, 85, 91–2; 1930–1945, 108, 110, 121, 137–8, 140–1, 145, 146, 149, 178–9, 188, 237–8; 1956 Suez campaign, 303–4; Palestine mandate and, 63–5, 68, 77, 84, 91–2, 99, 103, 108, 110, 134, 135, 144, 178–9, 188, 202–5, 229, 237, 284; in Palestine partition debate, 232–3, 249; post–World War II, 196, 202–5, 232, 234, 267; White Paper, 137–8, 145, 146, 178, 188, 196, 238
British Zionism, 63
Bryan, William Jennings, 59
Bryant, William Cullen, 27
Buber, Martin, 227
Buchenwald, 195
Bunche, Ralph, 235–6
Bund (General Jewish Workers' Organization of Russia and Poland), 33, 102–3, 123, 200
Burckhardt, Carl, 124
Burrows, Millar, 214
Byrnes, James F., 194, 222

Cahan, Abraham, 102–3, 104
Camp David peace agreement (1979), 313
Canaan, 4, 83
Canada, 236
Cantor, Eddie, 209
Carter, Jimmy, 313

A NOTE ON THE AUTHOR

Peter Grose is a Senior Fellow and director of Middle Eastern studies at the Council on Foreign Relations in New York City. A long-time foreign correspondent for *The New York Times,* he was bureau chief in Moscow and Israel and at the United Nations, and a member of *The Times* Editorial Board. He later served on the Policy Planning Staff of the State Department under Secretary of State Cyrus Vance. Mr. Grose is a graduate of Yale and Oxford universities, and wrote *Israel in the Mind of America* as a Research Associate at Columbia University's Middle Eastern Institute.

A NOTE ON THE TYPE

The text of this book was set via computer-driven cathode-ray tube in a type face known as Imprint. Designed in 1912 by Gerard Meynell, J. H. Mason, and Edward Johnston for use in their magazine of the same name, Imprint was the first original text type face to be specially designed for mechanical composition. Based loosely on Caslon Old Style, the lower-case letters are larger than Caslon and the overall look of the face is darker. Its success marked the beginning of type-face development by manufacturers of typecasting machinery, replacing the practice of adapting type faces hand-cut by punch-cutters working for type foundries.

This book was composed by Dix Type Inc., Syracuse, New York. It was printed and bound by R. R. Donnelley & Sons, Harrisonburg, Virginia. Typographic design was done by Joe Marc Freedman.